The Tainted Tea Tragedy

Murder Ink contains a book within a book. The one within, *The Tainted Tea Tragedy*, is told on the three pages beginning each *Murder Ink* chapter, with additional clues strewn throughout. There are at least two clues to a chapter (some would call them red herrings), and they are indicated by a teapot and teabag numbered sequentially. The cast of characters is introduced in the Contents, and Chapter 10, Justice, reveals the ending. To discover *The Tainted Tea Tragedy* aftermath—one year later—the captions under the figures shown in the Index may be read by holding the book up to a mirror. Those who peek early are despicable beyond words.

Murder Ink

Revived, Revised, Still Unrepentant
Perpetrated by Dilys Winn

EDWARD GOREY

Workman Publishing, New York

The Staffordshire salt glaze teahouse (England, circa 1745)
shown on the cover
courtesy Leo Kaplan Antiques, New York.

Library of Congress Cataloging in Publication Data
Winn, Dilys.
Murder ink.
Includes index.
1. Detective and mystery stories, English—Miscellanea
2. Detective and mystery stories, American—Miscellanea.
I. Title.
PR830.D4W49   1984   823'.0872'02   84-40321
ISBN 0-89480-768-4
ISBN 0-89480-777-3 (pbk.)

Cover photograph: Jerry Darvin
Cover and book design: Kathleen Herlihy Paoli

Workman Publishing Company, Inc.
1 West 39 Street
New York, New York 10018

Manufactured in the United States of America
First printing October 1984
10 9 8 7 6 5 4 3 2 1

DEDICATION

Who has not wanted to own a bookstore? I did. At times I still do, and it is then that I ring up Murder Ink® and ask wistfully, "How's So-and-So selling?" "Are he-and-she still customers?" And, utterly mawkish now, "Does anyone remember I once owned this place?"

Lately the calls have been infrequent. In part, I suspect, because there are now thirty mystery bookstores out there that surpass any fantasy I ever had of what mine should be like. They're carrying *everything*. They're organizing *everything*—mystery tours, mystery cruises, mystery dinners, mystery conferences, even mystery writer fan clubs.

Who could resist them?

It is these thirty I want to acknowledge. But twenty-nine of them will just have to understand that I will always reserve the warmest spot in my heart for Murder Ink®. And it is to the woman who now owns it, Carol Brener, that this *Murder Ink* is dedicated.

THANK YOU

M*urder Ink* owes favors to many, but most especially to Phyllis Brown, Sandy Christie, Kate Mattes, Gary Mollica and Peter Stern for solid information and superb snooping instincts; to Addee Key, who has surely read everything ever written; to Mike Chlanda, Jeannie M. Jacobson, Linda Johnson, Alex McHale and Michael Franklin, masterminds all; to Jim Huang and the many unsung moles at the *Drood Review*; to Frannie Ruch and Rona Beame, who epitomize the meaning of picture-perfect; to Kathleen Herlihy Paoli (and her kitchen staff: Drina Karp, Richard and Judith Rew) for knockout layouts; to Wayne Kirn and Joanne Strauss for their quick wits and quick turnarounds; to Michael (for his office) and Mary (for her disposition); and to Lynn Strong and Sally Kovalchick, the two fine editors who beyond any reasonable doubt aided and abetted and somehow found a way to make fun of it all; I can't imagine pulling a caper without you.

THE TAINTED TEA TROUPE

Lord and Lady Teasdale: Paul Rowntree and Stacey Wright. *Becca Teasdale:* Nancy Beard. *The Cad and the Colonel:* William Smith and William Reid. *The Nurse and the Secretary:* Carol Schimmer and Ronnie Simon. *The Vicar and the Publican:* George Spelvin and Frank Wright. *The Cook and the Gardener:* Margie Simon and Haig Shekerjian. *Upstairs and Downstairs:* Barbara Seaman and Kate Choler. *The Sisters of Mozart:* Regina Shekerjian and Caroline Rowntree. *The Perfect Butler:* Everett Roudebush.

Photography (unless otherwise noted): © 1984 Matthew E. Seaman Lightworker. *Costuming:* Aletta Vett, Theatre Department, SUNY, New Paltz, N.Y. *Props:* Bonnie Salmon, The Bankers' Daughters, Stone Ridge, N.Y. *Settings:* Mohonk Mountain House, New Paltz, N.Y.; DePuy Canal House, High Falls, N.Y.; the Schecter environs, including the most handsomely appointed home in the whole Hudson Valley. *Portcullis Pursuivant:* Theodore Arnold. *Story design:* Kathleen Herlihy Paoli. *Story line:* Pat Johnson, Sally Kovalchick, Dilys Winn.

CONTENTS

1. PLOTS
Yesterday, 6 pm, Just Dusk

TRACKING THE GENRE

JERRY DARVIN

Roudebush, the butler
Every house should have one.

MYSTERY HISTORY

THRILLERS

The Colonel
Who recaptures the Punjab nightly over dinner.

2. TROUBLE SPOTS
Yesterday, 11:18 pm, Perhaps

Jock, the publican

Whelks, the gardener
Affable tender of thorny problems.

3. SUSPICIONS
Today, 7am Sharp

Cook
Been in service 17 years.

Vicar Fogg,
whose penance in life is to
propose to Becca and be refused.
Seven times.

4. CRIMES
Today, Prior to Midday

*Ceramic portrait
of Staffordshire Hall,
the hallowed Teasdale home.*

JERRY DARVIN

Harriet the lovelorn

Leslie the cad

5. VICTIMS
Today, Teatime, 4:27 Precisely

6. BLOODHOUNDS
*Today, Twilight, A Shade
Past 5:46*

Bridie (upstairs) and Rosie (downstairs).

7. SIDE-TRACKED
Tonight, 8:01 and Ticking

*The Sisters of Mozart.
Hyacinth (flute) and Violet (cello).*

Lady Clare Fellows Teasdale   Hic.

Simon
Private secretary to His Lordship.

Becca Teasdale
A painter of very minor talent.

*House of Teas
official crest, eight years in the making.*

10. JUSTICE
Tomorrow, Light Dawns

*Lord John
Teasdale*   *The incipient deceased.*

INTRODUCTION

I live in a town so small it doesn't even have a bookstore, which, when I think about it, is ridiculous. There's not much else to do around here *but* read.

How do I cope? Long walks with hummingbirds.

Even so, I often find myself with agonizing withdrawal symptoms. When they hit, I charge down to the city, buy every title in sight, and binge.

What's my poison? Mysteries, of course.

Always have been, always will be. And like every other addict the world has ever known, I want to hook you all.

My first shot at it was a 522-page love letter called *Murder Ink*. This is the 416-page P.S. Can there be that much new to say? I think so. Where else but in *Murder Ink* would you find out what Miss Marple would look like if she had a little money, why the private eye's secretary has taken up data processing, which bookstores specialize in mysteries and are practically next-door to you, how to kill cardiovascularly, make a killing in a co-op, even plot a farewell toast and catch Mr. Hoover in several whoppers?

Who else but *Murder Ink* is on the tail of the Maltese Microchip, can sum up, in a sentence, breaking and entering, distinguish Eton from Winchester from the knot of a necktie and say "It's a secret" in twenty-five languages, including Hungarian?

Murder Ink, this time round, introduces you to the man who founded the CIA library, the woman who created six English pubs from her home outside Baltimore, the daughter of our thirty-third President and the bookman who comes in twenty-one colors.

What's more, *Murder Ink* compromises the entire English character in a droll little tale told in mug shots and text for the very first time. *The Tainted Tea Tragedy* is a book within a book. It is *the* definitive tea mystery (if you smell something fishy about it, it's probably a red herring).

So pull up a chair, put up your feet, pour yourself a cuppa and join us in our favorite brew: trouble.

(Gulp)

Dilys Winn

PLOTS

The official House of Teas crest, soon to be flaunted on china, silverware, linens, stationery and all House of Teas packaging.

It is the greatest event of my life and they are almost two hours late for it, all of them, even Clare, who was so keen on the house party in the first place.

When a gentleman has been honoured by our sovereign, when that sovereign says, here, old thing, have an OBE and ring up the Scriveners at the Royal College and have them work something out for you, and when that gentleman, yes, me, has waited patiently for eight long years for that crest to be completed, *and*, mind you, has gone to estimable expense to welcome it with a house party, and that party, *in toto,* is so ingracious as to be *over two hours late,* then I say do without me, chappies, and look to your back and your futures because I'm bearing grudges starting now.

I expect that *you* mightn't have taken to bed. Probably think it's silly. 'Tis. But at least here I'm in the good company of a book, whilst down there, in my own tea lounge specially redecorated for the weekend, at a time well past the one every last of them agreed upon and I topsied my schedule to accommodate, there's no one. What do you make of that, eh? Can they all've been held up on a train with a flat tyre, hmm?

Damn that Roudebush for deserting, too. Mind, I don't fancy a touch of the gout myself, but I'd've thought I'd've caught it, being the, so to speak, rich man; not the butler. He and I, we two, abed until we rot. Actually he'll only need a fortnight of no pressure on the foot before he can walk again. I'll want twice that before I'm in a mood to forgive.

Where Becca's got to is anybody's guess. She was asking Whelks for more front hall flowers earlier on, and some brighter colours for the table, and fair to make him daft with her "Bring me a primrose with the undulation of Donatello, Whelks, and a verbana plant with Gauguin's primitivism." Very polite he

Lady Teasdale dozes off.

was, too; just said, "Very good, miss," and acted like he'd heard a normal request. One day I expect to walk out and find she's taken her brush and done over the leaves on the trees to suit herself.

Undoubtedly Clare's holed up at her washbasin swallowing scent, more's the fool she; the trick went out with Pompadour. If she wants a go at it, then may's well be bold, I say; no more of this secret drinking business; and that damn nurse Simon hired for her can either see to it that she learns to hold it like a gentleman or find herself another post. Maybe off to Australia with Clare's cousin—the one who's so prompt to-night. Let the two of them do as they please on that kiwi farm of his. Some fit work for a gentleman, I told Clare; watching kiwis fornicate!

Harriet drops off a message for Simon in the usual place.

Cook prepares chicken soup for Roudebush, abed with gout.

It's a wonder I've not had the lot carted off to Bedlam by now: a sister who paints purple on her eyelids, a wife who drinks everything but tea, an in-law I've never met who stares at birds whilst they're doing naughty things—no wonder I've devoted myself to the firm.

It's Virgil I can't believe this rudeness of. An old Military man is never late, never, even with a sodding hole in his effing side. I rather wanted the first cup poured under the crest to go to Virgil, in memory of Her Majesty's Fifth Battalion. The next to Roudebush. Oh the times we shared, the tea breaks! The way we learned to brew and flavour it! And from such humble origins sprang up House of Teas, my House of Teas!

Half a moment—p'haps they've gone round to the shop instead. I'm sure I instructed Simon to put our at-home on the invitation, but that idiot could've got it backwards. Half an hour more I'll allow, then I'll pour a sleeping draught and the house party will just have to begin without me.

Pity, though; I was quite looking forward to a game of Piquet after dinner. Clare tells me Cousin Leslie is rather nimble with cards. Never mind; there's always tomorrow, after the musicale. Meanwhile, I'll just rest here and sulk. Maybe think about which apologies to accept and which I can turn down. They'll all feed me a pack of lies, you know. Every last one of them. Can't understand it myself. In my whole life I've never lied about anything small; I've told only two lies, actually, and one of them, of course, is about loving Clare. The other, well, I know it'll pop round one day and say, "Hallo, Your Lordship, piper-paying time, is it?" But that won't be to-night or this weekend.

FROM POE TO THE PRESENT

Dilys Winn

I have an untidy mind. It confuses dates, misspells names, amalgamates plots and mangles facts. And it does it unrepentantly, presenting its little distortions as Gospel when, in fact, they're fibs. For years I attributed the first mystery to Carolyn Keene, Nancy Drew's creator, even though I knew full well a gentleman named Poe deserved the credit. I'd read Keene first, and according to my personal mystery chronology she rated the honor.

For solid research, I defer to Howard Haycraft. Now, in a handsome retirement community in south Jersey, Mr. Haycraft and his wife spend quiet afternoons thunking the croquet ball through the wickets. But back in '41 Mr. Haycraft authored *Murder for Pleasure,* the

definitive mystery history, followed it up with *The Art of the Mystery Story,* the definitive mystery anthology, and then, with the assistance of Ellery Queen, issued his definitive mystery list, *The Haycraft-Queen Definitive Library of Detective-Crime-Mystery Fiction.* The list still stands as the best ever done.

I hope Mr. Haycraft won't think it bad manners if I approach things a little differently. Where he is orderly, I am not. Where he tells how, when, why, what, in chronological sequence, I crave a hodgepodge that pairs books of similar type rather than similar birth date.

I recognize five basic mystery categories: the Cozy, the Paranoid, the Romantic, the Vicious, the Analytical. (This leaves me no place for Rex Stout, but never mind; he really deserves a category unto himself.)

Of course, the Doyenne of Coziness is Agatha Christie, and the first book in the canon is *The Mysterious Affair at Styles.* Coziness, however, took another ten years to reach full kitsch, which happened when Miss Marple arrived in *The Murder at the Vicarage.* Alternately titled the Antimacassar-and-Old-Port School, the Cozies surfaced in England in the mad Twenties and Thirties, and their work featured a small village setting, a hero with faintly aristocratic family connections, a plethora of red herrings and a tendency to commit homicide with sterling-silver letter openers and poisons imported from Paraguay.

Special mention must be made of a Pseudo-Cozy: Dorothy L. Sayers. She teaches peculiar subjects (such as the art of bell-ringing) while she mystifies. Many Cozy readers appreciate this, and it's not uncommon to hear them remark, "Oh, I like a good read where I learn something. Mysteries teach me things!"

The Paranoid School began with Erskine Childers' spy novel, *The Riddle of the Sands,* and progressed through Sapper, through Ambler and Le Carré, to the Paranoid Politicals of Robert Ludlum. These books are characterized by a mistrust of everybody, particularly one's "control." Nothing dates faster than a Paranoid novel: this year it's chic to be wary of the Chinese; last year, the Arabs; the year before, the South Africans. Often, Paranoids are concerned with the reemergence of Nazis (e.g., Levin's *The Boys from Brazil*). Though not strictly Paranoid, the Dick Francis books belong in this category because of the hero's sentimentality.

The Romantics are one part supernatural to two parts warped intuition. The father of the Romantic novel is Wilkie Collins, and his *Woman in White* remains the classic in the genre. These books, under Mary Roberts Rinehart's supervision, evolved into the Had-I-But-Known School. From the Fifties on, the Romantic converted to the Damsel-in-Distress novel, typified by the works of Phyllis A. Whitney, Mary Stewart and Barbara Michaels.

An aberrant strain of the Romantic is the Romantic Suspense, championed by Helen MacInnes. As her books are old-fashioned (communism is a passé devil), she has been supplanted by Evelyn Anthony (who has stolen a leaf from the Paranoids and on occasion has gone after Nazism). A variant is the Historical Romantic Suspense. This is a splinter group: the Genuine Historical (i.e., any book written before 1918) and the Ersatz (written post–World War I but depicting the past).

Which brings us round to the Vicious. Carroll John Daly elbowed it onto the scene in the late 1920's with hero Race Williams, but in truth a nonwriter, Capt. Shaw of *Black Mask* magazine, was the man responsible for the genre's impact. These books all have a male protagonist, back-alley slang, enough booze to float the *Titanic* and a

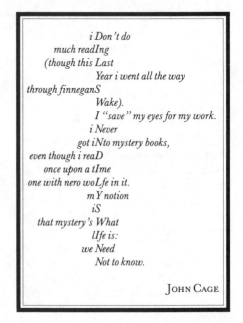

i Don't do
much readIng
(though this Last
            Year i went all the way
through finneganS
            Wake).
            I "save" my eyes for my work.
            i Never
            got iNto mystery books,
even though i reaD
    once upon a tIme
one with nero woLfe in it.
        mY notion
            iS
    that mystery's What
            lIfe is:
        we Need
        Not to know.

JOHN CAGE

BOOKS TO BE READ ALOUD

Anything by George V. Higgins. If you try to read these to yourself, you wind up moving your lips. Mr. Higgins loves dialogue, but it looks unintelligible on the page. It comes to life when you actually repeat the words. They are not the words, however, you would most want a maiden auntie to hear, nor kids under twelve. We suggest you read them out between deals in the poker game.

Anything by Wilkie Collins. Draw your chair close to the fire and gather the family round. These are old-fashioned stories with hammy, improbable plots that somehow sound wonderful if you pretend you're Lunt and Fontanne and emote for all you're worth. So much the better if it's storming outside, the phone wires are down and you have to read by gaslight. A lap rug thrown over your knees is not inappropriate either.

Anything by Stanley Ellin. Whenever anyone tells you mystery writers can't write, sit him down and read Stanley Ellin to him. Mr. Ellin is clear, direct and chilling. What's more, he is one of the few writers who has something to say to hard-boiled fans as well as classicists. His best for reading-aloud purposes: *Stronghold.*

Anything by Margaret Millar. You know how some people just seem to have the knack of saying things that get under your skin? Millar hooks you in the first paragraph. You might just as well begin reading her with someone else, or you're going to spend all your time chasing after friends saying, "Listen to this," and then reading out great chunks of books.

Anything by Dashiell Hammett. Take your Chandler friend by the hand, put a piece of tape over his mouth, and tell him to just shut up and hear how it ought to be done. *The Glass Key* puts to shame every other hard-boiled writer.

Dashiell Hammett

distressing way of blaming (1) the business partner or (2) the dame's father. Their partisans think of them as realistic. The best, bar none, of the Vicious writers was Dashiell Hammett; the worst, Mickey Spillane. Others include Chandler, Higgins, Leonard and Stark.

The Analytical School has the longest history. It began in 1841 with an errant orangutan stuffing a young girl up a chimney in Poe's *The Murders in the Rue Morgue,* where the solution was resolved by a process usually called ratiocination—a 50¢ word for logical thinking. The Analytical then forked into Reasoning by Intellect and Reasoning by Machine: the former, from Poe direct to Conan Doyle to Carr; the latter, from Freeman to Reeves to McBain.

Cross-reading among the categories is rare. A Cozy reader will semicomfortably pick up an Analytical but hardly admit that a Paranoid is part of the field. Similarly, a Romantic reader will sniff at the Vicious and insist they're outside the genre. According to Mr. Haycraft (and me), any book that focuses on crime is a mystery. So, readers should stop quibbling. This endless discussion of what belongs is really unnecessary; there's room for almost any style, as long as it concerns an evil. One could even make a case for calling *Crime and Punishment* a mystery. And who knows what lurks in next year?

Dilys Winn is the perpetrator of Murder Ink.

SIX BASIC PLOTS

Amanda Spivak

The Cozy

It is the morning after the dark and stormy night. The village is in an uproar: someone has stolen Miss Maple's marbles. A trail of muddy footprints leads direct to the tea table. The tea is served. When the table is cleared, a body is found beneath the (hand-knit) tea tablecloth. One swoon, one faint, two "Oh dears" later, the Inspector pops round. Miss Maple rings for more tea. The lights go out. The phone wires are down. The vicar delivers a boring homily. The lights come back on. Tea is served. The body beneath the table moves. It sits up and identifies itself: a younger son just sent down from university. Too upset to go home, he stopped by for tea. Miss Maple retires to the kitchen to prepare more scones. She comes upon her marbles in the flour canister (she'd forgotten she'd hid them there for safekeeping). Everyone adjourns to the library for more tea. The younger son announces his betrothal to Miss Maple's niece. Miss Maple promises them her marbles as a wedding present; they shyly request her tea service instead.

The Hard-Boiled

I was sitting at my desk wondering if Louie would take a disconnected telephone as collateral when a dame walks in crying. She drops her hankie. I yawn; I've seen a hankie before. Then some goon dehinges the office door, grabs the hankie and yells on his way out, "Move and you're dead." I borrow the dame's car (mine's been repossessed), tail Doorman to the Big House, ditch the car in the bushes and hunker down in time to see our esteemed Senator escort Musclemouth into his gunroom with all the enthusiasm I'd show a glass of Hawaiian Punch. Someone takes a pot shot at me from behind. I turn around and the dame's standing there. "I could have loved you," she says, "but you know too much." Someone takes a shot at her from north of my shoulder. Cordite mingles with Chanel No. 5. I hear another shot and duck, but too late; when I come to, her body's gone, the house's closed up and I'm forty-seven minutes older, but no wiser. I limp over to the car. There's a ticket on the windshield. I leave it as I found it and start walking, wondering how I'm going to pay for new door hinges.

The Gothic

Patience had none. As she flung down her embroidery, she beseeched her uncle, "Why, Uncle, why? Why can't I wear anything but nightgowns?"

"My child," he soothed her, "my innocent child." He stroked back her hair, allowing his fingers to trail its length, down, all the way down, past a slim bit of waist, a warm curve of hip, to a sweet rosebud dimly hinted beneath a cloud of nightie. "My child," he repeated, his voice husky with passion, "trust me."

"Oh, I do, I do, Uncle, truly I do," she assured him. "Why else would I gladly swallow that foul fetid tonic you press upon me, that strange elixir that saps strength from my limbs and makes memories grow dim?"

At this chilling revelation a lightning bolt smote the sky and thunder commenced. Above it all a pounding on the door could be heard. "Standforth, you scoundrel, open the door. It is I, Beauworthy, home at last from my study abroad with the Naik, the netsuke, the Nairobi Quartet. Attend my admittance at once, sir!"

"That voice," Patience swooned. "Have my prayers been answered, then?"

Her uncle clasped her in his arms, rubbing against her with a fervor that frightened her. "Tell me," he cajoled. "What prayers do you need when you have my protection?"

"Just this, Uncle." She glanced down at her sampler. " 'I pledge my heart, my hopes, my hearth to thee, dear Lord. Now find me a husband.' "

Standforth thrust her from him, ventured to the cabinet and returned with the elixir. "Here, child," he insisted. "Drink up before . . ."

The door crashed open, Beauworthy strode into the room and knocked the vial from his hand. "I shall relieve you of her now, Cousin," he smirked, then turned to Patience and said, "My own dear little sister, come away with me and we shall live together fulfilled to the utmost, as is our birthright." He stroked back her hair, allowing his fingers to trail its length, down, all the way down, past a slim bit of waist, a warm curve of hip, to a sweet rosebud dimly hinted beneath a cloud of nightie.

And off they went, happiness, after all, being only relative.

The Police

The kid seemed so young. Jesus, what kind of backup never heard of Old Main? Why'd they always give him the babies to sit?

"Pull in. I gotta take a leak. The box goes off, come get me, right? Don't go playing Superman. Got it?"

The kid smiled. Polite as all hell.

"Sure, Max. I know."

Max walked into Vinnie's and headed for the can.

"Eh, Max. Long time no see. How goes it, paisan? You got the pistol arm back now?"

"Better than ever, Vinnie, better than ever," Max lied, hating the reminder, the pictures that started in his head of Sammy and the punk with a sawed-off I-95 and the too little space for the three of them in the dink of a lunch-eonette over on Pine, with the owner at their feet missing most of his face, and the punk itching to let go again, and, wham, WHAM, white-hot, eyeballs rolling back, and the God-awful hospital with the dumb nurse saying he was lucky, not like Sammy, who rushed the punk and didn't make it, and then the pulleys, the weights, the pills, the fight to get reinstated and the fool doctor saying of course the feelings will come back, Christ what a lot of crap.

His hand started the shakes. Jesus, he needed a drink, but how'd he get it past the kid?

"Hey, Vinnie, gimme two blacks. Maybe a doughnut. I don't know, make it a Danish. I'll be right out."

He walked into the can, his head full of memories shaking loose, coming out his hands, in no way ready for the guy dealing and the buy so scared he panicked and something flashed and went in so fast he never had time, just thought It's so cold again. And then he dropped.

The kid was listening for their number, willing the box to call it, excited just thinking about a little first-day action, when the two guys ran out of Vinnie's, with Vinnie chasing them, blood streaming down, screaming at them and him and everyone and no one, "Come on, come on, it's Max, he's not gonna make it, ohmigod, he's not, come on, come on, come on."

The kid was in such a hurry, he jammed the car handle and nearly tore it off. Finally he got it working, open, and raced inside, straight to the can. When he got a look, he stopped dead, like he ran into a door.

"But that's my partner," the kid said. "My partner," and he began to cry.

The Spy

"Do you have it?"

"Perhaps."

"Show me."

"When the gentians are in bloom over Flanders . . ."

" . . . and the oleanders canopy Liège . . ."

"Hans!"

"Miles!"

"All clear?"

"Yes, I bribed the patrol. Quick, out the back door."

"The back way? No way! You're not Miles. Who are you?"

"What do you care? Give it to me!"

"Bloody hell I will. You'll have to kill me to get it."

"Come, be sensible. Give me the paper."

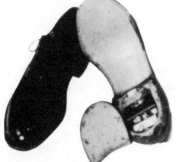

Will you speak to a heel?

"I'll have to make a call."

"All right, but be quick."

"Operator, ring double-oh, double-six, treble-nine."

"Let me hear."

I'M SORRY. THE NUMBER YOU HAVE REACHED IS NOT A WORKING NUMBER. PLEASE DIAL AGAIN.

"Enough of your delays! Hand it over now or I will call in Felix."

"You're bluffing. There's nobody here but us."

"Felix, introduce yourself to the gentleman. Ah, Felix, that was not kind. You know how much I dislike blood. And what do you have to say now, my friend?"

"Aaargh . . . . . You may . . . think . . . you've . . . won . . . but . . . but . . . I . . . swallowed . . . the . . . pa . . . pa . . . paper."

"Operator, get me double-one, double-two, treble-four. Maintenance? Send a clean-up team to remove one large . . . er, paper shredder. Yes, right away. Thank you."

The Horror

Charlie over at the Mobil station was the first. The way we figure, he'd turned on the answering machine so's he could work on Ernie's pickup without the phone ringing off the wall, and it was just his luck a few calls came in. The first one, it slammed the hood down and near to took off his hand. The second, it slipped the gear box and wasn't more than a minute after that, the third ring came through and must've short-circuited the horn. Jesse heard that, but by the time she thought to check, it was too late. Charlie must've tried to disconnect it and that's when it got him. Jesse said the place looked like a vat of green jello exploded and poor Charlie, his face was sort of melted into strips, like he'd been left on the burner too long. Jesse got out of there, but fast, and by the time she found us there wasn't a family in Machias with all its members living. We think we're the last ones left, but we don't know, any more than we know why it happened and if it'll ever stop. One thing's sure: we're not about to call anyone to find out.

Amanda Spivak has participated in The Summit Plot, *a conspiracy of four.*

THE LAST PRIVATE EYE
A MYSTERY STALWART IN ECLIPSE

Thomas Perry

Sometime next year Benton Fist, the last of the working private eyes, will close his office to take a job as security chief for a chain of fashionable clothing stores called Le Baudet avec Parapluie d'Or. He'll spend most of his time flying between the Costa Mesa and Dallas branches to administer polygraph tests to nervous employees. His receptionist, Chlo O'Flynn, who hadn't actually received a paycheck since 1958, has already started a new career in word processing. Her friends say she hasn't looked this good since the louse hired her.

In 1949 Raymond Chandler wrote, "The mystery story must take into account the cultural stage of its readers; things that were acceptable in Sherlock Holmes are not acceptable in Sayers or Christie or Carter Dickson." Chandler knew that the world outside the lurid book jacket was changing and that crime writers had to change with it. Nineteen forty-nine was the year when the number of people murdered in fictional English country houses exceeded the casualties of World War I: if the polite slaughter had continued unabated, the only imaginable inhabitants of Great Britain would be Inspectors roaming the empty countryside like hunters in search of extinct game. We have again reached the time for the crime writer to imitate Chandler's favorite animal, the cat. As it appears to be comfortably curled on one lap, its half-closed eyes watch for the next pair of human legs to bend and form the next lap. Now that Ben Fist and Chlo have straightened up and moved on, it's time to survey the field to see who's left.

It's still possible to use the mafia as a perpetual farm team for villains, but they've retooled and diversified. They can be presented as extorting money from the owner of the hero's favorite liquor store, but only at the store's main office, which is in another state. Go easy on the esoteric Cosa Nostra lore: one mafioso who wrote a best-selling confession reported that when his regime wanted to induct a new member a few years ago, nobody remembered how the ceremony was supposed to go so they had to improvise something for the occasion. And don't make these people look dumb—they own your bank.

Spies are still with us, but here, too, the novelist will have to compete with the reporter. The spy isn't William Buckley wandering through European restaurants mispronouncing his vowels in the presence of people who dress better than the maître d'. In the most recent case to make the newspapers, a spy supposedly divulged the identity of an important agent-in-place for eleven thousand dollars. A fictional spy wouldn't sell the plans for the Battle of Thermopylae for that kind of money. A fiction writer will also have to elbow aside the horde of real CIA agents who have retired to write their memoirs. They've given us all a wealth of useful details, but they've also managed to reveal that just about everything worth knowing is recorded by satellites and that spies spend very little of their time with beautiful women. And all those years they weren't dashing down the back alleys of Berlin to outflank the KGB; they were dispensing itching powder in Bolivia and working on a chemical to make Fidel's beard fall out.

The subgenre of the spy story that features Private Enterprise With Rabies has survived a couple of generations and may be good for one more. In these plots, corporation owners, sheiks, noblemen, Texas oilmen, generals or politicians, impenetrably disguised as corporation owners, sheiks, noblemen, Texas oilmen, generals or politicians, conspire to take control of whatever it is they don't control already. These stories still pass Chandler's test: things that were acceptable in Ian Fleming are still acceptable in Robert Ludlum. Since the world got used to heavily armed and well-organized evil in the 1930's, it's always been possible to imagine villains who have no motive except to dominate the earth. By the time James Bond first picked out a tuxedo that would look good over a Walther PPK, no villain needed to be provided with a more sensible motive than that. Does a criminal genius lurk in these pages? Then he must want to dominate the earth. And no doubt he's trained vast schools of tuna to stream across the world's oceans to do his evil bidding. There's never been a need to explain what the tuna get out of these schemes, or what anybody expects to do with the earth once he's got it dominated. Everybody likes to be a winner.

Plots that involve mere theft are still possible, but the changing nature of wealth demands a different kind of loot. Inflation has been fairly constant in Western countries since Pizarro came back from Peru with so much gold that nobody else could afford to buy anything. Now inflation has made thriller-caliber sums of money too bulky to carry off, hide and fight over in any reasonable way. Your corner supermarket's daily take is hauled to the bank in a fairly large armored truck. The repulsive little

PINKERTON'S ("The Pinks")

WE NEVER SLEEP

The original private eye belonged to the Pinkerton's National Detective Agency. It was their trademark, a large, unblinking, ever-seeing eye— the eye that never sleeps. This is the root of the expression "private eye," although many think the term derived from private investigator, abbreviated to P.I. Hard-boiled writers were not the first to steal inspiration from the Pinks. Conan Doyle beat them to it. Intrigued with the story of the Pink undercover agent who infiltrated the Molly Maguires, Doyle worked it into *The Valley of Fear.* Pinkerton itself got into the writing business. Allan Pinkerton hired a series of writers to perpetuate the Pinkerton exploits, and they did so—under his name—in eighteen novels.

guy on the opposite corner is a drug dealer, and he doesn't have time to count his money: he weighs it, after throwing away the small bills. The only bank robberies big enough to make a profit are done with computers.

Writers have begun to solve the currency problem by speculating in commodities. Donald E. Westlake has some thieves take a trainload of coffee, but the task is so difficult that it's not much better than honest labor. It used to be fairly convenient to use diamonds as pelf, but soon a Japanese company will produce a synthetic diamond that would make a jeweler smile in admiration and then stagger to his storeroom to shoot himself. The only really reliable form of wealth seems to be land, so the next group of villains may begin stealing real estate and transporting it to longitudes beyond the reach of the law. Major league greed will require the theft of whole continents, and by the end of the century armed robbery may be a subfield of plate tectonics.

There are still fine employment op-portunities for genuine criminals, but they don't tend to be the sort that makes fascinating reading. Many have to do with numbers: credit card numbers, au-tomatic bank teller codes, computer ac-cess numbers. Others are simple acts of fraud: turning back the odometers of used cars, counterfeiting trademarks, in-

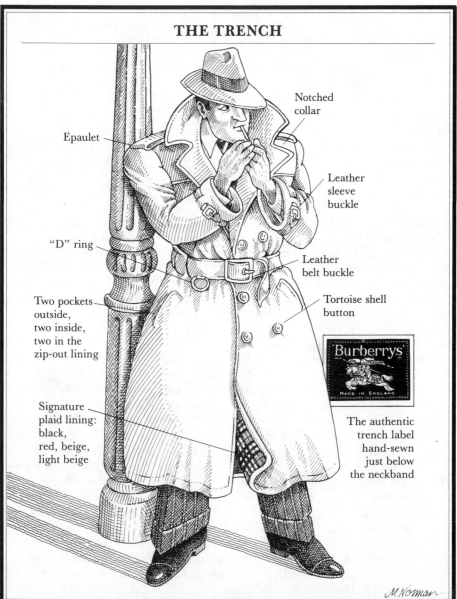

THE TRENCH

Notched collar

Epaulet

Leather sleeve buckle

"D" ring

Leather belt buckle

Tortoise shell button

Two pockets outside, two inside, two in the zip-out lining

Burberrys
MADE IN ENGLAND

Signature plaid lining: black, red, beige, light beige

The authentic trench label hand-sewn just below the neckband

M. Norman

MARTY NORMAN

fringing patents, and skimming. The modern hero had better be someone with a background in mathematics and a long attention span.

He will still need to be tough, because after performing his accounting feats, he still won't be able to get his adversaries to go quietly. This attribute of the modern hero must be carefully portrayed to convince a sophisticated readership. Everyone knows that the most aggressive and resilient people in our society are little old ladies. They've experienced depressions, childbirth, arthritis and the decline of the postal system—these people know no fear. If they were't so small, they'd bully the modern hero and not let him drive so fast. If little old ladies ran in packs the way villains usually do, no plausible plot could dispose of them. Thank God, Miss Marple was on our side.

The tough heroes we're used to will have to retrain quickly. Robert Parker's detective, Spenser, is well educated, a gourmet cook and a pretty fair carpenter, so there's a good chance he'll find something to do when the investigating business doesn't work anymore. Lawrence Block's man Matthew Scudder, who likes his bourbon sraight ("the way God made it"), is no chef, but he appears to be making his own liver into a pâté, and when that recipe is finished there's not much point in retraining.

A few writers such as Trevanian have tried to keep the tough hero in business by making him a master of arcane Eastern skills in the martial and erotic arts, but this won't work for everyone. The problem with Westerners who spend the years necessary to earn the black belt is that all of them had to. Each is the sort of person who has already spent an equal number of years earning punches in the mouth. They still get punched, but now they know how to roll backward without hitting their heads on the floor. Ask any competent orthopedic surgeon about the Eastern erotic arts, and he'll tell you that virtue is its own reward.

Physical ability has never been enough. The old private eye usually carried a police special .38, but if the new hero wants to survive he's going to have to keep up with the competition. The competition is carrying military-grade armament. Notable these days are automatic assault rifles like the Uzi and Ingram. There are refinements available to the imagination, if not to the average consumer, which may put the hero to considerable expense. There are silencers, Teflon-jacketed bullets, ammunition clips and infrared night scopes in such numbers that the sheer bulk of them may bring back the trench coat. Here's where the hero's mathematical skills will really pay off. He'll be the sort of person who can answer the following question: "If your Ingram fires 850 shots a minute, and you expect this gunfight to last ten minutes, how many rounds of ammunition should you have hidden in your socks?" He'll know that a snap-brim hat can hold fifteen or twenty rounds that may save his life.

The hero of the future will retain a few qualities of his predecessors. He'll still tell us more than he seems to about his past, he'll be alone more often than not, and he'll fight evil where he finds it because evil makes him angry. He'll win most of the time, though it won't do him much monetary good or ease the burden of his loneliness. And he'll survive until he comes up against the cadre of little old ladies who are assembling an aresenal of missiles that home in on his brand of whiskey in preparation for their plot to move the Bahamas up the St. Lawrence River into the Great Lakes.

Thomas Perry is the author of The Butcher's Boy, *which won an Edgar from the Mystery Writers of America,* Metzger's Dog *and* Big Fish.

A SLIGHT DEBATE
A Hard-Boiled Fan and a Country-House Fan Discuss the Genre

Marilyn Stasio
and
Richard Hummler

Scene:
A breakfast nook in an upper-middle-class suburban American home. A married couple, Mike and Margery, face each other across a glass breakfast table.

H.T. WEBSTER

MARGERY

Christie.

MIKE

Chandler.

MARGERY

Marsh.

MIKE

Who?

MARGERY

Ngaio.

MIKE

Oh, right . . . the New Zealander.
    (Sucks in gut.)
Spillane. *(Pause. Lasciviously.)* Mickey.

MARGERY

I'm simply not going on with this if you won't behave decently.
    (Pause. They glare at each other.)

MIKE

Ross Macdonald.

MARGERY

That's better. . . Margery Allingham.

MIKE

(Unbuttons his shirt collar and wrenches his tie away from his neck. Grins.)
Walker.

MARGERY

(Looks away from him nervously as she straightens the tea cozy.)
Who?

MIKE

Francix X. Walker, sweetheart. Detroit.
His detective is Mickey Reilly.

MARGERY

Hardly in the premier rank, I'd say.
(Pause) Michael Innes. No—make that
P.D. James. *(Pause)* I'm saving Innes.

MIKE

Gores.

MARGERY

(Pause) Are you making yours up?

MIKE

(Rolls up his shirt sleeves and slams his elbows on the table.)
Joe Gores. Nobody you'd know, baby. Just one of the greatest detective novelists in American crime fiction.

(Margery rattles her teacup ominously.)

MIKE

Don't gimme that, Maggie. Just because Gores writes about *real* people killing other *real* people for *real* reasons, instead of effete Oxford dons knocking each other off with African blowguns, doesn't mean you have to turn your nose up.

MARGERY

You've dribbled egg on your chin. *(Sniffs.)* Maybe I should have cooked it *hard-boiled.*
(Opens her newspaper—the London Observer—and screams.)

MIKE

(Slams down the Daily News.)
What the—

MARGERY

John Dickson Carr died.

MIKE

(Pause) Who?

MARGERY

You must be joking. He is *the* master craftsman of the century. The *ne plus ultra* of the locked-room genre.

MIKE

(Lights up, blows the smoke in her eyes.)
Figures.

MARGERY

And what is *that* supposed to mean?

MIKE

Only broad I know gets so worked up when some academic pedant kicks off.

MARGERY

(Picks up her knitting and begins to work the long needles savagely.)
And when Mickey Spillane dies, I suppose you won't disappear into some bar for a week of sodden grieving.

MIKE

(Crumples his empty Lucky Strike pack and tosses it into a plate of cold kippers.)
Listen, sweetheart—maybe guys like Parker and Stark have never seen the inside of a cathedral close, but they tell it like it is, not like it *was.*

MARGERY

Name me one who writes with the literary erudition of Nicholas Blake. Or the wit of Edmund Crispin.

MIKE

(Sullenly.) Raymond Chandler.

MARGERY

(A hoot of contempt.) And I suppose that John D. MacDonald is a better writer than Michael Innes.

MIKE

Okay, so that's how you want to fight?
(Pause. He spikes his orange juice with a shot of Jack Daniel's. She winces.)
MacDonald at least tells a good story. Those English biddies you read—you can't even follow the plot without a Ph.D. in Etruscan funerary statuary.

MARGERY

(Smiles grimly over her knitting.)
Any intellectual demand beyond the size of a woman's bra cup is utterly beyond the mental capacities of your heroes.

MIKE

(Stands up, grabs his coat.)
Let me put it this way. SHUT UP!

MARGERY

Why is it, every time we have this discussion you retreat into macho petulance? *(Pause)* Are you really going to wear that filthy trench coat to the office?

MIKE

Now, don't go giving me that macho stuff again. A little normal sex is healthier than all those repressed vicars and inbred toffs sitting around doing crosswords in the drawing room.
(Lurches over to her. Grabs her knitting.)
And when you stop wearing riding tweeds and those damned English brogues, then you can start telling *me* how to dress... *sweet*heart.

MARGERY

(Nervously.) The sense of societal... uh ... communality does get a bit thick with some of the older writers, I admit ...
(Fortifies herself with another sip of tea.)
But the familial social structure has a distinct advantage, I should say, over the blatant fascism of your lone-wolf avengers. *(Pause)* More tea?

MIKE

(Mumbling to himself.) Buncha chinless snobs... *(Pause)* Coffee.

MARGERY

(Sweetly.) I don't suppose you've ever analyzed the latent misogyny of the blood-and-guts brigade?

MIKE

(Gives his coffee a blast of Jack Daniel's.)
Don't get sarcastic with me or I'll shut a drawer on your fingers.

MARGERY

George V. Higgins, I believe. *(Pause)* And I suppose Travis McGee isn't a closet queen?

MIKE

(Mumbling.) Buncha chinless *faggots!*

MARGERY

(Furiously butters a scone.)
Adolescent mentalities attempting to compensate for their own impotence.

MIKE

(Getting more incoherent.)
Lester Dent... Henry Kane...
(Reaches for the bourbon bottle; knocks it over.)

MARGERY

Sexual sadists!

MIKE

(Draws himself up.)
I'm warning you, baby...

MARGERY

(Wildly shreds watercress.)
You want to destroy it all—the puzzle, the pace, the atmosphere, the literary clues. *(Pause. Sobs.)* The compound-complex sentence.

MIKE

(Draws a gun from his trench coat pocket.)
No jury would convict me.

MARGERY

Do you smell that soufflé in the oven? *(Pause)* It's your first edition of *The Big Sleep*!

MIKE

That does it, sweetheart.
(He shoots. She falls across the table, scattering the watercress.)

MIKE

Thirty-eight-caliber automatic. Makes a nice clean hole. Not too much blood. *(Pause)* She never did like blood.
(He grabs his throat. Chokes. Slumps back in his chair.)

MARGERY

(Weakly.) Potassium cyanide. Two grains. Chemical symbol: KCN. Crystalline salt with the following properties: colorless, soluble, poisonous. *(Pause)* Used in electroplating.
(She dies.)

MIKE

I won't play the sap for you, angel.
(He dies.)

— THE END —

Marilyn Stasio and Richard Hummler are divorced.

UNFINISHED MASTERPIECES

Judith Crist

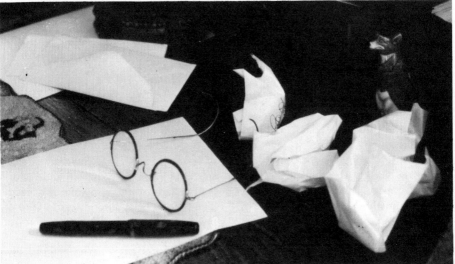

Page One, version 469.

We also serve who only sit and read. Let the uninitiate think we Mystery Readers serve the writers by our purchase and consumption of books and magazines and by our devotion, blind or very wise, to the masters of the craft and their creatures. We aficionados know that our greatest service has been our refusal to put down on paper, let alone publish, The Great American Detective Story that each of us carries around in his head. After all, we can devote a lifetime to perfecting plot and personnel as we consume the goodies the "public" writers provide and we grow fat on their creations. But we grow cautious, too, and taste humility from time to time as we encounter a more cunning crime, a cannier deduction, a tauter twist and better breath-bater than ever we

dreamed of. And so the revisions go on as standards are set higher and higher. We Readers remain closet writers.

I have spent my adult life in that closet, deposited therein by a paternal attitude that designated moviegoing and detective story reading as prime time-wasters. Even so, it was on the family bookshelves that I found Sherlock Holmes and then a host of others in a ten-volume set of *The World's Greatest Detective Stories* that the Literary Digest had apparently foisted on the household as a subscription bonus. And it was at the Saturday movie matinées that I encountered Warner Oland's Fu Manchu, Warren William's Perry Mason, Edward Arnold's Nero Wolfe, William Powell's Philo Vance, Ronald Coleman's Bulldog Drummond, Edna May Oliver's Hildegarde Withers, Peter Lorre's Mr. Moto, and Warner Oland again as Charlie Chan. These introductions at least fulfilled Hollywood's educational pretension: they led me to read the books.

But though in my adolescence as an aspiring writer I had no hesitation about attempting Dickensian sagas, Hemingwayesque stories and Thomas Wolfean *Weltschmerz,* I didn't attempt an unwritten mystery until graduate school. It came upon me suddenly—"Murder Cum Laude," a bitterly satiric view of academe, wherein a variety of scholars met their doom and a beautiful, slim and brilliant graduate student helped a charming, couth and educated cop (a novelty in those days, I assure you) determine whether it was the Shakespeare scholar, the doctoral candidate or the janitor who did it. A couple of years went by as I devised cleverly academic methods of murder, all of which had to go by the boards (college,

---

EXCUSE ME, MR. DROOD. HAVE YOU EVER BEEN TO POODLE SPRINGS?

Charles Dickens and Raymond Chandler died before finishing, respectively, *The Mystery of Edwin Drood* and *The Poodle Springs Story.* Attempts by others to complete them have been unsuccessful. Ed McBain, on the other hand, polished off *The April Robin Murders,* the novel Craig Rice was working on when she died.

---

of course) when I switched my professional interests to journalism and "Murder Makes News" got into my head. This was to be a bitterly satiric view of newspapering, wherein a variety of

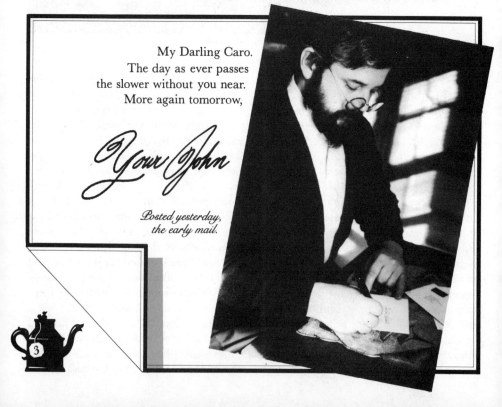

My Darling Caro.
The day as ever passes
the slower without you near.
More again tomorrow,

Your John

*Posted yesterday,
the early mail.*

3

columnists met their doom and a beautiful, slim and brilliant reporter helped a charming, uncouth and semi-educated cop (I had learned the facts of life) determine whether it was the publisher, the aspiring columnist or the copyboy who did it. My real-life reporting experiences with crime—most memorably a murder on the Columbia campus, suspicious deaths among wealthy elderly patients of a Connecticut doctor, the slaughter of a family with an eight-year-old survivor the possible killer—made me worry a lot about methodology; encounters with a couple of corpses and discovering the reality of "the stench of death" took some of the fun out of the murders.

But I soon found that my domestic interests superseded my professional life and had put "Marriage for Murder" into my mind. This was to be a bitterly satiric view of matrimony, wherein a variety of young couples met their doom and a beautiful, slim and brilliant wife helped her charming, couth and educated cop husband (it was no more than the gal deserved) decide whether it was the bachelor, the playgirl or the butcher who did it. While I was concentrating on avoiding any Northian taint to a martini-drinking Manhattan-couple tale, I found myself replacing it with "The Lying-In Murders," a bitterly satiric view of a maternity ward, wherein a variety of young mothers met their doom at the hands of the obstetrician, pediatrician or hospital trustee. In no time at all, or so it seemed, this had given way to "The Sandbox Slayings," wherein a variety of abominable toddlers were done away with by a mommy, a nanny or another toddler.

When my professional life, now that of theater and film critic, expanded to include television, however, domestic matters yielded to "Murder for Today," wherein a variety of morning-show guests were knocked off, on camera yet, and the heroine, no longer my vicarious

> # FIT PUNISHMENTS FOR THOSE WHO REVEAL THE ENDINGS OF MYSTERIES
>
> 1. Have them framed by Agatha Christie.
> 2. Have them waited on by the housekeeper at Manderley.
> 3. Have them stuffed up a chimney by an orangutan.
> 4. Have them interrupted in the shower by Norman Bates.
> 5. Have them licked to death by the Hound of the Baskervilles.

alter ego but the attractive, sharp interviewer on the show, determined on her own whether it was the anchorman, the producer or everybody's researcher-mistress who did it. For a while this one shared headroom with "The Critic Killer," wherein a drama critic was murdered in mid-review (multiple murders were becoming a bit too taxing) and his beautiful, slim and brilliant associate (reenter the dream alter ego) determined whether it was the producer, director or star of the show he was covering who did it. These two, in recent years, were replaced by "The Film Festival Murders," with an international cast, of course, and endless possibilities for doing away with the unbeloveds of my medium. I'm staying with it. On the other hand, a recent campus weekend with my son has started "The Cambridge Killings" buzzing in my brain . . .

But have no fear, you darlings of my noncinematic hours. We closet mystery concocters know that those who can, do; we, who like to think that we could if we would, are smart enough not to. Not yet. Meanwhile, we also serve. We sit and read.

Judith Crist was named Mystery Reader of the Year (1971) by the Mystery Writers of America.

ORGANIZED CRIME

K.C. Constantine

THE CAST:
  Mrs. Goode, librarian
  Mrs. Childe, patron of the arts
THE SCENE:
  A library checkout desk

CHILDE *(approaching counter):* I beg your pardon. Do you have the most recent book by K.C. Constantine?

GOODE: Why, I'm quite sure we do. Yes. There it is. On the New Arrivals counter behind you.

CHILDE *(getting book):* Oh, this is such a wonderful surprise. I wasn't sure you'd have it yet.

GOODE: Mercy, yes. We get all the mysteries. They're our most popular—after the best sellers, of course. We can never have too many mysteries.

CHILDE: I'm so glad, I don't know what I'd do without a good mystery to curl up with every night. Though I must say Mr. Constantine isn't very mysterious about whodunit.

GOODE: No, he isn't—or so I've been told. I started to read one of his books once, but the language was just too much for me.

CHILDE: Well, I like a little earthiness in my writers now and then.

GOODE: That's one way of putting it, I guess. But to me nothing beats a good Agatha Christie. She didn't have to use that kind of language to tell her stories. And *they* are *real* mysteries.

CHILDE: I suppose you're right. Still, I kind of like his—

GOODE: If you ask me, that man's books don't even belong in a library. Why, just last week a woman returned one the very same day she checked it out. She wanted me to put it in the trash—where it belonged, she said.

CHILDE: Well, it's not as though he goes around forcing his books on you, is it? I mean, he doesn't come around with a gun or something.

GOODE: I'd like to see him try.

CHILDE: Then how do you decide which books to get for the library?

GOODE: Our selection committee keeps up with all the trade journals—the ones that review all the books? And they decide on the basis of what the reviewers say and how popular the writer's books have been with our clients in the past.

CHILDE: So you don't even ask the writer whether—

GOODE: Madam, I don't know why you keep asking about whether we ask the writer this, that or the other. We don't ask the writer anything. The

writer has nothing to do with us.

CHILDE: Isn't that odd. The way you talk, one would think writers don't matter at all.

GOODE: My dear, once we have their books, they may as well be dead.

CHILDE: But if they were dead, they wouldn't be writing anymore.

GOODE: There are plenty to take their places, I assure you. See that fellow over there? *(Points. Mrs. Childe stares.)* There's a writer for you. He refuses to work at a decent job. Works at whatever comes along.

CHILDE: Maybe he doesn't make enough money writing to—

GOODE: Enough! Madam, he wrote for years and didn't make a penny. Now he's started to sell a few books, but look at him. Look at his clothes.

CHILDE: Do you have his books in here? Maybe I ought to read them.

GOODE: Of course we do. We've got them all. They all received excellent reviews, and then, too, he's a local fellow.

CHILDE: Oh, it seems such a shame that he isn't able to dress better.

GOODE: Well, it's no wonder. He simply won't apply himself to a job. Just works to make enough money to get by. Then he goes off and writes till all hours of the morning.

CHILDE: Needs a haircut, too.

GOODE: You may think so and I may think so, but do you know what he needs? I mean, what he really needs? He just thrives on seeing his name in print. You should've seen him the day his first book arrived here. Oh, he was practically dancing. Just laughing and happy. Pointing at his picture on the back of the dust cover and as excited as a child on Christmas morning.

CHILDE: Do you suppose that's what keeps him going?

GOODE: Absolutely. A fellow like that, all he needs is to read his reviews and,

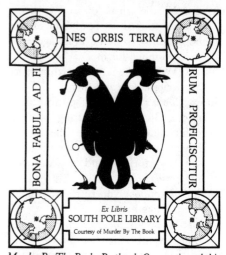

Murder By The Book, Portland, Oregon, issued this commemorative bookplate to all those customers who donated their used mysteries to the snowed-in scientists at the South Pole research station.

oh, now and then a letter from a fan telling him what a good writer he is. Keeps him going for weeks.

CHILDE: You know, sometimes I think about writing a letter to my favorite authors, like Mr. Constantine. Sometimes, when I think how much pleasure they give me, I'm almost tempted to put a dollar in the envelope—

GOODE: You want to do what? Send him a dollar? Whatever for?

CHILDE: Oh, I don't know. I guess sort of like a tip.

GOODE: Madam, he doesn't need tips. He's not a waiter.

CHILDE: Still, sometimes I get the eensiest twinge of—oh my, I don't know what it is. I've read all his books, and I got them all right here.

GOODE: My dear, you have to learn to control those twinges when it comes to writers. You must never ever send money to a writer. That's insulting.

CHILDE: You mean they'd be insulted?

GOODE: Not them. Me. I'd be insulted. I have devoted my life to giving books away so that literature would be available to everyone, to all the people. I do not deal in money. My mother was a librarian, and so was her mother and her mother before her. We have traced our lineage back to Colonial times. One of my ancestors, I'm proud to say, worked in Ben Franklin's first lending library. Madam, we deal in noble things here. We bring literature to the masses. We do not deal in money—that is unless, of course, your book is overdue.

CHILDE: I suppose you're right. Still. Sometimes I do think I'm getting something for nothing.

GOODE: How can you think such thoughts! My dear, until a book is read, it is nothing. Your reading it is what makes it a book. You are *not* getting something for nothing. You're reading, madam, and reading is work. It requires effort, concentration, perseverance. People who walk through our doors, madam, can truthfully say they have worked for everything they've got.

CHILDE: Still, I must admit there are moments when I think the writers deserve a little something.

GOODE: Believe me, writers have everything they can hope for. They've got

their books on our shelves. They've got their names in our catalogues. They've got their reviews, and they've got the supreme satisfaction of knowing that all the words between the covers of their books are theirs and theirs alone. What more could they want?

CHILDE: I suppose you're right.

GOODE: Don't take my word for this, madam. Go over to that poor wretch I pointed out and tell him you've read one of his books and how much you enjoyed it.

CHILDE: But I haven't read one! That would be a fib.

GOODE: It doesn't matter. He won't know. Just do it and watch his face light up. Watch him smile, listen to his profuse gratitude. Why, he'll probably get up and do a little dance for you. He's an excellent dancer. He's got wonderful rhythm. And it's his way of showing you how pleased he is that you like his work. Then ask yourself how you'd feel if you sullied all that by offering him a tip.

CHILDE: I guess that's why writers are different from you and me.

GOODE: So they are. Will you be checking this out?

CHILDE: Oh my, yes. And if it's as good as the last one, I'll sit right down and write Mr. Constantine a little note of appreciation. Oh, won't he be pleased! But I promise, I won't slip and mention anything so crass as money.

GOODE: Just remember tradition. Remember Ben Franklin and Andrew Carnegie. Those were two men who knew how to keep things in proper perspective. Remember what free lending libraries have meant to America, and you'll know just what to say to a writer.

CHILDE: Oh, I will, I will!

GOOD ENOUGH TO OWN

K.C. Constantine has never written a bad book (and that being the case, you'd think he'd tell us his real name). Check out the complete output, including:

The Rocksburg Railroad Murders
The Man Who Liked to Look at Himself
The Blank Page
A Fix Like This
The Man Who Liked Slow Tomatoes
Always a Body to Trade

K.C. Constantine is an ironclad pseudonym.

A WHIRLWIND VISIT TO FOUR ECCENTRIC MINDS

Michele Slung

Frequently on Saturday mornings when the doorbell rings, it's a pair of Jehovah's Witnesses. They're low-key, but their aim is high: they want to convert me.

I have not yet succumbed, but I have come to admire their technique so much that on occasion (this being one) I will usurp it and become the Writer's Witness—eagerly preaching the merits of a few special authors to anyone I can buttonhole.

Sui generis is the exact term for each of these writers, meaning "of its own kind." And just as flies are caught more easily with honey, so certain readers are hopelessly enthralled when confronted with a playful intelligence indulging in the offbeat. Admittedly, this Witness has had brief flings with some *sui generis* writers and then lost faith: early (but only early) Michael Innes was, for me, like being in the fun house of a theme park for smart people; and while I'll never renounce *The Burning Court* and John Dickson Carr, a little Henry Merrivale goes a long way. Ditto Gideon Fell. Consequently, there remains but a quartet of quirky, eccentric writers for me to ring doorbells about: Russell H. Greenan, Peter Dickinson, Jonathan Carroll and Delacorta.

There are strong fantasy elements running (never amok) through the works of these men and an imagination so huge that part of it, like an iceberg, is always submerged. Surprise plays an important role, too, making it a little difficult for us to keep our balance, yet who would begrudge a disorientation this delicious?

These, then, are specialists driven to invention, to juggling the real and the unreal, which they accomplish with the aplomb of a magician who's just managed to hide an elephant under a footstool. In some ways black comedy, a phrase we don't hear much anymore, applies to what they do. And when they're not being blackly comic, they're being satiric, or ironic, or sometimes simply... eccentric. The amusement they arouse—horrified giggles—mitigates the gore. Mr. Greenan's books especially contain some particularly vicious killings, but his wit, his deadpan tone, his screwball characters render them palatable.

Greenan's career, begun in 1968 with *It Happened in Boston,* smacks of the wacky, embodies the droll. It is pervaded by a lunatic misanthropy. In his cosmos paranoia rules, and we can't even trust the author to tell us the whole truth. From the porcelain pitcher in *The Secret Life of Algernon Pendleton* that's every bit as deadly a femme fatale as, say, Brigid O'Shaughnessy to the homicidal minister of *Heart of Gold* to the disintegrating caretaker in *Keepers,* Greenan makes sanity the exception, madness a fascination and addicts of us all.

Like Greenan, Delacorta does not shun violence. But the zaniness and cool, high style, the perversity and capital "R" Romance, the sheer Parisianness of his books divert so engagingly that the punches are absorbed almost without feeling them. Delacorta (pen name of the young Swiss Daniel Odier) established his reputation when a film was made from his novel *Diva*. Here, and in *Nana, Lola* and *Luna* as well, the hero's life *is* his art. Gorodish, the musician turned con man, for instance, makes criminal mischief abetted by the very naughty Alba, yet their "badness" is tinged with benevolence. Delacorta's stories are fast-moving, laconic, slightly kinky (*Luna* is *very* kinky), and there's no good way to describe them ... it's not really Humbert Humbert and Lolita playing Mr. and Mrs. North with a Gallic accent. Or is it?

With Carroll and Dickinson, we find far less visible blood and a more courteous sensibility; nonetheless, they bite. Peter Dickinson, whose first adult novel, *The Glass-Sided Ants' Nest*, appeared in 1968, is intensely cerebral. He skews the real world, converting it to an imaginary setting, as in his two masterpieces, *The Poison Oracle* and *King and Joker*, wherein an Arab kingdom and Buckingham Palace become as never before. We're plunged into these *in media res*, quickly needing to get our bearings so as not to be too far behind when the action begins in earnest, i.e., any murders. Learning to follow the proceedings of the first eight or so Dickinson novels, our brain cells are constantly engaged. And what a wonderful feeling when the premises become clear! As if we've survived a stiff workout!

Neither of Jonathan Carroll's two novels, strictly speaking, is a mystery. Still, they are squarely in the tradition of a benign Greenan, bearing no malice toward one's fellow man, but wanting to stretch the notion of reality just a bit and then pull the rug out from under our feet—with no hard feelings! In *The Land of Laughs*, Carroll's tour-de-force début, the youthful hero is mildly obsessed with a favorite childhood author and decides to write his biography. This turns deeply dangerous as the research takes him further and further into the looking glass' abyss. And that's Mr. Carroll just warming up with book one. Wait and see what a few more years will bring.

At this point I wish, like a real Witness, I could slip a booklet under your door. I can't, of course, but if what you've heard has intrigued you, you can read more on your own.

And before you know it, you'll be Witnessing, too.

Michele Slung is the editor of Crime on Her Mind.

SUI GENERIS

Jonathan Carroll
The Land of Laughs
Voice of Our Shadow

Delacorta
Diva
Nana
Luna
Lola

Peter Dickinson
The Glass-Sided Ants' Nest
The Old English Peep Show
The Sinful Stones
Sleep and His Brother
The Lizard in the Cup
The Green Gene
The Poison Oracle
The Lively Dead
King and Joker
Walking Dead
One Foot in the Grave
plus others

Russell H. Greenan
It Happened in Boston?
Nightmare
The Queen of America
The Secret Life of Algernon Pendleton
Heart of Gold
The Bric-a-Brac Man
Keepers

CANCRIMELIT
AN ENIGMA EVEN TO ITS PRACTITIONERS

Eric Wright

In 1982 Tony Aspler, a Toronto crime writer, got a small group of people together to establish the Crime Writers of Canada. At the time, if you had asked me to name six Canadian crime writers, I would have assumed you were making up questions for a fiendish version of *Trivial Pursuit*—questions that could be answered only by Derrick Murdock, the *Toronto Globe and Mail* crime reviewer and dean of CanCrimeLit. But these original organisers were right: a meeting was held, an association formed, and sixty or seventy people became members.

It's a nice group. We meet once a month in the bar of Massey College in Toronto to drink beer and complain about publishers, and a couple of times a year we get a speaker in—a coroner or a pathologist—to tell us what's wrong with our fictional crimes. We admit almost anybody for membership.

Part of the purpose of the organisation is to make Canadian crime writing known, to ourselves and the outside world, and to that end we have just announced the first Arthur Ellis award (named after one of our well-known hangmen) for the best Canadian crime novel of 1983. The terms of the award are typically and classically Canadian. A book does not have to be written by a Canadian, or be published in Canada, or even be set in Canada, but it has to be one of these—it has to *feel* Canadian. It is a national award, but no doubt when we feel strong enough we (note the pronoun) will consider allowing Arthur to be competed for openly, like the Edgar.

We are obviously going to get into trouble with this definition as we try year by year to agree on whether a book is eligible. It is a problem that the CanLit boys have been wrestling with for a long time: What is *Canadian* Literature? What is a Canadian? If a writer was born in Canada, is what he writes thereafter Canadian? Like Saul Bellow? What about someone like Brian Moore, who stayed only a while but took out Canadian citizenship? Which of his novels are Canadian? Can we include Malcolm Lowry? It's a lovely debate, but for the moment we can leave it to the CanLit boys to thrash out.

The realer problem for a Canadian crime writer who wants to use a Canadian locale is how, in these early days, to write a novel that will be on the face of it Canadian and be seen in 2044 to be one of the fathers of CanCrimeLit. We can

---

TORONTO CRIME FÊTE

The Crime Writers of Canada plan to host the 4th International Conference of Crime Writers in Toronto on October 8–11th, 1986. John North, committee chairman of the proposed conference, says, "We are projecting a four-day conference with lectures, discussions, workshops. We will announce the details as soon as we know them." In the meantime, anyone who wants to know more should write to Mr. North, 4 Plaxton Crescent, Toronto, Ontario, M4B 1L1, Canada.

sketch the problem by naming one or two writers who illustrate it and thus perhaps stake a claim for a bibliographical entry in future Ph.D theses. ("This early attempt to survey the ground recognised the difficulties of proceeding without maps, and for all its inaccuracies and omissions is still not entirely superseded.")

The difficulty is that like the early CanLit writers, we lack a tradition of our own except for Mountie-chasing-trapper stories, but we are conscious of the duty to create something future crime writers can imitate. The two major sources, the British and the American, are hard to adapt. The American private eye, for example. He operates more often than not out of Los Angeles, and Americans living in Oshkosh or even White Plains can accept the fiction that Los Angeles is as weird as the writers say it is. Even Spenser, in Boston, operates in a subworld that very few people have been near. But Canada doesn't work like that. The whole country is just a village strung out along a frontier, and most of us are familiar with or have friends and relatives in every part of the village. The idea of Sam Spade in Winnipeg is absurd—I went to school there, and there is nowhere to hide in that town. And as John Updike says about Toronto, how can you call it a city when you can't get decently mugged there? There isn't enough asphalt in our jungle yet to mount a proper manhunt. Another popular subgenre in American fiction is the man-against-the-mafia story, but in spite of the odd well-dressed corpse found beside the railway tracks with a neat bullet-hole in the back of his head, we don't really believe in the Canadian mafia—I mean, the people who buy books don't. For us the mob ends at Buffalo and we know the Mounties will keep it that way.

As for the British tradition, the two main subtypes, the wise, pipe-smoking police inspector and the clever academic amateur, are both equally implausible in a Canadian setting. Transplant them

ACCENTS: CANADIAN, ENGLISH AND STRINE

The American ear often cannot tell them apart but lumps them together as a commodity vaguely "foreign," with the Canadian being the most troublesome because one's inclination is to assume the speaker is an American with a peculiar affectation, or has a head cold, or maybe just suffers from a poor phone connection.

The tip-off word, however, is "about." A Canadian will pronounce it *aboat,* an Englishman will shorten it to *abat* and an Australian will veer Cockney and come out with *abaht.* The antecedents are a bit obscure but it's safe enough to say that the Canadians, swamped daily by the culture of their chums to the south, have derived something halfway between American and English, the Strines have retained the somewhat less than pear-shaped tones of their convict (often Cockney) origins and the English, well, they just continue to enunciate in a style they've been accustomed to at least since Runnymede. To sort things out, there are two noble texts: *The Canadian-English Dictionary* and *Strine,* a comprehensive overview (with wit) of the mother tongue down under.

The accent hodge-podge that is, by his own admission, Eric Wright, continues to baffle his students in Toronto. To their collective ear, he sounds Australian—this because his speech is an amalgam of his south London birthright and his lengthy sojourn in western Canada. An American would declare him a conundrum: a very classy Cockney. Furthermore, he can imitate all three renditions of "about" and sound authentic in each.

and they are immediately seen to be hot-house exotics which require an English climate of belief.

Five writers presently working in Canada illustrate the problem and some gropings toward a solution. (This is not an exhaustive survey, or a survey of any kind. For that the reader is recommended to Robert Weaver's article in the *Oxford Companion to Canadian Literature,* where Weaver has surveyed the history and summarised the practice of crime fiction in this country, with opinions and judgements.)

Our most prolific resident crime writer is Sara Woods, who has written a shelfful of court-room dramas, all set in England. Weaver does not mention her in his article, presumably because there is nothing Canadian about her work. At the other pole is Larry Morse, our Edgar-winning novelist for two books set in Los Angeles. These two writers avoid the problem, although Morse has settled his latest book in an island in the St. Lawrence; on the border, so to speak.

Howard Engel has created a genuine domestic whodunit. Engel's hero, Benny Cooperman, is a chopped-egg-sandwich eating, not very successful Jewish private investigator who specialises in divorce, but who three times so far has stumbled into bigger messes than his hometown, a thinly disguised St. Catherine's, usually affords. Cooperman is anti-heroic, funny, and very believable as a Canadian private eye.

Ted Wood, in *Dead in the Water,* has created another believable Canadian hero out of an ex-Toronto cop who is a one-man police force in an Ontario summer resort, just tough enough to handle some visiting American gangsters who take him for a dumb Canuck. *Dead in the Water* has been published in Britain and America, but not in Canada, which is another problem that Canadian crime writers sometimes have.

Engel and Wood have shown that

The Arthur Ellis Award, presented annually by the Canadian Crime Writers.

traditional subgenres can be adapted to Canadian soil, and a third, Tim Wynne-Jones in *The Knot,* is making a start on a genuine Canadian Gothic. Now that we have an association there will be more, but it is uphill work. When I sat down to plan my own book about a Toronto cop, I was told by a couple of people that Toronto was not a very rewarding location for crime fiction. They advised me to set the book somewhere more exotic, but since they were both Canadians I ignored them.

Future scholars will be in for some fun as they research and define the early examples of CanCrimeLit, especially if the purists in the CanLit crowd have any influence. For the present, though, in spite of theoretical problems, or problems of theory, we are enjoying an unreflective boomlet in crime writing, and most of us are happy with the definition of CanCrimeLit as writing on crime by an author eligible for membership in the Crime Writers of Canada.

Eric Wright won the Crime Writers' Association Award for best first crime novel, The Night the Gods Smiled.

An Edgar, a Raven,
a Dagger and the People
Who Own Them
THE
MOST PRESTIGIOUS
AWARDS

Mystery Writers of America
Founded 1945

National Headquarters: 105 East 19 Street, New York City

Regional Chapters: Boston, Chicago, San Francisco, Los Angeles

MWA issues three types of membership. Full membership is available only to those who have published in the field. Associate membership is open to those in allied fields, e.g., publishing and bookselling. Affiliate membership is granted to just plain fans. There is little difference between them, as all members receive the newsletter, *The Third Degree*, and all may attend the annual Edgar Allan Poe Award dinner.

Quoth the Raven,
"I'm tired of perching
on this roost. Nevermore!"

MWA Awards

MWA presents Edgars (for Edgar Allan Poe) and Ravens (ditto). Nominees are selected by a supposedly impartial committee and winners are chosen by that committee. The best novel and best first novel awards include:

1945 *Watchful at Night,* Julius Fast
1946 *The Horizontal Man,* Helen Eustis
1947 *The Fabulous Clip Joint,* Fredric Brown
1948 *The Room Upstairs,* Mildred Davis
1949 *What a Body,* Alan Green
1950 *Nightmare in Manhattan,* Thomas Walsh
1951 *Strangle Hold,* Mary McMullen
1952 *Don't Cry for Me,* William Campbell Gault
1953 *Beat Not the Bones,* Charlotte Jay
     A Kiss Before Dying, Ira Levin
1954 *The Long Goodbye,* Raymond Chandler
     Go, Lovely Rose, Jean Potts
1955 *Beast in View,* Margaret Millar
     The Perfectionist, Lane Kauffman
1956 *A Dram of Poison,* Charlotte Armstrong
     Rebecca's Pride, Donald McNutt Douglas
1957 *Room to Swing,* Ed Lacy
     Knock and Wait Awhile, William Rawle Weeks

1958 *The Eighth Circle,* Stanley Ellin
The Bright Road to Fear, Richard
Martin Stern
1959 *The Hours Before Dawn,* Celia
Fremlin
The Grey Flannel Shroud, Henry Slesar
1960 *Progress of a Crime,* Julian Symons
The Man in the Cage, John
Holbrooke Vance
1961 *Gideon's Fire,* J.J. Marric
The Green Stone, Suzanne Blanc
1962 *Death and the Joyful Woman,* Ellis Peters
The Fugitive, Robert L. Fish
1963 *The Light of Day,* Eric Ambler
The Florentine Finish, Cornelius
Hirschberg
1964 *The Spy Who Came In from the Cold,*
John Le Carré
Friday the Rabbi Slept Late, Harry
Kemelman

Edgar Allan Poe, awaiting dinner.

GRAND MASTERS AWARD

Agatha Christie
Vincent Starrett
Rex Stout
Ellery Queen
Erle Stanley Gardner
John Dickson Carr
George Harmon Coxe
Georges Simenon
Baynard Kendrick
John Creasey
James M. Cain
Mignon G. Eberhart
John D. MacDonald
Judson Philips
Ross Macdonald
Eric Ambler
Graham Greene
Dorothy B. Hughes
Ngaio Marsh
Daphne Du Maurier
Aaron Marc Stein
Stanley Ellin
Julian Symons
Margaret Millar
John Le Carré

1965 *The Quiller Memorandum,* Adam
Hall
In the Heat of the Night, John Ball
1966 *King of the Rainy Country,* Nicolas
Freeling
The Cold War Swap, Ross Thomas
1967 *God Save the Mark,* Donald E.
Westlake
Act of Fear, Michael Collins
1968 *A Case of Need,* Jeffrey Hudson
Silver Street, Richard Johnson
The Bait, Dorothy Uhnak
1969 *Forfeit,* Dick Francis
A Time for Predators, Joe Gores
1970 *The Laughing Policeman,* Maj
Sjöwall & Per Wahlöö
The Anderson Tapes, Lawrence
Sanders
1971 *Day of the Jackal,* Frederick Forsyth
Finding Maubee, A.H.Z. Carr
1972 *The Lingala Code,* Warren Kiefer
Squaw Point, R.H. Shimer
1973 *Dance Hall of the Dead,* Tony
Hillerman
The Billion Dollar Sure Thing, Paul
E. Erdman
1974 *Peter's Pence,* Jon Cleary
Fletch, Gregory Mcdonald
1975 *Hopscotch,* Brian Garfield
The Alvarez Journal, Rex Burns

1976 *Promised Land,* Robert B. Parker
The Thomas Berryman Number,
James Patterson
1977 *Catch Me, Kill Me,* William H.
Hallahan
A French Finish, Robert Ross
1978 *The Eye of the Needle,* Ken Follett
Killed in the Ratings, William L.
DeAndrea
1979 *The Rheingold Route,* Arthur
Maling
The Lasko Tangent, Richard North
Patterson
1980 *Whip Hand,* Dick Francis
The Watcher, K. Nolte Smith
1981 *Peregrine,* William Bayer
Chiefs, Stuart Woods
1982 *Billingsgate Shoal,* Rick Boyer
The Butcher's Boy, Thomas Perry
1983 *La Brava,* Elmore Leonard
The Bay Psalm Book Murder, Will
Harriss

Crime Writers' Association
Founded 1953

CWA Headquarters: The Press Club,
International Press Centre, 76 Shoe
Lane, London EC 4 3JB.

Membership is restricted to those who
have published in the field, with no
exceptions. Members receive
a monthly

newsletter, *Red Herrings,* attend monthly
meetings at the Press Club and the
yearly Gold Dagger Award dinner, at
which the best mystery of the year is
announced.

CWA Awards

CWA presents Gold and Silver Daggers
for the best English and the best foreign
mysteries of the year and the John
Creasey Memorial Award for best first
crime novel.

1955 *The Little Walls,* Winston Graham
1956 *The Second Man,* Edward Grierson
1957 *The Colour of Murder,* Julian
Symons
1958 *Somone from the Past,* Margot
Bennett
1959 *Passage of Arms,* Eric Ambler
1960 *The Night of Wenceslas,* Lionel
Davidson
1961 *The Spoilt Kill,* Mary Kelly
1962 *When I Grow Rich,* Joan Fleming
1963 *The Spy Who Came In from the Cold,*
John Le Carré
1964 *The Perfect Murder,* H.R.F. Keating
The Two Faces of January, Patricia
Highsmith
1965 *The Far Side of the Dollar,* Ross
Macdonald
Midnight Plus One, Gavin Lyall
1966 *A Long Way to Shiloh,* Lionel
Davidson
In the Heat of the Night, John Ball
1967 *Murder Against the Grain,* Emma
Lathen
Dirty Story, Eric Ambler
1968 *Skin Deep,* Peter Dickinson
The Lady in the Car, Sebastien
Japrisot
1969 *A Pride of Heroes,* Peter Dickinson
Another Way of Dying, Francis
Clifford
The Father Hunt, Rex Stout
1970 *Young Man, I Think You're Dying,*
Joan Fleming
The Labyrinth Makers, Anthony
Price
1971 *The Steam Pig,* James McClure

THE FALLING DAGGER

The CWA dagger (*see picture*) used
to stand upright, but it kept top-
pling over, no one knows why. After
numerous failed attempts to—so to
speak—get it on its feet, the dagger
was permanently laid to rest. Winners now receive one that is lying in
handsome repose. Just like a corpse.

JERRY DARVIN

THE INK PLOTS

A once-in-a-lifetime award, presented solely in the pages of *Murder Ink*. Recipients, who have yet to be officially notified of their award, were chosen by the editor.

An Ink Plot and a napkin to Lawrence Sanders for "The Delaney Deli," a superb lesson in sandwich making.

An Ink Plot and a trail of bread crumbs to Mary Fitt for "Lost in the Maze," an ongoing battle to overcome recalcitrant shrubbery.

An Ink Plot and a bundling board to Charles McCarry for "The His-and-Her Maneuvers," an overwhelming commitment to working through the male/female relationship.

An Ink Plot and an alpha wave to Andrew Coburn for "Frayed Nerves," a paean to everyday pain and angst.

An Ink Plot and an I ♡ New York button to Jack Finney for "Back Aches," a Gothamite's guide to the past.

A TRIBUTE TO THE SHORT STORY MASTER

Eleanor Sullivan

Without Frederic Dannay, who knows what state the mystery short story would be in?

Bluntly put, no one in modern times has done more to popularize, develop, promote and nurture the most challenging method of telling a mystery—the short story form. Fred's advocacy of it dates back to the Thirties, when he and his cousin Manfred B. Lee (the two shared two writing pseudonyms, Ellery Queen and Barnaby Ross), acting as the entire staff, published their first magazine devoted entirely to detective fiction. Called *Mystery League,* the venture folded after just four issues (October 1933–January 1934) "for business and financial reasons," wrote Anthony Boucher in the Book Review of the New York *Times,* 1961, "having nothing to do with its quality, which was high."

In 1941, with the moral and financial support of Lawrence E. Spivak, publisher of *The American Mercury,* Fred's dream was rekindled with the fall début of *EQMM.* In planning that pioneer edition, Fred told Spivak he wanted it to be the most perfect issue ever conceived. Replied Spivak, "Fine, and what will you do for an encore?"

Mr. Spivak shouldn't even have raised the question. The man who placed Allingham and Hammett, among others, in the premiere edition, followed them next time with Christie and Sayers, and went to bat third time up with Edgar Wallace and Jacques Futrelle. During his tenure as *EQMM* editor-in-chief, a position he held from the magazine's inception until his death in 1982, he actively sought out new authors as well as established writers whose work in translation would be new to English-speaking people. Among the many firsts Fred managed to record for *EQMM*: the first story in English by Borges and the first story anywhere by Stanley Ellin.

Fred's daily routine took some getting used to. When I was hired in 1971, I learned that I would work out of the *EQMM* office in New York City while Fred would stay sequestered at home in Larchmont. His methods for conducting editorial business were ingenious. Every morning a special-delivery package was sent to him. It included my reader's reports, but they had to be attached to the *backs* of the manuscripts so that Fred would not be influenced by them before he had a chance to form his own opinion. Stories he wasn't interested in were mailed back to me, now with my report stapled to the front page. To it would be added, in red ink, either a simple "No" or a "Discuss." If the latter, a numbered list of words or phrases would follow, often as many as a dozen items. Fred would call me, and I'd read off the numbers, one by one. Each of his phrases

Frederic Dannay always double-crossed his Q to indicate two authors were responsible for Ellery Queen's work.

The first issue of EQMM, *with a cover designed by former adman Fred Dannay.*

triggered his memory about a point he wanted relayed to the author (in the event he thought rewriting would help) or sometimes reflected a point he wanted to make to *me*, about why he was rejecting that particular story. Can you imagine a more privileged tutorial? I should have been paying *him*.

Fred was a tenacious editor; he never gave up trying to give a story a final polish. Joe Gores recalls that one of his submissions required four revisions to appease Fred's taste—including one Fred requested *after* he'd finally accepted the manuscript. He said he'd run the story without the change, but . . . Joe reread the piece one more time and agreed to rework it; Fred was right. Was it all necessary? Well, this was the story that won Joe Gores the Edgar for best mystery short of the year. That's what happens when a very talented writer and an extremely talented editor collude.

Sometimes there'd be art problems to discuss. At first I dreaded telling Fred when one arose—until I learned how much he loved the challenge. I suppose it shouldn't have surprised me to discover he enjoyed solving difficult problems; this was the gentleman, after all, who was famous for issuing challenges to the reader and then outwitting them. I still don't understand how he managed it,

but when I'd call him up with a layout problem I thought was unsolvable, he could not only visualize but fix it!

More than once, Fred wondered why he worked so hard over his story introductions and the anthologies— probably no one read them anyway. And he wasn't joking, despite the fact that in his lifetime a collection of his story introductions, *In the Queen's Parlor,* became a much valued collector's item and his *Queen's Quorum* was recognized as the major critical work ever done on the detective short story. I agree with Henry Morrison, who once speculated that the intimate tone and valuable information in the introductions played a large role in the success of *EQMM*.

At home, on a shelf, where I pass by it almost every day, sits a copy of *The Golden Summer,* the one novel Fred wrote by himself. It's inscribed "To Eleanor from Ellery—and Daniel Nathan," which was Fred's birth name. When he gave me the book, he warned me not to expect a romantic vision of childhood, growing up with his family in Elmira, New York. He was, he insisted, extremely mercenary at the age of ten. Stanley Ellin wrote of the book and the young man revealed in its pages, "He was full of vague fears and alarms, and had a streak of avarice long and wide enough for any full-grown adult. Yet he was also sensitive, imaginative, full of loves and loyalties and, above all, an intuitive master of the fine art of improvisation." I suspect the initial motivation for taking on the production of the magazine was grounded in that avarice. But I am certain it was the sensitivity and imagination and loves and loyalties that made it the unique success it is.

To me, Fred Dannay will always be editor-in-chief of *EQMM*. I am privileged to have known him.

Eleanor Sullivan is the editor of Ellery Queen's Mystery Magazine.

AMASSING INTELLIGENCE
IN SEARCH OF TRUTH IN FINE CONDITION

Walter Pforzheimer

Once upon a time, in my mid-prep school days back in the late 1920's, I became a rare book collector. Nobody made me do it; I guess I came into it naturally, as my father and two uncles were collectors and bibliophiles. I started off by putting together the works of a second-rank nineteenth-century American author, Frank R. Stockton. Of course, one had to know his famous "The Lady, or the Tiger?" to get through College Boards, but I enjoyed reading many of his works—some fifty-five titles. By the mid 1930's I had them all, including some original manuscripts, much of his correspondence and many of the original illustrations done by such as Charles Dana Gibson and A.B. Frost. My father, meanwhile, was building up *his* collection, which focused on Molière and Royal French bindings. When it became clear I was hooked on collecting, he announced it was my twenty-first birthday coming-of-age gift. I still own it.

I spent the war years in Air Force Intelligence and in February 1946 was asked to join the newly created Central Intelligence Group (CIG, which became the CIA in 1947), America's first peacetime centralized intelligence organization. I soon found myself surrounded by veterans of the OSS, which I knew very little about, having had virtually no contact with it during the war. A few books on the OSS slowly began to trickle forth in the late Forties, however, and I bought them to read. I even found a few books on World War I intelligence in secondhand bookstores and bought them, too. (They were generally pretty dreadful stuff by self-proclaimed spies.) None of this, mind you, was gathered with thoughts of starting an intelligence collection. It was for information only.

I think it was in January of 1950 that David Randall, the great rare book specialist at Scribner's, brought me face to face with a beautiful copy of *The Spy of the Rebellion* by Allan Pinkerton, possibly one of the worst books by one of the worst intelligence officers who cluttered up the intelligence channels of the Civil War. I bought it. And a little while later Randall sold me Margaretha Gertruida Zelle Mcleod's last visa application to enter France—which she had twice signed with a flourish with her better-known nom de danse, Mata Hari.

But my collecting "day of reckoning" came when my old friend Bill McCarthy asked me to drop by. He had a small intelligence report written during the American Revolution, which he thought I might like. I did. I bought it and turned to leave. "By the way," he ventured, "I have another item you might find interesting." He brought out a lengthy order-of-battle letter dated July 26, 1777. The last paragraph was the finest expression of our profession that I would ever see:

> *The necessity of procuring good Intelligence is apparent & need not be further urged—All that remains for me to add is, that you keep the whole matter as secret as possible. For upon Secrecy, Success depends in most Enterprizes of the kind. . . .*

The signature on that letter was G. Washington.

Here was a letter by the greatest intelligence office in our history prior to the advent of General William J. Donovan as director of the OSS in World War II. What to do? What could one do? Confronted with the Washington letter (my collection now boasts three more), I knew I would have to try and build the best private American collection of books and historical materials on intelligence that could be brought together.

Please don't think of this as a "spy" collection; it's a good deal broader, encompassing espionage, counterintelligence, unconventional warfare (covert action, psychological warfare, sabotage, subversion), military intelligence, economic intelligence, escape and evasion, and more. Basically, the collection is limited to books, monographs and periodical articles in the English language. It now constitutes 130 three-foot shelves of nonfiction, about twenty shelves of Congressonal publications on intelligence, subversion and espionage, and literally hundreds of folders, each with an appropriate article or monograph. Then, too, there are truly volumes of mounted clippings files on related exotica.

There are about fifteen shelves of spy fiction in my collection, but I regret most of it. It came as a shock to me when a practitioner of the art of writing mysteries included spy fiction along with detective novels, police stories, etc. Much as I dislike it, I had placed spy fiction on a different pedestal. There are exceptions, of course, some so close to the real thing as to have some value. Somerset Maugham's *Ashenden* comes immediately to mind. James Fenimore Cooper's *The Spy.* Robert Asprey's *The Panther's Feast. Command Decision* by William Wister Haines is a delight for those of us who grew up in World War II's air intelligence service. And for sheer excellence there is Joseph Conrad's *Under Western Eyes,* much superior to his *Secret Agent.* And no one should skip Compton Mackenzie's spoof, *Water on the Brain.*

Vicar Fogg forgot his hymnal.

Lord Teasdale's library, including *No Friendly Drop* (Henry Wade), *More Work for the Undertaker* (Margery Allingham, chapter 24 dog-eared) and *Teapots in Pottery and Porcelain,* the Queen's Stationers.

BASIC INTELLIGENCE

Bibliographies

Constantinides, George C. *Intelligence and Espionage: An Analytical Bibliography.*

Scholar's Guide to Intelligence Literature: Bibliography of the Russell J. Bowen Collection...

U.S. Defense Intelligence College. *Bibliography of Intelligence Literature: A Critical and Annotated Bibliography of Open-Source Literature.*

Official Histories

Foot, Michael R.D. *SOE in France: An Account of the Work of the British Special Operations Executive in France, 1940–1944.*

U.S. War Department, Strategic Services Unit. *War Report of the OSS (Office of Strategic Services) 2 Vols.*

U.S. Intelligence

Cline, Ray S. *The CIA: Reality vs. Myth.* This incorporates and supersedes the author's *Secrets, Spies and Scholars* (1976) and *The CIA Under Reagan Bush & Casey* (1981).

Dulles, Allen Welsh. *The Craft of Intelligence.*

Kent, Sherman. *Strategic Intelligence for American World Policy.*

Troy, Thomas F. *Donovan and the CIA: A History of the Establishment of the Central Intelligence Agency.*

Wriston, Henry Merritt. *Executive Agents in American Foreign Relations.*

British Intelligence

Masterman, Sir John C. *The Double-Cross System in the War of 1939 to 1945.*

Jones, Reginald Victor. *The Wizard War: British Scientific Intelligence, 1939–1945.*

Soviet Intelligence

Barron, John. *KGB: The Secret Work of Soviet Secret Agents.*

——. *KGB Today: The Hidden Hand*

Hood, William. *Mole.*

Myagkov, Aleksei. *Inside the KGB: An Exposé by an Officer of the Third Directorate.*

U.S. Congress, House Permanent Select Committee on Intelligence. *Soviet Covert Action (The Forgery Offensive).* Hearings, 1980. Washington: U.S. Government Printing Office, 1980.

Surprise Attack and Deception

Betts, Richard K. *Surprise Attack: Lessons for Defense Planning.*

Daniel, Donald C., and Katherine L. Herbig, eds. *Strategic Military Deception.*

Knorr, Klaus, and Patrick Morgan, eds. *Strategic Military Surprise: Incentives and Opportunities.*

Congressional Publications

U.S. Congress, Senate Select Committee to Study Governmental Operations with Respect to Intelligence Activities. *Final Report* (Senate Report No. 94-755). Books I–VI. Washington: U.S. Government Printing Office, 1975–76. This *Final Report* of the Committee chaired by Senator Frank Church covers the most extensive Congressional hearings on the U.S. Intelligence Community ever held. As there is no adequate single book covering all of these U.S. intelligence activities (particularly CIA) during the 1950–1975 period, these volumes make interesting reading. Book IV contains the "History of the Central Intelligence Agency" by Anne Karalekas of the Committee staff. (The "History" has also been published commercially by the Aegean Park Press, Laguna Hills, California, 1977.) While somewhat biased and uneven in some areas, particularly on the role of clandestine collection and covert action, this "History" is probably the best single text publicly available on the history of the CIA.

U.S. Congress, Senate Select Committee on Intelligence and House Permanent Select Committee on Intelligence. These two Congressional oversight committees were established in 1976 and 1977, respectively. Periodically, they issue sanitized *Hearings* and *Re-*

PICTORIAL PARADE

...*ports* on general problems and activities of the U.S Intelligence Community or on specific aspects of intelligence. As such, they are important reading in this field.

Cryptologics

Beesly, Patrick. *Room 40: British Naval Intelligence, 1914–18.* New York: Harcourt Brace Jovanovich, 1982. The British cryptologic effort in World War I, including the Zimmermann Telegram. This book does not include material on the Ultra secret.

——. *Very Special Intelligence: The Story of the Admiralty's Operational Intelligence Centre, 1939–1945.* New York: Doubleday, 1978.

Bennett, Ralph. *Ultra in the West: The Normandy Campaign, 1944–45.* New York: Charles Scribner, 1980.

Calvocoressi, Peter. *Top Secret Ultra.* New York: Pantheon Books, 1980.

Clayton, Aileen. *The Enemy Is Listening.* London: Hutchinson, 1980.

Hinsley, Francis H., with E.E. Thomas, C.F.G. Ransom and R.C. Knight, *British Intelligence in the Second World War: Its Influence on Strategy and Operations.* New York: Cambridge University Press, Vol. 1, 1979; Vol. 2, 1981; Vol. 3, Part I, 1984. (Vol. 3, Part II, the final volume, will cover from D-Day to the end of the war and will probably not be published until 1985.)

Holmes, Wilfred J. *Double-Edged Secrets:*

U.S. Naval Intelligence Operations in the Pacific During World War II. Annapolis, Md.: Naval Institute Press, 1979.

Kahn, David. *The Codebreakers: The Story of Secret Writing.* New York: Macmillan, 1967. This major history was published before the exposure of Ultra.

Kozaczuk, Wladyslaw. *Enigma: How the German Machine Cipher Was Broken, and How It Was Read by the Allies in World War Two.* Frederick, Md.: University Publications of America, 1984.

Lewin, Ronald. *The American Magic: Codes, Ciphers and the Defeat of Japan.* New York: Farrar Straus Giroux, 1982.

——. *Ultra Goes to War: The First Account of World War II's Greatest Secret Based on Official Documents.* New York: McGraw-Hill, 1978.

Montagu, Ewen E.S. *Beyond Top Secret Ultra.* New York: Coward, McCann & Geoghegan, 1978.

U.S. Department of Defense. *The "Magic" Background of Pearl Harbor.* Washington: Government Printing Office, 1979. (This work, numbered Vols. I–V, actually consists of eight volumes, as Vols, II–IV each consist of a volume of text and an Appendix volume.)

Weber, Ralph E. *United States Diplomatic Codes and Ciphers, 1775–1938.* Chicago: Precedent Publishing, 1979. This interesting history of early American cryptology of course includes no material on the Ultra secret.

Welchman, Gordon. *The Hut Six Story: Breaking the Enigma Codes.* New York: McGraw-Hill, 1982.

Winterbotham, F.W. *The Ultra Secret.* New York: Harper & Row, 1974.

Wohlstetter, Roberta. *Pearl Harbor: Warning and Decision.* Stanford, Calif.: Stanford University Press, 1962.

Yardley, Herbert O. *The American Black Chamber.* Indianapolis, Ind.: Bobbs-Merrill, 1931. This book on aspects of the American cryptologic effort in the years 1916–1929 of course contains no material on the Ultra secret.

People say, "What is your oldest book?" I mention the Bible, which surprises them. The word "spy" appears some eighteen times in the Bible, and there are perhaps a dozen spy stories in the Great Book. In passing, one need only mention Moses' sending agents to spy out the land of Canaan, in the Book of Numbers; and in the Book of Joshua, Chapter 2, one learns of Joshua sending spies into Jericho. One other early noteworthy: the famous Trojan Horse in the eleventh century B.C. Allen Dulles, himself the son of a minister, always claimed that this was the first great deception operation, and perhaps it was. But wasn't it also really a horrendous failure of Trojan counterintelligence?

In my opinion, the earliest book in English given over to intelligence is *Memoirs of Secret Service* by Matthew Smith, published in London in 1699. This involves the plot to remove (kill?) King William from the British throne by his Jacobite opposition, who were being protected by the King of France near Versailles. If Smith is to be believed, he infiltrated the Jacobite center, discovered who the plotters were, where the weapons were cached and the date of the operation, thus saving the throne! He felt forced to write of his work in order to be paid. The Parliament was so angry at his forwardness, they ordered his book burned by the common hangman. For this reason, it is a rare book indeed. I treasure my copy, the only one, to my knowledge, inscribed by Smith to the Lord High Chancellor of England.

I should also mention my most favorite title—actually a twenty-one-page monograph entitled *Proceedings of a Board of General Officers . . . Respecting Major John André, Adjutant General of the British Army,* published in Philadelphia in 1780, by order of the Congress. These *Proceedings* were the result of an advisory board, assembled by General Washington after the capture of Major André with the plans for the defenses of West Point in his boots (given to him by General Benedict Arnold). The Board, which consisted of such luminaries as Lafayette and Baron Steuben, recommended that André be hanged as a spy. There followed a correspondence between Washington and the British regarding an exchange for André. Washington agreed, provided the British return General Arnold for André. This General Clinton, the British Commander, had to refuse. And so, at high noon on 2 October 1780, Major André was hanged. Washington quickly bundled up the *Proceedings* and his appended correspondence and sent them off to the Continental Congress in Philadelphia. It is therefore doubtful that this monograph could have been printed before mid-October; nevertheless, it proved so popular that it was reprinted in six other cities in the Colonies before the end of 1780. Three of the seven editions of 1780 are in my collection. No library has all seven. The pamphlet was so in demand, it was even reprinted in Dublin, Ireland, in 1781. When I bought my copy of the Dublin edition, it was only the third known copy; two others have since turned up. I consider the *Proceedings* to be the cornerstone of a collection of American publications on intelligence service, and of all the thousands of items in the collection I would say that it is my favorite—next to the Washington letter.

For those who wonder where the final resting place of my collection will be, it is destined for the Beinecke Rare Book and Manuscript Library at Yale. May the good librarians there have mercy on its soul.

Walter Pforzheimer was the first legislative counsel for the CIA, then became curator of the Historical Intelligence Collection (established by Dulles). He is an adjutant professor at the Defense Intelligence College and has been called "the dean of intelligence literature collectors."

CHAMPIONS OF THE CAUSE
AMERICAN MYSTERY BOOKSTORES

Desdemona Brannigan

I do not suggest this idly: There is nothing quite so eccentric as the mystery bookstore owner. Living in a world of guns, black cats, skeletons, blunt instruments, bloodcurdling screams, customers who affect trench coats and deerstalkers, who crave endless gore washed down with endless cups of tea (or endless slugs of bourbon), the mystery shop proprietor is nowhere near so balanced as Dr. Freud would have thought healthy. But are trend-setters generally?

These are the folks who make the rules. *They* decide what's a mystery and if it's worth carrying. *They* decide who shelves where (D.L.S.? Over there between James and Cross. Hammett? He's wrestling Chandler for space). *They* decide which writers we'll meet (by arranging autograph parties), what we'll read next (via chatty newsletters), and some of them seem determined to make experts of us all—by inviting us to join discussion groups, mystery tours, fan clubs, even detective dinners.

Clearly crazy, the lot of them. And perfectly wonderful. Herewith, thirty delights. Please encourage them.

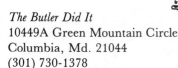

The Butler Did It
10449A Green Mountain Circle
Columbia, Md. 21044
(301) 730-1378

Gail Larson (who schedules store hours so as not to intrude on softball practice) provides the most comprehensive mail-order service you or anybody else has ever heard of: her regular monthly catalogue lists fifty new hardcover titles, fifty paperbacks, twenty-five used sought-afters, twenty-five British imports and, usually, mention of an upcoming autographing party. Besides, the logo is adorable.

Crime House
175 E. Queen St.
Toronto, Canada M5A1S2
(416) 365-1338

If you owned a mystery bookstore, what color would you paint it? Peter and Maryan Grima opted for bloodred, which probably has the Victorian who originally built the house spinning in his you-know-what. A garrulous, cerebral sort, Peter freely acknowledges he learns as much from his customers as they do from him. Rather perfectionistic, the Grimas tried out at least five logos before settling on one. Regular newsletter (scrunched up type, alas).

Criminal Proceedings
2526 E. Webster Place
Milwaukee, Wisc. 53211
(414) 332-9424

Old-fashioned, in the best possible sense. Lionel Johnson has manipulated every square inch of his L-shaped space to accommodate handsome wood shelves, Charlie Chan, the better of the vintage movie stills and all matter of Sherlockiana. Name the book, Lionel will ferret it out for you. No newsletter, but give him time. The shop's barely a year old and still developing.

Escape While There's Still Time
207 E. Fifth #105
Eugene, Ore. 97401
(503) 484-9500

The droll name says it all: this is *the* place in the great Northwest to fritter away all your free time, surrounded by every kind of great escape fiction imaginable—from cozy to hard-boiled to Gothic to police procedural. Fluctuating hours, so please call first. (Listen, who's to say you'd run a shop differently? The nice thing about being small is you have a certain flexibility.)

Fantasy, Etc.
808 Larkin St.
San Francisco, Calif. 94109
(415) 441-7617

You have to love Charles Cockey, a man of whimsy, honesty and humor. Says he, "Fantasy, Etc. was set up to reflect my own personal tastes in reading, the 'etc.' allowing me unspecified leeway in oddities that might otherwise not show up in a science-fiction or mystery store—everything from eighteenth-century Gothic weirdness on up. How many stores can boast both *The Monk* and *Melmoth the Wanderer* as perennials?" He concludes, "Everything is for sale except the cat."

Foul Play
10 Eighth Ave. (at W. 12 St.)
New York, N.Y. 10014
(212) 675-5115

Beware the secret door—it even creaks! Specializing in all the stuff that's current, the store has perhaps earned much of its notoriety for its unique collection of T-shirts—the best sellers being the one emblazoned "I haven't a clue" and the other stating "It's a mystery to me." Also: "I love Agatha Christie (Spenser) (Dracula)" and "Elementary, my dear Watson." Much mail order and kindly ministrations from resident experts Sunny Clark, Patricia Smith.

Grounds For Murder
Old Town Mercado
2707 Congress St.
San Diego, Calif. 92110
(619) 294-9497

Beneath a wall of weapons (blowgun, ax, dagger, noose et al.) Phyllis Brown presides over a truly impressive array of mayhem, including what mayhaps be the vastest collection of kids' and young adults' mysteries anywhere. Also at hand: foreign-language mysteries, Britain to a fare-thee-well, first editions and humble used books. Wait for it, there's more: mystery tours, scrumptious detective dinners, a newsletter and a store-sponsored fanzine, *The Crime File,* which has included (a) an original mystery, (b) readers' evaluations, (c) tidbits and gossip, and all manner of ephemera. Phyllis arranges talks, parties, merely *everything*.

I Love A Mystery
29 E. Madison St.
Chicago, Ill. 60602
(312) 236-1338

Recently relocated, but still in the Loop area. Ever the purist, owner John Morginson disdains all save books, and only the better written ones at that. A small selection of the elegantly written is what John aims for, and he has no intention of lowering his standards by widening his scope.

Moonstone Bookcellars
2145 Pennsylvania Ave. N.W.
Washington, D.C. 20037
(202) 659-2600

A half and half—half mystery, half science fiction, with mysteries maybe getting the short end of it. About a five-block walk from the White House and worth the trip if just to meet owner Phil Grosfield, a sort of universal papa to every stray who walks in the door. Excellent mystery magazine coverage, and for science-fiction buffs a wonderfully bizarre creature on coffee cups, carrying cases and T-shirts.

Murder By The Book*
212 E. Cuyahoga Falls Ave.
Akron, Ohio 44310
(216) 434-2112

Spanking new in that it just opened its doors, but otherwise mostly old with an emphasis on recycled Hammett, Chandler and the gentlemen MacDonald (no matter how they spell it). A catalogue issues forth periodically; for further queries, contact Ms. Sanford.

Murder By The Book*
1574 S. Pearl St.
Denver, Colo. 80210
(303) 871-9401

Claims the brightest customers in the country (three of them banded together and won $10,000 for solving the Robins family mystery). Now owned by Shirley Beaird and Chris McPhee, one of the original partners was Nancy Wynne, author of *The Agatha Christie Chronology*. Accordingly, the store sponsors The Greenway Group, named for Dame Agatha's home and devoted to her partisans. Currently instituting mystery weekends, special dinners, autograph-

ings and an exquisitely gruesome greeting card line, the store features, evermore, a splendid selection of crime fiction lovingly depicted in a newsletter.

Murder By The Book*
2348 Bissonnet
Houston, Tex. 77005
(713) 524-8597

Proving yet again that fine things come in teeny packages, this brainchild of Les and Martha Farrington displays new editions front and center, bargains just beyond in a cozy backroom. Need advice? Les and Martha really can help, and love to. In addition, they host a "Whodunits" course. Please check for next one to be scheduled.

Murder By The Book*
3729 S.E. Hawthorn
Portland, Ore. 97214
(503) 232-9995

Jill Hinckley and Carolyn Lane were so worried that the scientists at the South Pole Research Station would have no mysteries to read during the nine months of the year they were cut off from the rest of the world, they nagged their customers into donating great batches to them. To commemorate the event, South Pole Library bookplates were issued. Wouldn't you kill for one? Ever creative, the women sort their store titles by type, among them "Yardbirds," "Innocent Bystanders," "On the Run." In their spare time they send out, they say, "a more or less monthly newsletter."

Murder By The Book*
197 Wickendon St.
Providence, R.I. 02903
(401) 331-9140

Locked-room savant Kevin Barbero likes nothing better than to draw up a chair and tell you about his favorite subgenre. Being affable, however, he'll just

*Murder by the Book—all of them—would have you know that they are not a chain of Kentucky-fried mysteries. The stores share nothing but an abiding love of the mystery.

as willingly draw up his chair and let you tell him about yours, whatever that might be. Small, cluttered, splendidly disorganized as a result of a recent move; you may never want to leave.

Murder Ink®
271 W. 87 St.
New York, N.Y. 10024
(212) 362-8905

The pioneer. Opened June 14, 1972, by Dilys Winn and purchased five years later by Carol Brener, under whose auspices the business has thrived, its stock has, at least, tripled, the hours have been standardized and the mail, you'll be glad to hear, has been answered with reasonable promptness. The emphasis is on the books—both for the collector and for the more casual reader—but also on hand are mysteries on tape, on record; the better of the computer games; the infamous Murder Ink T-shirt, Maltese Falcon and Sherlockian tea set. Several newsletters a year and a must-visit.

Murder Undercover (Kate's Mystery Books)
2211 Massachusetts Ave.
Cambridge, Mass. 02140
(617) 491-2660

The only store with an alias—Kate's Mystery Books, so dubbed in recognition of the personable owner Kate Mattes, who charmed Robert B. Parker into building bookshelves and Jane Langton and Charlotte MacLeod into planting pachysandra in the front yard. A row of skulls guards her desk, whence she oversees monthly meetings of the Judas Goats (the Parker fan club), produces (a tad irregularly) a very friendly newsletter and gazes fondly at her ample stock, including an in-depth selection of New England authors and settings. Truly the most original window shades ever, replete with lurker, rocker and scaredy-cat. Mail order? Sure.

Mysteries From The Yard
616 Xenia Ave.
Yellow Springs, Ohio 45387
(513) 767-2111

Who's that peering through the eyelet curtain? Mary Frost-Pierson, of course, whose turn-of-the-century house holds, in her words, "shop, back stock and family, polished hardwood floors and a dining area for all the parties! My customers and I will use any excuse whatsoever and Sundays invariably include munchies and a slew of old mystery videos." Ms. Mary is "not particularly bloody-minded." More to her taste: genteel crimes and polite forms of larceny. Impossible to go here and not have a grand time.

The Mysterious Bookshop
129 W. 56 St.
New York, N.Y. 10019
(212) 765-0900

The mastermind here is Otto Penzler, bona-fide workaholic, who not only runs the store (abetted by, if you can believe it, Miss Christie), but publishes *The Armchair Detective,* runs The Mysterious Literary Agency, is editor-in-chief of The Mysterious Press and in his spare time whips off an Edgar-winning encyclopedia. The ground floor is all paperback, up the spiral staircase are the hardcovers, and in Otto's special domain is the finest mystery collection—floor to ceiling, and the room's not small—in any of the bookstores. First edition enthusiasts consider this a second home, and Sherlockians tend to sigh contentedly within its walls.

The Mystery Bookstore
2266 N. Prospect Ave.
#209
Milwaukee, Wisc. 53202
(414) 277-8515

The only mystery bookstore to issue

an annual award, a soft sculpture called "The Mysterious Stranger." First winner: Tony Hillerman. The shop headquarters the monthly meeting of The Cloak and Clue Society, a group of dedicated die-hards, and organizes a bimonthly newsletter called *Crime-in-Suite 209.* Among the more innovative and adventuresome of the shops, though still a relative newcomer.

The Perfect Crime
Gateway Shopping Center
1958 E. Sunrise Blvd.
Ft. Lauderdale, Fla. 33304
(305) 764-2525

Crime, southern style. Mostly paperback, but with a nice quantity of remaindered hardcovers. The very newest of the mystery bookshops, and owner Richard Beaupré promises the stock will increase as its customers do.

Quest's End
220 The Commons
Ithaca, N.Y. 14850
(607) 272-2221

Shares space with a science-fiction/fantasy bookstore, not quite equally. According to Marianne, who works here, the owner's name is Alex Skutt, but the "real boss is the cat, Sara, who lies in the window and demonstrates her contempt for the world." Comments on the books by staff and customers are posted on the shelves. You're welcome to impart what you will, provided it is legible, pithy and fit for company.

Rue Morgue
942 Pearl St.
Boulder, Colo. 80302
(303) 443-8346

The bookstore with a glorious past. Rue Morgue is the recently opened retail division of Aspen Bookhouse, which has been delighting mail-order customers for

approximately a dozen years. With backing such as this, you can expect Rue Morgue to excel in posting mysteries, which it does. Tom and Enid Schantz mail an annotated newsletter to customers ten times a year. Their first love is still Sherlockiana, but send on your want lists; they're equipped to handle them beautifully.

San Francisco Mystery Bookstore
746 Diamond St.
San Francisco, Calif. 94114
(415) 282-7444

Owner Bruce Taylor turns churlish when someone wants more from him than books. But wittily so. As he explains, "No T-shirts, trips to exotic lands or balloon rides. We sell books. But once a year we do put on a Nero Wolfe dinner. And we have signings for local authors. And long live Tony Hillerman. And William Marshall. Cornell Woolrich, too, but . . ."

Scene of the Crime®
13636 Ventura Blvd.
Sherman Oaks, Calif. 91423
(213) 981-2583

Ruth Windfeldt is the one everyone else copies. As well they might; no one else has near her style. She was the first woman since Agatha Christie to stage a murder on the Orient Express (on one of her recent tours for mystery fans), she houses the largest, most sumptuously presented collection of detective fiction on the West Coast and she is the first person to combine *two* favorite fantasies: the opening of a mystery bookshop *and* the opening of an adjoining tea shop, where cabbage roses climb up the walls, Persian rugs scatter underfoot and oak gleams throughout. The food? Mouthwatering. Ditto the books. You owe it to yourself to check Ruth out first.

Science Fiction and Mystery Bookstore, Ltd.
752½ N. Highland N.E.
Atlanta, Ga. 30306
(404) 875-7326

As the name implies, a bit of both worlds, mystery and science fiction. The reading corner features an armoire, wingback chairs and a don't-hurry ambience nurtured by cofounders Bill Amis and Mark Stevens. In winter months, Sunday tea includes a pot of Fortnum and Mason's best, cucumber sandwiches and pastries; summer Sundays command wine spritzers. All this and something to read, too! Absolute heaven.

Sherlock's Home
5614 E. Second
Long Beach, Calif. 90803
(213) 433-6130

Granted the book selection is admirable and the catalogue serviceable, but some say the real reason to frequent Beth and Chris Caswell's haven is for the gift selection—lots and lots of games, mugs, totes, bric-a-brac, stocking stuffers and so forth. Despite the name, you can be a more hard-boiled fan and still be comfortable browsing here.

Sleuth of Baker Street
1543 Bayview Ave.
Toronto, Canada M4G3B5
(416) 483-3111

The pride of Canada, with proprietor Mr. Singh more than willing to act as unofficial welcomer for the 4th International Crime Congress scheduled in two years' time. At hand right now, a panoply of crime fiction, the best from both sides of the border and across the sea. Clearing house for all mystery authors venturing north and favorite haunt of those living nearby.

Spenser's Mystery Bookshop
314 Newbury St.
Boston, Mass. 02115
(617) 262-0880

Andy Thurnauer, who would never lie, swears "Spenser's second office, which he occupied in *Promised Land* through *Rachel Wallace,* is two blocks southeast and his Marlboro Street apartment a few blocks north." Another of the space sharers, the cohabitant this time being Marlowe's Used Books. Emphasis on the hard-boiled, and Andy's personal favorites, the vintage paperbacks, specifically old Dell mapbacks.

Uncle Edgar's Mystery Bookstore
2864 Chicago Ave. S.
Minneapolis, Minn. 55407
(612) 874-7575

The best-named of the bookstores, Uncle Edgar's abuts its spines with Uncle Hugo's, the science-fiction shop. Don Blyly owns both, but Jeff Hatfield is the expert-on-premises for Edgar, Scott Imes for Hugo. They sell worldwide, debunking the myth that New York and L.A. garner most of the foreign sales.

Whodunit
1931 Chestnut St.
Philadelphia, Pa. 19103
(215) 567-1478

Owner Art Bourgeau has the distinction of being the only shop proprietor to have written mystery fiction: *The Most Likely Suspects* and *A Lonely Way to Die,* two good-old-southern-boy hard-boileds, published by Berkley. The shop is more for buyers than for browsers, more of a business than a passion, but the books are all here—Art just doesn't want to have conversations about them.

Desdemona Brannigan says as much as she loves bookstores, she'd never want to own one. She couldn't handle all that joy.

TROUBLE SPOTS

Perhaps

Thundering Thermopylae! What was that! Brought me off the bed like rhinos were charging. Never forget that time in Rajasthan . . . was that it, Rajasthan? Get my bearings now . . . north, I think, up from the Hill Station, seems to me . . . damn lovely, too, before—that's it, that's the ticket! Srinigar! Had that pretty little houseboat. 'Course, it absolutely stank . . . heathen maid absolutely no use a-tall. Wasn't sorry when it fell apart; just too bad it didn't sink, could've used the wash. Hold up, hold up! *Chrandigar, that's* the charge! Remember now clear as this morning . . . I was changing my boots and had to go

Harriet borrows a trinket.

gaming off with one on and t'other flapping . . . But a leader leads, and the men knew I would not fail them. My men!

Thermopylae! *More* footsteps!

Old place is noisy as a boarding house. Better food, 'course; Cook sees to that, but comings, goings, half the night! Wouldn't live here myself; no, I would not. Bones'd never thaw. Fires straight into July, I shouldn't wonder, and devil take the heat! And a damn fool name for a house, too! "Staffordshire Hall!"

Thorring Thermopylae! Again! Where's a candle? Where's my stick? Can't go patrolling without my stick. On with it, Virgil, on with it!

Who's next-door? Cousin, is it? Must be. Guests on the one side, them on the other, makes sense. Now where's that noise again? Downstairs? Can I get down this way? Forage, Virgil, forage . . . like that midnight in Poona, when the sabre-tooth snapped the tentpole and it was up to you to take command and bring it down. Was it Poona? Yes, yes, Poona, I'm almost sure of it. Great whacking noise those teeth made! Had dreams about it for months. Gunned it right in the third eye, too, fell like a tree, even the Gurkhas couldn't believe it . . . sahibed me to death.

Lord Teasdale and his loofa.

Hallo, then, where does this go? Nasty small space, isn't it? Must be servants' wing. Take a peek, they won't mind. One girl, but where's the other? Bed not slept in yet? I say, wicked little thing, isn't she? John has something on the side, does he? Can't full blame him with Clare that way. She'd put off a saint, which we all know John never was one of. Thought surely he'd marry Caroline. "My Caro, my Caro," all I heard from him, even said it in his sleep. Told me once he'd made a vow to write her every day of his life. Can't imagine why he didn't marry her. Father must've put his foot down, before John made the money. Sorry to high heaven now, I should think, with the crest and the house and the grounds and the prestige from town; heard he was invited to the Royals' for tea last month; can't do better than that, can you?

Who's in here, nice little suite, wouldn't mind it myself, would I? Cook, of course. Nothing new here.

Stop, Virgil, listen... shhhh... there, right there it was, on to it. The game room? What's here to make a noise? Hallo, what's this... the Piquet score? Can't understand losing like that! Rather good with a deck, I don't mind admitting.

Leslie formally introduces himself to Bridie.

Sorry about tea. The card did say Promptly Seven. Would've trained if I'd known he wanted me sooner. Enjoyed the walk... bracing... reminded me of that trek in Nepal, from base camp to the Yak & Yeti. Silly name for a hotel... food was fine, though, none of that yak butter, no matter what they named the place.

What now! French farce this house is, with doors going all night long! Now who? Back up the stairs and find out and report to John. Am I the only one here on his side? Poor fool. Bought a wife with money, and an elephant house, and what does it get him? Look, look at this brass one ... parading down the hall like she was in a ballgown! Brooches on, no less. And whose room might that have been... Becca's? Clare's? She's gone in the morning, I'll see to that.

Must write this down, official report for John. Not that I can't trust the mind, clear as water after all these years. Know today and yesterday and Army days just like new. Even remember when Roudebush wore a fourteen collar, and that would choke him now! Thermopylae, how he would run for us! Best damn tea I ever had! I'll stop in tomorrow and pay my respects! Imagine! Roudebush with gout! Sugar in tea. Do it every time.

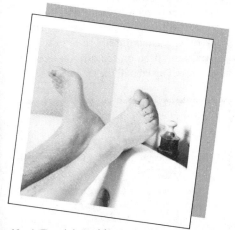

Lord Teasdale and his tootsies.

THERE'LL ALWAYS BE A SORT OF ENGLAND

Martha Grimes

In a wonderful Monty Python routine, the cast is cloistered in an English manor house. The subject is murder. Could there be any other in an English manor house? Everything else—tea, port, chat, crackling logs—is subordinate to the murder and to the entrance of Inspector Hound. (Or better, Chief Inspector. Seldom a Sergeant, more often a Superintendent or, if the gang is having an especially bad time of it, a Commander like P.D. James' Adam Dalgliesh. There are very few Commanders to go round, so if the murderer winds up with one, he's hit the jackpot.)

Now, the Python gang busy themselves with ruining one another's alibis through the near-holy device of the Train Schedule.* Roderick claims he could not possibly be guilty because he was in the dining car on the 5:15 from Swindon at the time of the murder. "But the 5:15 *has no dining car,* Roderick," says Elizabeth sweetly. "It's the *6:07* that has a dining car!" Ah, farewell Roderick's alibi, but also farewell to Elizabeth's, as dear Auntie quickly reminds her that *she* couldn't have taken the 4:27 from Waterloo and eaten that cheese toastie because *the 4:27 has no snack bar.***

The viewer continues to be snowed under with the minutiae of the departures, arrivals and dining facilities of BritRail.

And speaking of snow. To see a character out there in the dark and the snow, tripping over—"Well, but it must be a *log,* Roderick! But whatever are those funny tracks?" The reader is quite familiar with the workings of Roderick's mind by now, especially since he's wearing skis.

These are but two of the sacred and marvelous banalities of the British crime "thriller." We who love to read such books can muster up many more: the library (where the characters go not to read, but to die); the unquenchable thirst for tea and/or port (with nasty things in their dregs); dim outlines in the fog (that are seldom those of friends); riding to hounds on frosty mornings (where something rather untoward waits on the other side of the hedge); valets or butlers being unspeakably subservient (because they are unspeakably disguised). In addition to all of the above, the suspects (meaning one's relations) always seem to be wearing tennis togs or twin-sets. The Colonel, however, is in black tie and chalking his cue-stick.

One could go on for quite a spell. I have myself used all these conventions

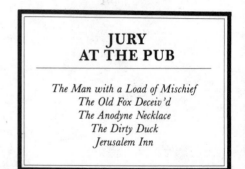

JURY AT THE PUB

The Man with a Load of Mischief
The Old Fox Deceiv'd
The Anodyne Necklace
The Dirty Duck
Jerusalem Inn

---

*There can never be too much importance placed upon this.
**Ditto.

shamelessly, while telling myself that Shakespeare was never afraid of a cliché.

A reviewer once said that I wouldn't be caught dead with a body in a library. Actually, I'd be happy for my imagination to trip over one. Either that or a murder at the local vicarage, or a terrible unpleasantness at the Turf Club. Most of all, I crave a bit of unscrupulous mayhem on a train.

The England of the mystery novel (or "thriller," as they say) is a cliché, and British-mystery lovers know it. But still we want all those lovely conventions, as long as we can believe in them. If we toss a book aside, the failure is not in the cliché, but in its failure to convince—which might be a contradiction in terms, but I don't think so.

Perhaps the primary convention of the British thriller is its chicken-coop quality. It is claustrophobic. There are certain places where the suspects are invariably found: in the manor house or the parsonage or, if the writer is forced for reasons of plot, some hovel of the "lower" classes or an "office." Regardless, there is still that attempt to keep the quarters close, pristine and as sterile as an operating theater. One always seems to come upon the people, even those in the hovel or the office, just as they are pouring tea or as the secretaries are having a go at ruining a boss' reputation. It is almost Jamesian, the way the reader doesn't actually see them *work*.

Even when the characters are outside, they might just as well have stayed home. I cannot remember a suspect ever actually walking along Oxford or Regent Streets (unless it is dead dark). Oh, the character can talk about having bought that lovely length of Liberty lawn, but one never *sees* her in Liberty's, pillaging the sales tables. One sometimes gets the impression that all the characters are incipient agoraphobes who hug their libraries and drawing rooms to them for security's sake (only to get murdered in

THE SLAUGHTER SCHEDULE

MILES	STATION	am (TFb)	am (TFb)	am (Y)	am (D)	am (E)	pm (TB)	pm (S)
Dep.	**UPPER SLAUGHTER**	6:25	7:55	8:05	10:00	11:15	2:10	7:30
2¼	LOWER SLAUGHTER	6:31	8:01	8:11	10:06	....	2:16	7:36
9	BODY-IN-WATER	6:46	....	8:27	....	11:46	2:50	....
10½	WATER-OVER-DAMN	6:57	....	8:30	....	12:02	3:00	....
11½	TROUBLED WATER	7:11	....	9:10	....	1:00	3:15	....
15¼	**CRUMPET-UPON-JAM**	7:20	8:50	9:20	....	1:10	4:20	4:27
21	CLUE UNDER CLUE	....	9:25	9:55	....	1:30	5:00	8:01
22¼	**NERVES ON EDGE**	8:20	9:45	10:50	11:30	1:40	5:01	9:50
23	THEREABOUTS	8:26	9:50	11:10	....	1:50	5:15	....
25 Arr.	**LONDON**	9:00	9:55	11:30	12:35	2:07	5:17	10:3

(SECOND CLASS ONLY)
EFFECTIVE
FRIDAY THE 13TH
TO SUNDAY NEXT

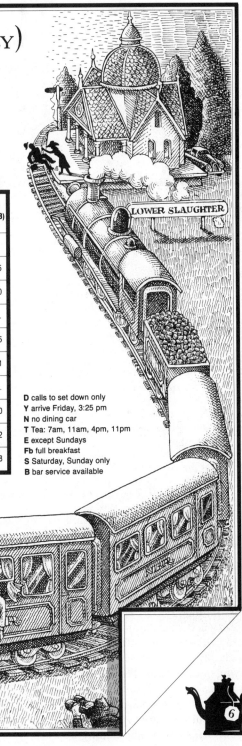

STATION	am (TFb)	am (NFb)	am (S)	am (Y)	am (BT)	pm (BN)	pm (T)	pm (TFbB)
Dep. LONDON	6	7	8	9	2	3	4	5
THEREABOUTS	6:10	7:10	8:10	9:10	2:10	3:10	4:10	5:25
NERVES-ON-EDGE	7:17	7:25	8:25	....	2:20	4:00	4:25	6:00
CLUE UNDER CLUE	7:27	8:25	8:40	10:17	3:15	5:00	5:00	....
CRUMPET-UPON JAM	7:30	9:00	8:50	11:00	3:17	....	5:30	6:25
TROUBLED WATER	8:01	....	9:00	11:05	4:00	....	6:00	7:11
WATER-OVER-DAMN	8:20	....	10:00	11:07	4:05	....	6:10	....
BODY-IN-WATER	8:40	....	10:05	11:09	4:10	....	6:20	7:30
LOWER SLAUGHTER	8:54	9:54	....	11:56	4:54	....	6:54	8:02
Arr. UPPER SLAUGHTER	9:00	10:00	....	12:00	5:00	6:00	7:00	8:08

D calls to set down only
Y arrive Friday, 3:25 pm
N no dining car
T Tea: 7am, 11am, 4pm, 11pm
E except Sundays
Fb full breakfast
S Saturday, Sunday only
B bar service available

TRANSATLANTIC TRAUMA

Many people find it odd that an American should choose the genre of the British crime novel. Or, I should say, have the gall to choose it. In particular, there are the British customs officials who hide their smirks behind their hands when I tell them why I'm in their country: to do "research" (or whatever you call sitting around in pubs) for my next British mystery. They leave me cooling my heels while they go off and "research" the problem (or whatever you call having a cuppa).

Nothing intimidates me quite so much as going into the local station. I start laughing before I even tell the constable or desk sergeant that I need information. That way, I figure we can laugh at me together. (I've had cards made up to prove who I am. Everybody I give one to hands it back, as if the card were on loan.)

And then there are the British friends who delight in pointing out my errors. You can't buy Hershey's chocolate in England. I slipped up and called petrol "gas." My spelling's American (well, so is my publisher). And there are the public relations officials at New Scotland Yard who feel I am mucking about in their manor and advise me to write about what I'm familiar with, presumably New York or L.A. cops.

There would be room left over for angels to dance on the pinhead of what I know about the workings of the American police force. I doubt many Americans know much more about city or state police than what we find out when we're burning rubber at 80 m.p.h. and that familiar light starts whirring behind us and we hope it's an ambulance. Does your True Brit know one whit more about London's Metropolitan Police? No. When I was wandering around Victoria Street, looking for New Scotland Yard and accosting first this and then that British citizen, not one of them knew where England's finest were located. Who finally set me in the right direction? An American. So there.

M.G.

them, finally). They *talk* about going up to town, popping in to Harrods, catching the earliest train—endlessly, endlessly—but one doesn't see them carrying those dreadful little plastic tea cups up and down the aisles of an actual train. Here, claustrophobia is honed to a fine art; the suspects are never allowed off the train, not even for questioning by what-

ever police force has jurisdiction. The officer comes aboard instead.

Still . . . Roderick was a fool to imagine the *Swindon* train would be encumbered with a *dining car* . . .

Martha Grimes is the author of the Superintendent Jury crime novels, the title of each being a venerable pub.

DERAILING BRITISH RAIL
The Mystery Writers' Favorite Prank

Hugh Douglas

Trains of every kind, named expresses, night mails and smelly little local puffers, have been a favourite setting for crime writers and their readers since the crime novel was born. They have inspired authors to make the wheels of fear spin in their readers' minds as no other mode of transport could.

What's so special about the railroad that ships, airplanes or automobiles don't have? Why does *Mystery of the Blue Train* capture attention on the bookstalls while *Mayhem on the Queen Mary* would hardly rate a second glance? What is there about the grinding of iron wheels on iron rails that sets the adrenalin flowing like a rogue oil-well?

Ships and planes have been used successfully by crime writers, of course they have, but as a location they suffer from the disadvantage that they're not really in our world as they travel: their routes don't relate to real life or death, so they are soulless phantoms orbiting beyond man's environment until the moment they touch land. And then, seaports or airports are not at the heart of cities—where people live, love and commit violence against their fellow man. Even the motorcar is a capsule sealed off from humanity. Look down on a highway and you see little automated ants rushing to and fro, starting, stopping, and missing one another by a hair's breadth as if directed by some kind of

formic radar. And who ever heard of a whodunit about ants, for heaven's sake?

The train is different. It has all the good qualities that other modes of travel offer to the crime novelist, but it has more. Although quite isolated from its environment, the train never ceases to be a part of it. A real world of houses, villages, cities, fields, cows and even people passes by the window. Yet this world is quite out of reach, unable to affect the traveller for good or ill. Reality is just beyond his fantasy world, but quite unattainable. The wheeled thing rolls on, out of the reader's control. There is no escape. In this enclosed space the tension heightens all the way to journey's end.

The train is a universe of its own. It is confined, remote and comfortable. Whodunit victims always travel first class, so their blood soaks into the thick plush cushions, leaving no vulgar mess. Indeed, the whodunit train resembles that other favourite venue of the thriller, the secluded country house, with the compartment as closely confined as a smoking-room. Here must be no vulgarity, no undue ostentation.

But unlike the country house the reader's companions on the train are strangers—or so he thinks. Who are they? Who is victim and who villain? Half a dozen people eye one another, reading (or is it lurking?) behind a newspaper, dozing fitfully, or glancing apprehensively from window to fellow passengers and then to the door. The train rushes into a tunnel and the overhead reading lamp clamps a mask over the face of the man opposite, turning him from a benign Dr. Jekyll to a savage Mr. Hyde. Can he really be as sinister as he looks, or is he one of the red herrings with which the whodunit's track is strewn? And who is that old lady knitting in the other corner? Her eyes are everywhere. Is she waiting for the chance to thrust a No. 10 needle six inches into someone's heart, or is she dear Miss Marple biding her time to unravel the problem?

Truly, travellers are strange bedfellows. Bedfellows? My God, the sleeping car is lethal. Here is the most isolated place in the whole world, a tiny square of space, lonelier than the summit of Everest. And what are all these switches, buttons and bolts for? Does the door lock securely? It is impossible to try it without opening it again. And will the distant clanging of the bell be answered by the steward, or will it bring some sinister caller?

It's bad enough when the train is moving; noise covers up other noises, the scream or gunshot will never be heard over the clickety-clack of the wheels, the roar of the tunnel will shut out the stealthy footstep in the corridor, the engine's strangled whistle will drown the cry of danger in the next sleeping berth. But what happens when the train stops in the middle of nowhere? Trains do. The Orient Express stuck in snow-filled waste, deep with drifting fear. Help could not reach it; escape was impossible. This prison was as secure as Devil's Island, as well guarded as Sing Sing, but it held the person who had wielded the knife in the night, and he might wield it again.

A wakeful man in a sleeping car is the loneliest man on earth.

Day restores the scene to that comforting, comfortable country house, filled with elegance and peopled with feudal staff. In the dining car, the stewards show all the attentiveness of old family retainers and breakfast is as generous as it would be for a house party in Devon, with only the food-loaded sideboard missing. But in the train there can be no relaxed feeling for long, because murder has been committed and work is in hand to solve the crime. While the innocent hover in fear, the murderer's confidence crumbles. He is as much the victim of the confined space as of the detective's skill.

The train journey has shape, and shape is what the writer is seeking when he plans his novel: within a time-scale the crime will be perpetrated, discovered and solved. Journey's end will reveal all, convict the guilty and release the innocent. It is very tidy.

Of course, not all novelists confine their story to the train: the crime can pursue the traveller home, and then his detectives go to work on time-tables, proving the impossible by a mere thirty seconds between trains—for the railway time-table is the train crime writer's *vade mecum,* as essential as his typewriter.

Alas, the heyday of the train was the heyday of the railway whodunit, when trains were drawn by lumbering dinosaurs that left behind them a trail of fire, smoke, steam and mystery. Diesel or electric locomotives are clinically clean and lacking in romance, and it is largely their fault that the train no longer attracts the crime novelist or his reader. But memories are memories. The classics of the genre still are read and re-read by those who seek a glimpse into the lush past, taking their crime elegantly and with a whiff of nostalgic smoke.

Hugh Douglas loves trains almost as much as mysteries; as well he should, since he works for British Rail.

MURDER BY DEGREE
The Case of the Screaming Spires

Reginald Hill

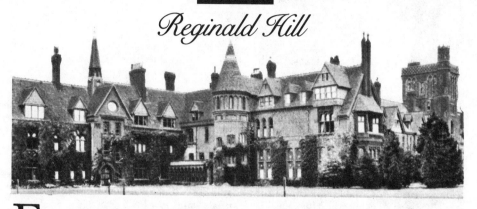

Every crimiculturalist knows that mayhem breeds best in hot-house conditions. First find your closed community, then drop a mould-warp into the humus.

Jane Austen in her well-known advice to Agatha Christie (among others) says, "Three or four Families in a Country Village is the very thing to work on." As a rural parson's daughter she was clearly aware that the best bestialities took place out of town, and it was a dull weekend when, swollen by house-party guests, Daddy's congregation didn't contain at least one gifted amateur detective to every three homicidal maniacs.

But had Jane Austen lived a century later, when her sex was beginning to be disadvantaged by higher education, she might have modified her advice to include the great centres of learning.

After all, she might have asked, what is a university but a large village? What is a college course but a continuous house party? And is it not a truth universally acknowledged that students and teachers alike perform short stints of work punctuated by long periods of idleness which can most profitably be filled by crime and its solution?

It might be useful at this point to extend our list of universally acknowledged truths about the world of higher education. So self-evident are they that they need as little statistical support as the basic tenets of other branches of entertainment fiction, *viz.* cowboys smell nice and shoot straight, foreigners smell nasty and spy, spilt blood will out and blue blood will tell.

The following bear the same stamp of authority.

(1) *Students are sex-mad.* When you look at them, it's obvious. When you can't look at them, it's because they've gone to an orgy.

(2) *Students are unbalanced.* Prof. A.E. Housman, the well-known expert on rustic violence, wasn't joking when he

> *I hate academic mysteries. As soon as I come across the word "don" and it's not someone's first name, I close the book.*
>
> Fran Lebowitz

FINAL EXAM

Addee Key, Proctor

1. Who staged a sit-in at the University of Calleshire and made C.D. Sloane cope with it in *Parting Breath*?

2. What subject was taught in the Bantwick University English class?

3. In which university did Professor Gideon Oliver teach in Elkins' *Fellowship of Fear*?

4. In Carol Clemeau's *The Ariadne Clue,* what subject did Professor Antonia Nielson specialize in?

5. Amanda Mackay's Dr. Hannah Land is a Professor of Political Science at which southern university?

6. Balaclava Agricultural College and Professor Peter Shandy are featured in four novels. Name them and their author.

7. *Campus Killings* by Jessica Martin, *Coast Highway 1* by Elizabeth Ward and *Murder in the English Department* by Valerie Miner all co-exist in the same western state. Which one?

8. Detectives Lamarre and Prendergast in Peter Fox's *Trail of the Reaper* solve a case at the University of _____ .

9. Kate Fansler, from the mighty pen of Amanda Cross, has taught at which Ivy League colleges?

10. Cite the Andrew Taylor novel concerning a university's medieval manuscript problems.

CORRECT ANSWERS:

1. Catherine Aird 2. crime fiction 3. Heidelberg 4. Classics 5. Duke
6. Charlotte MacLeod's *Rest You Merry, The Luck Runs Out, Something the Cat Dragged In* and *Wrack and Rune*
7. California 8. London 9. Columbia and Harvard 10. *Caroline Miniscule*

GRADE:

10 correct answers = A 8–9 right = B 6–7 right = C
5 and under = fail; please reread all books on the list.

Addee Key is a librarian with a phenomenal memory in southern California.

said, "Cambridge has been an asylum to me in every sense of the word." Come exam time, the mental wards install bunk beds.

(3) *Students are dishonest.* They steal food, books, bicycles, lingerie from clothes lines and small change from locker rooms. Also, it is well known that they use the small change they steal to pay for drugs and examination questions other students have stolen.

(4) *Students are revolutionaries.* The only students who are not left-wing anarchists are those who are right-wing terrorists.

As for the teaching staff, suffice it to say that a university lecturer is a student who liked it so much, he didn't want to leave. And a professor is a lecturer who excels.

But to be attractive to the crime novelist, it is not enough for a section of society just to breed potential criminals. The business world, or the Church, can do that quite as well. It must also breed potential detectives.

Here the crime writer can prove in a flash what educational psychologists have been debating for centuries—the theory of the transfer of training. At its most basic in nineteenth-century England, it asserted that a good classical education inculcated habits of thought and attitudes of mind that fitted a man to administer an Empire. But the claims go beyond the classics and extend to any academic disciplines requiring the application of logic and reason. And how easy it is to point to many influential figures in modern life who have moved freely between the Groves of Academe and the Corridors of Power!

Yet, even with this evidence, many scholars continue to believe in the theory of the transfer of training.

Arthur Conan Doyle realised its implications when, searching his mind for a detective hero, he recalled the diagnostic techniques of his old medical professor.

UNDERSTANDING ACADEMIA

O' (Ordinary) Level.

These are exams taken by students who wish to leave school at the age of fifteen. (They must be in attendance until that time.) A student takes a different exam for each of his subjects, so it is not uncommon to hear someone say, "Yes, I got seven O' levels." This means he passed all seven.

A' (Advanced) Level.

These exams are given to students who have remained in school another two years and wish to qualify for college. They are roughly equivalent to the American College Boards. Again, a student will take them in his major fields of study and three to four A' levels are generally acceptable for college entry.

"He read history at Balliol."

At the Oxbridge colleges, a student does not "study" a subject; he "reads" it.

"He was sent down last year."

A student who has been "sent down" has been ejected from his college. This can be for many reasons, ranging from academic difficulty to disciplinary action.

Red Brick Universities

Generally speaking, any academic institution other than Cambridge or Oxford. Primarily those in the midlands.

THE CLASSIC CRIME COURSE

Clytemnestra killed her husband Agamemnon.

Electra convinced her brother Orestes to kill Clytemnestra and her lover Aegisthus in order to avenge their father.

Oedipus married his mother Jocasta and slew his father Laius.

Theseus killed the robber Procrustes, slew the Minotaur and attempted to abduct Persephone.

Phaedra fell in love with Hippolytus, her stepson, and eventually hanged herself.

Erebus, son of Chaos, was the personification of darkness and the symbol for the land of the dead.

Achilles killed Hector.

Prometheus defied Zeus and stole fire from Olympus.

Laocoon was killed by serpents after warning the Trojans to beware of gift horses.

Polynices slew his brother Eteocles, which made him a chip off the old block—Dad was a murderer, too, name of Oedipus.

Pandora was nothing but trouble.

R. Austin Freeman drew similarly upon personal experience in creating his famous forensic scientist, Dr. Thorndyke. And Jacques Futrelle was the first to give his detective formal academic status when he created, perhaps, the greatest logician of them all—Prof. Augustus S.F.X. Van Dusen, "The Thinking Machine." Futrelle sank with the *Titanic*. Van Dusen, having made such light work of Cell 13, almost certainly escaped.

This early establishment of the suitability of top academic minds for detective work has been followed by the evolution of the student into the state of potential criminality already described. And since World War II, donnish detectives and campus crime novels have abounded. Indeed, for a while it seemed as if all those lecturers who were not filling their long idle periods by committing crime must be writing stories about it.

This brings us to a final point of interest about the academic setting.

Library shelves are full of books set in countries, cities or social environments which the author has observed only in his mind. Shakespeare never went to Bohemia, Poe never visited Paris. But the academic setting is rarely used except by those who know it personally and often intimately.

Herein lies the difference between the "truth" of the academic mystery and the "truths" of other forms. Those who look closely at such matters must confirm, albeit reluctantly, that six-guns were low on accuracy, cowboys were high out of as well as in the saddle, some foreigners are quite nice, some aristocrats are quite nasty, and most villainy goes undetected.

But few who move and work in our universities and colleges have not at some time been aware that under many a swirling gown lurks the blade of the assassin, and under many a scarlet hood prick the ears of the bat. Words are the grains of sand heaped up against a tide of blood. And if there sometimes seems a shortage of bodies, it may be because in these places the dead keep on walking rather longer than in the world outside.

Here, then, for the subtle palate, are soufflés of death and violence served on plates of gold. Taste them in comfort and let who will go down those mean streets, tiptoeing through the cadavers with Chandler and Chase, to whom (among others) Jane Austen said, "How horrible to have so many people killed! And what a blessing one cares for none of them!"

Reginald Hill is the author of An Advancement of Learning, *a crime novel with a professional touch.*

OXFORD VS. CAMBRIDGE
THE DARK BLUES HAVE THE MOST

Margaret Yorke

GEORGE HALCROW

More mystery stories are set in Oxford than in Cambridge. More fictional sleuths are Oxford than Cambridge men. More crime writers live near Oxford than Cambridge. Why?

First, is it true? Yes. Dorothy L. Sayers and Peter Wimsey, Edmund Crispin and Gervase Fen, Michael Innes and his quotation-capping Appleby score instantly for Oxford, whose sporting teams are distinguished from the light blue of Cambridge by their dark blue colours. Then comes J.C. Masterman with *An Oxford Tragedy* and *The Case of the Four Friends*, Katherine Farrar with *Gownsman's Gallows* and *The Missing Link*, and Robert Robinson with *Landscape with Dead Dons*. James McClure lives in Oxford; Elizabeth Ferrars lived there for five years; three of Gwendolyn Butler's books have Oxford settings. John Le Carré and Geoffrey Household both went there. G.D.H. Cole, a Fellow of All Souls, wrote many detective novels in partnership with his wife Margaret, but she went to Cambridge; Anthony Price went to Oxford, and lives nearby, but sent his Dr. Audley to Cambridge: two half-hits for the Light Blues here?

So what about "the other place,"

which is what Oxford persons call Cambridge? P.D. James lived there, her poetry-writing Commander Adam Dalgliesh was certainly at Cambridge, and her *An Unsuitable Job for a Woman* has a Cambridge setting. To support her, there is Glyn Daniel and his sleuth Sir Richard Sherrington. V.C. Clinton-Baddeley's Dr. David is a Cambridge don; Margery Allingham's Campion went to Cambridge. Peter Dickinson, Robert Charles and Brian Cooper all went to Cambridge. So did J.B. Priestley, whose comprehensive works include a detective novel, *Salt Is Leaving*.

Scenes-of-crime investigation is important when solving mysteries. Let's examine these. Oxford is centrally placed in England, the hub of road and railway lines radiating in all directions on the way to many other places. Cambridge is out on a limb, long ago a port but now an end in itself. Oxford has varied, hilly countryside around the city. Cambridge lies amid flat fenland ex-posed to cobweb-dispersing winds. Oxford is a grey city, its buildings stone, though the re-faced colleges now gleam palely golden as when they were first built in the days before polluted air blackened their façades. Cambridge is a city of colour; many of the colleges are built of mellow brick, and old frontages in the town have been preserved by planners who have hidden modern blocks away from immediate view.

But the biggest difference lies in what is central to each city. In Oxford, the colleges border busy streets: most of those at Cambridge lie along the banks of the tranquil river, each linked by its own bridge to the verdant parkland and gardens on the farther side. In Oxford, the rivers run around, not through the city, and few colleges are alongside them. Both cities have Bridges of Sighs: Oxford's crosses a street; Cambridge's, water. But at Oxford, over all, looms the motor industry that grew from a cycle repair shop. Cambridge, however, has no

THE OXBRIDGE MYSTERIES

Oxford

Jeffrey Archer, *Not a Penny More, Not a Penny Less*

Adam Broome, *The Oxford Murders*

Gwendolyn Butler, *Coffin in Oxford; A Coffin for Pandora; Dine and Be Dead*

G.D.H. and M.I. Cole, *Off with Her Head*

Edmund Crispin, *Obsequies at Oxford; Dead and Dumb; The Moving Toyshop*

Colin Dexter, *Last Bus to Woodstock; Silent World of Nicholas Quinn*

Katherine Farrar, *Gownsman's Gallows; The Missing Link; At Odds with Morning*

Tim Heald, *Small Masterpiece*

Michael Innes, *Operation Pax; Seven Suspects; Hare Sitting Up*

J.C. Masterman, *An Oxford Tragedy; The Case of the Four Friends*

Dermot Morrah, *The Mummy Case Mystery*

Raymond Postgate, *Ledger Is Kept*

Robert Robinson, *Landscape with Dead Dons*

J. Maclaren Ross, *Until the Day She Dies*

Dorothy L. Sayers, *Gaudy Night*

Howard Shaw, *Death of a Don*

Margaret Yorke, *Cast for Death; Grave Matters*

Cambridge

V.C. Clinton-Baddeley, *Death's Bright Dart*

Adam Broome, *The Cambridge Murders*

Robert Charles, *Dead Before Midnight*

Brian Cooper, *The Path to the Bridge*

Dilwyn Rees, *The Cambridge Murders*

P.D. James, *An Unsuitable Job for a Woman*

R. Lait, *Switched Out*

Harvard Has a Homicide, Too

Amanda Cross, *Death in a Tenured Position*

Timothy Fuller, *Harvard Has a Homicide*

Victoria Silver, *Death of a Harvard Freshman*

ANATHEMA

In 1497 Dr. Thomas Langton presented Pembroke College, Cambridge, with what has come to be known as the Anathema Cup because of its Latin inscription pronouncing a curse upon whoever steals it (no one's tried). This silver cup, eight and a half inches tall, dates back to 1481. It is not, however, the oldest piece of silver at Cambridge; that honor rests with Trinity Hall's Founder's Cup, given to the college by Pope Innocent VI, who established the college in the 1300's.

Anathema: *from the Greek, meaning a denunciation of something or someone. Originally used by ecclesiastics in excommunicating the faithless.*

Hemlock: *a poisonous herb, which is not a bad thing to put in an anathema cup. Also the name of a group (Hemlock Society) devoted to dying when and how they choose.*

comparable industrial complex.

Both universities have much the same student population, but Oxford has more colleges and some are small, tucked away in dark corners. Cambridge colleges are generally large; the eye is led ever upwards and one is aware, always, of the sky. The heavens are not conspicuous above Oxford, where the climate is prone to fog and the atmosphere induces introspection.

Oxford's lead in the crime fiction stakes notwithstanding, Cambridge has a Chair in Criminology while Oxford has only a small research institute. Nigel Fisher, however, Professor of Criminology at Cambridge, was himself at Christ Church, Oxford, and was a Fellow of Nuffield College before he went to Cambridge. Colin Dexter, though, went the other way: he left Cambridge for Oxford, where he sets his mysteries. Nicholas Blake (C. Day Lewis, later Poet Laureate) was at Oxford, then became Clark Lecturer at Trinity College, Cambridge, and later Professor of Poetry at Oxford. Is this evidence or a red herring?

Cambridge, strong on science, deals with criminological facts whereas our subject here is crime in fantasy. To invent it, you may have to leave Cambridge. (P.D. James lives in London.) It cannot be coincidence that eight writing members of the Crime Writers' Association live within fifteen miles of the center of Oxford and only two live as close 'to Cambridge. On this evidence the verdict must be that Cambridge persons, living beside tranquil water under the wide sky, need no escape into a world of fantasy: where is their Tolkien or Lewis Carroll? Oxford persons, pressured amid their busy streets under darker, lowering skies, suffer from more blues.

Margaret Yorke lives fourteen miles from Oxford, has worked in the libraries of two Oxford colleges and has a sleuth who is an Oxford don, Dr. Patrick Grant.

THE GARDEN
Thou Bleeding Piece of Earth

Avon Curry

Gardeners and crime writers have quite a lot in common, not least that they are both fond of a good plot. Writers, like horticulturists, have to labour at improving the groundwork: you can start off with a good idea, but it's the way you tend it that produces a good crop—either of blossoms or of salable words.

Gardening is particularly basic to the British. You know, it's said that if you give a quarter of an acre to a Frenchman, he'll plant a vine and invite a pretty girl to share the vintage; a Japanese will grow enough rice to feed a family of ten; an Englishman will lay out a lawn and sit on it to drink tea.

A crime writer will at once see a quarter-of-an-acre garden as the answer to one of the three great problems in plotting a mystery—how to get rid of the body. The perceptive reader would be well advised to look out for a passing remark about how well the roses are growing compared with those next-door, because it's under that rose bed that the deceased is sleeping. If you allow your garden to run wild, undergrowth is a useful camouflage for the quickly hidden corpse and provides good descriptive stuff when you begin talking about the heavy boots peeping out among the bluebells, or the tangle of blond tresses among the brambles.

Gardeners often burn their rubbish. If you take the trouble to establish the character ("plant the idea," as we significantly say when chatting about plotting) as a thoroughgoing efficient husbandman, you can justify the big incinerator in which bodies can be reduced to ash. I recall a garden incinerator proved very handy to that well-known "husbandman" M. Verdoux. The drawback in Britain is that the weather's seldom dry long enough to keep the bonfire going for the requisite time—so that brings us to the compost heap.

Compost is very "big" in British gardening at the moment. There was a time when to talk about it branded you a crank, but now you're an ecologist. Foolhardy would be the policeman who dared open up a keen gardener's compost heap without the very best possible evidence that a corpse was providing a large part of its bulk. Moreover, compost heaps are messy things. Smelly, too, the uninitiated believe. Policemen are more than likely to leave them alone so that the corpse is left in peace where the convocation of politic worms can keep busy.

Gardens are a good excuse for collecting the tools of death. You have only to look at the names of chemicals sold to garden-lovers—"tox" on the end of the word means, of course, that the mixture is extremely toxic; words that include the consonance "kil" or the straightforward "slay" or "bane" speak for themselves. One might almost say that in many garden-lovers there lurks a hater of other life forms—and a murderer is after all a person with enough hate to want to kill another human being.

Modern gardening chemicals are extremely dangerous. If you read the instructions—and I strongly recommend it both as a piece of academic research and as a practical life-saving exercise—you'll see you're to wash at once if a spot lands on your skin, that you're not to inhale the spray, that children mustn't get at it, or even pets. In the early days of DDT, puppies and kittens died from licking flea-killing powders from their coats. DDT has gone, but worse things have replaced it. Bear in mind, too, that the effect of these contaminants is, alas, irreversible; the poison builds up with every tiny drop.

So the easiest way to get rid of your enemy is to rent the house upwind of him, and spray your roses every time there's a strong breeze. If may take a while, but by and by he ought to get very sick if he will insist on sitting on that lawn of his.

For the knowledgeable gardener, poison need not come out of a bottle. There are deadly plants all around us, in every lovesome plot, God wot. The most innocent products can provide the most efficacious alternative to the bare bodkin. The potato, for example. Good to eat, unless you allow the tubers to become green through exposure to light, in which case the skin becomes very harmful. The leaf of the rhubarb plant (*Rheum rhaponticum*) is very toxic, although the stalk is used in pies and preserves. Ivy is poisonous. So is laburnum—remember *My Cousin Rachel*?

Nor need you actually grow the plant yourself. Once you have weeded your own garden, it dawns on you that hedgerows and wastelands are teeming with lethal growth. The datura is a member of the same family as the harmless tomato and potato. Deadly nightshade. Hemlock . . . there's a historic aid to death: Socrates drank a brew of hemlock at the behest of the Athenian rulers.

THE BORDER PATROL

Passing Strange
(Catherine Aird)
Death in the Greenhouse
(John R.L. Anderson)
Dead Heads
(Reginald Hill)
Green Grow the Dollars
(Emma Lathen)
Suddenly While Gardening
(Elizabeth Lemarchand)

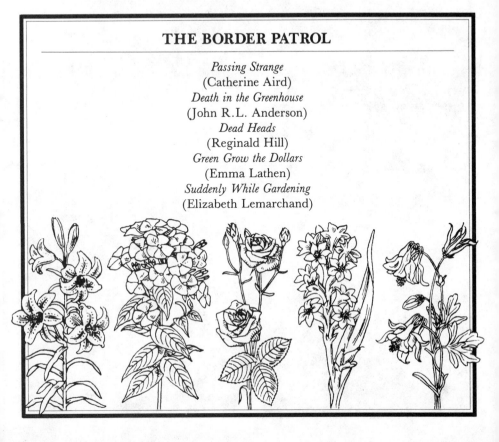

RUE

His Lordship inspects a faulty root system.

Vicar Fogg's nemesis.

Lord Teasdale and Whelks conferred every morning from eight till half past. The topics covered: freesias, forsythia and the climate for rue. Then Lord Teasdale handed Whelks a letter, bade him good morning and returned to the house. Whelks trimmed near the servants' wing till it was time to cycle to town for the early post.

Persephone, walking off her morning mouse.

Whelks is disturbed by unexpected trampling.

WHO SAYS LIFE AIN'T A BED OF ROSES?

In the words of Sgt. Cuff, "I haven't much time to be fond of anything, but when I have a moment's kindness to bestow, most times, the roses get it."

Nero Wolfe would demur. To him, nothing is as sacred as his hours spent with Theodore tending the top-floor orchids. Rare is the phone call he will allow to interrupt his botanical interlude, practiced daily, some would say religiously.

Be it roses, orchids or a rather ordinary herbaceous border, few things so rouse the mystery character to hyperbole as things that bloom. Among the more famous horticulturists: Senator Wentworth, Webster Flagg, Father Bredder and, of course, dear Jane Marple.

The garden is a plot staple of the cozier type of mystery. Its familiarity is rivaled only by the maze, into which walk vicars and virgins, lords and lay-abouts, total strangers and tipsy relatives with such alacrity, one could assume there were real gold in the goldenrod. The maze is always just high enough to hide a hand raised in anger, just dense enough to disguise the seething mass waiting therein to strike. What's understood, though never stated, is: once in, ever in, though not quite in the state nature intended.

Mushrooms... perhaps you don't want your victim dead, only out of his head: a handbook on fungi will soon tell you which to offer him, as in *The Documents in the Case.*

I can hear male readers saying that although gardening opens up endless varieties of poison, this is a very tricky and feminine form of murder. Those who like action-murder might prefer to deliver a hearty clout with a spade or shrivel the opposition with a weed flame-gun. The motor-mower or the mini-cultivator might run amok at the psychological moment—but you need a big garden to justify big equipment. Your small-scale gardener, your patio-gardener, must rely on having the victim trip up and hit his head on the Alpine rockery; or perhaps he could fall face down among the water-lilies in the decorative pond (*Nymphaea capensis* is a good bright blue variety, recommended for contrast to the drowned features when he is fished out).

There's nothing like a little knowledge of horticulture to make you aware that life is precarious, that the prize at the Flower Show is only gained by eternal vigilance against enemies natural and unnatural. The crime-writing gardener is acutely aware of an under-meaning in the famous lines from the *Rubáiyát*:

> How oft hereafter rising shall she look
> Through this same garden after me—in vain!

But the crime writer who sets his murder in a garden wants you to look in vain—at least until the end of the book. He has a splendid chance of mystifying you, because it's standard practice for a garden-lover to direct your attention to the good things and distract you from the spindly growths or the rogue intruders. You must have heard the excuse: "The rhododendrons aren't at their best now—you should have been here last week."

Indeed you should. That was when he was suffocating his victim with the plastic bag in which the fertiliser was delivered.

Avon Curry is a member of the Royal Horticulture Society.

THE PUB
A Sober Study of Darts, Pints and Sullied Reputations

Hadrian Schwartz

There's a certain type of mystery in which the author strolls you up the High Street, past the post office, past the doctor's surgery, past the old Bermondsey place with its dishevelled lawn, and deposits you in The Bunch of Grapes.

There, the Squire stands you to a lager and you reciprocate. When he leaves, you have a friendly game of dominoes with a North Country lorry driver. Just as you're finishing up, a stranger with a peculiar stain on his waistcoat asks to be directed to the loo. You oblige. As you're settling your bill with Teddy, he suggests you bring in your own tankard and put it there, third peg from the left, over the counter. Before you can answer, Daft Willie intrudes. He offers you his peanut brittle tin. You decline. He cries. You accept, carefully wiping the candy before pretending to eat it.

It's all very low-key, and you have a thorough good time of it. Until the author invites you to leave.

If you've read as many mysteries as I have, you know you're now in for big trouble—which will hound you throughout the book.

On the walk home, a little the worse for lager, you take a wrong turning, and instead of manoeuvring the High Street you're skirting Miller's Pond. Oops. You slip, of course. As you right yourself, you see it. A silver kilt pin. The Squire's?

Hurrying now, you cut 'cross the gully. Two shadows. Whispers. A snatch of North Country accent?

Exhausted, you arrive at Lady Sarah's. She ushers you into the game room and sits you east; opposite, calmly shuffling, a gentleman with a stain on his waistcoat.

And then to bed, where you fret the night away dreaming of clay-covered peanut brittle tins and empty tankards swooshing left, right, left.

It helps at this point to get a pen and neatly xxxxx out The Bunch of Grapes. Like every other pub in every other village mystery, the name is a pseudonym. This time, it's The Grapes. Next time, The British Queen, or The Three Tuns or The Cheshire Cheese. But actually, though the author can't admit it or he'd spoil his plot, the pub's real name is The Red Herring.

Here, more alibis are created, more suspects congregate, more clues are uncovered, than anyplace else in the whole book. Undoubtedly, you will be suckered in by every single one of them. Who could mistrust something he sees or hears in a place that goes back at least two hundred years?

The typical Red Herring Pub was built in the time of Cromwell. Its sides bulge as though distended by gas. Its door lists in a permanent curtsey to the street. Its exterior, as well as many a patron, needs a nice coat of whitewash. Inside are two small rooms. The left has a dartboard, the dominoes, the walk-in fireplace, the regulars' tankards and the slew of red herrings. The right has the wives. (It's usually empty.) Both have sagging floors and tiny paned windows with the original glass still intact. Shapes are barely recognisable through them.

The publican lives upstairs. In fact, he was born there. He is one of the three men in town who make a decent living, the other two being the butcher and the turf accountant. He has calluses on his palm from pulling pints, an endless supply of not-quite-clean aprons, and he arbitrates all arguments by calling Time and closing the bar.

He also sets up more red herring situations than anyone else in the story. It is he who picks up a discarded match-book and remarks, "Fancy that, the Savoy Grille. Someone just been to London, eh?"; who warns Simon he's had a bit of enough and sends him on his way, alone, with a step unsteady and a mind besotted by gin; who loans Colin the weed-killer and Derek the van.

It is he who serves the Inspector a half-and-half and a passel of half-truths, which he repeats as gossip.

The publican himself is not a red herring. He is obviously too busy tending to Rodney's shandy to step across the way, filch Mrs. Greer's locket, hide it and establish an alibi. He hasn't the time to stiletto the Duke, cycle to the dump and heave the knife, and be back for Opening. But as sure as his shandy is a half-pint beer to a half-pint cider, his pub is a red-herring breeding ground.

Think about it. An author can't always be arranging house parties to introduce his suspects. What's more logical than having them stop by the Local for a quick one?

An author can't always rely on conversations being heard outside the French windows. Where better to plant them than in the adjoining booth at the neighbourhood free house?

DARTS

The one game in town that can safely be "thrown." In darts that means letting all three of your missiles zing away. Winning score between two players is 201; between three or more, 301. Bull's-eye equals 50 points. If you throw a bull, you are not obligated to stand a round, but it's considered nice if you do.

*Yesterday, 5 P.M.,
at The Red Herring Pub,
Upper Slaughter.*

"One lager and lime, one
Amaretto and Benedictine, like
the last time, right-o?"

An author can't always expect the parlour maid to discover and return the button (cigarette lighter, woolly scarf, initial handkerchief, loose key). Who better to notice it than the publican?

There's no such thing as an innocent conversation in a mystery pub. What seems harmless at the time will evolve, two chapters later, into a clue. Similarly, no one who goes to a pub is entirely innocent. A page or so further on, one learns the sociable drinker needed an alibi. That these clues and these alibis have little to do with the actual solution of the case should by now be second nature to us. But it's not. We grab hold to the bitter end, staunch in our conviction that what transpired in the pub is of utmost importance. And so it is, or we'd have solved the mystery in the very first chapter and hated the author ever after.

Real pubs are markedly similar to fictional ones. There's the same whimsical choice of names, the same Cromwellian architecture, the same hard-working publican (only usually it's two publicans, a husband and wife). Darts are played; so are dominoes. (Stakes, however, are low: a penny forfeit if you can't go.) Lager outsells gin, gin outsells whisky and lemon squash is more popu-

lar than Coke. Tankards are hung over the bar, but they're often bawdy—not like those in mysteries—with naked females forming their handles. Visitors use one room, the regulars use the other (and that would play havoc with a mystery plot).

The biggest point of difference is that publicans rarely own their pubs. They belong to Whitbread's or Watney's. The free house has almost disappeared, and today publicans are managers rather than owners. Still, the décor is their own and so is the atmosphere.

A recent three-day swing through six London pubs disclosed no red herrings, either. Nobody in them, including me, had found a long-lost glove or noticed a bloodstain on a lorry trunk. A constable had not checked in, and no one had seen a tattersalled Continental asking directions. Mugs were rinsed without a thought to saving them for prints, and plowman's lunches were downed without a single instance of ptomaine, never mind arsenic.

In real life, The Bunch of Grapes is no Red Herring. But I've yet to close the file on Ye Olde Tea Shoppe.

Hadrian Schwartz is a regular at The Blubbering Whale.

LOCKED-ROOM MILESTONES

Kevin Barbero

In the locked-room mystery (the "impossible crime"), the stakes are doubled: the puzzle demands not only a determination of the guilty party, but also an explanation of a murder that seems to transcend all earthly laws—a deed that apparently could not have happened.

What is widely regarded as the first detective story is also the first locked-room mystery: Edgar Allan Poe's *The Murders in the Rue Morgue* (1841).

The Irish author J. Sheridan Le Fanu toyed with the locked-room concept in a short story as early as 1838, and in his classic novel *Uncle Silas* (1846) his solution was similar to Poe's. Israel Zangwill's *The Big Bow Mystery* (1892) offered variations on both method and culprit, and in the same year Conan Doyle's Sherlock Holmes solved his most baffling locked-room case, "The Adventure of the Speckled Band."

The year 1907 brought Gaston Leroux (today most famous for his *Phantom of the Opera*) and *The Mystery of the Yellow Room,* as well as Jacques Futrelle and his Thinking Machine triumphing over "The Problem of Cell 13" in an inverted tale whose hero, on a bet, works his way out of an impregnable prison.

G.K. Chesterton's crime-crushing priest débuted in 1911 with *The Innocence of Father Brown,* the first of five collections of Father Brown stories. Chesterton was a master of paradox with a real feeling for the macabre. Among the best examples: "The Miracle of Moon Crescent," "The Oracle of the Dog" and "The Dagger with Wings."

S.S. Van Dine borrowed a trick from Edgar Wallace (and established an alibi that has since become a cliché) in *The Canary Murder Case* (1927), while Ellery Queen, who would return to the locked-

MOON DOOM

The locked-room situation that's never been tried (so far): the space capsule, with one lonely astronaut about to orbit the dark side of the moon, where for a few minutes he will become incommunicado with NASA. When they once again are able to monitor his vital signs, he has none. Whodunit? How? You figure it out.

PICTORIAL PARADE

THE OLD MAN'S CASES

Poor Gideon Fell. Poor Patrick Butler. John Dickson Carr liked H.M. best of all his characters. He indulged him in twenty-two novels, two short stories. (And how he put up with the stench from the cigar is beyond understanding.)

The Plague Court Murders
The White Priory Murders
The Red Widow Murders
The Unicorn Murders
The Magic Lantern Murders
(Punch and Judy Murders)
The Peacock Feather Murders
(The Ten Teacups)
The Judas Window
Death in Five Boxes
The Reader Is Warned
Nine—and Death Makes Ten
(Murder in the Submarine Zone)
And So to Murder
Seeing Is Believing
The Gilded Man
She Died a Lady
He Wouldn't Kill Patience
The Curse of the Bronze Lamp
(Lord of the Sorcerers)
My Late Wives
The Skeleton in the Clock
A Graveyard to Let
Night at the Mocking Widow
Behind the Crimson Blind
The Cavalier's Cup

Dr. Gideon Fell, John Dickson Carr's 250 pound eccentric, surveying Carter Dickson's work.

notable achievements included a comprehensive lecture on the locked-room phenomenon in *The Three Coffins* (1935). The undisputed master of the locked-room setup, Carr, writing as Carter Dickson, ushered in Sir Henry Merrivale; among his notable cases, *He Wouldn't Kill Patience* (1944), a dandy inspired by a challenge from Carr's colleague Clayton Rawson (a room is sealed from the inside with tape, a death occurs, the tape is undisturbed, yet a plausible—though highly improbable—solution is presented).

Rawson himself created a magician sleuth, Merlini, whose initial case in 1938, *Death from a Top Hat,* proved his most difficult. (It was complicated by the arrival of a whole cult of conjurers.)

Mystery critic Anthony Boucher was so partial to the form, he adopted the name H.H. Holmes (actually the alias of a real murderer) and penned, among others, *Nine Times Nine* (1940).

Edmund Crispin tackled the locked-room situation in 1946 with *The Moving Toyshop,* an impossible puzzle with comedy overtones. More remarkable is the fact that Raymond Chandler, renowned for the tough-guy private eye, came up with an oddball, little-known example of the locked room called "Professor Bingo's Snuff" (1951).

More recent contributions to the subgenre include Maj Sjöwall and Per Wahlöö's *The Locked Room* (1973) and Michael Innes' *Appleby and Honeybeth* (1983). Among the "puzzle" anthologies, Hans Stefan Santesson's *The Locked Room Reader* (1968) and Edward D. Hoch's *All but Impossible* (1981) stand out.

The classic study in the field remains Robert Adey's *Locked Room Murders* (1979), which lists over a thousand examples of the form.

Kevin Barbero is the owner of Murder By The Book, a mystery bookstore in Providence, Rhode Island.

room theme more than once, made perhaps his most startling use of it in *The Chinese Orange Mystery* (1934), in which bewildering backwards clues offer a hint regarding the sealed-room problem.

Inspired by Chesterton, John Dickson Carr created Gideon Fell, whose

WATCH YOUR BACK

THE GOTHIC HOUSE

Peter Blake

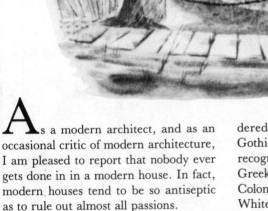

As a modern architect, and as an occasional critic of modern architecture, I am pleased to report that nobody ever gets done in in a modern house. In fact, modern houses tend to be so antiseptic as to rule out almost all passions.

But people certainly do and did and will again get passionately murdered and otherwise discomfited in so-called Gothic houses. Actually, most of the "Gothic" houses that people get murdered in are not, strictly speaking, Gothic at all; they are just about any recognizable or unrecognizable style: Greek Revival, Romanesque Revival, Colonial Revival, Plantation, Stanford White (every village in the East has at least one attributed to White—who died of gunshot wounds himself, of course—and most of these attributions are incorrect) and, most dependably, the style best known as "Charles Addams."

I don't recall a single place in which I have ever lived in the U.S. that did not have at least one Charles Addams house: it was usually two stories in height (plus mansard roof); most windows were broken and/or boarded up; its front porch was in a state of collapse, barely able to support the cobwebs strung between its slender (and partly splintered) pillars; its siding was termite-infested; and the paint was peeling throughout. The steps leading up to the porch had long rotted away; the foundation walls (if any) had settled in the general direction of China; and at night shutters (usually dangling from a single hinge) would swing and bang mournfully. Whenever there was a thunderstorm, lightning would be sure to strike the mansard roof, like a sword of fire.

There used to be a Charles Addams house at the end of Long Island, between Bridgehampton and Sagaponack. Everybody *knew* that someone had been murdered inside that terrible wreck. The story went that she (the victim) had been all alone, that there had been no will, and that no one had been able to locate any next of kin. Hence the title to the disaster area was clouded, and the property could not be sold. (That's a ridiculous scenario to anyone who knows what's what; the next of kin obviously had to have been at least marginally involved in the bloodbath.)

The house was leaning at an angle the Tower of Pisa would have envied when I decided one day to trespass on the premises (bodyguarded by my then eight-year-old son and a team of killer dogs). The exterior had been posted liberally with NO TRESPASSING signs; the floorboards on the entrance porch gave way with a crash; the front door screeched; and the walls and ceilings sighed. Rats scuttled, bats whizzed by, and so did ghosts. We looked for black widow spiders and original copies of the Federalist Papers.

However, by the time we reached the stairs to the attic (where those priceless Federalist Papers were sure to have been stashed away), we had giant butterflies in our stomachs and the killer dogs were in a state of shock. There seemed to be a great many bleached bones scattered about this Haunted Mansion (they turned out to be droppings left by Colonel Sanders' army), and there seemed to be an awful silence—made more awful by whimpering sounds (my own).

It was in the middle of a sunny summer day, but inside that Haunted Mansion it was very dim and very cold and clammy. We never made it to the attic, where the most telling clues were undoubtedly on display.

My son and I went back a year later, and the Charles Addams house had simply vanished. It had not merely been struck down by one final bolt of lightning, leaving a burned-out cadaver; it had literally dropped out of sight, like a whodunit clue left too long unobserved.

Except . . . except that late one night, after a long party in Sagaponack, I drove back heading west on Sag Road, toward Bridgehampton, and suddenly there was this bolt of lightning, to my right, crashing into the now vacant lot, and I caught sight of it in my rear-view mirror. And there, in this flash of lightning, stood the old "Gothic" house in all its glory, as if entirely new, long before it had been touched by Charles Addams' brush. And on the porch I saw the figure of a lady clad in gossamer cobwebs, and the figure of a brutish man, and something clearly against the felony statutes was about to be done to her, with an ax. I quickly stepped on the gas and made it to my own, dispassionate modern house in record time.

Peter Blake is chairman of the School of Architecture, Boston Architectural Center, and author of Form Follows Fiasco: Why Modern Architecture Hasn't Worked.

CO-OPS, CONDOS AND CONJUGAL CELLS

Sanford Nesbitt

Give me your tired, your poor, and I will show you a typical city dweller who lives on a double-digit floor with what little view there once was now obscured by maximum security bars, which he just spent the weekend installing. For the privilege of living thus, with less light than a mole requires, less air than a fish deems healthy and less space than an anorexic occupies, this poor tired urbanite pays dearly—so much, in fact, that he almost never thinks of his condo or his co-op as his home. He thinks of himself as caretaker to an investment and what we commonly hear him say is, "I can get $150,000 for it right now and if I keep it up and wait a few years, who knows?"

Indeed. The problem is to find another place for that $150,000. Of course, if he's willing to settle for a bit less than what he has, I might know of something for him. Follow me now to the newest get-rich-quick scheme since some sucker actually bought the Brooklyn Bridge (and suggested to his friends that they might want a piece of the action, too).

Like the Brooklyn Bridge scam, this is legal only as long as you keep one step ahead of the cops and have a very fast-talking lawyer.

I know you want out of your white elephant and I offer to take it off your hands. Very legitimate. I then approach your neighbors, introduce myself as the new sharer and confess I'd like more room, if they're thinking of selling, please let me know. I luck out (this version of the scenario needs a little luck).

Soon I have cornered the market on apartments in the building. In fact, I now own everything in it. It, through careful planning, wise investing (and filing with the attorney general's office) is now ready for my big government swindle. I own this building for two years. Then, working day and night like a demon in pursuit of the all American dream, I sell all the apartments out within one year. I can now take the lower tax return. Nice, if I can pull it off.

I might prefer version two in get-rich-quickdom. I found a co-op corporation. I then trade the corporation my building for all its stock. I have now circumvented dealer status, which will save me a bundle.

A variant: I sell my building to a "good friend." We have arrived at a very complicated contract with a fluctuating price adjustment clause(s). This says that the buyer has to buy from me (crafty soandso) at a relatively high price, but it's an inflated price. This is not so difficult to manage as one might assume, tax laws being as bizarre as they are. Tax shelters in which you get a four to one write-off (I put in $1 and get a $4 deduction) are trickier to get away with. My real estate machinations are less likely to be challenged, particularly if I'm satisfied with only one a year.

The difficulty in all of the above is having a nest egg large enough to start the process rolling. Those with tax scam schemes on their brain might prudently look to buying smallish brownstones with six or less apartments, rather than tackle, say, the U.N. Plaza complex.

The co-op and condo business began in New York under rent control, which, supposedly, was a way of controlling profit (6 percent return on the amount of the investment). Because of the creative manner in which landlords filed their tax returns, they made much more. When the clamp-down came, and it did, though some might say it's still only in progress, landlords wanted out. Their goose laying gold eggs began dropping pyrite ones. The solution: sell, and fast. First target of opportunity, of course, was other landlords. Landlord #1 sold out to #2 sold out to #3 and so on. This created a spiral effect upwards and was fine until there was nobody left to sell to (diminished profits = no takers). This brought us up to the late freewheeling 1960's, when derelict buildings went begging. No one knows the name of the first con artist who said, "Hey, let's sell to the tenants," but this became the birth of the co-op and the condo.

Is there an advantage to one and not the other? Generally, real estate experts and those with financial finagling on their minds will favor the co-op. It is more readily transferable, you don't need approval of a board to buy in and you get the almighty deed for it, which makes banks smile upon you—they see it as supremely fine security, which makes it easier to borrow against.

Those of you with aged relatives kindly disposed towards you, however, might try and persuade them in the direction of a co-op, which is willable. You will have to pass muster with the co-op board to claim it, but unless you have obvious crime world connections, you

MARTY NORMAN

Despite the best advice (John D. MacDonald: Condominium) *the condo craze has swept Florida.*

will probably sneak through. (A casual check through several co-op boards uncovered no instances when a will was contested, though that's not to say, yours couldn't be the first.)

What happens if the feds get wise to you?

Then, my friend, you get to discover the delights of the conjugal cell. That's if you behave yourself; prisons

The red house, Mississippi Correctional Facility.

only allow this nicety for ideal comportment behind their bars (not that dissimilar from the ones that used to sit over your co-op and condo windows and aren't you the lucky one—someone else had to install them!).

Mississippi claims credit for pioneering in the conjugal cell movement. They started conjugal visits at least as far back as 1918, when inmates built the visit facilities themselves out of lumber scraps. This gave rise to their nickname: red houses, which they are still called, although they are now often of brick and sometimes of aluminum siding.

To qualify for conjugal visits, both male and female prisoners must show proof of marriage (no, your word is not good enough). Women prisoners must practice birth control. Generally speaking, you are allowed a conjugal visit every other Sunday from one o'clock until five, which may not be much, but it's better than the alternative.

Conjugal cells are complete with all the mod cons: bath or shower, sink, bed, dressing table, closets, bed linens. Be-

THE SAFE HOUSE

It is on a small, privately owned island surrounded by mined water and accessible only by boat, provided the pilot has a map of the minefield. The front door is secured by a chain, a dead bolt, a Medeco lock and a beeper alert direct to the White House. The back door does not exist. The windows are of triple thickness two-way glass (you can look out, they can't peek in). There is a radar scanning system on the roof. There is one Doberman for every square yard of lawn, which has been criss-crossed with tripwires. To enter, you must pass a voice check, fingerprint check, palmprint check and show a secret service badge.

fore you enter, however, you and your visitor will be searched. If your visitor demurs, no visit.

In an effort to maintain family relationships, Mississippi has also established a weekend visit program, again only for the married and those with clean prison records.

Most states now view the conjugal programs as civilized, humane ways of treating prisoners and though some infractions have been noticed, the rules governing inmate conduct are usually upheld. To fully appreciate the program, the nicest arrangements are those at minimum security facilities (the higher the number, the closer the security—Marion penitentiary, for example, is rated 6, whereas Allenwood Prison Camp is a 1.

Just as with co-ops and condos, there is snobbism among prisons. Fort Worth, Texas, has a nice reputation. Leavenworth, Kansas, on the other hand .... Regardless, all are rent-free.

Sanford Nesbitt lives in a pig sty.

OUR CRIME-RIDDLED CAPITAL

George Hanover

The one and only time I was in Washington, I was eight years old and traveling to Florida with my parents and my brother. It was on the way, so we stopped. (I was more interested in what was coming up next: Williamsburg—and horses!) I don't remember very much about our stay except we poked our noses through the White House fence, elevatored up and climbed down the Washington Monument and my brother and I chased each other from one end of the Smithsonian to the other, then stood in front of the Treasury Building waving dollar bills while our folks took our picture. I still have it and I

am sorry to say, to my old sad eyes, it seems a very concise, exact and trenchant description of what Washington was, is, and probably always will be: little nobodies impressed with money.

In this respect, Washington is not so different from the typical small town, where the have-nots gawk at the haves, then sashay around in imitation of them.

What happens when the have-nots want more? Bloody murder. After our picture was taken, my parents told my brother and me that we could keep the money. I immediately lunged for his. He wouldn't let go. I wound up flat out on the pavement with a cut lip and a torn

ROYAL RUCKUS

Robert Barnard, *Death and the Princess* (Perry Trethowan at Buckingham Palace)

William F. Buckley Jr., *Saving the Queen* (Blackford Oakes and the Queen's bedchambre)

T.E.B. Clark, *Murder at Buckingham Palace* (George V's Silver Jubilee)

Peter Dickinson, *King, Queen, Joker* (Princess Caroline and trouble)

Jack Higgins, *Exocet* (the Queen's security system and the Falklands)

Reginald Hill, *Who Guards the Prince?* (English Prince and American President)

dollar bill in my hand, which my parents then confiscated. That night I stole my brother's Hershey bar from his suitcase. We didn't talk again till Charleston.

And you wonder where crime writers get their ideas from!

Washington, by my own example, breeds envy, jealousy, greed, rage, vengeance, retribution, sour grapes and a raw struggle for power, all among quite pretty landmarks. Does that sound like the goings on in every small town you ever heard of, from St. Mary Mead in England to Podunk, U.S.A? It should, principally because every crime writer and his brother (including me and mine) seems hell-bent on using Washington as the setting for a "village" mystery.

We have only succumbed to the eminently suitable. Like all the villages, Washington, too, has its "characters." What is a President but a windier mayor with a little more money to worry about? Spinsters? Washington has plenty of those; they're called government secretaries and they've been running the town since they graduated Radcliffe. A

local team to root for? Redskin tickets are so hard to come by, they've become willable. A fumbling police force? Need you be reminded of CIA blunders, Pentagon miscalculations and FBI manhunts that lasted for years and came up empty-handed?

Washington even has its small-time hoods, who bungle break-ins; its village drunks, who wind up in the tidal basin; and its teachers with a mission, though usually this means they leave Georgetown with a passel of microdots and head for the 'Stambol Express.

Probably the best practitioner of the small-town Washington mystery today is/are R.B. Dominic, who also is/are Emma Lathen (a consortium of two, the Misses Mary Latis and Emily Hennissart). They've dawdled in Washington five times, most recently with *Unexpected Developments*, and before with *The Attending Physician*, *Murder Out of Commission*. *There Is No Justice* and, initially, *Murder in High Places*. I suppose it would be fair to say the books are gossipy; granted, the gossip is manufactured—no roman á clef here—but the plots are propelled by it, an endless succession of one character libeling another, backtracking with lies, and generally taking swipes at the "haves," be they hospital bigwigs, political honchos, whomever. Fairly reeks of small townitis, doesn't it? You bet. The Washington mystery par excellence. And very often, just as in the Lathen books, the senator who's in trouble, the bureaucrat who's cornered the market on chicanery, has about him the stench of money unaccounted for.

The one village trait the Dominic books lack is the landmark syndrome. Dominic is not one to linger warmly on the more attractive edifices along Pennsylvania Avenue. There are no mini city tours (D.C. in a day, a subgenre of its own). No, Dominic's Washington is concerned more with jobs than offices.

Of course, as with every small town,

THE MARGARET ADMINISTRATION
MISS TRUMAN GOES ON RECORD

The daughter of our thirty-third President spent her student days majoring in history and minoring in mysteries, and now, more years later than her looks will admit to, she's found a way to combine the two interests: a series of crime novels using Washington landmarks and government positions as background.

To date, Miss Truman has committed murder on Capitol Hill, in the White House, on Embassy Row, in the Smithsonian and even among members of the Supreme Court. Yet she confesses, "No one has ever accused me of writing a political novel. I'm afraid I'm old-fashioned. I don't believe in using real people to further fiction; it's silly to have them doing things they'd probably never have considered. Harry Truman, in other words, will never appear in one of my mysteries. For that matter, neither will Margaret."

Miss Truman lays the blame for reading mysteries squarely in her father's lap. "I picked up the habit of reading mysteries from my parents, but Mother also read Westerns, which Father and I passed on. We stayed with the MacDonalds and the Creaseys, and we'd trade titles after we were finished with them. Today I read McBain's 87th Precinct books, and I've enjoyed some of the Emma Lathen banker novels, too. I don't know many mystery writers, but long ago a friend introduced me to my favorite, John Creasey. The first thing I said to him was, "Well, hello, Inspector Gideon," and he said, "You're perfectly right, you know. I based him on myself—his looks anyway."

For research, Miss Truman picks up the phone and calls old friends. "When I was working on *Murder at the White House,* I needed to know about the Lincoln bedroom, so I called up the curator and told him I had to have a plan of the second floor. I didn't tell him why. When I met up with him a year later, he said, 'Well, well, well, no wonder you needed my floor plan.' I told him, 'Yes, but everything was exactly where I remembered it.' "

Like many writers, she doesn't start work until "I feel my editor breathing down my neck. My first draft is dictated, and when it's been typed up I start slashing at it. I find writing fiction difficult and painful. It's far easier to deal with nonfiction. Then I have more than my imagination to work with; I have facts."

Which comes first, the victim or the killer? For Miss Truman it's the former. "I always start by deciding whom to murder, then whom to name as chief suspects. After that's set, I start thinking about the method. My victims may not be thoroughly evil, but they're certainly not particularly likable. It seems a pity to read about characters you're fond of, dying."

Summing up, Miss Truman says: "I hope people find my books easy to read and enjoyable. I like mysteries myself, and that's what I expect from them. I don't think there's much more you can say about them than that—that they're entertaining."

The mysterious trio.

there are some families that set the style, tone and priorities of the citizenry as well as rule it. So be it with Washington. Quaintly called the First Family, they remain the trend-setters even if they move away. Case in point: Margaret Truman.

Harry's little girl has dropped a few bombshells of her own, including cutting a throat in the Lincoln bedroom, garotting a raffish secretary of state, and redecorating a chief justice's chair with bulletholes.

The trend Miss Truman started: First Family mysteries. Swelling out their number, Elliott Roosevelt's *Murder and the First Lady*, in which Eleanor sniffs out a few clues in a rather sweet, old-fashioned way, rather like the village matriarch inspecting mantelpieces for dust.

Does the apple, one wonders, fall far from the tree? Certainly not. The paterfamilias of the First Family mysteries would have to be Abraham Lincoln, who wrote "The Trailor Murder Mystery"

for the Quincy, Illinois, *Whig* of April 15, 1846. "Trailor" was based on one of Lincoln's cases when he was a defense attorney and concerns three brothers, a neighborhood, a mysterious disappearance, buggy tracks, a doctor's testimony, a trial and a comeuppance. Howard Haycraft, a great detective (of sorts) himself, dug up the fact that Lincoln was a devotee of Poe. You could not, however, prove this by his style

Ninety-one years later, another President joined the mystery First Families: Franklin Delano Roosevelt. Unlike Abe, Margaret and Elliott, FDR didn't actually sit down to write the story out. He passed his idea on to six authors— Anthony Abbot, Rupert Hughes, S.H. Adams, Rita Weiman, S.S. Van Dine, John Erskine—each of whom wrote a chapter and more or less resolved FDR's idea of absconding with $5 million without leaving any clues. Originally published as "The President's Mystery Story" in *Liberty* magazine in 1935, the

Queenie's birthday.

The Queen's birthday.

work was reprinted under the title *The President's Mystery Plot* in 1967 with a new final chapter by Erle Stanley Gardner. Roosevelt's royalties were donated to charity.

The offshoot of the First Family mystery is the First Family detective, in which an author's closest association with real First Families comes from history books, which he studies diligently to enable him to spew out a "what if..." Typical of the genre, *The Fala Factor,* in which author Stuart Kaminsky wonders "what if Fala were kidnapped and the first family were asked to pay ransom and...." William DeAndrea charged into this field with his Teddy Roosevelt mystery with somewhat more success, but the medal of honor really ought to be awarded to G.J.A. O'Toole for *The Cosgrove Report,* which is the (fictional) inquiry into the death of President Lincoln by a Pinkerton detective.

I confess I am just about up to my neck in the Potomac with Washington mysteries, but just when I thought I couldn't possibly want to read one more, somebody shoved a copy of Charles McCarry's *Tears of Autumn* in my hands and I changed my mind. Mr. McCarry possesses a talent so huge, maybe the rest of us ought to declare a moratorium on Washington books and leave the field to him.

Does all this make you think our small town is getting a bit overcrowded? It is, but we've devised a system for culling out. It's called incarceration and several have been subjected to it, among them, David St. John, a pseudonym for Watergate participant E. Howard Hunt. Haven't heard from him for a while now.

That's the way it is with small towns. Some are carried out feet first and some are simply forced out.

George Hanover lives at the corner of Q and A streets.

A JAUNT THROUGH THE (HEMLOCK) FOREST IN SEARCH OF TERRIBLE EDIBLES

Ruth H. Smiley and Carolyn Fiske

There are approximately 750 species of plants in the United States and Canada that are either partly or entirely poisonous. Among them:

Deadly nightshade. Virtually everything about the plant is poisonous—leaves, stems, flowers, seeds. Interestingly enough, it belongs to the same family as the potato and the tomato. Active ingredients are topane alkaloids, atropine and hyoscyamine. Symptoms: fever, visual disturbances, burning of the mouth, thirst, dry skin, confusion and a splitting headache. **Castor bean.** One bean contains enough ricin toxin to kill an adult. The bean, however, must be chewed; if swallowed whole, the hard protective coat prevents absorption and poisoning.

Buttercups. The leaves, seeds, roots and flowers of this dainty yellow plant have been known to cause convulsions. Other common plants with similar poisonous properties are the azalea, rhododendron, iris, daffodil, jonquil, oleander, hyacinth, morning glory, poinsettia and lily of the valley, often associated with funerals. Mountain laurel is so potent that it was known to the Delaware Indians as the "suicide plant."

Snakeroot. A white wild flower known for its writhing root system. Among its illustrious victims were Nancy Hanks, mother of Abraham Lincoln, who died by drinking milk from a cow that had grazed on snakeroot.

Dumb cane (a.k.a. dieffenbachia, elephant ear, mother-in-law plant). An attractive white speckled plant that, when chewed, produces swelling of the tongue, lips and palate, making it difficult, if not impossible, for the victim to ask for help. There are reported cases of death by suffocation when, as a result of violent swelling of the tongue, the victims were unable to breathe.

Apples. The seeds are quite bitter and contain cyanic poison, which accumulates in the body and builds up over a period of time. This circumstance partly compensates for the fact that one must eat a large quantity of the seeds for the desired effect. Symptoms: nausea, vomiting, stomach cramps, difficulty in breathing, muscular weakness, dizziness, convulsions, stupor.

Apricots (also cherries, prunes, plums and almonds). All contain cyanogenetic glycosides in the leaves, stems, bark and seed pits (not the fruit, alas).

Wild cherry branches. The twig of this tree contains cyanic poison.

Red elderberry branches. Use the toxic stem to make a blowgun or peashooter. When blown, the blower, not his target, is the real victim. Be sure not to confuse this twig, which has a red center pith, with the benign black elderberry, which has a white pith.

Rhubarb. The leaf (not the commonly eaten stalk) contains oxalic acid, which has a corrosive action on the gastrointestinal tract and can cause massive hemorrhaging. Spinach also contains some of the same toxins.

Ruth H. Smiley, a botanist, and Carolyn Fiske, an attorney, stroll the verdant acres of Mohonk Mountain House looking for terrible edibles.

DEMONS AND DNA

Chloe McGinty

A gremlin was on the bed and Faust was on the night table. Spielberg was propped up behind the headboard and Stephen King was taped to the bureau mirror. The closet was jammed with plastic ectoplasm, half-stuffed werewolves, missiles with humming implants and the entire robotics cast of *Star Wars*.

She absolutely loved her room, but that was before the spot.

It was small, dank and black like a clogged-up pore, and one day it wasn't there and the next it was, as simple as that. A little inky squish clinging to the window. When she tried to rub it off, it caught at her thumb and she got stuck, pinned to an ordinary pane of glass by the ball of her finger and godknowswhat.

She screamed for her mother.

Her mother couldn't help. She used Ajax and water and Brillo and elbow power and a scrub brush with a squirt of ammonia and a butter knife with a smear of olive oil and a kitchen knife that slipped and nicked and stung and finally some dental floss because she had to try *something* and it just might have worked.

Then she called *her* mother, whose dirt vendetta was the talk of three boroughs, but the phone kept on ringing. She'd left early for bridge because the game was at Judith's and if she missed the turning, which she usually did, she didn't want to be late.

"All right," her mother said. "We'll call Daddy."

Daddy at that moment was splicing genes in an ill-lit laboratory in the air-constricted bowels of the Vanderbilt Center for Advanced Continuums. He was poking at them with a uranium toothpick that cost 19 million dollars and was considered a bargain. He answered on the fourth ring.

"What is it, Jean?" His tone implied he was very busy.

"Little Jeanie's stuck to the window and I can't get her off."

"Do the best you can and I'll deal with it when I get home," he told her, in the manner of a man overcome with work, then banged down the receiver.

He turned his attention to his nuclear microscope and focused it down to the 817th power, so the genes looked like suspensions on a bridge. A very handsome bridge, maybe the Golden Gate. Then he took aim and wielded his toothpick. "Gotcha!" he cried with a glee usually reserved for opening Christmas presents. "Gotcha again!"

Back at home, the Jeans were no better off than Daddy's genes.

"Daddy says," her mother tried to sound cheerful, "Daddy says nothing to it. I'll smash the glass and the shock will make you let go."

Jeanie didn't think so, but she

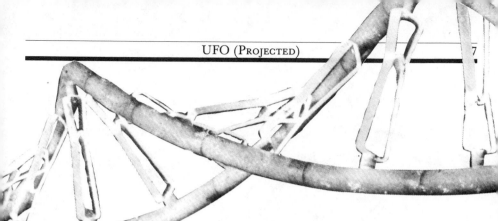

DNA double helix.

agreed to be brave and let her mother try, no matter how it hurt.

Meanwhile, the spot was seething, turning red as a boil. Then indeed it boiled over. Millions of little black spots spurted out and fastened themselves to whatever was handy, including Mr. Spielberg's lip and Mr. King's chin. Now both Jeans were stuck in many places and there was nothing to do but wait for Daddy.

While they waited, they counted.

Four black spots on Mommy's knee, seven at the nape of her neck. A dainty trio on little Jean's wrist and a dozen, maybe more, clustered on her badly scuffed instep.

Seventeen scattered on the rug, until one flopped off and they both went to step on it, a clear mistake. It dislodged and spiraled to the desk lamp. When it touched the bulb, it puffed like a pimple, angry and red; then it erupted.

The spots were multiplying too fast to count: Mr. King's teeth all filled in and the whites of Mr. Spielberg's eyes; the gremlin looked like a victim of the tarbrush and the cover of *Faust* could no longer be read. They bulged the keyhole, occupied all the open spaces in the wicker headboard, and the closet door handle was now twice its size.

The Jeans began to moan and the

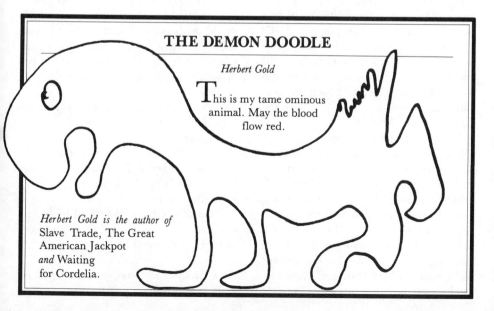

THE DEMON DOODLE

Herbert Gold

This is my tame ominous animal. May the blood flow red.

Herbert Gold is the author of Slave Trade, The Great American Jackpot *and* Waiting for Cordelia.

DNA molecules fold into a double helix with one sugar-phosphate chain twined around another. The side-groups stretch at right angles between the two, each interlocking with its opposite number, for a base on one chain which can only be partnered by a particular base on the other.

bemused spots went blue as they listened. The moans became a word and the word became Daddy. Daddy, Daddy, Daddy, Daddy.

Daddy was splicing away, thrusting and parrying with a panache not seen since Errol Flynn retired. And with each cut, each gash, something out there got very mad and punished the bedroom, splicing everything in it.

The black dots increased and so did the red ones, though the air was so thick with them you couldn't really tell. The room looked like a checkerboard in motion, with one major exception.

Their names were Jean. They were mother and daughter and mother and daughter and mother and daughter and mother and daughter and each one was identical, down to its chant: Daddy, Daddy, Daddy, Daddy.

He wiped the uranium knife on the cotton swab, carefully placed the swab in the contaminate holder, removed the knife blade from the holder and put each in the specially fitted section of the chamois-lined case that held them overnight. He took the vials of ooze and the patch strips of goop and double helix of dangling blops, opened the refrigerator and neatly shelved them, vial on top, patch in the middle, blops at the bottom, with the other concentrates.

Driving home, he gave half a moment's thought to whether Jeanie was still stuck to the window or Jean had gotten her off. Then he turned his attention to the basketball scores.

He knew something was wrong the minute he parked. His one-car garage was now a two-car garage, and the door leading to the kitchen was now a Dutch door, with a handle on the top and a handle on the bottom. The kitchen he could barely recognize. Refrigerators bumped into dishwashers, sinks and drainboards collided with cabinets, and there were chairs all over the place: on tables, under them, crashed to the floor . . . still multiplying.

He raced upstairs.

The flight took twice longer than he remembered. No wonder: the stairs *were* twice longer.

"Jean!" he screamed. "Jeanie!"

They looked at him, looked at him, from every corner of the room. Life reflecting his art.

He should have known all along: if you're going to splice genes, you've got to expect a splice-of-life story.

Chloe McGinty is a woman of many possessions; some would call her two-faced.

SCI-FI MYSTERIES

Baird Searles

Why, one wonders, the mutual nonalignment treaty between science fiction and detective fiction, particularly since back in the heyday of weekly story magazines many of the cent-a-word toilers in the pulpy vineyards wrote both?

Maybe the only answer is that science fiction is supposed to stretch the mind, mystery fiction to sharpen it, and creating something that both stretches and sharpens is difficult.

Nonetheless, there are successful examples of the intermingling of the two disciplines. Herewith a list of admirable sci-fi mysteries.

The Caves of Steel by Isaac Asimov is set in a future Earth that is hideously overpopulated and polluted. Detective Lije Bailey and his android partner, R. Daneel Olivaw, solve a murder in this messy society, which discriminates against robots. In the first of two sequels, *The Naked Sun,* a murder is committed in a world teeming with robots but low on humans; the murderer can only be a robot, but that's impossible since robotic programming precludes harming humans. In the second, *The Robots of Dawn,* the victim is a robot. But is this murder?

Darkworld Detective by J. Michael Reaves is hard-boiled sci-fi on the planet Ja-Lur. The hero wears a trench coat, and the interrelated stories have such names as "The Big Spell" and "The Maltese Vulcan."

The Demolished Man by Alfred Bester answers the question: Can murder be committed in a telepathic society where almost nothing can be concealed? A very tricky howdunnit.

Do Androids Dream of Electric Sheep? by Philip K. Dick is set in another nasty future. The "hero" is a bounty hunter; his prey, androids masquerading as humans. It's one long chase through the unpleasant urban landscape of the next century. (Filmed as *Bladerunner.*)

Double Star by Robert Heinlein neatly updates a familiar construct: an egotistical and none too successful actor is coerced into doubling for a kidnapped politician of interplanetary note. When the politician dies . . .

Fire, Burn! by John Dickson Carr is a backwards-in-time story in which a contemporary British Inspector steps out of a cab into the Scotland Yard of 1829 and applies his investigative techniques to a crime of the period.

MARTY NORMAN

The Golden Witchbreed by Mary Gentle chronicles the adventures of the first Envoy from Earth Dominion to the governments of the planet Orthe. As she travels around Orthe's complex semimedieval cultures, the Envoy realizes that someone is determined to kill or at least discredit her. When one of Orthe's rulers is murdered, she must find the killer. This is an extraordinary job of creating a realistic, working, alien society.

The Lord Darcy Series by Randall Garrett consists of classically constructed mysteries that just happen to take place in an alternate history (King Richard died young, John took over and didn't do badly). In this untechnological Earth, "magic" (really parapsychological powers possessed by only a few) works, but the urbane Lord Darcy triumphs with ruthless deduction. Great fun.

The Murder of the U.S.A. by Will F. Jenkins bombards America with three hundred atomic bombs (the novel predates the H-bomb) and Lt. Burton must solve the mystery of which country did it.

Needle by Hal Clement combines chase and deduction, since the cop and the criminal are aliens best described as intelligent symbiotic viruses. When the quarry takes refuge on a strange planet (Earth), each inhabits the body of a native "host" and the criminal becomes a needle in a . . .

Police Your Planet by Lester Del Rey concerns an Earth colony on Mars, a corrupt government and an investigator from Earth disguised as a deportee.

The Squares of the City by John Brunner is a story of intrigue and murder in a South American country very like Bra-

zil. To avoid civil war, the president and a rival political leader manipulate people with an advanced form of mind control. The novel follows, play by play, an actual championship chess game of 1892.

The Tenth Victim by Robert Sheckley proposes a future where murder is a sport, organized for the thrills of the television audience. If you're taking part in the game, you have to do your detecting *before* the crime: anyone could be your assassin.

Time and Again by Jack Finney sends a man of our time back to the New York City of the 1880's. He traces the suicide of the ancestor of a friend, which leads to blackmail and a case of arson—the infamous World Building fire. The evocation of the New York of another era is stunning, and this novel has become a deserved classic.

MARTY NORMAN

There are also various series revolving around a charismatic agent or sleuth with an entire galaxy in which to find trouble, often with extraterrestrial races whose alien physiologies and morals can vastly complicate life (and death). The most popular: the Claudine St. Cyr novels of Ian Wallace; the Jan Darzek series by Lloyd Biggles, Jr.; the Sybil Blue Sue novels of Rosel George Brown; James H. Schmitz's Telzey Amberdon stories; and the inevitable twenty-first-century hard-boiled detective, Mathew Swain, written about by Mike McQuay.

Baird Searles is coauthor of A Reader's Guide to Science Fiction *and* A Reader's Guide to Fantasy.

THE ULTIMATE MYSTERY TOUR
BY TRAIN, LIMO, LINER AND ARMCHAIR

Regina Monello

Day 1

Scheduled departure date: Agatha Christie's birthday, the eleventh hour. Full-day excursion to St. Mary Mead via 4:50 from Paddington, the Blue Train and the Orient Express. Visiting the vicarage (notable for its extraordinarily mundane stained-glass window), the grange and the local handicrafts centre, where we are taught how to make Belgian eggheads. Arrive Miss Marple's larder in time for lunch (antidote included in package price). Afternoon transfer to cycle for tour of nearby tea plantation, knit shoppe and chance to purchase stolen goods at fence. Return to Bertram's Hotel, where notable train enthusiast Georges Nagelmackers presents an overnight discussion of Nagelmackers' Compagnie Internationale des Wagons-Lits et des Grands Express Européens. Gentlemen are advised to wear black patent-leather shoes for walking. It is suggested that women pack a red silk kimono and binoculars.

Day 2

Optional tour of Mexico with Sylvia Angus and Mrs. Wagstaff; of the coast of Denmark with Poul Orum and D.I. Jonal Morch; of a Tahitian island with Claire McCormick and John Waltz; of the Caribbean with Michael Gillette and Eric Pendleton or Patricia Moyes and Henry and Emily Tibbett. Half-day optional tours also available: fishing in Oregon with Richard Hoyt and John Denson, P.I.; fishing in Shinglebourne with Alan Hunter and George Gently. For those who feel guilty if they do nothing on their vacation, a special outing with Jane Langton and the Kellys' baby-sitting nephews is offered. Participants should purchase the following guide-books for these (respective) tours: *Dead to Rites, Scapegoat, Club Paradise Murders, The Cortès Letter, Angel Death, Siskiyou Two-Step, Gently Between the Tides* and *Natural Enemy.*

Day 3

The highlight of the day is the karate lesson at the School of Hard Knocks, reached by southern California freeway and circuitous back alleys. Our car is repossessed at lunch (tuna on rye with a bottle of rye, served with vigorish). Quiet afternoon at leisure in hospital. Those with ice in their veins will continue on to the Burberrys factory and the pistol range (blanks extra). The night is spent with a little sister in Santa Barbara.

Day 4

Fens, marshes and abysses viewed from the trunk of a car. In the morning we enjoy a Busman's Honeymoon and in the afternoon, following a quick snack of Five Red Herrings, we venture forth on a Hangman's Holiday. If enough tour members express interest, we will schedule a translation of the Latin inscription on the Oxford bridge. Under no circumstances will tour leaders Advertise for

Poison, Carcasses, Teeth or Unpleasantness. Wine salesman Montague Egg joins the tour for cocktails (complimentary glass of wine provided to toast the winners of the cricket match). The excursion concludes with bell-ringing and a fierce headache. For full viewing of the body, a monocle will be necessary. Those wishing to participate in Day 4 must present a Dawson Pedigree to the tour leader or wait downstairs while the others are guided through the Bellona Club and Tallboys.

Day 5

The day's shot.

GOING TEN ROUNDS WITH A ROLLS

Round One:
Chauffeur opens door on left; you're waiting on right. Chauffeur wins.

Round Two:
Chauffeur wears coat and tie; you wear a shroud. Chauffeur wins.

Round Three:
You shout a question through partition; chauffeur answers you on intercom.
Chauffeur wins.

Round Four:
You ask chauffeur to drag Main; he counters with suggestion you shake a tail. Draw.

Round Five:
At sixty miles an hour, the loudest noise you hear is that of clock ticking; at sixty
miles an hour the loudest noise the car makes is that of bomb ticking. Rolls wins.

Round Six:
You sport the two-tone look (blond at ends, black at roots); car sports two-tone look
(gun-metal grey and blood-red). Rolls wins.

Round Seven:
You open windows with suction cup and glass cutter; windows can be opened by
pressing a button. Rolls wins.

Round Eight:
You horn in on the mob; car blows its own horn. Draw.

Round Nine:
Car has lock on engine; you know how to pick lock. You win.

Round Ten:
You run out of gas; car takes you for a ride. Rolls wins.

Double-occupancy boot.

Day 6 through 9

- 2 Nights in the outback
- 1 Night in the sewers of Paris
- 4 Days of limited sightseeing. Guides: Max Carrados; Duncan Maclain
- All accommodations: softcovers promised
- Free bookworm issued every hour
- All tips included (bribes, optional)

Day 10

Side Tour of Fort Knox.

This handsome tribute to post-Depression architecture was completed in December 1936 at a cost of $560,000. A sturdy blend of granite, steel and concrete, the building houses a two-level steel-and-concrete vault divided into compartments. The vault door alone weighs nearly 30 tons. As we gaze to our left and our right inside the vault, we will see standard-issue mint bars of almost pure gold and coin-gold bars resulting from the melting of gold coins. The bars are somewhat smaller than the average house brick, approximate dimensions being 7 x 3⅝ x 1¾; they contain approximately 400 troy ounces of gold with an avoirdupois weight of about 27½ pounds. We shall have an opportunity to test the security measures firsthand (previous groups have commented on its proficiency). The Depository does not sell souvenirs, but to compensate one may leave the premises for a tour of Bullion Boulevard in an armored truck guarded by mean army officers. All cameras must be checked at the entrance, and you are asked not to draw detailed maps of the Vault Room.

Day 11

Shrine of Ronald Knox.
Shrine of Father Brown.
Temple dedicated to Rabbi Small.
Evangelism and TV Ministry under the auspices of John D. MacDonald. If we are notified a day in advance, special dietary requests can be met.

Day 12

The group will divide into smaller groups. Those with English accents will be placed onboard the Basle Express (if the group exceeds the car's capacity, the overflow will be escorted to Australia and put on The Long Straight), with Freeman Wills Crofts acting as conductor. Those with perpetrator boots will steal into Harlem with Chester Himes. Those in public office will be remanded to The Gallows of Chance and those mediaevalists among us will be sent to Newgate for Low Treason. We shall all meet at The Estate of the Beckoning Lady for dinner, where the evening's entertainment will be a presentation by the Augusts, a comedic troupe. There will be a special midnight showing of the mystery double feature, *Corpses on Caravan* and *Hot-Wire Kid in a Winnebago*.

Day 13

Quick visits with Charlie Chan in Honolulu, Inspector Ghote in Bombay, Bony in Queensland and Nancy Drew in River City. We hop over to San Quentin to hear the prisoners sing, then lace up our brogues and saunter over to Interpol to see if we're wanted. While there, we leave a message for a medium with Mignon Warner. Before we say farewell to the world as we've known it, we take a sail in the (blood-red) sunset on a houseboat with Travis or a sailboat with Johnson—women only are invited. Meanwhile all men with Sandhurst training will commandeer the *QEII* and watch Prince Andrew drift out with the tide.

Special mini tours

- 7 Days studying spiders and candlelight in a Gothic house. Minimum of 7 nighties required.
- 1 Week in jail—you get to choose which!

Regina Monello has seen it all.

THE EXTREMELY SHADY PAST

Peter Lovesey

F og, swirling through the streets of London. Footsteps quickening. They stop. A moment of silence, then an agonised scream. Blurred shapes running. The blast of a police whistle. The beam of a bull's-eye lamp directed onto a lifeless form. Another victim.

Meanwhile, the great detective sits in his rooms in Baker Street before a blazing fire, reading the Personal Column of the *Times*.

For atmosphere, the counterpoise of teacups and terror, cosiness and crime, the Victorian mystery is supreme. The architects of the popular detective story—Poe, Dickens, Wilkie Collins and Conan Doyle—built citadels of suspense that still dominate the scene. Any mod-

ern author setting a story in the Victorian period starts with the knowledge that hansom cabs and London fogs are redolent of Holmes and Watson.

And how productive the nineteenth century was of motives for murder! The need to achieve security by inheritance, or life insurance, or marriage; the risk of losing it when scandal threatened; the equating of sex with sin; the stigma of insanity; the things that went unsaid. Our world of social welfare and easier divorce and psychiatric care has removed many of the bad old reasons for murder. How uninspiring, too, by contrast with times past, are the modern weapons—the gun with telescopic sights, the car-bomb and the hypodermic syringe. Give me Jack the Ripper's knife or Neill Cream's bag of poisons or Lizzie Borden's ax!

Of course, the historical mystery has reached back beyond the nineteenth century, millenniums before the first police officers appeared on the streets. Ancient Egypt of 4000 B.C. (*Death Comes as the End*), Tang China (*The Chinese Bell Mur-*

facts and that those facts arise naturally from the plot. If we want a history lecture, we can go to college.

The fascination of a mystery set in the remote past is easily explained: it provides an escape from modern life. But we are not at the mercy of a science-fiction writer's fantasizing. The world we enter is real and under control.

BRITISH TOURIST AUTHORITY

ders) and Alexander's Greece (*The Great Detectives*) have all been used as settings, while characters as various as Machiavelli, Richard III and Ben Franklin have been featured. Treatments range from documentary novels researched from actual cases, such as Michael Gilbert's *The Claimant* and John Cashman's *The Gentleman from Chicago,* through brilliant pastiches like Lillian de la Torre's *Dr. Sam Johnson, Detector,* to extravaganzas like Anthony Price's *Our Man in Camelot,* in which the CIA becomes involved with King Arthur. The trend is toward more fantastic plots, more dazzling tricks, with a strong infusion of humour. All we ask of the historical mystery is that it tell a story consistent with known

There is a framework of fact. Even the most extravagant plots conform to historical truth. Yes, the CIA does become entangled with King Arthur. Read about it and see!

And the greatest of all fictional detectives has tangled with the worst of criminals (*Sherlock Holmes Versus Jack the Ripper*) and discussed psychology with Sigmund Freud (*The Seven Per-Cent Solution*), while his old adversary is launched on a whole new career of crime (*The Return of Moriarty*). Thank heavens Holmes is alive and well and reading the *Times* in London!

Peter Lovesey won the Panther-Macmillan prize for Wobble to Death.

ONCE UPON A CRIME

If today can't get any worse and tomorrow (according to Scarlett) will undoubtedly get better, what about yesterday? Judging by the literature, it wasn't safe to walk the streets. Among the authors on patrol in the Victorian era: Peter Lovesey, Julian Symons, Nicholas Meyer, and P (for Philip) W (for Whitwell) Wilson.

Mr. Lovesey's yesteryear output (a random sample: *Wobble to Death; A Case of Spirits; Mad Hatter's Holiday*) includes *Waxwork,* the archetypal Victorian domestic drama culminating, naturally, in murder. At its center, a strong silent woman and more than a little erupting frustration, not always hers.

Mr. Symons, in *The Blackheath Poisonings,* plays out a saga in two family mansions, each described with the loving attention to historical plausibility that one would expect from a scholar and his hand-picked advisers (the details, Mr. Symons assures us, come not from imagination alone, but from curators with a devotion to accuracy). It all adds up to a cunning tale of Victorian living conditions both beautiful (physically) and awful (emotionally).

Mr. Meyer, who first stepped back in *The Seven Percent Solution,* relocates there for *The West End Horror,* a March 1895 Holmesian adventure. (Surely no creature has been beset as often as Holmes by menacing gaslight, except, possibly, Ingrid Bergman.) Like its predecessor, *West End* has no trouble proving glibness predates turn-of-the-century.

Mr. Wilson wrote three novels back in the mid-Forties featuring England in 1809, 1893 and 1912. For ambience it is hard to fault them; for plot, well, the less said, the kinder. Still, they're worth a try if you crave accurate representation of the Westmoreland district and upper classes bereft of funds. The titles, reading first to last, are *Bride's Castle, Black Tarn* and, assuredly the best, *The Old Mill.*

One of the newest writers to insert himself into the Victorian milieu is James Sherbourne. In *Death's Clenched Fist,* *Death's Gray Angel* and *Death's Pale Horse,* he combines three passions: Victoriana, horse racing and New York City. His ongoing character, racing correspondent Paddy Moretti, tackles corruption, recalcitrant animals and horse-and-buggy gridlock long years before Rockefeller had a center and twin towers blighted the cityscape.

Stepping even farther back, Raymond Paul's Davy Cordor, a cub reporter for the New York *Sun,* covers crimes in the city circa 1836, and his memorable case, *The Thomas Street Horror,* concerns a "Queen of the Pave," i.e., a prostitute, unattractively murdered.

Also way back then, Joyce Carol Oates' *Mysteries of Winterthurn,* and more distant yet, J.G. Jeffreys' *Suicide Most Foul* (the Battle of Waterloo). Also gamboling through history: Falkirk's *Blackstone,* Joan Fleming's *Screams from a Penny Dreadful,* Christie's *Death Comes as an End,* Butler's *Coffin for Pandora,* Selwyn's *Verity* series and a slew of Carrs, including *Bride of Newgate, Devil in Velvet, Captain Cut-Throat, Fire, Burn!, Scandal at High Chimneys, Witch of Low-Tide, Demoniacs, Most Secret, Papa La-Bas, Ghosts' High Noon, Deadly Hall, Hungry Goblin, Murder of Sir Edmund Godfrey* and (as Carter Dickson) *Fear Is the Same.*

There is, however, another form of historical mystery, one in which the characters live in the present but the crime that dominates their thoughts occurred years ago. The classic example would be Josephine Tey's *The Daughter of Time,* in which Detective Alan Grant, recuperating in hospital, becomes obsessed with proving Richard did not smother the little princes in the Tower. Grant's reconstruction of events is not only plausible, but so highly probable that *Daughter of Time* has been used in university history courses.

For those readers anxious to tackle an unsolved crime themselves, a good place to begin is with the custodian of your local historical society, who will be only too pleased to trot out puzzlements for your detective impulses.

SUSPICIONS

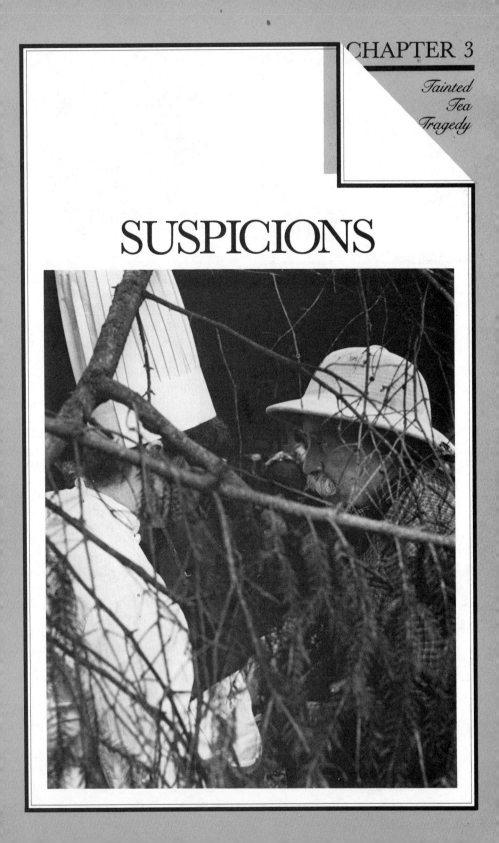

TODAY
7 AM

Sharp

The Colonel prepares to gallop off, 7:25 A.M.

Y ou think I don't know what's going on here, Colonel? There's more than flour in this brain, I mean to tell you, much more. When he says to me, "Cookie," he says, butter not melting in his mouth, "Now, Cookie, you've got eight for meals Friday dinner through Sunday lunch. See to it, will you?" Give him a see-to, I will. Not tuppence extra did he hand me to do with. What does he think? No matter how I wring the chicken, it won't spit coppers, now, will it? Not for me to say, I'm sure, but there's a bit of peculiar going on round here since he's put his hand in.

*Bridie and Rosie
airing linens and grievances, 7:00 A.M.*

"Economy, Cookie," he says, "one more meal from the joint, shall we?" Tish, wants to economy, does he, then why bring her here? Fancy piece, that one is. Little Missy tarts herself up real fine when she's a mind to. And don't think I don't know whose bed's not been slept in alone since she got here! Nurse indeed. Playing doctor's more the likely.

Not that I notice, I'm sure. I've got a handful as it is without taking time to look in anyone's personal business, I mean to say, but Louis let go, and Walter and first footman, and that young back parlour girl, and in she walks, this missy, and what does *he* say? "More to go, more to go, Cookie; maybe you next if you can't improve your crust!" "My crust!" I say. "Well, excuse me, Mr. Know-it-not-at-all, my crust is the first bid at Whitsuntide Supper, so there."

Don't think I'm complaining, dear me, not my type at all, but having to serve up with just the two girls and Rosie so clumsy and Bridie mooning about for a husband, what's to do, I ask you! 'Course the girls will always stay, I suppose, what they're paid won't feed birds. But there's hardly staff left to run the house decent. Reflects on His Lordship, it does. And him wanting things nice for this weekend. I try my best, I do. I do have my pride in my kitchen. But eight! For all meals! And some of them eaters fair to huge ones—begging your pardon, Colonel. Not that I'm suggesting, of course, but a bug in the right ear, Colonel, I would much appreciate it. Only's right, I should think, what with Himself and Mr. Roudebush in here every morning these days.

"Move over, Cook," Mr. Roudebush says to me, "please to move over for His Lordship." Then I hardly gets to shift before they're pulling for the flour

nel, or I'll hand in, I will. I haven't seen things like this since the both of them were in here morning to noon to night brewing up those first tea batches, that's what this was like. And the money just as hard to come by then as now, I mean to tell you, though I wouldn't mind a bit of a look at the books about *that*. Doing sandwich spreads now, Himself says, if they can find a pleasing taste. Not much use for that, I shouldn't think. Who doesn't know how to put up a decent fish paste? Still, if it will help His Lordship,

His Lordship breakfasting; egg, grilled tomato, toast, Teasdale Tea with cream and three sugars.

Her Ladyship and her morning pick-me-up (chilled Amaretto). 11:13 A.M.

and the sugar and the butter and my word, the eggs those men used! Yesterday was it, they took all my baby limas. Day before because of them I ran out of 'cress. I admit it to you with an honest heart, Colonel, if they came round today, what with eight to cook for and shrimp so dear, I'd not let on I have them.

I don't expect clean-up, of course, that wouldn't be right, not from them, but Rosie's got to cover downstairs now, too, and her so awkward and all, it's impossible, impossible. Changes'll have to be accounted for, I tell you that, Colo-

and him so smart with people's wants and all, then glory to him, nothing else. But I won't be sorry when they stop mucking about in my kitchen. I tell you, Colonel, they do make a mess-up.

One more on-my-mind, if you don't mind, Colonel. I am putting up special for tea, to celebrate the crest, like? Now, you don't be late and miss it, will you?

Right, then. Off you go. Enjoy your ride, and when you're back ring and I'll have elevenses all laid on for you.

I do like the Colonel. But he does natter on so and who's the time for it?

TEMPEST IN A TEAPOT
The Care and Brewing of Tea

Jeanine Larmoth

To brew the best tea, it is as necessary to have a spinster as it is to have a virgin for a truffle hunt. Only a spinster can provide that atmosphere of coziness, knickknackery, and chintz so important to the taste. Tea is made, of course, by first installing a hob on which to hang the kettle, then scattering antimacassars liberally about the room, and finding the cat. A collection of flowerpots with African violets is helpful, but not essential.

The ultimate tribute to the teapot, its temple, the tea shop, and its vestal virgin, the spinster, was paid by Agatha Christie in *Funerals Are Fatal*. The genteel companion, Miss Gilchrist, kills her employer with a hatchet all for the love of a tea shop. Instead of a faded picture of an old beau on her bedroom wall (ready to be brought into service should a séance arise), there is a photograph of a tea shop she once had, called The Willow-Tree. A victim of the war. Like a mother with a very special child, she babbles about the blue willow-patterned china, or the jam and scones she used to prepare, or trade secrets for making brioches and chocolate éclairs. She is more often seen with flour on her hands than blood. Miss Gilchrist's obsession for the return to gentility a tea shop would afford is so great she kills for a pittance, and is taken away to the meting out of justice, happily planning the curtains.

So much tea is poured in a mystery, one comes away a bit squelchy after reading. So many sweet biscuits are served one could build a hundred Hansel-and-Gretel houses. Tea is the great restorer. It seeps into the nooks and crannies of the soul. It is oil on troubled waters. It is applied, like a hot compress, wherever it hurts, with a faith and fervor that could only be bred in a conscientiously, securely, puritanically Protestant country such as England. Prayer is for Papists; whisky for shock.

There is something crisping about tea. None of the florid, suspect luxury of coffee. Tea cries out to stiffen the lip, and be on with it. Tea quenches tears and thirst. It is an opening for the pouring out of troubles. It eases shyness, and lubricates gossip. While it is not in itself sympathetic, in the right hands tea acts as a backing force to tender ministrations. The mighty to the lowly assuage with tea, cure for body and soul.

Tea pours with equal grace from glazed brown pots or vast cauldrons of furbelowed silver. It washes through kitchens, where the lino cracks and the housewife offers a cuppa char, or slips, a perfect amber arch, into gold-stippled cups on the lawn of a stately home—its crystalline, chuckling voice covering any awkward moments with delicacy.

There are proper teas and, perhaps, improper teas, high teas and low. A proper tea is offered by an overbustly, oversolicitous matron who feels you look peaked and in need of immediate sustenance. A proper tea should, therefore, be substantial: Marmite eggs, meat pies, sandwiches, cake, the lot. The substance of a proper tea is not actually different from high tea, which has stood in place of supper for hundreds of years for thousands of English schoolchildren. To be truly British, tea should be imbalanced in favor of carbohydrates—therefore, bread-and-butter sandwiches, plus sandwiches (kept nicely moist beneath a dampened napkin) and cakes.

A CUPPA CALAMITY

MARTY NORMAN

Make your pot of tea in the usual way, but when you pour the tea into the cup, do not use a strainer. Ask your subject to drink the tea, then to swirl round the dregs and invert the cup over the saucer. Suggest he or she turn the inverted cup in the saucer three times in a clockwise direction and say, "Tell me faithful, tell me well, the secrets that the leaves foretell." Then you, as leaf reader, take the cup in two hands and peer at the patterns the leaves have made. If you see any of the following shapes, your tea drinker should make no long-range plans.

SHAPE	MEANING
Clock	*Illness; if at bottom of cup, death*
Cross	*Trouble*
Key	*Robbery; if at bottom of cup*
M	*Someone has evil intentions toward you*
Nun	*Sorrow*
Parrot	*Slander*
Raven	*More trouble*
Scythe	*Danger*
Snake	*Enmity*
Wings	*Messages; the nearer the bottom of the cup, the worse the news*

Prepared by The Tea Council Limited.

Tea is best brewed in the brown pot. Otherwise, any china pot. The pot is "hotted up" with boiling water, which is allowed to sit for a moment before it is tossed out with an air. A teaspoonful of tea added for each cup, and one for the pot. The water for tea is of such moment, gentlemen traveling abroad often require special spring waters lest they encounter a foreign admixture to their favorite bouquet. The water must not boil a moment beyond its open, rolling bubble or the mineral content becomes proportionately higher. The brew then steeps for three to five minutes. Certain teas grow bitter if left longer, so second pots may have to be prepared for second cups. If tea is too strong, water will thin it, but not reduce the bitterness. Tea can be deep and opaque or very little darker than water. In order that the flow never falter, a jug of hot water should stand by the jug of warmed milk and the sugar bowl (no lumps, please).

Because England is inclined to be damp and chilly, and the houses drafty, the teapot may—though this is common—be given a little coat of its own, called a cozy, to wear to the table. A tea cozy is floral and quilted chintz, or a lumpish, unrecognizable crocheted affair made by an abysmal aunt. Some pots are further accoutered with tiny, tea-stained sponges attached to their nozzles to prevent drips.

The container in which the tea is stored is an understandably regal affair of antique Indian brass, lead-lined wood, or exotically devised porcelain, and is called a caddy. When the tea is a swirling maelstrom ready to be served, a strainer is placed over the cup to be sure the tea is clear. The strainer, as is proper with ceremonial vessels, has, in turn, its own resting place above a little stand or hooked over the slop bowl. Despite the revolting name, a slop bowl is a superbly proportioned, exquisitely decorated piece of china. To add the final, mystical

THE TEA OBSESSION
The Ten Foremost Controversies Concerning Tea

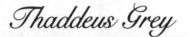

Thaddeus Grey

A tea-tasting session conducted by Thomas J. Lipton, Inc.

Hot or cold?

Iced tea is an abomination only the Americans deem drinkable.

Bagged or loose?

With loose tea, there can be a dreadful strength inconsistency from cup to cup. Bagged tea not only is tidier—demanding no awkward, leaking strainer—but infallibly serves up one perfectly brewed cup. Please, *never* reuse a teabag.

Thaddeus Grey sips Bovril.

TEA COUNCIL, U.S.A.

Sugar or honey?

For a proper tea, sugar lumps, accompanied by sterling tongs, are obligatory. The granulated form is more suitable for tea picnics and such. Honey is to be taken only when one is convalescing.

Glass or cup?

Serving tea in a glass is acceptable only for those of Eastern European origin; we who are not prefer the grace and delicacy of china. Soup belongs in mugs; nothing else, certainly not tea.

Green or black or oolong?

Green tea has been steamed immediately after plucking, which prevents fermentation, and is most heavily comsumed in China and Japan. Black tea (Orange Pekoe, for example) is deeply fermented, full-bodied and most heavily favoured in the West. Oolong rests midpoint between the two, the best-known leaf size being Lapsang Souchong, a smokey blend.

High or low?

High tea is really no more than supper for the working classes, centering on indelicate portions of meat pies and custards. The peerage, ever grateful to Anna, seventh Duchess of Bedford, who established the custom of taking tea, prefer slim finger sandwiches with the crusts neatly trimmed.

Herbal or sipping?

The herbals lack caffeine. Bur root improves the skin; licorice root, hops and passion flowers induce sleep; valarian root and balm mint appease headaches; eyebright soothes tired eyes; sassafras and sarsaparilla root flush out blood impurities; gentian root placates an agitated tummy. Sipping teas are dishwater in colour, with little caffeine, little taste and little to commend them.

Distilled or tap?

Well-water, with a heavier-than-normal concentration of sulfur, is ideal. But tapwater is serviceable, and distilled waters an extravagance.

Lemon or cream?

Lemon adds a certain piquancy, which some like to temper with a clove in the center of the wedge. Cream should never be used in conjunction with lemon. Clotted cream, from Devon, is for teacakes, not tea proper.

Claridge's or Lyons?

Does the world's proudest hotel serve a better tea than the humble corner tea shoppe? Yes.

note to the ceremony, a silver bell may stand on the tea table with which to ring for the servants for more cake, more milk, more hot water, or the police.

Tea kettles, apart from making tea, hot water for bottles, and singing, are very important utensils in a mystery if you haven't a letter opener, and wouldn't use one if you had. To unstick an envelope, you send whoever else is in the kitchen out of it. Be sure not to arouse suspicions, or they may dash back in and surprise you.

When the room is empty (check behind the fridge and stove to be sure), fill up the kettle. Put the kettle on the fire. Bring to a boil. Be sure to wait for a steady jet of steam. This will be about seven minutes for an average kettle. Keep an ear cocked. Hold envelope over steam. Slip knife under flap. Pry open very gently. Pull out contents, and read will, letter, or shopping list. If latter, scan for hidden meanings. If interrupted, slide knife into garter, and hide envelope behind stove, being sure to fold the flap backward to prevent resealing.

Make tea with leftover water.

Sometimes, spinsters get tired of their High Street shopping-and-tea-after routine, and take the cheap Thursday train to London for the sales, and to switch suitcases and catch murderers at the station's Left Luggage. After her adventures, the spinster may choose to refresh herself by having tea in the lounge hall of a hotel, or take it on the return train.

Tea on the move may be the best tea of all. Served on British Railways, it is a rush and clatter of dishes which jump up and down—apparently from the excitement of travel—all the way from London to Plymouth, and back again, if they're not required. In the dim light of declining afternoon and three-watt bulbs, the crockery sits at empty tables in a state of eternal preparedness, as if endlessly waiting a macabre Mad Hatter's Tea Party—passengers advancing, eating, from table to table as the train runs along. The sandwiches—small circlings of tomatoes, sliced hard-boiled eggs, or fish paste on limp white bread, its crusts resolutely removed for refinement, and swathed in mayonnaise—contribute their own lifeless air, faintly enlivened by a tossing of mustard cress, and augmented by downtrodden, but resilient fruitcake. Thus, the bottom-heavy tradition of starchy foods at teatime is upheld, even in transit.

The civilizing effects of tea, perhaps more than the building of roads, or even the drinking of gin, has been one of the largest contributions England made to

THE GREAT ENGLISH TEA BREAK

Wake-Up
(Crack of Dawn)
Brought to you in bed (by a kind mummy, a thoughtful host) to give you the strength to start the day. Usually unadorned, but sometimes streaked with milk and sugar. Alongside: an austere biscuit.

Elevenses
(Work Respite)
Midmorning perk-up, often accompanied by a sweet roll and delicious gossip. Heavily sugared and quite pale with milk.

Tea Proper
(Late Afternoon)
The major event of the day, occurring between 4 and 6 (the later the hour, the higher the tea). Served with sugar lumps, room-temperature cream (lemon only as a last resort), bitty sandwiches and a nice gâteau to round things off.

Solace
(Bedtime)
Taken in meditative sips just prior to donning nightclothes. Minimal milk, no sugar and never a second cup.

HOUSE OF TEAS
SANDWICH SPREADS
(PENDING)

Chipped 'cress with macademia
Potted shrimp with leek juice
Royal pear with minced plaice
Greengage and lemon
mayonnaise

Gooseberry tidbits with cream
Sprouts and carrots julienne
Nutmeats and raisin suspension
Ghee kebobs in pita (in
production)

*Lord Teasdale
pouring a celebratory
tea for two.*

civilizing her empire. For centuries, wherever the flag waved, it was an amiable way for people to gather together under pith helmets or parasols for a well-mannered chat about breaks in the weather and aphids on the roses, to push sweet morsels with creme fillings in their mouths, and forget the ruddy natives hiding in the bush.

Jeanine Larmoth has sipped tea in well-appointed homes and grand hotel lounges.

THE INVALID'S TRAY

Violet St. Clair

A untie is sick. Has been for years. She took to her bed in '37 for reasons she's quite forgotton and has been going steadily, if slowly, downhill ever since.

She accepts breakfast at eight, luncheon at one, tea between four and five, dinner at half-seven and a cocoa nightcap at just past nine.

Her mornings are occupied with re-writing her will and her afternoons with receiving the doctor. She has terrible nightmares in which someone is either garroting her with the bell pull, smothering her with her pillows or poisoning her by tinkering with her food tray. She ought to pay more attention to the last.

Great-Uncle Patriarch is also in bed, sent there by an embolism that refuses to dissolve. It presses on the corner of his brain that garbles speech and causes incontinency.

His mornings are spent on his right side, facing the sun, and his afternoons on his left, focussing, as best he can, on the secret panel in his desk.

He is spoon-fed three times a day by people he can barely recognise. One of them makes him very uneasy and his tremors upset his egg cup. He ought to have it analysed.

Clara, slightly concussed from a fall down the stairs, will be abed a fortnight. Her counterpane is speckled with petals from a nosegay, get-well cards and wrappers with bits of chocolate clinging.

She spends the day confiding in her diary and the night sleeping with it beneath her pillow. Fierce headaches make her prone to napping, and when she awakens a tray is on the bedstand. Upon sampling its custard, she becomes violently ill. She ought to try to stay awake more often.

Alec is recovering from a wound he won't let anyone tend to. In fact, no one's ever seen it. Lately, he's developed a cough, and he's suggested that no one come in his room lest they catch it. His trays are left outside his locked door.

These poor wretches—hypochondriacal, chronic, accidental and deceitful—are the mainstay of the old-fashioned whodunit. All must be fed (except the last, who could really get up and serve himself, but then he'd have no alibi). All must be killed or almost killed before too many chapters slip by. And their tray is the perfect way to incapacitate them.

Every decent invalid's tray is bordered with pill bottles. The smart villain will replace one of them with another of his own prescription. If Nurse assumes the big pink pills are the usual big pink pills, who can blame her?

The tray also contains a napkin (for wiping off prints), a white linen place mat with hand-tatted edges (for hiding the knife under), an oversize spoon (for administering the toxin), a toast rack (to hold the blackmail note), a tea cosy (to be thrust halfway down the larynx as a gag) and a single rose (to fatally prick a weakened hand).

Some trays also come equipped with a hypodermic. While Miss Prendergast is off in the pantry fetching the bouillon cube, the villain is squirting out its shot of B_{12} and filling it with a Tanzanian virus for which there's no antidote.

Upon her return Miss Prendergast notices the needle is slightly to the left of where she put it, but that doesn't stop her from taking it Upstairs and injecting sweet old Auntie with it. It's only later, when queried by the Inspector, that she remembers how it seemed to move.

And, of course, every respectable invalid's tray has a splendid variety of dishes to fiddle with.

A nice cup of tea, for example. Murderers have little difficulty in raising the teapot lid, inserting a quick-dissolving poison, lowering the lid and leaving the room before anyone suspects what they're up to. One invariably assumes they were just checking to see if the water needed hotting up.

And let's not forget the water glass itself. This tumbler contains eight ounces of death which the tray-bearer will insist the victim drink right up, for her own good. Sometimes the victim's nerves overcome her, and she spills the contents. This is a brief reprieve, nothing more. So the dear thing can swallow her pills, the water-bearer will insist on refilling it—usually from the very tap which the killer has polluted.

Then there's the custard. Made from fresh eggs. At least they *were* fresh until some nefarious soul neatly pin-pricked each and every one of them, carefully dripped in a poisonous ooze and then put them back on the shelf.

Porridge, too, has a nice lumpy consistency appealing to a villain, and one can bank on its being included every morning. Its greyish colour is also an asset if one is dealing with impurities.

Other bright spots, for the villain, on the invalid's tray are: the jam pot; the sugar bowl; the milk pitcher; the soup bowl; the applesauce dish.

It never happens, however, that the killer serves the tray himself. He is more likely to be out of the house at feeding time, establishing an alibi by playing bridge with the Wittsentides in Yarmouth. Thus killers must do their tinkering well ahead of time. Occasionally, this isn't possible, and the killer must go up the stairs, down the stairs, up again, down again, until he accidentally bumps into whoever is carrying the tray. An elbow auspiciously placed, a subtle jostle, and his task is accomplished: the tray has been lethalized. Ofttimes, he's even too late to do this and must rely on getting to the tray before it's removed from the invalid's room. Or, wait for the next feeding time.

No matter. As Alec passed on to Auntie, Great-Uncle Patriarch and Clara: Never eat in bed.

Violet St. Clair owns Blue Cross stock.

THE DINNER PLATE

Carlotta Ogelthorpe

If I had an enemy and that enemy were fond of reading English murder mysteries vintage 1920–1930, I wouldn't wait for Monday. I'd start my diet today. I'd turn down all invitations to lunch, brunch, tea, high tea, supper, dinner and between-meal snacks—especially if that enemy were planning on preparing them personally.

You see, of the many conventions established during the so-called "Golden Age" of detective fiction, the one most rigorously followed was, if you had to eliminate someone the table was as good a place as any to have a go at it. In those mysteries the main course was usually served with poison as a side dish. The victim would proceed to the sideboard, innocently ladle the turnip purée onto his plate, return to his seat and, two forkfuls later, slide off his chair— permanently immobilized. If the stately

home that guested him was stately enough, he wouldn't even have to fetch his own plate; a helpful, albeit sinister member of the staff would bring his portion to the table for him. Regardless, the outcome was the same: two forkfuls later, down he'd go—fatally stricken by the piquantness of the white sauce. In those mysteries, dinner conversation always included the phrase "I believe the sole did not agree with Reginald. Carruthers, please ring Dr. Watney."

The dinner plate became the poisoner's playground. I suppose its popularity was due to the fact that, with the possible exception of the blunt instrument, nothing was as easy to use. It didn't have to be aimed (like the gun) or personally brought into direct contact with the body (like the knife). It was simple to figure out how much poison to use: when in doubt, you merely doubled

---

DISTURBED DINNERS

Marian Babson, *Death Warmed Up*.
  Jean Ainsley's Executive Meal Service is threatened.
Leo Bruce, *Death with Blue Ribbon*.
  Carolus Deane with Catering and Cookbooks.
Beverly Byrne, *Murder on the Menu*.
  Former chef gets embroiled with Pâté and Brioche.
Dorothy Cannell, *The Thin Woman*.
  Ellie Simons, overweight gourmet.
Tim Heald, *Just Desserts*.
  Simon Bogner—London's Board of Trade—with chefs and restaurateurs.
Emma Lathen, *Murder to Go*.

John Putnam Thatcher and fast-food "Chicken Tonight."
Virginia Rich, *Baked Bean Supper Murders*.
  Widow Emily Potter in Maine fishing village—with recipes.
——*Cooking School Murders*.
  Widow Potter at cooking school in Harrington, Iowa—with recipes.
J.C.S. Smith, *Nightcap*.
  Jacoby, security officer for the Pinnacle Room, posh restaurant in N.Y.C.
Julie Smith, *The Sourdough Wars*.
  Rebecca Schwartz, the youngish, talented San Francisco attorney, confronts the war of the bakers.

THE CHOCOLATE MOUSSE MURDER

Marty Norman

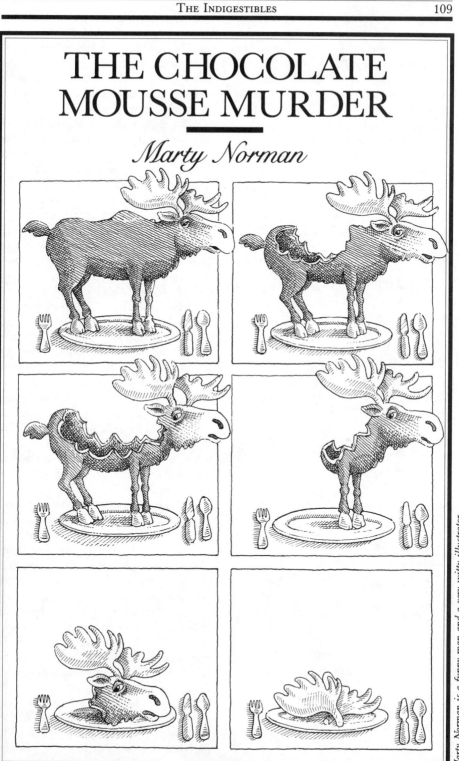

Marty Norman is a funny man and a very witty illustrator.

the dose. It was also a snap to get the victim to ingest it. After all, everyone ate at least one meal a day. And the English were—still are—notoriously insensitive in regard to food. A slightly off-taste bit of potted meat would not have seemed odd to them. They'd hardly have noticed.

No, it definitely wasn't safe to eat in those books. There were arcane poisons, of course, which one had to go to Brazil to collect or, even worse, sign the chemist's registry to purchase. But by and large, toxic substances were available at the drop of a grudge. Botulism was fre-

THE ULTIMATE COOK-OFF

The Silver Palate

Madame Butterfly
vs.
Lizzie Borden

The Silver Palate is delicious, both the book and the gourmet food shop. The perpetrators: Julee Rosso and Sheila Lukins.

quently induced. Mushrooms were nurtured in the dank of the cellar. Weedkiller decimated two-legged rats. By the time the chubby sleuth waddled onto the scene, it was too late to administer the antidote—if indeed there was one.

The dinner plate is still being toyed with in detective fiction, only now the Americans have gotten in on the act (Fred Halliday's *The Raspberry Tart Affair*; Nan and Ivan Lyons' *Someone Is Killing the Great Chefs of Europe*). There is also a counter-trend: books featuring fat sleuths' must-haves rather than the poisoners' menus (*Madame Maigret's Own Cookbook; The Nero Wolfe Cookbook; the Mafia Cookbook; Murder on the Menu; Dining Out with Sherlock Holmes*).

What is this fascination? Why is food to the mystery what Watson is to Holmes, inseparable best friend? One theory intimidating enough to make Freud take to his couch is that there is virtually no sexual activity in the mystery and food is used as the surrogate. Many psychiatrists have noted that the number of pounds of overweight can be directly correlated to the number of kisses, etc., not received. (Don't blame me: I didn't invent the theory, I'm merely repeating it.)

There are some foods in mysteries it's never safe to trust. Dover sole, baked or poached. Porridge. Ladyfingers. Any cream sauce. Eggs, unless they're hardboiled. Chocolates, if they're given as a present. Warm milk. And, of course, any sort of spirits. The Case of the Deadly Decanter has been written at least a hundred times, and there's probably a fiend out there typing up another one right now. When analyzed, the sediment always contains enough poison to fell a hippopotamus.

Who's putting all these bad things in the victim's mouth? Certainly not Cook. Granted, she has the disposition of Attila the Hun, but her weapon would be the meat cleaver. No one in and around the

THE CONSUMMATE "MINCEUR" DISH

Jacques Pépin

SCALLOPS OF SALMON AVEC CURARE BUTTER À LA BELLE-MÈRE*
For 1 corpse

3 oz. salmon scallops, red and fleshy
2 tbs. hacked shiitake or Amanita phalloides
1 large truffle, thinly dissected
dash champagne
4 tbs. butter
salt and pepper to taste
½ tsp. curare, preferably homemade (if you have the right tropical plant)

Place salmon, mushrooms, truffle, champagne, salt and pepper in unlined copper skillet. (Unlined copper serves as a catalyst for the working of the ingredients.) Cook briefly over medium heat. Arrange fish and garnish on plate. Using a whisk, add butter and curare to remaining juices in skillet to create a light, foamy sauce. Pour over scallops and serve immediately. (Although best served hot, it is also perfectly effective when served cold.)

The curare in the light beurre blanc has the advantage of being tasteless, low-calorie and, as a special bonus, paralyzes the insides, therefore preventing swallowing and consequently guaranteeing a great loss of weight. This will produce a beautiful body, thin and magnificent in its last repose.

I hope you like my recipe. Please test it on someone else before trying it yourself.

Jacques Pépin is the author of La Technique, La Méthode *and the companion volume to his PBS television show,* Everyday Cooking with Jacques Pépin.

---

*M. Pépin is not seriously suggesting you combine, then ingest these ingredients. Please be advised that the recipe is poisonous and should not, under any circumstances, be prepared or consumed.

kitchen, in fact, is a desecrator of the dinner plate. The washing-up girl has no time; the butler has no motive; the serving girl never has her hands free.

No, the poisoner is usually someone from Upstairs, or an Upstairs associate such as the lawyer or the doctor. Poisoning is a well-to-do crime. It's neat. It's tidy. It's rather elegant.

What I would prefer, if I may be so bold as to instruct my enemy, is to be allowed to eat my meal in peace and *then* be done in. The owners of New York's elegant Four Seasons restaurant concur. They suggest that, in the manner of Sing Sing, you give the condemned a hearty meal. After all, at one time you and your victim were rather intimate. You did share things together—be it a love affair, a family relationship, a corporate decision. Accordingly, you owe it to your victim to let his last meal reflect the gloriousness of his former role in your life. Bring on the golden egg caviar with the gold caviar spoon. The Trockenbeeren Auslese in a vintage coinciding with the date of your first encounter. The Havana cigars (smuggled). The cognac (Hennessey X.O.). The freshly peeled crayfish tails with morels flown in from the Himalayas. *Then* as you stroll from the restaurant, *then* as you turn into a convenient dark alley, *then* set about finalizing matters. *That's* good manners.

If you feel you simply must monkey around despite the admonishments from me and the Four Seasons, let us remind you of peppered duck and shrimp with mustard sauce. Both have the necessary robustness to disguise a poison. And they have not been, forgive us, done to death. If you will settle for just making your victim deathly ill, we suggest off-season oysters from polluted waters. They'll cause hepatitis.

One other thing: may I invite you to dine with me Saturday next?

Carlotta Ogelthorpe dines alone.

READERS, YOUR GOOSE IS COOKED
NOW SAY GRACE

Naomi Buttermilk

Nobody wants to have dinner at my house and I'm not a bit surprised. As a consequence of devouring two mysteries a day for the past twenty or so years (talk about a misspent youth), I have decided that there is only one correct thing to do with food: poison it.

More detective novels than I care to name have insisted that the ideal cup of bedtime cocoa contains one level teaspoon of cocoa for every heaping teaspoon of arsenic, that bonbons are suitable only if they've been dipped first in nitrobenzene, that a white sauce must always be accompanied by a fillet of strychnine amandine and that a truly amiable hock will be plastered with cyanide pellets before being decanted.

Clearly, in a detective novel the general rule seems to be if you're going to ask someone to suffer through a helping of *Amanita phalloides,* then really make him suffer—coat it with hemlock for starters. Equally clearly, my decline-to-dine friends fear this is what I'll serve them if they show up. Nonsense, I might not go to all that bother; another thing mysteries have taught me is that food needn't be ingested to be hazardous to one's health. A frozen leg of lamb, for instance, makes a fine cosh, as anyone who's read Roald Dahl's wicked little tribute to the freezer compartment, "Lamb to the Slaughter," will attest.

I concede, however, that the real reason I'm not out pricing meat lockers or chatting up obliging chemists is that I strongly suspect if I kill a chum in the vicinity of the kitchen, I'll be caught by a detective who likes to cook, or one who likes to eat.

With few exceptions, mystery sleuths come in two sizes: Lge and XLge. Fattest by a cookie crumb or two is Rex Stout's Nero Wolfe, who weighs in at 1/7th of a ton. Waddling right behind him are John Dickson Carr's Gideon Fell, Dashiell Hammett's Continental Op, Earl Derr Biggers' Charlie Chan, Erle Stanley Gardner's Bertha Cool, Joyce Porter's Inspector Dover, Charles Dickens' Inspector Bucket, George Simenon's Jules Maigret, John Le Carré's George Smiley and Dame Agatha's Hercule Poirot, all of whom could do your couch a favor if they declined sitting on it.

Bertha and Dover are the junk food lovers. She gobbles up pecan waffles after first dousing them with enough syrup to raise Atlantis; he litters the corridors of Scotland Yard with candy wrappers.

Maigret, to my mind, is the most romantic of the tubbies, preferring to take meals with his wife, work permitting. Mme. Maigret's culinary efforts have nudged her husband to the 200-pound mark and have led a publisher to immortalize her recipes in *Mme. Maigret's Own Cookbook,* a hefty hardback volume of several years ago. I tried a few of her suggestions; found a swift swig of Calvados made them quite tasty.

Poirot's palate is hard to understand. He favors marrows and tisanes, yet has been known (in *Funerals Are Fatal*) to polish off more elegant fare: pâté de fois gras, sole véronique, escalope de veau milanaise, poire flambée with ice cream, Pouilly-Fuissé, then a drop of Corton. But to prove that he's still a Philistine in his gut, Poirot guzzles crème de cacao at the meal's conclusion, when a decent port is at hand. Well, what can we expect from a man whose head is shaped like an egg?

A word should be added here about the tendency of the English mystery to start off each breakfast with kedgeree, which is a strange thing to do with fish,

---

TAKE YOUR ORDER, LUV?

Jane Garmey

Angels on Horseback: oysters wrapped in bacon and grilled under the broiler. Substitute scallops for the oysters, and you have *Devils on Horseback.*

Bubble and Squeak: potato and cabbage leftovers fried together in hot fat and usually served with *Wow Wow Sauce,* a spicy, hot sauce that has a vinegar, mustard and Worcestershire base.

Cawl Mamgu: a Welsh recipe containing leeks (the national emblem of Wales) in cawl (Welsh word for "broth," pronounced *cowl*).

Cullen Skink: a Scottish soup made from smoked haddock and cream, with a golden colour and smokey flavour.

Eton Mess: a concoction of strawberries, soaked in kirsch and mixed with crushed meringues and much whipped cream. Owes its name to the best-known public (private) school in England, where it is traditionally served on the annual prize day.

Flummery: a slippery, white custard jelly that was a favourite of Mrs. Beeton. Dull on its own, but much enlivened if served with fresh raspberries.

Gooseberry Fool: believed to date back to the fifteenth century, this sublime mixture for serious eaters is made from whipped cream, gooseberries and a bit of sugar.

Hindle Wakes: an ancient Lancashire recipe for chicken, cooked with prunes, lemon and vinegar. Thought to have originated with the Flemish weavers who came to the area in the fourteenth century.

Kedgeree: traditionally served for breakfast in large, draughty country houses, this mixture of smoked haddock, hard-boiled eggs and rice was brought back from India by generations of empire builders.

Poor Knights of Windsor: an English version of French toast, served with raspberries and cream.

Singin' Hinnies: Northumberland scones, cooked over a griddle.

Soles in Their Coffins: a Victorian recipe in which sole fillets are stuffed in potatoes, then surrounded by shrimps and mushrooms. Particularly appropriate for funerals and wakes.

Spotted Dick: a simple, steamed pudding, "spotted" with raisins and currants and beloved by pudding fanciers.

Syllabub: the British answer to zabaglione, dating back to Elizabethan times when it was made with milk still warm from the cow. Now a rich confection of stiffly whipped cream, sherry and lemon juice.

Toad in the Hole: Yorkshire pudding, with the addition of sausages cooked in batter. Popular with children and a stand-by for high tea.

Jane Garmey is the author of Great British Cooking: A Well Kept Secret.

A HOMEMADE BREAD-AND-BUTTER NOTE

Bert Greene

The truest crime is one of culinary passion. Where else but in the kitchen of a stately home in England would a cook bake a gilded wheaten loaf and with gastronomic cunning send it on to the drawing room in time for tea, still warm and accompanied by a prawn butter? Yet the discerning nose detects—what? The bite of jalapeño peppers? Perhaps. That would be a lovely end to tea. But cyanide, ah, that would be a lovely end to the unwary tea drinker.

The Lovely End to Tea

WHEATEN LOAF

2 tbs. granulated yeast
2 cups warm water
3 tbs. blackstrap molasses
5 tbs. honey
5⅓ cups stone-ground whole wheat flour
1½ tsp. salt
3 tbs. unsalted butter, softened
1 egg white
⅔ cup sesame seeds (approximately)
2 tbs. butter, melted

1. Dissolve yeast in warm water in large bowl. Add molasses and honey. Let stand 10 minutes.
2. Stir in 3 cups whole wheat flour. Add salt and 3 tbs. butter. Beat with wooden spoon until smooth. Slowly add more flour, ½ cup at a time, until a stiff dough is formed. Turn onto floured board; knead 10 minutes.
3. Place dough in large, greased bowl. Cover; let rise in warm place until doubled in bulk, about 1½ hours.
4. Punch down dough. Knead 5 minutes; return to bowl. Cover; let rise until doubled in bulk, about 1 hour.
5. Punch down dough. Knead 5 minutes. Divide dough in half. Roll each half lengthwise into sausage shapes, about 10 inches long each. Beat flat with hands; fold dough into thirds. Brush each loaf with egg white; roll in sesame seeds to coat completely. Place in two buttered

10 x 5 x 3-inch bread pans. Cover; let rise 50 minutes.
6. Heat oven to 350°. Bake bread until loaves sound hollow when tapped, about 45 minutes. Turn out on wire rack. Brush top with melted butter to add sheen.
Makes 2 loaves.

PRAWN BUTTER

2 cups deveined, shelled, cooked tiny shrimps
½ cup lemon juice
1 cup unsalted butter, softened
2 tbs. chopped fresh basil
2 tsp. minced anchovy fillets
2 jalapeño peppers, seeded, deveined, minced
¼ tsp. salt
Pinch cayenne pepper
1 tbs. coarsely ground black pepper

1. Combine shrimps and lemon juice in small bowl. Let stand, covered, at room temperature for 1 hour. Drain.
2. Cream butter in large mixing bowl. Beat in basil, anchovy, jalapeño peppers, salt and cayenne pepper. Fold in shrimp; taste and adjust seasonings.
3. Spoon shrimp mixture into small earthenware crock. Sprinkle top with black pepper. Cover. Refrigerate at least 5 hours.
Makes about 1 pint or enough to satisfy two plump loaves and several healthy appetites.

The Lovely End to the Tea Drinker
Poison to taste.

Bert Greene is the author of the delectable Greene on Greens.

and to take tea at the drop of a hat (chet). In Frances Iles' *Malice Aforethought,* for example, Dr. Bickleigh sips a cup on eleven separate occasions before he commits his first murder; then things slow down—between murders one and two, there are only four trips to the ubiquitous tea trolley.

For those intrepids brave enough to attempt cooking in an English mystery manner—or manor—I commend two texts: Jeanine Larmoth's charming *Murder on the Menu,* which reminds us that only in Britain would a biddy tack a pinup of a teashop to her wall, moon over it and, indeed, kill for it (Agatha Christie's *Funerals Are Fatal*) and Julia Rosenblatt's *Dining with Sherlock Holmes,* which includes recipes Mrs. Hudson could have used, such as eggs with gunpowder butter, to fight back when the sniper was taking pot shots at her in Holmes' quarters.

Holmes, by the way, is one of the select group of mystery heroes who can eat like a pig and not get fat. James Bond is another and the third is Lord Peter Wimsey. And now that *The Lord Peter Wimsey Cookbook* is out, you can pop in your monocle and follow Wimsey's fancy—from his and Harriet's wedding breakfast to the Wimsey family solicitor's chambers luncheon to a Scottish holiday casserole of stewed beef prepared by the inimitable Bunter.

To return to 1/7th of a ton, to the gentleman whose girth demands a specially constructed desk chair, it must be said that no figure in the history of mystery fiction, which dates back to 1841, has eaten quite so well, nor quite so much. Nero Wolfe and his chef, Fritz Brenner, and his good friend Marko Vukcic, owner of Rusterman's restaurant, combine the knowledge of Craig Claiborne with the grace of M.F.K. Fisher, and if you need convincing, pick up a copy of *The Nero Wolfe Cookbook* and eat your heart out.

Ellen Kreiger, president of the Wolfe Pack, a band of loyalists who convene each spring for a Wolfe cookbook-derived banquet (last year's choices: beef braised in red wine, lamb-stuffed eggplant, carottes flamandes, salad with devil's rain dressing and lemon-sherry pudding with brown sugar sauce), says they are also trying to stage the feast described in *Too Many Cooks*. Until a date is set, club members have to console themselves by stalking the streets of Manhattan in search of a real-life counterpart to Rusterman's.

Although his following is not nearly so vast as Wolfe's, Robert B. Parker's Boston-centered private eye, Spenser, is attracting readers with insatiable appetites for both gore and garnishes. Soused shrimp are a favorite of his, and in style he's not unlike an uncouth Harry Palmer, Len Deighton's gourmet spy, who is as much at home with a Cuisinart as with a codebook. Only fitting, since Mr. Deighton once wrote a regular cooking column, taught cooking classes professionally and includes the cookbook *Où Est le Garlic?* among his collected works. In a parallel career switch, the mystery author Nicolas Freeling used to teach cooking school professionally and includes *The Kitchen* among his titles.

In kibbutzing with Joan Kahn, editor at St. Martin's Press, over which mystery has the most memorable eating sequence, Miss Kahn asked, "Do people eating other people count?" and we both agreed that the Alfred Packer Memorial Trophy (Mr. Packer is the only man in the United States to be tried and convicted of cannibalism) ought to go to Stanley Ellin's *Specialty of the House.*

All things considered, the next time someone accuses me of reading mysteries because I'm hungry for violence, I'm going to tell 'em nope, I'm just plain hungry.

Naomi Buttermilk's life has gone sour.

DEAD DRUNK ON MEAN STREET
AN UNHAPPY SAGA OF OVERINDULGENCE

Simon Brett

Like most writers, I hold sacred the first drink at the end of the day's work. (A large Bell's on the rocks, thank you very much.) Charles Paris, though sharing my taste in whiskies, does not share my abstemiousness. Nor, I fear, do most of the other characers he bumps into in the course of a plot. In my crime world—and others past and present—the citizenry abide by beer, bitter, bourbon and a variety of more baroque potables. It has come to this: if a literary prohibition were suddenly introduced whereby all references to alcohol had to be expunged from crime fiction, the genre would not only dry out, but completely dry up.

The ubiquitous butler would wander the library with an empty tray.

The jolly publican would turn surly and go on the dole.

The master detective, denied an interview with the pub patron conveniently indiscreet about "that nasty patch of business a few years back," would be evermore unable to solve a crime—a situation perhaps not unexpected in real life, but with fiction readers do tend to want a tidy wrap-up.

Even the hard-boiled would find things impossible. Private-eye heroes would no longer be able to ingratiate themselves with villains by drinking them under the table. Gone, too, spiking highballs, concocting Mickey Finns, switching glasses and deducing the evening's companion was a woman from the imprint on the rim. Did you just feel the foundation of the genre tremble?

Mysteries *require* liquor. In much the way many of us *require* air. It provides work (wine salesman Montague Egg), snobbery (James Bond's "shaken not stirred" martini), rococo hobbies (Nero Wolfe's beer-cap collection, for instance), atmosphere (Constable Thackeray's connoisseur approach to the ales of Victorian London), physical description (Van der Valk's nose with its broken veins from too much drink) and ultimately—salvation (my poor Charles is so tanked in *Murder in the Title* he falls, thus avoiding impalement by a sword shoved through a stage flat).

Amazing, isn't it, how all these sleuths manage to achieve remarkable feats of deduction and derring-do through their respective alcoholic hazes. No amount of booze seems to rot the little grey cells. Still, there is one bastion of sobriety, one teetotalling dissenter among the pages: Adam Hall's Quiller. He doesn't drink "because it would affect his reaction time." (Nice to have one among us conversant with reality.)

Actually, my informal poll of the genre (I read friends' books) reveals that we crime writers pretty much use the words "drinking" and "thinking" interchangeably. Gavin Lyall's Major Maxim downs a couple of lagers while typing out reports; in *I, the Jury,* Mickey Spillane's Mike Hammer spends a whole Sunday emptying his fridge of beer and most of

Monday polishing off highballs in a bar, while trying to remember where he put a vital clue; Sam Spade holds a Bacardi wake the night following his partner's death; and the Continental Op cheerily embarks on a three-day bender in the course of an investigation.

Well, to each his own manner of dealing with stress, I say.

The Op, though, may be overdoing it. At one critical point in *Red Harvest* he swills gin and laudanum. Now, that really *is* mixing your drinks, which perhaps accounts for the supreme self-justification following: "I would rather have been cold sober, but I wasn't. If the night held more work for me, I didn't want to go to it with alcohol dying in me. The snifter revived me a lot. I poured more of the King George into a flask, pocketed it, and went down to the taxi." A.A. meetings, I am led to believe, hear almost identical vindications nightly. They are considered the ramblings of a diseased man.

Women have reached parity under the table, so to speak. They, too, hoist a few. Antonia Fraser keeps Jemima Shore well stocked with white wine (a very good white wine at that), Jane Dentinger supplies Jocelyn O'Roarke with the headier brandies, and let's not forget to toast the elderberry wine sorority.

But books, even mysteries, reflect life, and there wouldn't be such a fuss made over liquor in them if it didn't play such a significant part in real crimes. Drunkenness is at the bottom of many

WILLIAM HAMILTON/CAMERA PRESS

The East End's Jack the Ripper Pub, within walking distance of the crime scenes (most of which are now sites of parking garages and office buildings). The publican here does not wear a Leather Apron—the name by which Jack was first known.

TIPPLERS

MARTY NORMAN

Be it said once and for all time, Nick and Nora Charles mix the perfect martini.

They might consider sharing a shaker with Philip Atlee's Joe Gall; to admit he's partial to them is to understate the case. Matt Helm, Donald Hamilton's hero, would also appreciate an invite; he, too, fancies the drink adorned with an olive.

The wine faction is represented by Linda Barnes' Michael Spraggue, part owner of a Napa Valley winery, and Dorothy L. Sayers' devoted, oenological sleuth, Lord Peter himself, who, on one occasion, must prove his identity by pinpointing a series of wines, by taste ("The Bibulous Business of a Matter of Taste").

Curt Cannon, who raucously proclaims *I Like 'Em Tough*, will settle for any whiskey, but Robert B. Parker's Spenser is rather choosy: in *The Widening Gyre* he opts for Murphy's Irish Whiskey. Shell Scott, Richard S. Prather's leading man, is an aficionado of Hudson's Bay Scotch, and belying his name, Donald E. Westlake's Dortmunder is seriously committed to Amsterdam Liquor Store bourbon. Preferring a whole brewery (or distillery) are Bill Knox's Colin Thane, Richard Grindal's Mike MacDonald and Nicholas Blake's Nigel Strangeways.

The beer contingent spans both sides of the Atlantic: in England, the chaps downing a pint include Ruth Rendell's Inspector Wexford, Peter Lovesey's Sergeant Cribb and Leslie Thomas' Dangerous Davies; stateside, the brew guzzlers are Paul Engleman's Mark Renzler, Rex Stout's Nero Wolfe, James Crumley's C.W. Sughrue.

Mr. Crumley deserves the D.W.I. originality award. In *Dancing Bear*, Milton Chester (Milo) Milodragovitch sips peppermint schnapps.

riots and even more domestic disputes, and who will deny Lucrezia Borgia mixed a mean cocktail? Marie Lafarge, in her campaign to remove her husband with arsenic, put "enough to poison at least ten persons" in his eggnog. What's more, George Chapman added a dash of antimony to his wife's brandy and soda, and Richard Brinkley livened up a bottle of stout with cyanide and killed two (neither of them the one he was out to get). Harlow Fraden and Dennis Wepman were a bit classier—when they eliminated Fraden's parents, they added the cyanide to champagne. For many years now, poisoners have recognized the value of strong drink to hide the taste of their embellishments. Art, in the guise of the thriller, is merely imitating life.

Not to be outdone by reality, detective fiction has provided so many examples of substances doctored to kill that the mystery reader may even experience a touch of disappointment when an investigator finishes a drinking bout with no worse effects than a hangover.

Simon Brett is the author of the flamboyantly witty Charles Paris crime novels. He writes sober; Charles acts drunk.

MYSTERY TOASTS

Michael Cader

1. The Graceful Goodbye
May old acquaintance be forgot.

2. The Backslapper
Forget your mouth,
Forsake your gums,
Watch your back
'Cause here it comes.

3. The Traitor's Curse
I pledge allegiance
   to the flag
   of whatever state I'm in
And hope to find
   my martini glass
   contains no bugs, just gin.

4. The Cozy's Salute
To the clue in the garden,
The footprint washed to sea,
And the sweet smell of almonds
In the curmudgeon's tea.

5. Burnt Toast
I made this toast
   when I got home
   and caught the wife and parson.
I lit a fire to his seat
   and kicked him in the arson.

6. The Mercenary's Opening Salvo
Can't pay, won't slay.

*Michael Cader is barely
old enough to drink.*

SINISTER ORIENTALS
Everybody's Favorite Villains

Robin W. Winks

When Goldfinger's Korean body-guard, Oddjob, was given the shock of his life by James Bond, he was simply dying for The Cause, yet one more Sinister Oriental gone to his just reward. After all, as Goldfinger had told Bond, Oddjob was "simple, unrefined clay, capable of limited exploitation." He was above the Chigroes, to be sure, since he was not half-caste (only Dr. No, half Chinese and an obvious if emaciated descendant of Fu Manchu, rose above what Somerset Maugham would have called "The Yellow Streak" in Ian Fleming's work), and while wily enough, he obviously was created simply to be outwitted, as Fu Manchu's only purpose seemed to be as a foil to Sir Denis Nayland Smith.

If one smells a giant rat from Sumatra in all this, one is meant to, for the Mysterious East has been a staple of the entertainment industry ever since hack writers took the sounds but not the sense from Thomas De Quincey's *Confessions of an English Opium Eater*. The rise of the "penny dreadful" to its peak in the 1840's and the success of Wilkie Collins' *The Moonstone* in 1868 were two stages on the path toward a persistent English, and later American, fascination with the Orient, a fascination both pejorative in content—as when Egyptians were dubbed Wogs, for "Westernized Oriental Gentlemen"—and at times highly respectful. The persistent tone of Western popular interest in the Orient has been

one of high ambiguity coupled with creative drift.

The drift has been toward greater respect joined with greater fear, and the appearance of the Sinister Oriental as hero or villain in Western thriller and detective/spy fiction has usually coincided with a period in which China, or latterly Japan, played a role in world affairs. Orientals were sinister because they were inscrutable (or, as the music halls had it, they couldn't get pregnant in the normal way), "able to live off the smell of a greasy rag," and addicted to "half-hatched eggs"—or so the *Westminster Review* told its readers in 1866.

The notion of an inexplicable East bites more deeply than this, however, for the journals of early explorers and voyagers reported upon "strange and wondrous" sights as early as Marco Polo's visit to the Court of the Great Khan. If Magellan's chronicler, Pigafetta, could assert that within the contemporary Philippines there was a race of men with ears so large they curled them under as pillows, then the Victorians might equally well insist that the Chinese, Japanese, Malays and others engaged in incredible sexual practices, devoured birds' nests and were persistently hung over from ubiquitous opium dens. The great Kraken, the gigantic octopus creature that legend placed in the South China Sea (later to transfer it to the Sargasso), was shown with hooded eye and beak, the very caricature of an Ori-

FAR EAST RECLAMATION

Chinese "mystery."

Not all Orientals plead at the bar sinister. Harold Gray, the creator of Little Orphan Annie, influenced by Charles Dickens and Joseph Conrad, introduced the Orient through the Asp—a slim, black-clothed, Far Eastern protector of capitalism, i.e., of Daddy Warbucks—and through Punjab, a turbaned South Asian who frequently appeared to rescue Annie from the sinister West. In the late 1930's Hugh Wiley introduced to *Collier's* magazine a Chinese detective, James Lee Wong, who soon moved on to the silver screen in the person of Boris Karloff and later Keye Luke (who had been Charlie Chan). At the same time, John P. Marquand created an immaculate detective, Mr. I.O. Moto, who appeared in five books within seven years. In 1957 Marquand unsuccessfully revived him for the book *Stopover: Tokyo.* And beginning in 1949 Dutch diplomat Robert van Gulik introduced Western readers to Judge Jen-Djieh Dee, modeled on a seventh-century Chinese magistrate. Wise and always controlled, Judge Dee would contrast sharply with the madcap Hong Kong police of William Marshall's *Yellowthread Street,* proving not only that the left hand knows not what the right does, but that the Orient can produce its Laurel and Hardy, too.

R. W. W.

ental. Bamboo splinters under the fingernails, the Chinese water torture, child brides, bound feet—all were indications of a culture that knew better than the West how to construct the exquisite Torture Garden of pornography.

In general, the Sinister Oriental was Far Eastern, not South Asian. There was no lack of thriller literature about India, rampant with *thuggee,* widows' funeral pyres, cobras in the bedcovers, rampaging elephants and cursed jewels. But the Indian never took on the same sinister connotations as did, in particular, the Chinese. Those who have read Collins know that he admired the Indians of *The Moonstone* and reserved his harshest judgments for such figures as Godfrey Ablewhite and the retired Anglo-Indian officer John Herncastle. Perhaps the fact that the British came to know the Indians well, as they became part of the empire, removed some of the sense of distance on which mystery thrives. Since Americans had little interest in South Asia, few American thrillers appeared with Indian settings.

East and Southeast Asia were another matter. With the evolution of the energetic and respectable "boys' magazines" out of the penny dreadfuls, Asians became simpler if no less villainous. By the 1870's the "penny packets of poison," as one critic called them, had rolled out the entire inventory of horrors: rape, bloodsucking, burial alive, cannibalism, lingering and exquisite torture, the dissection alive of a victim's face. This was too strong for the boys, so S.O. Beeton's *Boy's Own Magazine* (1855–66) and the Religious Tract Society's *Boy's Own Paper* (1879–1967) set a higher tone. Nonetheless, the Chinese continued to be wily, and in *Boys of England* one read of the heroic battles of upright traders who sailed home from Canton with their costly cargo, only to be attacked by "Malay scum...Chinese, Japanese, Javans, Papuans, Pintadoes, Mestizoes," and even a few Spaniards and Portuguese. All this was simply a romanticizing of the very real threat posed by sea Dayaks and pirates out of Borneo. So "Christian" a writer as Charles Kingsley, author of the treacly *Water Babies,* could write: "You Malays and Dayaks of Sarawak, you . . . are the enemies of Christ . . . you are beasts, all the more dangerous, because you have a semi-human cunning . . . I will blast you out with grape and rockets."

Four contributions to popular fiction probably did more than all others to promote the notion of the Sinister Oriental. The first of these, oddly, did not depict the Oriental as sinister so much as sinuously enterprising and wickedly clever: E. Harcourt Burrage's Chinese hero, Ching Ching, of the "celestial charm." He too had his own boys' journal, *Ching Ching's Own* (1888–93), and one of the books that were spun off, *Daring Ching Ching,* won a substantial readership among adults in England.

The second, and far most important, contribution to the creation of the Sinister Oriental was Sax Rohmer's Dr. Fu Manchu, who sprang into diabolical life during the period when the Yellow Peril was perceived to be at its most insidious. Racism was at its most virulent just before, during and immediately after World War I, when so benign a Canadian writer as Agnes Laut could warn her fellow countrymen against the "dangers within, not without," of letting down the barriers to "too many Jappy-Chappies, Chinks, and Little Brown Brothers." Rohmer, who had been doing research on the Chinese District of London, created his Devil Doctor to meet a public mood and sent him into the world in *The Mystery of Dr. Fu Manchu* in 1913. Fu Manchu moved onto the silver screen in 1923. (For a full account of Rohmer's creation, see *Master of Villainy: A Biography of Sax Rohmer* by Cay Van Ash and Elizabeth Sax Rohmer.)

A third major contribution to the image of the clever Chinese was Earl Derr Biggers' Charlie Chan, the member of the Honolulu Police Department who works on the side of Good and who coins quasi-Confucian (and sometimes very funny) aphorisms. It may be ar-

gued that Chan was an antidote to the notion of the Sinister Oriental, and that *The House Without a Key,* which appeared in 1925, was the first of a series of replies to the yellow-robed evil Doctor, but the Chan of the books—as distinct from the amusing Chan of the films—often casts a chilling shadow over his ratiocinations.

Finally, who can forget the first issue of *Detective Comics,* which appeared early in 1937 and for one thin dime gave the reader a healthy case of the shakes? A malevolent Chinese peered out from the cover, and inside the story of "The Claws of the Red Dragon," by Maj. Malcolm Wheeler-Nicholson and Tom Hickey, carried one into San Francisco's Chinatown and face to face with the Yellow Menace. By 1939 the Orientals of comic book thrillers had taken on an increasingly Japanese look, and through the war they would supplant the Chinese—bestial, red of tooth and claw.

Today the Japanese have recovered their features, and it is once again the Chinese who present a sinister face to us. But we are somewhat more sophisticated now, and certainly more ambivalent in our views of Asian societies. To the true mystery fan, no one did more to correct the balance than the Dutch diplomat and Sinologist Robert van Gulik, who began to reconstruct from actual records the cases of his fictional seventh-century Judge Jen-Djieh Dee. Between *Three Murder Cases Solved by Judge Dee,* first published in Tokyo in 1949, and *Willow Pattern,* published in 1965 (other, less interesting books were to follow), van Gulik provided a chilling, sometimes truly sinister, historically accurate and balanced picture of Chinese justice at work. *The Manchurian Candidate* may have kept the stereotype alive; Judge Dee freed the aficionados.

Robin W. Winks reviews mysteries for the Boston Globe. He is a professor of history at Yale Univeristy.

TWO-TIMING DAMES

Allison Wentworth

Pink is not their color, and they've never developed a fondness for true blue, either. It's blood red that tips their nails and jet black that swathes their bodies, usually in a sweep of taffeta that crackles like crisp new hundred-dollar bills.

Dames have been around since the Thirties, but they hit their prime in the Forties and Fifties. They seduced Spade and lately they've been hectoring Parker—and dumber than that, they just don't come.

Dames have one recurring fantasy: a little house with twenty-seven rooms in it, a mink in every closet and a white telephone by the poolside. Every morning, if they had their way, a six-foot gent would exit their bed and on his way out drop some bills on the dresser (nothing smaller than a fifty). Then they'd spend the day boozing it away, gambling it away beside a man who'd pat them on the fanny every time they rolled a seven.

Books about dames appeal primarily to men. They never see what the broads are up to till it's too late, and they have no recourse but to black-and-blue their jaw or ventilate their belly.

Men, be they the private-eye hero or the private-eye reader, are tripped up by dark seams stretching up impossibly long legs. A waft of gardenia perfume numbs their thinking. Their eyes get clouded by a toss of hair that's whiter than any pillow cover.

> *I* adore the old mysteries with their wicked rajahs and barons and the lurid beautiful spy who walked like a serpent—wouldn't you just love to be able to do that!
>
> BARBARA CARTLAND

"Will you marry me when you
are free?"
"Hic."

...hic...hic...hic...

It's not uncommon for such men to think of these dames as red herrings. "Poor kid," they say about a gal who'd sell her mother, "she needs a break." They know she's not quite on the up and up, but they'd rather not face it. It's easier for them to treat her as a diversion instead of the instigator.

So the hard-boiled dame functions as a red herring. Unless, as sometimes happens, a woman is reading the book. Women know all the dame's tricks. They know only a female with a yen for black taffeta could arrive at the murder scene in time to commit it, not to be framed by it. They know it's no accident the black-mailer was iced once her letters were returned to her. They know if there's any confusion she's at the bottom of it, if there's any death she committed it.

Still, the dame is an ersatz red herring. The sentimental will think her guilty—but not really. The cynic will spot her for what she is—a two-timing broad.

When they're not in the swing of things themselves, dames are champion red-herring droppers. Who put one of Saul's cigars in the dead man's ashtray? Who gave Lewis the ticket to a performance that was canceled? Who told Herman to drive her car past the bank at eleven sharp? Who indeed.

The old-fashioned peroxided dames, with earrings that got lost and diaries that got stolen, are quickly vanishing from the crime writer's lexicon. But they're being replaced by hippie dames, twenty-year-olds who never wear bras and never forget their dexies. These women are not so different in anything but dress. Their morals can be likened to the Easter bunny's, their language smacks of the Fifties truckdriver's. But deep down there is about them a lingering scent of gardenia, a glimpse of a seam going clear to the thigh. They, too, are seemingly vulnerable; they, too, find a susceptible private eye to do their dirty work. They don't usually die at the end of the book, but they get sent home to their parents—and to their mind that's tantamount to death.

How did women get started in the role of red herring? They had all that free time on their hands in which to scatter clues (women almost never work in mysteries, unless it's as a governess) and so they became targets of opportunity.

The next time you read of a woman waiting in a private eye's office, and he opens the door to find her sitting there on the edge of his desk, a long leg beating time against his chair, pay attention. The dame ain't there for his health.

Allison Wentworth is a feminist.

WATSONS
BLESSÈD INFERIORS

Frederick Arnold

It's a toss-up whether the hero's best friend is a red herring or an albatross.

If there's a clear footprint, he walks across it.

If there's an equally clear finger-print, he invariably smudges it.

If there's a vital phone message, he forgets to relay it, and if there's a hand-writing specimen, he misidentifies it.

In short, if there's a wrong conclusion to jump to, he swings into it with the enthusiasm of Tarzan on the vine.

A Watson (who needn't be a male) is chronically inept, possibly genetically so. He is also the biggest troublemaker since Cain. As he blunders from room to room (pocketing clues as he goes), he keeps up a barrage of questions so inane, it's a wonder his chum bothers answering.

Every now and then, a scholar (with more than a dollop of Watson in his soul) will suggest the hero's friend is a stand-in for the reader. He is supposed to say all the things we would, if we were in his place. His insights are our insights, so the theory goes, and his confusion is our confusion. Perhaps the reader ought to sue for character defamation.

Actually, Watsons exist because, without them, who would lay down the trail of red herrings?

If there is one thing Watsons excel at, it's pointing the way to the fork on the left when the killer has blithely gone on his way to the right. A confirmed mystery addict will recognize this duplicity for what it is, and not be bothered with it. The novice often traipses down the wrong path with him.

To qualify as a Watson, a character

RICHARD KALVAR/MAGNUM

A comrade-in-arms, literally.

must have more faith in the hero than Rockefeller has dimes. And that faith must be absolutely unshakable. Example: The hero picks up a book of Serbo-Croat poetry (not in translation). To the best of a Watson's knowledge, his friend has never been in Serbia or Croatia, has never read a word of the language be-

SLEUTHS AND SIDEKICKS

Elizabeth Lange

*Take one from the left column and one from
the right column and match them up.*

Sleuths	Sidekicks
1. Sexton Blake	*a.* Chick & Patsy
2. Dr. Daniel Coffee	*b.* Mr. Ricardo
3. Sir Denis Nayland Smith	*c.* Insp. Roberts
4. Albert Campion	*d.* Henry Satterthwaite
5. Lamont Cranston	*e.* Bunter
6. Capt. José da Silva	*f.* Dr. Motial Mookerji
7. Insp. Wilfred Dover	*g.* Harold Bantz
8. John J. Malone	*h.* Dr. Petrie
9. Dr. Thorndyke	*i.* Sgt. Love
10. Sherlock Holmes	*j.* Jeff Marle
11. Col. March	*k.* Magersfontein Lugg
12. Perry Mason	*l.* Dr. Watson
13. Mr. and Mrs. North	*m.* Tinker
14. Joseph Rouletabille	*n.* Capt. Hastings
15. Judge Dee	*o.* Archie Goodwin
16. Rabbi David Small	*p.* Louis Calling
17. Lord Peter Wimsey	*q.* Sgt. Bull
18. Henri Bencolin	*r.* Insp. Todhunter
19. Modesty Blaise	*s.* Hugh Lanigan
20. Bertha Cool	*t.* Insp. Fox
21. Insp. Purbright	*u.* Harry Vincent
22. Insp. Gabriel Hanaud	*v.* Col. Primrose
23. Grace Latham	*w.* Martini
24. Insp. McGee	*x.* Christopher Jervis
25. Nick and Nora Charles	*y.* Sainclair
26. Nero Wolfe	*z.* Hoong Liang
27. Henry Gamadge	*aa.* Maggie Cassidy
28. Roderick Alleyn	*bb.* Insp. Blount
29. Max Carrados	*cc.* Willie Garvin
30. Evan Pinkerton	*dd.* Sgt. MacGregor
31. Harley Quin	*ee.* Asta
32. Nick Carter	*ff.* Paul Drake
33. Nigel Strangeways	*gg.* Donald Lam
34. Hercule Poirot	*hh.* Wilson
35. Spenser	*ii.* Emmy
36. Henry Tibbett	*jj.* Hawk
37. Old Man in Corner	*kk.* Clarissa
38. Valentine	*ll.* Chief Insp. Masters
39. H.M.	*mm.* Miriam
40. Homer Evans	*nn.* Polly

Answers:

1-m; 2-f; 3-h; 4-k; 5-u; 6-hh; 7-dd; 8-aa; 9-x; 10-l; 11-c; 12-ff; 13-w; 14-y; 15-z; 16-s; 17-e; 18-j; 19-cc; 20-gg; 21-i; 22-b; 23-v; 24-r; 25-ee; 26-o; 27-g; 28-t; 29-p; 30-q; 31-d; 32-a; 33-bb; 34-n; 35-jj; 36-ii; 37-nn; 38-kk; 39-ll; 40-mm.

fore. Nevertheless, when he remarks that there's an amusing grammatical error in the third stanza, a Watson not only believes him but maligns the author for his slipshoddiness.

The best Watsons (i.e., the ones who most frequently succor the enemy under the misapprehension that they are abetting the innocent) are never the same age as their heroes. It doesn't matter if they're older or younger; they simply must not be on a par with the hero on any level, even a chronological one. Besides, if they're older, the hero gets to twit them for being forgetful, and if they're younger, he gets to tease them for still having a lot to learn.

Watsons are also good for establishing alibis. For the killer. They are the ones most apt to remark, "Why, Lord Z and I were on that train together. He never left my sight for a moment," thereby confounding the Hero Detective until he reminds his pal of his penchant for dozing off without realizing it.

The red herring-est aspect of a Watson is, of course, his total inability to solve a case on his own. (Think of the Old Man in the Corner's Polly and the Thinking Machine's Hutchinson Hatch.) He has an uncanny ability to do all the legwork and have all the pertinent information in front of him (including a few things he really doesn't think matter—such as that old love letter he retrieved from the trash basket which he's shown to no one) yet not be able to see the solution. He must present his findings to the Great Detective, who will then carefully explain to him what it all means. Left to his own devices, a Watson would march even farther down that path. And this *despite* the evidence.

Unlike other red herrings, Watsons never lie. But they have an unfortunate tendency to repeat anything they hear, so killers frequently whisper lies in their ears which they then naïvely perpetuate. This is what trips up the new mystery reader. He assumes trusty Watson would not be gulling him, when, in fact, he is.

Although we're calling this specific breed of red herring a Watson, after the most famous of them all, it really ought to have another name, reflecting the first character who represented the type. The problem here is, the first one was so dim-witted he neglected to tell us his name. You probably remember him, though, as a chronicler of Dupin's tales. Yes, Edgar Allan Poe, originator of most whodunit conventions, also gave us the friend of minus intellectuality. Why he entrusted this oaf with the task of narrating the stories is beyond our comprehension, but others have followed, and it's a safe bet if the narrator isn't the killer, he's the hero's best friend, the red herring *par excellence.*

Frederick Arnold says that since he has two first names, he is his own best friend.

SECRET HANDSHAKES

Don't you secretly suspect if you shook hands with Nero Wolfe it would feel like the doughnut after all the jelly's been squeezed out?

Don't you secretly suspect if you shook hands with Lord Peter Wimsey it would feel like a baby's bottom that's been sprinkled with talc?

Don't you secretly suspect if you shook hands with James Bond it would feel like you'd been stirred, not shaken?

Don't you secretly suspect if you shook hands with Miss Marple it would feel like a skein of wool?

Don't you secretly suspect if you shook hands with Sherlock Holmes it would feel like Basil Rathbone?

Don't you secretly suspect if you shook hands with Stephen King it would feel like something green and slimy and the minute you let go, your arm would fall off?

THE MYSTERIOUS STRANGER

Ahab Pepys

His name is Legion, he's from out of town and he subsists on a paltry diet of red herrings tossed his way by an uncaring author with plans for his impending disappearance—in a crowd.

His middle name, of course, is Godsend, defined in the mystery lexicon as a device visited on the reader from out of the blue for the simple reason that the plot was desperate for it.

His surname is X and his resumé shows deployment as a whisper in the fog, a threat on the phone, a shadow on the walk, a knock on the door and even, alas, a shot in the dark. He's been down on his luck, just passing through, part of the mob scene and sometimes, gloriously, the brains behind the job.

Considering how often we bump into him, the most peculiar thing about him is that the impression he leaves is extraordinarily vague: a muffled voice, hard to tell whether it's male or female; a dim outline, at once short and tall, fat and lean, kindly and menacing; a blur, racing away before we can ask why it's thrust this ticket in our hand, why it's shoved us toward the path of the oncoming bus, why it alone imparts that little piece of trivia that is the key to the case.

Inconsistent the mysterious stranger may be, but he is adamant on one point: he does not sidle in unnoticed; he has the whole town talking.

Example. Someone is buying up all the property on the North Side. The Ramseys sold first, to a broker acting, he said, on behalf of a client who preferred remaining nameless. (That's our friend, the mysterious stranger.) Next the Weatherfords sold out, then the Weisses, the Cobbs and the Robelard-Finns, and all to the same broker, still acting on behalf of the same unspecified someone. When seven more parcels of land were snapped up, the mayor grew nervous and called up the broker. "If you don't mind my asking," he asked, "is there something going on here that I should know about, and just who is behind it?" The broker was none too helpful: he'd been dealing, he confessed, with purchase orders slipped under his door and a bank in Geneva that issued checks in substantial amounts at the drop of a number, not a name. (Switzerland, come to think of it, is the spiritual homeland of the mysterious stranger. An entire country that refuses to divulge names. But back to our story.) Panic has now hit Smalltown. Will the mysterious stranger want all the houses? Will the bad side of town now become the good side? Mass hysteria prevails and the scramble is on to unload houses, stores, schools, factories, even churches, before disaster—nameless, faceless—hits. And guess who's buying up at rock-bottom prices? Not bad, considering the mysterious stranger has yet to open his mouth to close a deal. Who cares that in the end the mysterious stranger turns out to be a local with a little inside information? Certainly not the author.

Another example. The young wife is alone in the house. It's late at night. The phone rings. She picks up. "Hello. Hello. Hello?" she says. No one answers, but

Harriet and Simon discuss matters with utmost propriety.

INAPPROPRIATE LAUGHTER

Some things are never funny, such as: a Lord kept waiting two hours by his guests; a portly toe besieged by gout; a proposal refused for the umpteenth time; long johns joined to knock-knees; a valuable cameo gone missing.

someone's out there breathing at her. Very ominously. Who else but our mysterious stranger, who says more without saying a word than most husbands and wives manage to confide to each other in a lifetime—which, by the by, this wife on the line hasn't much left of. Who's on call as suspect number one? Of course.

Still another example. The trial has dragged on for weeks. Everyone is bored, not to mention numb. The judge can barely prop himself awake on the bench. The jury is, collectively, rummaging in its pocket for a stick of gum.

The lawyers on both sides are hemming, hawing and idly padding their expense accounts. Even the accused is acting a tad blasé, which is somewhat remarkable in that it's his life in the balance. Suddenly there's a commotion at the back of the courtroom: a mysterious stranger enters. She sashays down the aisle with all the subtlety of Bette Midler playing bride. The judge is so enraptured, he raps his knuckles with the gavel. The jury swallows its gum. The lawyers rifle through briefs trying to identify the surprise visitor. And the victim, he stares, shakes, sweats, trembles, blanches, gulps, collapses in sobs and finally confesses. All this and the mysterious stranger has not said a word. Clearly, this intense a plot device, generating excitement and retribution with little more effort than it takes to wiggle, is too good for an author to throw out. Never mind the reader has different feelings about it, that's immaterial.

There are five textbook-perfect mysterious strangers. Control, in any spy novel you care to name; the bankrupt private eye's first client on any rainy Tuesday morning; the police informer who hangs out on the street corner in the beginning of the book and at the end is flat on his back, pennies on his eyes, in the gutter; the witness held incommunicado at the hotel by the Federal Witness Protection Agency (which will later "misplace" the stranger); and the ghost drifting gauzily along the north turret. Women used to be mysterious, if not strangers, but since the advent of women's liberation they're no longer allowed that prerogative.

How can we distinguish a mysterious stranger from a mere minor character? By the whiff of red herring he extrudes, but of course.

Ahab Pepys is known to many as the face on the post office wall.

HOMOSEXUALS
UNIVERSAL SCAPEGOATS

Joseph Hansen

Dave Brandstetter, death claims investigator for Medallion Life Insurance, first drove up a storm-lashed California canyon and into the awareness of mystery readers in 1970, in a novel called *Fadeout.* He was not the first homosexual detective in fiction; that distinction belongs to Pharaoh Love.

Pharaoh Love, however, is no hero. In *A Queer Kind of Death,* he becomes infatuated with the murderer and covers up the young man's guilt. This makes for lively plotting in a savagely funny novel, but in no way upgrades the traditional treatment of homosexuals in detective fiction. Pharaoh Love is thoroughly corrupted by his sexuality, and the other homosexuals in the novel make up a veritable freak show, as they do in Baxt's two sequels. In one, a boy is called "Lad, A Dog." Where does comedy leave off and cruelty begin?

The hideous little assassin in *The Maltese Falcon* is tagged a "gunsel" by Dashiell Hammett. The word means "homosexual." It has nothing to do with guns, though a thousand writers afterward thought so. Raymond Chandler, on the evidence of his letters, had about the same regard as Hammett for homosexuals. And in the Chandler novels they are without exception weaklings, cowards, degenerates.

Ross Macdonald kept the faith of his literary godfathers, Hammett and Chandler, and did his share of exploiting homosexuals for their negative value. His handling of a pair of middle-aged, little-theater type homosexuals in *The Drowning Pool* may pretend at sophisticated tolerance, but adds up to a very thinly veneered disgust.

Unlikely as it seems, the homosexuals in Dorothy L. Sayers' mysteries come out of the same stock bin. Her sneers may be masked by British politeness, but the contempt is there. Other great ladies of the Golden Age of Detective Fiction were equally disdainful. Ngaio Marsh often included a willowy male actor or ballet dancer in her London backstage mysteries for our condescending amusement. And a thatched cottage in a cozy Agatha Christie village sometimes housed a pair of tweedy ladies in sensible shoes who bred dogs and, it went without saying, slept together—poor things.

Still, it is only fair to remember that until after World War II stereotypes flourished in mystery fiction. A few years ago, a Los Angeles radio station asked me to choose twenty-two mystery short stories to read on the air. I accepted eagerly, piled up a mountain of books and began reading. What I met with, in the work of highly regarded and fondly remembered writers, sickened me. Their pages and plots teemed with ignorant shiftless blacks, avaricious Jews, unscrupulous Orientals, cutthroat latinos, wispy females, every insensitivity imaginable. It took a a lot of reading to locate twenty-two stories not laced with grossly offensive characters and passages.

If you weren't a white male of north European ancestry and equipped with at least one extra Y chromosome, you were fair game for abuse by writers, male and female, good, bad, indifferent, whose cast-iron Underwoods filled the pulps and slicks of the 1920's , '30s and '40s with thrillers—until the Anti-Defamation League and the NAACP cried, "Enough!"

The niggers, spics, kikes, chinks, greasers, treacherous redskins disappeared from radio, film, television, and from the pages of *Dime Detective* and *Saturday Evening Post* alike. But while Stepin Fetchit blacks faded from the movies, Franklin Pangborn, the prissy hotel clerk, and Grady Sutton, the sissified bank teller, remained. While Mr. Kitzel, the caricature Jew of the Jack Benny program, was silenced, the pansy department store floorwalker—"You're breathing on my car-*na*-tion!"—was not. Queers were still good for a laugh, and who was going to complain?

Queers were also still good as twisted murderers and cringing suspects. Instances are far too numerous to list, but the weird young man in Joyce Porter's *Dover One,* who disjoints his victims and stores them in the deep freeze, leaps to mind. As does the poor victim in Bart Spicer's *Act of Anger,* who is deemed so loathsome for flirting with a lad that a jury acquits his killer.

But all the books I have mentioned were published years ago. Surely things have changed. They haven't. In *Stick,* Elmore Leonard gives us Chucky, a fat, cowardly, murdering drug dealer, quiveringly enslaved by the very product he peddles. Evidently worried that Chucky isn't sufficiently repulsive, Leonard adds a clincher: the creature is homosexual. Wouldn't you know it? His homosexuality is never proved, has no function in the plot, but we are frequently reminded of it. No, times have not changed.

The often thoughtless, always callous, sometimes vicious treatment of homosexuals in mystery novels began to anger me a long time ago. Why must reading mysteries, which I enjoy, so often entail enduring slurs at myself and my kind? And what could I do about it? I was a writer with a string of pseudonymous paperback novels to my credit, all of which dealt straightforwardly with homosexuals and how they really live. One of these was even a mystery. So I had honed my skills.

I went to the typewriter determined to correct in *Fadeout* as many misconceptions about homosexuals as I could in fifty thousand words. The idea that homosexuals are fit only to be hairdressers I swung at first, giving my hero a job the mystery tradition gives only to the manliest of men. Homosexuals are said to be unable to maintain lasting love relationships. Dave's with Rod Fleming had endured over twenty years, ending only with Rod's death from cancer—this in contrast to the nine marriages and eight divorces of Dave's thoroughly masculine father. On these and other points in the

---

REALISTIC PORTRAYALS

Vermilion and *Cobalt,* Nathan Aldyne
Family Trade, James Carroll
The Second Curtain, Roy Fuller
Fadeout, Death Claims, Troublemaker,
The Man Everybody Was Afraid of,
Skinflick, Gravedigger and *Backtrack,*
    Joseph Hansen
Looking for Rachel Wallace, Robert B.
    Parker
On the Other Hand, Death, Richard
    Stevenson
Dead Man's Thoughts, Carolyn Wheat
A Reason to Kill, Eve Zaremba

UNSYMPATHETIC CHARACTERS

Dress Gray, Lucian K. Truscott, IV
Still Missing, Beth Gutcheon
Death Drop, B.M. Gill
The Talk Show Murders, Steve Allen

ANTI-SEMITISM AND THE MYSTERY

For all the reasons a reader may be drawn to English mysteries of the Twenties and Thirties—nostalgia, a certain elegance of phrasing and tone, that classic plotting—there is an equally good reason for slamming the books shut and tossing them from one's home: a strain of anti-Semitism that runs deep, constant and pervasive. Most of the better-known authors are guilty of it, even the two whom we might innocently expect to be exempt from such palaver, Dorothy L. Sayers and G.K. Chesterton. For a woman who spent the latter part of her life composing religious tracts and a man who chose to make his sleuth a cleric, these two showed remarkable insensitivities toward Jews. The obvious question is why, and the answer—whichever that might be—still leaves their attitudes indefensible. Is it sufficient to suggest that they were merely reflecting society's opinion? That, by and large, most Jews at the time were tradesmen who were never invited in the front door, who were, if you will, not even "downstairs," but rather "outside," thus perfectly suitable for snubbing? Yes . . . well, snubbing is one thing, slurring quite another, and the number of gratuitous insults dangled upon Jews in these books quite exceeds the reprimands, slights and minor indignities suffered on anyone else. Something more powerful is operating here than a casual disdain of the outsider; it is a virulent, insidious attempt to verbally annihilate a race. Let the psycho-historians figure out reasons. But let us no longer blithely ignore the anti-Semitism Sayers and Christie and the bulk of the Golden Agers perpetrated. It is as much a part of their books as the corpse. And just as unlikable. And, in most cases, even more offensive.

novel, I was not joking. I was trying to set the record straight at last.

The fact is, homosexuals are as various as any other group of men and women. There are the strong and the weak, the decent and the corrupt, the bitter and the forgiving, the successful and the failures, the timid and the brave. And in the Brandstetter books I have tried to depict them in their infinite variety, along with the so-called normal folk with whom their lives, like it or not, are daily intertwined. I try always to be even-handed, never to exploit, to write apology or propaganda, but to mirror life faithfully, for better or worse—two of my homosexuls *are* murderers.

Dave Brandstetter is the only constant in these books. He is a deeply decent, caring man, ruthless when he has to be, with a strong sense of justice but able to temper justice with mercy. It upsets some reviewers that he can possess these virtues and still be homosexual. Old stereotypes die hard. But letters from strangers, and words from strangers when I am out among them, suggest that by persisting in what seems to me the unsensational revelation that homosexuals are much like everyone else, I have changed a few hearts and minds.

When writers fall back on ugly stereotypes, they betray their trust and make an already tough life tougher still. Whether mysteries or not, honest novels allow us for an hour or two to escape the confines of our familiar selves and, in effect, become someone else. Rarely in life can we know a real human being as completely as we come to know good fictional characters. When a writer scrupulously models his characters on the way men and women really are, he opens to his readers the opportunity to widen and deepen their understanding of others and themselves, and this can only make the world a gentler place for us all.

Joseph Hansen is the author of Backtrack.

THE DEVOUT
VICARS, CURATES AND RELENTLESSLY INQUISITIVE CLERICS

Catherine Aird

Clergy in the mystery are part of the literary tradition, even though they don't go back quite as far as Cain and Abel. This, the first murder of all, certainly began a long connection between religion and crime. Another Biblical link was forged a little later than the Old Testament—in the Apocrypha.

If you remember, it was the Apocrypha that included the two tales about the prophet Daniel which are said to be the original mysteries. The earlier was "The Tale of Susanna and the Elders," in which certain malicious charges were laid against the blameless Susanna; the prophet Daniel proved her innocence in the classical manner—by demonstrating that the evidence given by two separate accusers did not hang together. The second was "Bel and the Dragon," in which the miscreants were confuted by as nice a piece of circumstantial evidence as you'll find outside a crown court.

Daniel's successors in detection have been many and various—and ecumenical. Father Brown, the lovable little priest with the endearing traits of dowdiness, untidiness and a complete lack of pretension, was one of the first. Rabbi David Small is one of the latest. In between have come both Uncle Abner (a religious detective if ever there was one) and a succession of vicars of the Church of England—to say nothing of an archdeacon or two. (Promotion comes late to fictional clergymen engaged in solving mysteries; they have to be satisfied with another sort of preferment.)

But what they have all had in common, these detective clergy, is the ability to reason. If they had faith as well, and I am sure they did and do, all I can say is that it doesn't come into the story the same as their deductions do. It is their logic that we admire. Cogent argument seems to come so easily to these incumbents of the page. Be this a Jesuitical nicety or a rabbinical pilpul, clerical detectives indeed convince us.

Of course, they have advantages over other amateur sleuths. A thorough grounding in theology, for a start. After all, what is the modern detective story but an extension of the mediaeval morality play? That earlier art form was simpler—the Devil invariably entered from stage left, and you always knew who he was—but it is essentially the same. Our hero now seems able to recognise the Bad'n or the Rotten Apple in the Barrel or the Sinner or the Unfortunate Victim of Circumstance (according to period) with the same sure facility.

Not only do our clerical heroes instinctively know the difference between right and wrong, but they have a professional interest in making sure that Good Triumphs over Bad in the last chapter—if not sooner. Then there's all this experience of the confessional. The Depths of Human Wickedness have already been plumbed by these unshockable men, and this is a great help in the detective story. They have cut their milk teeth on the World, the Flesh and the Devil, so by comparison little foibles like Wine,

DIVINE READING

Catherine Aird, *The Religious Body.* C.D. Sloane finds Convent life a challenge.

E.M.A. Allison, *Through the Valley of Death.* Brother Barnabas investigates death in his monastery in 1379.

Robert Barnard, *Blood Brotherhood.* St. Botolph's Monastery beset visitors.

Douglas Clark, *Death After Evensong.* Masters is called to the Vicarage.

Edmund Crispin, *Holy Disorders.* Gervase Fen is at home in English cathedral town.

Dorothy Salisbury Davis, *A Gentle Murderer.* N.Y.C. Priest, Father Duffy, faces difficult decisions over a parishioner.

Colin Dexter, *Service of All the Dead.* D.C.I. Morse at St. Frideswides.

Umberto Eco, *The Name of the Rose.* William of Baskerville is sent to a Franciscan Abbey (Italy) to investigate, 1327.

Michael Gilbert, *The Black Seraphim.* James Scotland, pathologist, takes medical leave to visit Melchester Close.

——, *Close Quarters.* Melchester Cathedral's Dean invites his police nephew to straighten the wayward in his Close.

Dorothy Gilman, *A Nun in the Closet.* Sister John and Sister Hyacinthe investigate property willed to their order.

Joe Gash, *Priestly Murders.* Sgt. Terry Flynn has problems with Chicago's South Side Church.

S.T. Haymon, *Death and the Pregnant Virgin.* D.I. Ben Jurnet faces worshippers at the Shrine of Our Lady of Promises.

——, *Ritual Murder.* A choirboy's murder challenges D.I. Ben Jurnet.

Tim Heald, *Unbecoming Habits.* Simon Bogner, of London's Board of Trade, is needed at the Beaubridge Friary.

Isabelle Holland, *A Death at St. Anselms.* A woman administrator, Rev. Claire Aldington, finds her Episcopalian responsibilities weighty indeed.

William X. Kienzle, *Assault with Intent; Death Wears a Red Hat; Kill and Tell; Mind over Murder; The Rosary Murders; Shadow of Death;* Father Koestler, of the Detroit Diocese, all volumes.

Ralph McInerny, *Bishop as Pawn; The Grass Widow; Her Death of Cold; The Loss of Patients; Lying Three; Second Vespers; Seventh Station; Thicker than Water;* Father Dowling, St. Hilary's Catholic Parish, Illinois—all volumes.

Sister Carol Anne O'Marie, *A Novena for Murder.* Sister Mary Helen, retired professor, is now at S.F. College for Women, researching more than books.

Ellis Peters, *The Devil's Novice; The Leper of St. Giles; Monk's Hood; A Morbid Taste for Bones; One Corpse Too Many; St. Peter's Fair; The Sanctuary Sparrow; The Virgin in the Ice.* Brother Cadfael of the Benedictine Monastery, St. Peter and St. Paul (1139), featured in each.

Monica Quill, *And There Was Nun.* Sister Mary Teresa, and two other nuns, in their Frank Lloyd Wright house in Chicago, are the last of their order—but are not above getting involved in whatever comes.

John Reeves, *Murder Before Matins.* Insp. Coggins and Sgt. Sump in the Tathwell Abbey affair. (Toronto)

Walter J. Sheldon, *The Rites of Murder.* Features Bishop Paul J. Burdock—Washington, D.C.

Charles Merrill Smith, *The Reverend Randollph and the Avenging Angel; The Fall from Grace; The Holy Terror; The Unholy Bible; The Wages of Sin.* Series features Randollph, of the Church of the Good Shepherd, Chicago. Prior to becoming an Episcopalian, he was with the L.A. Rams and played quarterback.

Women and Song come as very small beer indeed. They've heard it all before.

This isn't the only advantage they have. Besides being well versed in the ways of the world—at a respectable distance, of course—their occupation leaves them time and energy in which to pursue villains. Evensong never seems to clash with a dénouement when the amiable Archdeacons of Thorp and Garminster, creations of C.A. Arlington, D.D., are solving a gentle mystery. This author, incidentally, was at one time Dean of Durham—a novel combination of Dean and Chapter.

Another real-life clergyman who wrote detective stories was Monsignor Ronald A. Knox. It was he who in 1928 laid down the famous "Ten Commandments" (it is quite difficult to get away from the analogy, isn't it?) for the writing of detective stories.

Yet the peculiar situation of all these literary men of the cloth is even more felicitous than their just having ample time between Matins and Compline. Their parochial duties actually give them a good reason for being where the action is. This far from small matter is normally a sore trial to those authors whose detectives are amateur—but it is no problem with the ordained. It might only be collecting for the organ fund; it is more likely to be making arrangements for that uniquely English form of infighting known as the parish fete. But somehow it always seems perfectly appropriate for the vicar to be there, whatever the setting.

This goes for where you will find him, too—cottage or castle—for nothing so spans social life as the visiting list of the parish incumbent. Not only is there no one quite so well placed to appreciate the passion aroused by, say, the church flower-arranging rota, but there is no one better to whom the confession of the murderer in the last-chapter-but-one can be made. A case, you might say, of a good living meeting a bad dying . . .

Then there's the distaff side. There may as yet be few detective nuns (though the play *Bonaventure* by Charlotte Hastings comes very near to this), but the

When healthy as a horse is no longer applicable . . .

convent has been used more than once as a setting for murder. And we must never forget it is the wool from black sheep that is used for nun's veiling.

But there: I've nearly left out something important. Most amateur detectives have a love-life that—let's face it—can get in the way. More often than not it comes between the Mountie and his getting his man and, at the very least, distracts the mind from the serious business of crime. Far easier the division of the human species into men, women and clergy. By all means, let the curate cast a flirtatious eye at the leading lady in the choir, but leave us with the certainty that, however much our hero may pontificate about being sure that other people's sins will find them out, he hasn't committed any of his own. Unfrocking has no place here: *Clerical Error*, C.E. Vulliamy's tale about a clergyman, concerns something quite different.

Some detective stories in the canon (if you'll forgive the allusion) go further still and are actually set in the church. Charles Dickens began this with his *Mystery of Edwin Drood*. We don't, in fact, know what was to be found in the crypt of Cloisterham Cathedral and now never shall because the author died before finishing the book—but naturally we suspect the worst. Another book centred round a cathedral is Michael Gilbert's neatly titled *Close Quarters*. The town is Melchester, and the setting is what may be aptly called the other sort of precinct: a cathedral close.

Men of the cloth don't always come into the story in a detective capacity. Dorothy L. Sayers, a noted theologian in her own right, left the detection to Lord Peter Wimsey but gave us two affectionate pen portraits of Anglican clergymen. The Reverend Theodore Venables in *The Nine Tailors* and the Reverend Simon Goodacre (Magdalen College, Oxford) in *Busman's Honeymoon* are happy specimens of their kind—and Goodacre is a

nice name for a clergyman when you consider that the churchyard is often known as "God's Acre." (Venables isn't far from Venerable, either.)

Emma Lathen, in her customary pithy way, gives us an evocative vignette of a Catholic priest, Father Doyle, taking action after a murder in *Ashes to Ashes*. Josephine Tey in *Brat Farrar* goes further. She allows her rector, George Peck, to destroy evidence that would have spoilt what in a detective story can't very well be called a happy ending.

> *"George!" said Bee. "What became of the pen?"*
>
> *"The stylograph? I lost it."*
>
> *"George!"*
>
> *"Someone had to lose it, my dear. Colonel Smollett couldn't: he's a soldier, with a soldier's sense of duty. The police couldn't: they had their self-respect and their duty to the public to consider. But my conscience is between me and my God. I think they were touchingly grateful to me in their tacit way."*

And if you like the connection to be vicarious, remember that Conan Doyle's Sherlock Holmes appears at least twice in clerical disguise—in "The Final Problem" and "A Scandal in Bohemia."

So do read on. Preaching and detecting do go hand in hand in an acceptable plurality (even if only a bishop actually gains by translation). Whatever your theological persuasion, you must agree that Satan versus Godliness is the onlie begetter of the detective story. . .

Finally, brethren, let me assure you that Caesar's wife has nothing on your detective clergyman. Not only is he above suspicion but, dear reader, there is one thing in this uncertain world of which you can be absolutely sure: the Vicar didn't do it.

Catherine Aird lives in Canterbury and is the author of The Religious Body.

CRIMES

F eisty, aintcha? Think yer stayin' in there, well, yer not. Got me bloomin' clippin' shears all ready fer yer little roots and snip snip, ta ta, off yer go. Wi' such a talkin' ter as I just got, not bloody likely I'll let 'im find yer 'ere t'morrow.

"Purple, Whelks? Who said purple?" 'e says ter me. "I detest it, pull it all out before the post, will you?"

me, "Rembrandt's purple. Please be so kind as to inspire me with some purple along the walk."

Pinks, purples, them's all mad hatters. Oughtter be put away. Pave 'er over, fer all I care. Not me trade, after all; cobblin's mine and decent at it, too. Not that anyone's likely ter give me a chance again, bloomin' luck.

In once more and the key's thrown, they told me. Last chance now, Whelks, wi' the guv'nor 'ere. Give yer an opportunity ter get a clear name, who'm I ter say no? Couldn't stand it in, but maybe 'ere's worse.

Lady Teasdale takes her medicine whilst Harriet reads aloud Mrs. Beeton's suggestions for confining compost. 11:36 A.M.

Rosie breaks the second-best creamer. 10:45 A.M.

Well now, if 'e detests purple so much, whyn't 'e take it up wi' that fine sister of 'is and leave me be? "Painting purple this week, Whelks," she says ter

Town's more me sort. Good man, that Jock, maybe'll find me a spot near ter the pub. Need a little life, I do. Girls ter pinch, ter take ter me room. What's 'ere ain't worth missin' a snore.

Miss Becca's got the smell o' paint and Her Ladyship, ah, that's a rum one. That little Rosie ain't bad, but Jock's got 'is way and I don't mess wi' 'im, not when 'e's standin' the bill a bit, till I get a few bob ahead. T'other one, she's got marriage in 'er eye, scare me 'ere ter the

Liffey if I touch 'er. No, town's fer me, if I can sneak a bob or two.

Oh, look at this one comin', purple ter the nines again, and trailin' the Vicar. The saint and the stuck-up, them two, make a book of 'em. Every day 'e asks 'er fer a walk and she 'ands 'im the box and the paintin', and like as I can see, t'aint changed yet...just gettin' more purple. Haint the talent of a schoolgirl. Vicar finds 'er fascinatin'... just stares at 'er fer hours while she paints posies and says so sweet like wi' a trillin' "Now, Philip, yer in me light, please ter move." And 'e moves, bloody fool! Less borin' if 'e read the Good Book, yer would think, but 'e haint opened it yet 'cept ter quote fer 'er pleasure. Be glad when they go in the 'ouse; give me a bit by meself 'fore I takes off ter town.

Now, back ter yer, me lovelies, out yer comin'. Up. Up. Up. Gone fer t'day. Been walkin' 'ere, I see, by the window. Who'd be doin' that 'cept a no-good? Have ter climb over the bush ter get in there. Speak wi' Roudebush, I better, 'fore I gets ter town. Can't 'ave 'im

Becca catching the morning light, as is her wont. 10:30 A.M.

thinkin' I ain't takin' notice o' what's not right. Bugger's worse than 'Is Lordship. Never seen such airs, not even on the warders.

Now, who's that movin' about this time o' the mornin'? Must be one o' them nobs come down fer the do. What a muck-up yesterday. Colonel walkin' up the drive that much too late and the cousin not till even later. Rich ways ain't so polite, now, be they? Get me a lot wi' better manners when I finds me own spot. Do a punch-up if they treat me bad, see 'ow they like it.

Might be worth a couple o' bob ter me, this weekend. Shine up Colonel's boots after 'is ride, that oughtter count fer a bit. Don't look like much of a tipper, but the Lord'll see I gets me due. T'other gent's a proper one, ain't 'e? Spiffy fit ter see the Queen, and pants so tight 'e can't sit down. Guess that's what took 'im so long gettin' 'ere—'ad ter take little steps so's not ter tear 'em.

Gettin' on ter time fer puttin' me shears up and placin' away me shovels. Town's fer me. More'n ready fer me whistle-wetter, I be.

T'morrow, me beauties, t'morrow. Off wi' yer 'eads!

Simon and Lord T. discuss the appointment with the solicitor Monday next. 9:55 A.M.

LAUNDERING MONEY
Numbered Accounts and Other Tax Shelters

Stanley H. Brown

If there is a technical definition of "laundering," it probably goes something like this: the rerouting, or conversion in any way, of hot untaxed money or other assets into untraceable or apparently legitimate cash or assets. Needless to say, there are no textbooks on laundering; nor do bankers, lawyers or others connected with the money and its movements want to talk for the record on who does it or how.

What is known about the process comes pretty much from the few instances in which the authorities have managed to get people into court or before congressional committees. A small-time hustler named Jerry Zelmanowitz spent some time testifying before a Senate subcommittee on how he turned stolen securities into clean cash for the Mob. Until he came along (he would have us believe), your typical thief would keep the money, jewelry and other disposable assets but throw away whatever securities were stolen. Zelmanowitz says he changed all that by taking the securities to Europe, where he set up accounts in various banks, transferred money around by Telex to establish a pattern of legitimate transactions, then introduced his stolen stocks and bonds into the system he had set up. Typically, the stolen paper would be used as collateral for loans, the proceeds of which could then be invested for legitimate purposes. As long as the loans were outstanding, nobody paid any attention to the collateral sitting in the bank vaults.

Meanwhile, Zelmanowitz had created a nice pool of usable capital for his clients. They could repay or keep refinancing their debt, or even default on the loans and let the bank dispose of the collateral.

The trouble with this method is that some bank clerk might decide to check the numbers on the securities against lists of stolen property.

A couple of years ago Chemical Bank in New York discovered its facilities were being used for another kind of laundering. Employees of the bank were routinely changing the small, dirty bills that are the retail currency of the heroin trade. The $1 and $5 bills that come out of your wallet, or some old lady's snatched purse, are cumbersome to deal with. You can't fly down to Mexico with laundry bags full of money to buy more dope. So the dealers simply found themselves some bank employees who would exchange the small stuff for $50 and $100 bills. The bank lost nothing in the process, though the employees, against federal regulations in effect since 1974, failed to report the $10,000-plus transactions. What they also neglected was declaring as income the bribes they received from the dealers—about 1 percent of the money they laundered. The U.S. Attorney's office figures that more than $8 million in dirty cash was handled through Chemical Bank.

Any legitimate business that takes in a lot of cash provides a way to clean up dirty money. One thief used some of his money to buy a diner. He would relieve

The balmy Bahamas, where the banks are more crowded than the beaches, the vacationing embezzlers outnumber the common tourists.

the cashier, then put some cash in the till and ring up some phony sales. He gradually increased the amount of cash he would process, so as not to attract attention. When he wasn't satisfied with the rate of flow, he bought a second and then a third restaurant. Now he had a business big enough to allow him to travel lavishly on an expense account, ostensibly to scout out locations for other restaurants around the world.

Every method of laundering has endless variations. Many involve banks and corporate entities in such places as the island of Jersey and the Duchy of Liechtenstein. False but convincing identities abound—so much so that the U.S. Passport Office has been considering a tightening of the passport-issuing process. After all, you have only to get the real birth certificate of someone of your sex and age who is dead. One traveling representative of a crime syndi-

cate had more than twenty U.S. passports that he used as identification for opening foreign bank and securities accounts. He reasoned that since many billions of dollars move by Telex every day through the money markets of the world, no one bank would ever be able to sort out honest from crooked money.

Thus money can have a life of its own, irrespective of its origins. The purpose of laundering is to create that new identity. The most important element in the success of such operations seems to be patience. But that is also the trap, because if you've scarred your conscience by committing a heavy crime, you've already lost your patience with the straight and narrow. And once that happens, you're going to leave tracks. And they're going to get you.

Stanley H. Brown is the author of A Tale of Two Cities: Houston & Detroit.

U.S. STEAL

Hamilton Banks

MARTY NORMAN

Embarking on a life of crime is not one of those things you should assume you have a natural aptitude for; the consequences, if you don't have innate talent, are perfectly awful—namely, maximum-security prisons. That's if you're lucky enough to have the feds catch you. Private security forces can be brutal. As the saying goes, they take no prisoners.

There is, however, a guide for the illicitly inclined. Called the combat bookshelf, it's a catalogue of titles issued by Desert Publications.

Safe & Vault Manual

Referred to as the "safeman's bible," this slim volume includes every detail of every nook and cranny of myriad safes and vaults. Among the topics covered are hand, screw and key combination changing, drilling procedure, drilling locations, complete list of factory tryout combinations and a chapter on time locks.

Fitting Keys by Reading Locks

The latest in a long series of locksmithing manuals, this one explaining how to "eyeball" a lock, then make a key to fit. Clear, clean drawings. A nice companion to *The Lock Pick Design Manual,* which was originally designed for use by the federal government to effect surreptitious entries.

Handcuffs

Just in case you don't learn your lessons well, this valuable pamphlet (approximately 50 pages) discusses handcuffs and shackles from as far back as the 1800's to those in service with U.S. marshals today.

Agent's Handbook of Black Bag Operations

Described as the book the "Watergate 5" should have read, this text details operational planning, plan of entry, operational considerations (entrances and exits), operational clothing requirements and a sample plan of action from an actual FBI memorandum detailing a "for-real" black bag job.

Hand-to-Hand Combat

A complete basic training course, including alertness exercises, silencing techniques, counters to knife attack, blows, kicks and throws. All this in six well-balanced lessons.

Techniques of Harassment

Sure-fire methods of exacting revenge or, as the catalogue states, "guerrilla warfare reduced to the lowest common denominator." No moral or legal assessment is made, they add, implying that one man can become an army, striking from the shadows to reduce his target to a veritable basket case. They do caution, however, that the book is for entertainment only. We say, make of it what you will.

Sun, Sand & Survival

True-life accounts of men who survived by grit alone, not expecting search parties to come looking. Of particular interest to those planning capers in Vegas or sojourns in the Bahamas is the listing of desert-survival techniques. Ideal for outwitting Southern Hemisphere elements.

Wiretapping

The contents include interception of a suburban residential telephone, interception of a firm's data communication to a computer service, and interception of conversations over the direct-distance dialing network between two specific individuals in different cities. A copy of existing wiretap laws has been appended.

Devil Dogs

An analysis of guard dogs, with chapters on obedience training, the dog as weapon, surprise attack training and the guarding of prisoners.

Hamilton Banks is a consultant to the Franklin Mint, the Denver Mint, the Philadelphia Mint, the Danbury Mint and the Pepper Mint.

COUNTERFEITING
THE ARTISTIC APPROACH
TO MONEY

Gerald Petievich

Quick, name the face on the fifty-dollar bill.

All counterfeiters believe in an outrageous fantasy: that they can, secretly, through their own efforts and with a few pieces of printing equipment, create wealth. Counterfeiters are dreamers. Their nemesis is the product itself. Like the man who spent a year building a boat and when he was finished realized it wouldn't fit through the door of his workshop, they always seem to forget that funny money can only be passed out one bill at a time.

In this age of modern printing methods, anyone with modest printing skills, a copy camera, a light table for making offset plates, an offset press and some paper can run off a million dollars or so in about a day's work. Most counterfeiters, unless they've "borrowed" a legitimate print shop for an evening, take great care to find a secret location for the printing to take place. They like to pick out-of-the-way spots where the rattle of the printing press won't draw attention. Some counterfeiters, in order to avoid the problems inherent in "borrowing" or renting a headquarters, choose to print right in their own homes and invariably discover that the best way to muffle the locomotive-like sound of the offset press is to place mattresses against the walls. Most of them think they're the

CAT BURGLAR'S KIT

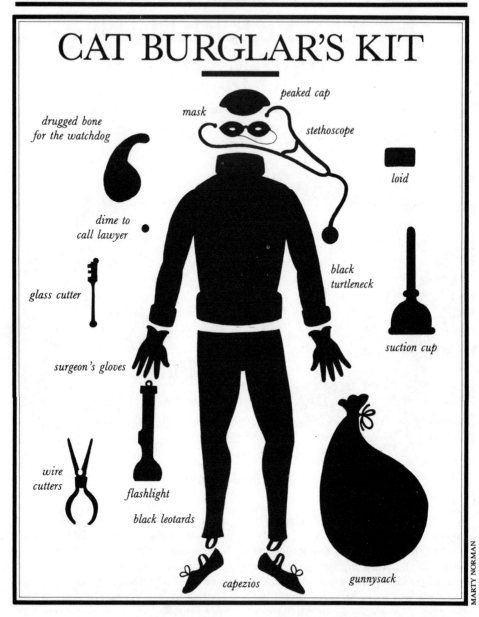

drugged bone
for the watchdog

mask

peaked cap

stethoscope

loid

dime to
call lawyer

glass cutter

black
turtleneck

suction cup

surgeon's gloves

wire
cutters

flashlight

black leotards

capezios

gunnysack

MARTY NORMAN

first to discover this technique, which, by the way, works fairly well.

The makers of funny money take steps to obtain printing equipment and other supplies clandestinely. They like to use an alias when purchasing their press or copy camera and sometimes hire a front man to purchase the paper and inks. In one instance, counterfeiters robbed a legitimate printer and drove off with his press and equipment in a rental truck; though they went to all this trouble to avoid leaving any trace of their activities, one of their group turned out to be a police informer and they were caught before the bills were printed.

Most counterfeiters are actually successful in printing counterfeit money. Almost all of them print at least a million dollars' worth. Whether they pick a million because of the magic sound of the word or because after all the trouble and risk it wouldn't be worth it to settle for less, the real problems start once the money rolls off the press. First, the counterfeiter realizes that fresh bills just don't look like the average bills in circulation. After experimenting, he will probably discover one of the common ways to make new bills look like old bills: some variation of soaking the money in a brackish solution of anything from coffee grounds to brake fluid and drying it by means of an oven or a hair or clothes dryer.

With the final product ready for the market, the counterfeiter makes his first attempt to set up a distribution network. He offers to sell the counterfeit bills for 10 to 20 percent of their face value and finds out that there are few buyers.

Counterfeiters are always after a "money man," someone with the funds to pay two or three hundred grand for the million in "queer." It takes only a short while for the more intelligent to figure out that a man who has two or three hundred thousand dollars of genuine money isn't about to trade it for *any* amount of counterfeit bills.

Then the counterfeiter decides to pass his first bill, and another problem presents itself: in order to make a profit from a pass, he must purchase something and this cuts into his profit margin. He then considers all the ways one might pass a whole stack of counterfeit bills. Each of these involves risk because large cash purchases invite scrutiny, and certainly one can't take a load of funny money into a bank and ask for change.

And then it hits him.

The green ink is still under his nails when it dawns on him that the only way to make a profit from the whole venture is to pass one bill at a time, making small purchases and keeping the change as a

---

THE PRISON PRINT SHOP

In California a counterfeiter who was serving time for printing his own version of a cashier's check successfully ran off ten thousand dollars in twenty-dollar bills while in the prison print shop, supposedly for vocational rehabilitation. With the help of his wife (he was allowed conjugal visits) he smuggled some of the bills out, and the first the authorities learned of his escapade was when an inmate who felt slighted at being left out of the caper informed the warden what was going on.

When questioned by the guards about his inside-the-walls counterfeiting venture, the culprit readily admitted his guilt and confessed that the hardest part was planning the print run: it had to be completed in one day, since the guards searched the shop every night without fail. He managed to print his bills in a three-hour period while the shop teacher was writing reports in his office.

G.P.

---

profit. Though disappointed that all the effort he's put into the project has resulted in such a prosaic endeavor, he starts his passing spree. From that point on, it's Russian roulette: how long can he pass bills without a clerk or shopkeeper detecting one and calling the police or the Secret Service?

When he gets caught, the counterfeiter realizes for the first time that it was the end itself that was his undoing—that detection was inevitable and that one single twenty-dollar bill is all it takes to send the whole effort into a tailspin.

Gerald Petievich is a special agent of the United States Secret Service and the author of The Quality of the Informant, To Live and Die in L.A. *and* To Die in Beverly Hills.

THE ARSENICAL BUN: OR, COURTING DISASTER ET CETERA

Edward Gorey

A is for Arsenic someone thought fun
To include in the icing on top of a bun.

B is for Bats that swoop out of the air
And squeaking inaudibly catch in one's hair.

C is for Cord of a moderate length;
To use it requires a dollop of strength.

D's for Dirigible seen in the distance:
It hangs in the sky with a baleful persistence.

E's for the East from where patently comes
A sinister person who lurks in the slums.

F is for Fog of the pea-soup variety
Whose onset occasions a vile impropriety.

G is for Genuine which this is not:
The real one's been taken to further a plot.

H is for Hoop and a stout one at that;
Its ricochet progress has knocked many flat.

I is for Idiot met on the moor;
He appears unperturbed, but the light's
    rather poor.

J is for Judge whose address to the jury
Is compounded of errors, omissions and fury.

K is for Kris with a blade that is wavy;
One wonders why somebody smeared it
    with gravy.

L's for a Letter that lay in a trunk;
Its contents explain how the dinghy was sunk.

M is for Madhouse wherein is confined
A lady whose friends drove her out of her mind.

N is for Nowhere, at least on the map;
Our being directed here looks like a trap.

O is for Opal, an ill-omened jewel:
The fate of its owner bids fair to be cruel.

P is for Precipice crumbling away;
Where was it you said she went
    walking today?

Q is for Quilt wrapped around a nude torso:
A sick-making sight that could scarcely
    be more so.

R is for Ray from a wicked invention
That dissolves at a distance the parts you
    don't mention.

S is for Suicide, so it would seem—
Then who was it uttered that unfinished
    scream?

T's for Tarantula; what a good chance
To study the native approach to the dance.

U's for Umbrella, discovered beneath
A piece of old sacking, along with some teeth.

V is for Vengeance planned far in the past;
Although often delayed, it's been taken at last.

W's for Water; it pours through the sluice;
Quite soon even swimming will be of no use.

X is for X, the mad genius of crime,
Who's escaped the police for the
    seventeenth time.

Y is for Yonder where something is lying
Which proves, seen close to, to be somebody
    dying.

Z is for Zero, the hour of doom;
It will strike any minute, but none knows
    for whom.

Suspects

Teacosy

Fishpaste Sandwiches

Victim

Clue

Doggy

Napkin

Teacup

EDWARD GOREY

Edward Gorey won a Raven from the Mystery Writers of America for set and costume design for Dracula.

POISON PHARMACOPOEIA

Rodger J. Winn, M.D.

There's no accounting for taste. To guide you through the toxicologic data, we offer the following scenarios and their appropriate poisons.

The classic poison: arsenic. Often called "inheritance powder" because of the tendency of family members to use it on each other, this white, odorless, tasteless powder is readily available in ant pastes and weed-killers, and provides a broad range of acute and chronic clinical spectra. For the get-it-done-in-a-hurry job, a dose of about 1 gram is more than enough. Within 3–4 hours the victim lies deathly ill, with vomiting and diarrhea followed in 24–72 hours by death from circulatory collapse. A supersleuth may make a diagnosis on the basis of the characteristic garlic breath of the victim and can confirm his suspicions with a single urine specimen. If the diagnosis is made after death, analysis will utilize the victim's hair and nails for testing arsenic levels. For a slower death, a pinch of arsenic a day will lead to the victim's progressive weakness, baldness, development of roughened skin and characteristic white ridges of the nails (Aldrich-Mees lines). Eventually, the poor imbiber begins to experience hoarseness, a hacking cough, and sensations of cold and numbness in his limbs that can progress to permanent paralysis over a matter of years. The intriguing aspect of chronic arsenic poisoning as a homicidal modus operandi is that the poisoner may build up his own tolerance to arsenic by taking tiny amounts over a long period. (Careful, too much leads to death, not to tolerance.) Thus he may serve sumptuous suppers liberally spiked with arsenic and, unlike his victim, emerge horse-healthy. One should be warned, however, that arsenic does not always work: the historical example of this is Rasputin's refusal to react to the poison.

The horrible demise: strychnine. Within 15 minutes a fiend can relish the sight of his quarry racked by convulsions that lift him off the floor but still leave him fully conscious to suffer the excruciating pains of the powerful spasms. The lightest stimulation—the shining of a light, the gentle nudge of a foot—can set off another round of the bone-creaking contortions. Strychnine is for the victim you wish to torture before you kill. A most seriously unpleasant death.

Please pass the mushrooms: Amanita phalloides. The use of this deadly poison in a delectable package allows the poisoner to be well on his (or her) way to the hinterlands by the time the victim succumbs. Even the most sophisticated gourmet will not notice the tiny white gills and wartlike scales that differentiate the deadly *Amanita phalloides* from *Agaricus campestris,* the common, edible mushroom. Since cooking does not remove the toxins, a hot meal can be prepared without diminishing the deleterious effects. All is well and good for 12 hours before the onset of vomiting and diarrhea, which still may not require medical care for another 24 hours. By this time the patient may go into circulatory collapse. If he is lucky enough to escape thus far, you can be sure that in 3–4 days he will begin to turn yellow as his liver decays. A bonus to the poisoner is that unless the history of the mushroom meal is elicited—a nicety easily overcooked by the critically ill—tracing the poison source is very difficult.

The poison in the fake tooth: cyanide. Every spy worth his alias knows instant death is preferable to the tortures from his sadistic enemies. He bites down, and the convenient cyanide pellet embedded in his bridgework acts in a matter of seconds. This is due to cyanide's ability to bind the body's internal breathing apparatus. Found in nature in bitter almonds, and peach and apricot pits, the tip-off to cyanide's presence is the intense smell of bitter almonds on the victim's breath. Because the body cannot use the blood's oxygen, the skin of the individual turns a violent pink—this despite his difficulty in breathing. However, the combination of almond breath and bright pinkness can lead to an early diagnosis, and a quick-witted hero can rescue the incipient corpse with an amyl nitrite pearl.

The blowpipe poison: curare. Isolated from *Chondrodendron tomentosum,* curare blocks the spread of impulses from the nerve to the muscle, thereby paralyzing the victim. Minutes after the injection (usually by a curare-dipped dart, since curare is not effective if eaten) there is a flushing of the face and a soft cough. The muscle paralyses start in the head so that the poisonee may have drooping of the eyelids, double vision because of weak eye muscles, difficulty swallowing due to secondary throat-muscle paralyses and, finally, respiratory failure due to his inability to move the muscles of the ribs and diaphragm. Though almost impossible to trace after death, the effects of curare are instantly reversible by the intravenous injection of one ampule of Prostigmin.

Come into my parlor: the black widow. This petite little lady, about half an inch long with an hourglass on her belly, spends much of her time in unsavory places (privies), and so genitals and buttocks are favorite attack sites. The sharp

THE DOCTOR'S LITTLE BLACK BAG

The tireless, faithful family practitioner is a walking arsenal, equipped with:

Insulin—to drive down the blood sugar, causing convulsions and death.

Potassium—to slow the heartbeat and eventually cause it to stop.

Calcium—to send the victim into kidney failure and coma.

Barbiturates—to fatally slow the metabolism.

Amphetamines—to irrevocably speed up the metabolism.

Oxygen—to remove the drive to breathe in a victim with emphysema of the lungs, resulting in a condition known as carbon dioxide narcosis.

Not quite in the little black bag is the *air bubble,* but who better to inject it than the physician?   R. W.

bite is similar to the slight tingling of a needle and may possibly go unnoticed. The pain begins in one half-hour as the poison affects the nerve endings. The ascending cramplike sensations starting in the legs or abdomen eventually become severe spasms; if touched, the victim's abdomen has a boardlike rigidity. (This mimics closely the clinical picture of a perforated ulcer, and medical evaluation may go totally down the wrong path.) The patient is anxious, in a panic, and appears acutely ill since he is bathed in a cold sweat and has a thready pulse. The severe spasms last a day, then slowly subside over the next 48 hours. Death is rare, however, from a single bite. Perhaps it would be best to have several of these venomous females on hand.

Another troublemaker is the South American brown spider, recognized by the violin markings on its back. The bites of this Latin import are very painful and become agonizing after 8 hours, leaving a large, swollen, black-and-blue area. The venom attacks the blood cells in about 36 hours, rupturing them so that the victim passes urine dark with the breakdown products of his hemoglobin. He progresses to a state of jaundice, kidney failure and shock.

Vapors through the vent: carbon monoxide and nerve gas. Carbon monoxide has the advantage of accessibility for our would-be assassin. This odorless, tasteless gas is formed from the incomplete combustion of carbon products such as coke or charcoal, and it takes little technical knowledge to hook a tube from an automobile exhaust pipe into a room vent or to leave a low-lit hibachi in a room for heat, enabling the gas to do its insidious job. Carbon monoxide has a tremendous affinity for the body's hemoglobin, binding closely and tightly to it so there is no room for the blood to carry the life-supporting oxygen. Thus, although the victim actually gets enough oxygen, he is unable to deliver it to his tissues and dies from lack of it. Of the two stages of deterioration, the first is characterized by headaches, giddiness, increasing shortness of breath with exertion, and ringing in the ears. This progresses to a drunken condition, with agitation and confusion, during which there is a noticeable impairment of judgment; though the victim knows something is wrong, he makes no attempt to leave the noxious environment. (Even nicer for

ESOTERIC POISONS

Nobody knows them better than Douglas Clark, who has tinkered with castor-oil beans (*Premedicated Murder*), peppercorns (*Golden Rain*), salad oil (*The Gimmel Flask*) and plain old water (*Sick to Death; Dread Water*). Runner-up in the exotica contest would be V.C. Clinton-Baddeley, who, in *Death's Bright Dart,* concocted a poison of ant's brew. Third place goes to Alisa Craig for her satisfying botulism endeavor, *A Pint of Murder.*

The delinquent dab.

Dispensary contents (itemised account drawn up by Harriet):
Caroid and bile salts, 12 tablets. For neuralgia attacks. (Purchased over the counter, Boots Chemists, Upper Slaughter.)
Atropine drops. Combats redness in eyes, hand tremors. (Prescription authorized by Bentley Cummings, RCMD. Chemist's registry signed by H. Lovelorn.)
Soporific (dosage: 1 tsp. per cup of black tea before bedtime).
Tincture of Amaretto and Benedictine, for sipping (eases melancholy, despondency). On hand in litres.

Lady Teasdale's dispensary.

the would-be assassin is the fact that if the victim recovers, he generally has complete amnesia and can offer no incriminating evidence.) In the second stage, the skin turns a shade known as cherry red and breathing becomes more labored, occasionally exhibiting a Cheyne-Stokes pattern: periods of 30 seconds of no breathing followed by 6–8 rapidly increasing deep breaths, then again the absence of breathing. The victim begins to twitch, convulses, then slips into unconsciousness and probably death, just prior to which his body temperature may rise to 108°. Death usually comes in the first 2 days after massive exposures but may be delayed as long as 3–8 days. Even if the victim recovers, his troubles are not over: late-occurring sequelae include severe psychological reactions, i.e., overtly psychotic behavior.

Nerve gas is indicated for the more deadly *coup de grace.* Killers with names such as Tabun, Sarin or T-46, Soman, DFP or DCP, all work in like manner. They prevent the breakdown of acetylcholine, which transmits impulses from the nerves to the muscles, and thus induce hyperexcitability in the victim. These substances are colorless, basically odorless, and can be inhaled or absorbed by skin. The initial symptoms are runny nose, wheezing and chest tightness, followed by excessive salivation, inability to tolerate light and, finally, paralysis and death. Old gases may take 20 minutes to work, but newer improvements have cut down the time, making the administration of the antidote—atropine—almost impossible. A particularly sadistic scenario may find the victim in possession of a syringe filled with the antidote, but too paralyzed to squeeze the plunger and save himself.

EMERGENCY ALERT

Josephine Bell relinquished her medical practice in the mid-Fifties, but her mystery medical career carries on—notably with *Stroke of Death,* concerning a country M.D., and *The Trouble in Hunter Ward,* in which St. Edmunds Hospital comes in for its share of problems. Sarah Kemp's M.E., Dr. Tina May, exists in *No Escapee* and Michael Gilbert's pathologist James Scotland is on medical leave in *The Black Seraphim.* Should the kids come down with something, try Edward Candy's Royal College of Pediatricians (*Bones of Contention*) or Bantwich-Bannister Children's Hospital (*Which Doctor*). If it seems you haven't a prayer for survival, how about medical missionary Dr. Mary Finney, whom Matthew Head sent to Africa (*The Cabinda Affair*) and Paris (*Murder at the Flea Club*)? If your pet takes sick, Barbara Moore suggests an appointment with Gordon Christy, her doctor of veterinary medicine (*The Doberman Wore Black*).

The gardener's caper: rat poisoning. As any sly weekend gardener knows, rat poison offers the convenience of the nearest hardware store and a believable alibi—one needed it to tend the weeds and the rodents, didn't one? For human as well as furry fare-thee-wells, there are two effective poisons: thallium, one of the leading homicidal agents in the world, and the warfarin drugs.

Thallium has been removed from U.S markets since 1965 because of its lethality, but it is readily available in European settings. Odorless and tasteless, the chemical blends superbly with sugared grain, making a delectable feast for rodents and a taste tidbit for those humans with a sweet tooth. The action is slow, first declaring itself with diffuse pain and severe constipation 3–4 days after consumption. Supersleuth can make a diagnosis of it at this early stage by detecting a peculiar dark pigmentation around the roots of the hair. During this period the victim is often thought to be hysterical or psychologically disturbed rather than poisoned. In the second or third week after ingestion the victim begins losing his hair, not only on his head but also on his body—except for the middle third of his eyebrows and his pubic hair. His skin appears dry and scaly, his heart beats rapidly and various nerves become paralyzed so that his eyelids may droop, his feet drag, blindness ensue. Ultimately, death occurs with pneumonia and congestion of the lungs. Like arsenic, thallium can be added in small dabs and the homicide accomplished over a period of months.

In the United States rat poison has been replaced mainly by warfarin, which interferes with the blood-clotting system. The victim exhibits signs of increasing bleeding such as nosebleed (epistaxis), gum bleeding (gingival hemorrhages), black-and-blue marks (ecchymosis), bloody urine (hematuria), bloody vomit (hematemsis) and bloody bowel movements (melena and hematochezia). A disadvantage to the evildoer is that this poison affects humans only slightly, so that large amounts are needed. The potion does mix well with corn porridge, however, and a series of good hearty breakfasts can do the job. The antidote would be large doses of vitamin K.

Rodger Winn is a physician in New Jersey.

HOW TO KILL CARDIOVASCULARLY

Millie B. Fitt

Things the Health Club never taught you:

- The Marjorie Craig Face-Lift
- The Jack LaLanne Lip-Smacker
- The Suzy Chaffee Chatter-Box
- The Jackie Sorensen Last Gasp
- The Charles Atlas Strong-Arm
- The Richard Simmons Gut Reaction
- The La Costa Money Belt
- The Prudden (Bonnie, Suzy) 1–2 Punch
- The Victoria Principal Callous Dallas Treatment
- The Golden Door Slam
- The Elaine Powers Power Play
- The Joe Weider Muscle-In
- The Linda Evans Long-Suffering Technique
- The Arnold Schwarzenegger Barbarianism
- The Bruce Lee Kickback
- The Jane Fonda Stomp

Millie B. Fitt bellyaches.

FEROCIOUS DOOMSDAY WEAPONS
SARCASM AND THICK WRISTS

Warren Murphy

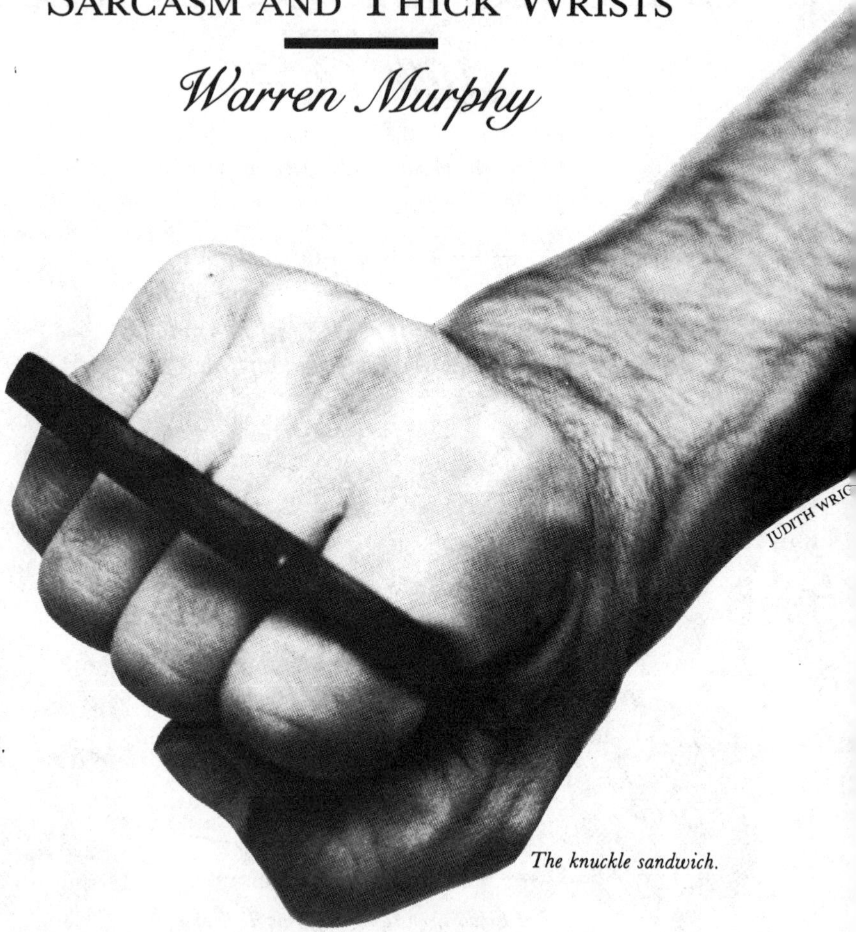

The knuckle sandwich.

A wise man (from the Los Angeles *Times*) once said the *Destroyer* books were "hilarious satire." Another wise man (also from the West Coast, but let's not draw inferences) called the series "a mad parody on the [splatter] genre." Dick Sapir and I—we created the series a zillion titles ago—wouldn't mind if they lobbed more encomiums our way. Meanwhile we'll survive, which is more than can be said for most who meet up with

Remo and his trainer, Chiun, a carping, racist, eighty-year-old Korean who is reigning Master of Sinanju, an ancient house of assassins-for-hire.

Though given over to death and the piling up of bodies, the Destroyer's violence is curiously bloodless and ungraphic, which prompts a lot of reader letters. Most of the mail is addressed to Chiun and answered by Chiun.

Occasionally, we peek.

Dear Exalted Master Chiun:

I want to learn the secrets of the art of Sinanju. Where can I learn to be like Remo?—Spencer, La Jolla, Calif.

Dear Botherer-of-His-Betters:

Have you tried a zoo?—Chiun, Master of Sinanju

Dear Exalted Master Chiun:

Really. I'm serious. Please give me an answer.—Spencer, La Jolla, Calif.

Dear Misbegotten Creature:

I presume from your unpronounceable and idiotic name that you are a barbarian white and therefore basically uneducable. You can never learn Sinanju.—Chiun, Master of Sinanju, Reduced to Being a Pen Pal

Dear Exalted Master Chiun:

But you taught Remo. Why not me? It's the wrists, isn't it? All the Destroyers say Remo does things because he has thick wrists, but they never say how. Climbing up buildings, wiping out gangs . . . it's the wrists, right?— Spencer, La Jolla, Calif.

Dear Spencer La Jolla, Calif.:

All that you think you know about Sinanju, you have learned from reading the so-called Destroyer series, written incompetently and inaccurately by two fat people who have grown wealthy off my labors. These two scribblers could look at a wheatfield and describe a train wreck, so what you think they have taught you about Sinanju is a mirage, a trickster's illusion. But I will make you a gift. The wrists have something to do with it. Breathing has more to do with it. When I was first deceived into teaching Remo, he had wrists like chicken necks and he wheezed like a sump pump.—Chiun, Master of Sinanju and Trainer of Fools

Dear Exalted Master Chiun:

I still don't understand. First you say it's wrists and then you say it's breathing. I want to know exactly what it is.—Spencer, La Jolla, Calif.

Dear White Thing:

You give new depth to the word "moron." The breathing makes a man invincible; the wrists enable him to demonstrate that invincibility. Breathing and wrists. They are all. It is fortunate that the secret of Sinanju is not the mouth or you would be the most feared man in history.—Chiun, Master of Sinanju and Correspondent with Monkeys

Dear Exalted Master Chiun:

I don't think it's fair. In other books I read, we always find out how heroes kill. What kinds of guns they use and exactly where they want to put bullets into somebody's head to get maximum coverage of the wall behind. How they slash with a knife and twist with a garrote or whatever. From the Destroyer I learn nothing. All you tell me is wrists and breathing.
—Spencer, La Jolla, Calif.

Dear Idiot:

Do not presume to tell me what other idiots do. They are butchers, lunatics, crazed killers. We in Sinanju are assassins. If you do not understand the difference between a noble assassin and a wanton killer, you can understand nothing.—Chiun, Master of Sinanju, Who No Longer Suffers Fools Gladly

Dear Exalted Master Chiun:

I think somehow I have offended you. My humblest apologies. I sought only to bask in your reflected glory and wonder, thereby to improve myself.— Spencer, La Jolla, Calif.

Dear Spencer La Jolla, Calif.:

Whites cannot improve themselves. In glimpsing my perfection, you have done the best you could. Consider yourself lucky.

With moderate tolerance for you, I am,

Chiun,
Master of Sinanju

Warren Murphy *is the coauthor of* Grand Master. *He does not have especially thick wrists.*

THE ASSASSIN'S ARSENAL

David Penn

The pen may be mightier than the sword, but all too frequently it is a damn sight more inaccurate than the pistols it portrays.

In the whodunit, it is only rarely that the correct portrayal of the murder firearm is crucial to the mechanics of the plot, since the emphasis is on logic and the pleasure is intellectual. It matters little to the reader that the author has played safe with an anonymous "pistol," or has invented an exotic "Münslich eight-millimetre flat butt," or has chosen a real ".38 Special Colt Cobra revolver," unless the type and performance of the firearm form a significant part of the deductive process. Such plots are understandably rare, since sufficient technical knowledge for correct interpretation is unusual among readers and practically unheard of among mystery writers. Exceptions do occur, of course, for instance in the well-known naturalist Colin Willock's *Death in Covert,* a classic mystery based on a detailed and accurate knowledge of shotguns and game shooting in England, or in John F. Adams' *Two Plus Two Equals Minus Seven,* not so much a whodunit as a where-did-I-go-wrong. This is narrated by a too-clever-by-half pistolero whose perfect murder goes awry, and who suffers the indignity of being framed for a crime involving a cheap and aesthetically unpleasing Saturday Night Special with which he would never have soiled his hands.

If, however, a firearm is to be the Means to an End in a mystery, I do believe that its role should not strain too far the bounds of logical probability. One eminent English mystery writer managed to contrive a story around the ability of a loaded automatic pistol to fire itself by the contraction of its working parts after it had been left lying around in freezing conditions. Such an occurrence may not, in absolute terms, be impossible. Indeed, there is a known case of a shotgun capable of discharging itself without an intervening human agency by means of the effect of climatic change on its stock. Yet the design of an automatic pistol makes the chances of such an accident highly improbable, since the violence of its operation requires substantial bearing surfaces in the firing mechanism, and the degree of contraction of the metal, which would be compensated for in some degree by spring pressure keeping the parts in proper relationship, would not suffice to disengage them on even the coldest English day. On this occasion our illustrious author followed Sherlock Holmes' dictum that "when you have eliminated the impossible, whatever remains, however improbable, must be the truth" beyond the bounds of improbability and into the realms of incredibility.

When the focus of our attention moves an inch or so from the cerebral world of the Country House to the private-eye or the thick-ear thriller, the *mise en scène* is all. Technical inaccuracy or infelicity of language can puncture the illusion of a hero who is, with certain humorous exceptions, always tough, worldly-wise and competent, whether he be the rumpled sardonic romantic of Chandler or Gavin Lyall, or the sophisticated psychopath of an Ian Fleming. There is a school of thriller, epitomised by the spy stories of the Sixties and by Frederick Forsyth and Sam Gulliver in the Seventies, in which a bravura display of arcane technical knowledge plays a major part in the book's appeal. The police procedural is equally dependent on the author's ability to visualise a gritty reality through blood-boltered spectacles.

Some writers in these fields, such as Donald Hamilton or Richard Sale (author of the amazing extravaganza *The Man Who Raised Hell*), are familiar with firearms and incorporate them easily into their plots. Others manage to disguise their ignorance or error by a dis-

You're fired!

play of straight-faced confidence that convinces all but the true *amateur des armes* of their veracity. In *The Day of the Jackal,* Forsyth arms his assassin with bullets specially loaded with a mercury blob in a cavity, alleged to have a wondrously mind-blowing effect upon their victim. Far out, but no way would they work. Len Deighton is a past-master at the convincing memorandum and bolstered up *The Ipcress File* with such a wealth of apparently genuine detail that some alarmist souls voiced concern about undesirable security leaks. All I can say is, if the "Extract from Handling unfamiliar pistols, Document 237.HGF, 1960" is for real, heaven help our secret servants. The anonymous hero of *The Ipcress File* is armed with "a hammerless Smith and Wesson, safety catch built into grip, six chambers crowded with bullets . . . in an accompanying box were twenty-five rounds, two spare chambers (greased to hold the shells in tight)." Impressive. Except that no hammerless Smith and Wesson is six-shot—it's only five and the safety mechanism does not in strict terms incorporate a "catch," since it does not intercept the motion of an already cocked mechanism but rather prevents an uncocked mechanism from being moved. Deighton means "two spare cylinders," not "chambers." Smith and Wesson has never supplied additional cylinders for the purpose of rapid reloading, since on all models, hinged-frame or side-swing, they take a

few moments to remove. With the exception of a little-known Spanish revolver, spare-loaded cylinders went out of fashion when percussion muzzle-loading revolvers became obsolete. Greasing the chambers of the cylinder has a number of highly undesirable possible side effects which would outweigh any benefits.

In some curious way, many thriller readers feel that an author who displays technical ignorance in his writing has

Spinning the chambers.

somehow betrayed his hero by undermining their confidence in his ability to cope with the worst a hostile world can throw at him. A glossy idol cannot withstand a crack, and even a scruffy matte-finish anti-hero can only afford clay on the outside of his boots. This disenchantment is reflected in letters of protest by technology buffs from Bangor to Bangkok. Whether or not such a reaction is a little immature is beside the point, since if that is the audience for whom the author has aimed, he should at least make an effort to deliver the goods. Dick Francis never subjects his fictional jockeys to experiences that he could not himself survive, and writers from the sublime Gavin Lyall to the prolific J.T. Edson go to some lengths to find out whether the gunfights they chronicle are within the bounds of probability.

Perhaps the best-known target of the armchair experts was Ian Fleming. Fleming's fortes were pace and an ability to convey the risqué glamour of an afflu-

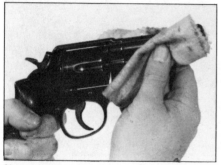

Chamoising the barrel.

GUN LORE

In its heyday, the British Empire made three immortal contributions to the vocabulary of the crime writer: "cordite," the "dumdum" bullet and the "automatic revolver." Thanks, I suspect, to Raymond Chandler's education at Dulwich College, an English public school whose Cadet Force would have been issued with cordite-loaded cartridges, he always used this term when referring to any smokeless powder and it has passed into the English language as a generic term for nitro propellants. True cordite bears a remarkable resemblance to whole-meal spaghetti, was given widespread use in small arms only by Britain and her Empire, and is now obsolete. "Dumdum" derives from Dum-Dum, an arsenal in India where early experiments in expanding rifle bullets took place. Its name took the fancy of the British Press and has symbolised inhumane projectiles ever since. Many a journalist and novelist has been castigated unfairly by so-called firearms experts for employing the phrase "automatic revolver." Such apparent contradictions in terms have existed, the British Webley-Fosbery being the best known, but the Spanish "Zulaika" and the American "Union" were also produced in tiny numbers, and the phrase was used by American advertisers to enhance the conventional self-extracting revolvers.

D.P.

ent consumer society beginning to glitter after twenty grey years of austerity. Despite his intelligence background, however, Fleming's knowledge of firearms was sketchy. The .25 Beretta of his early books was at least concealable, and deadly enough if the brain or spine was hit, but it had been subjected to some dubious modifications. To file the firing pin to a point was to invite a punctured primer, an escape of gas and perhaps a lightly grilled shooting hand. The taped skeleton butt would present no improvement in concealability over the standard skinny stocks and would invite all sorts of sticky trouble, such as a difficulty in removing the magazine. Fleming was eventually taken firmly in hand by a Scottish firearms expert, Geoffry Boothroyd, who is characterised as the Armourer in *Dr. No*. Boothroyd suggested that Bond be armed with either a .32 Walther PPK automatic or a Smith and Wesson .38 "Centennial" revolver. While both were an improvement over the Beretta, they were themselves idiosyncratic choices, since Boothroyd must have been well aware that the PPK, introduced in 1931 and perhaps still the best pocket automatic made, was available in the significantly more effective .380 ACP calibre as well as the decidedly anaemic .32. The "Centennial" is a compact, well-made and powerful .38 Special snub-nosed revolver, but a concealed hammer weapon capable of double-action fire only and fitted with an unnecessary complexity in the form of a grip safety. Why Boothroyd selected this revolver when the equally compact and powerful but more versatile Smith and Wesson "Chiefs Special" and "Bodyguard" revolvers were available has always mystified me.

The Fleming/Boothroyd axis also demonstrates the danger of trying to graft on someone else's expertise, since Boothroyd suggested that the "Centennial" be carried in a split-front Berns-Martin holster, an advanced design for the day that could be used as either a belt holster or a shoulder holster and allowed a very quick draw with good security against accidental loss. Fleming loved the idea and duly sent Bond forth equipped with a PPK automatic and a Berns-Martin holster, to a chorus of anguished groans from the shooting fraternity since the Berns-Martin was made

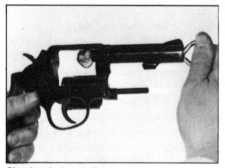

Cleaning the barrel, first swipe.

only for revolvers, not for automatics. As a crowning irony, in recognition of his care in references to firearms, Ian Fleming was presented in 1964 with a "Python" .357 Magnum revolver by Colt's, a company whose products had appeared almost entirely in the hands of the bad guys in his books.

Stern injunctions against loquacity preclude turning this chapter into a gunman's *vade mecum,* but having bitten the hands of many authors whose works have given me hours of pleasure, I feel obliged to turn pundit for a page or two.

I do not wish to probe too deeply into the gory business of wound ballistics, but it is wise to bear in mind that the projectile fired from a gun is a simple means of transmitting energy to the target. This energy is wasted, and becomes a potential hazard to innocent bystanders, if the projectile either misses or passes right through the victim. The purpose of this release of energy may be to kill, if the shooter is an assassin or a humane hunter, or to cause the recipient to cease and desist from whatever action he happens to be engaged in. Where the police and military are concerned, it is this "stopping" effect that is essential and any subsequent fatality is an undesirable side effect. There is little correlation between the ability of a weapon to kill and its ability to administer an instant and staggering shock. As an analogy, if a bag of oats is stood on its end,

and a rapier is thrust right into it, the sharp slim blade will slide through and transmit little shock, but an identical thrust with a blunt walking stick will not penetrate and will knock the sack over. This analogy holds good for pistol bullets, where bigger and blunter is better, but is not entirely valid for modern high-velocity rifle bullets, working at velocities in excess of 2,500 feet per second, where other criteria obtain and the most wounding effect is caused by cavitation. As a rule of thumb, .22, .25 and .32 pistols and revolvers are thoroughly capable of killing if they hit a vital organ, but they do not transmit enough energy to provide reliable stopping power; .38 and 9 mm pistols are effective about 50 percent of the time, and modern .41, .44 and .45 cartridges are effective about 95 percent of the time. In practise, the effect does not seem to be cumulative, so two .38's do not carry the same clout as one .45. All shotguns can be considered effective and messy up to forty or fifty yards, and all modern high-velocity rifles are also reliable one-shot stoppers.

Second swipe.

In *Open Season,* David Osborn writes:

> *The rare, British-manufactured seven-millimeter H & H magnum twin barrelled breech-loading rifle has, at 300 yards, a velocity of 2,450 feet per second and a striking impact of 1,660 pounds, enough to kill a charging elephant in-*

stantly or knock a ¾-ton bull moose not just to his knees but completely off his feet. . . .

Now, David Osborn has clearly done a lot of hard research into firearms, but he has perpetuated an all-too-common and erroneous assumption that, because a bullet generates an impressive striking energy, it is capable of physically knocking the victim off his feet. Newton's second law remains on the statute books, and this says that if the bullet can knock the victim over, the firearm will knock the shooter over. The armchair theorist fails to take into account the effects of inertia. I know it happens in the movies, but the effect is created by a brisk and timely heave on a piano wire attached to the hapless actor's belt. The real effect is a shock to the nervous system causing sudden loss of control and resulting in collapse, somewhat akin to a marionette when the puppeteer releases the strings.

Robert Churchill, one of the foremost English forensic ballisticians between the wars, wrote:

It is a paradox that in the great majority of offences involving a pistol the people concerned knew next to nothing about the mechanism or potentialities of the weapon. In many cases the fatal shot is the first and last they fire in their lives. Crime guns are usually ill-kept, often mechanically faulty, and commonly loaded with unsuitable or improvised ammunition.

As a basic standard of competence, an untrained person in a stressful state and shooting a pistol can miss a stationary figure at seven yards and a running one at seven feet. A skilled pistol shot in control of his emotions can reliably hit a stationary figure at a hundred yards and a moving one at twenty-five.

A pistol may give the same sort of comfort as a teddy bear on a cold dark night, but its virtues are light weight and

compactness. It is a defensive arm that can be carried along or concealed when a rifle would be a hindrance or an embarrassment. Its virtues become positive disadvantages when the weapon actually has to be fired. A riot gun or sawn-off shotgun is a much more effective weapon favoured by both sides of the law when trouble is expected.

Machine guns, submachine guns and full-size rifles find little favour with the criminal classes since they are large, expensive to acquire and feed, and distinctly unhandy to get in and out of motorcars. In America, overenthusiastic use of machine guns also tends to attract

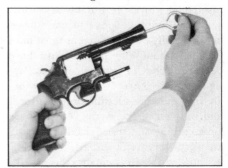

Removing the swipe.

the unwelcome attentions of the FBI, while the trusty shotgun remains a local problem. Criminals are as cost-conscious as any other laissez-faire capitalist and see no need to invest money in fancy hardware when any old 12-bore will do perfectly. Terrorists, who have a different image of themselves and may expect to have to do some serious fighting if things go wrong, are entirely another matter.

While on the subject of criminals and motorcars, it is well to remember that firing pistols at the tyres of moving cars is a pointless exercise, since they are difficult to hit and very hard to deflate. Thanks to Ralph Nader, the laminated steeply raked windscreens of modern American cars have an amazing ability to withstand pistol bullets and shotgun slugs, although the firm of KTW has marketed Teflon-coated steel bullets to combat this problem.

Criminals rarely use holsters. It is easy to drop a pistol down the storm drain but thoroughly embarrassing to disengage a holster from a belt or beneath the armpit while attempting to outstretch the long arm of the law.

The "secret weapon" is by no means confined to the realms of spy fiction. The SOE and OSS developed a plethora of highly specialised weapons during the last war, including lapel daggers, tyre-slashing knives, and pistols that fired automatically when the arms were raised in surrender (and presumably also when one was waving goodbye to one's loved ones). A fully equipped agent must have weighed about 800 pounds and have been subjected to permanent metal fatigue. The silencer was especially beloved of these clandestine organisations, and the best of them, the .45 ACP De Lisle carbine and the Welrod .32 pistol, are very, very quiet indeed. "Silencer" is, however, a misnomer; the British term "sound moderator" is a more accurate description of the device, its main function being to keep a firearm from sounding like a firearm by muffling noise. The principle of operation is identical to a motorcar silencer, and the Maxim design is indeed still used on tractors. Points to watch are that silencers work well only with subsonic bul-

lets, since supersonic projectiles make a loud "crack" as they pass through the air; that a revolver cannot be silenced effectively by conventional means because the gap between cylinder and bar-

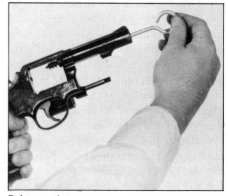

Balance testing.

rel allows gas to escape rapidly, thus creating noise; and that, to be effective, a silencer must have a large volume. The two-inch tube stuffed onto the end of a snub-nosed revolver by the movie hitman would be singularly inefficient. Satisfactory silencers for .45 and 9 mm weapons are about 18–24 inches long and about 2½ inches in diameter. Someone has even invented a "silent grenade," which resembles a suit of armour for an octopus since several silenced barrels radiate from a central sphere. Each barrel is loaded, Roman candle fashion, with multiple charges. When the infernal machine is set into motion, it hops around like a laryngitic crackerjack broadcasting its bullets among the duly astonished multitude.

Having highlighted a few pitfalls in the field of firearms, and left many still unilluminated, I close with the wise words of the Western gunslinger: "Speed's fine, pardner, but accuracy's final."

David Penn is Keeper of the Department of Exhibits and Firearms at the Imperial War Museum, London.

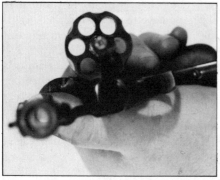

Prior to loading.

CROOK BOOKS

Mike Chlanda

I root for the bad guy. If he's planning a caper or divvying up the loot from the last one, if he's been in jail or is up on charges, if his living room is so loaded with merchandise (lifted, of course) that it looks like an Amway depot, that's my man. That would also be my woman, but I just haven't met one recently.

Anti-heroes are fun, literally. Consider John Archibald Dortmunder, Donald E. Westlake's criminal manqué. Been arrested twice (for robbery) and will undoubtedly go up a few more times before he packs it in. Known associates include Kelp, an ex-con who specializes in stealing cars with M.D. plates; Murch, a crook who lives with his mom for reasons too Krafft-Ebing for me to go into; and once in a while, Roger Chefwith, whose interest in railroads extends to hijacking them. Dortmunder et al. romp through *Bank Shot, Jimmy the Kid, Nobody's Perfect, The Hot Rock, Why Me?* and even a couple of pretty funny movies.

When Westlake gets tired of being funny, he turns mean and calls out Parker. Originally issued under the Richard Stark by-line, the Parker series is now being published under Westlake's real name. Like Dortmunder in one respect only: Parker takes jewels. In *The Black Ice Score*, for example, he's contracted to steal a mess of African diamonds from the museum for an African consortium. Nobody ever laughs at Parker, and if you think the love of a good woman turns a man mellow, Claire has failed her sex.

The toughest, grittiest, most realistic (I think) of the crook books are those of George V. Higgins, whose Eddie Coyle (a small-time hood) and Coogan (an enforcer) work against the system in Boston. *The Friends of Eddie Coyle* spotlights hoods, wise guys, punks and a slew of street smarts. *Coogan's Trade* centers on high-stakes gambling and fixed card games. Switching upscale, Higgins' *Choice of Enemies* centers on government corruption in the person of the Speaker of the Massachusetts House.

Other crook books to consider: Jack Higgins' *Luciano's Luck,* which slips Lucky out of Greenhaven Prison and into confrontations with such disparate types as a mafia capo and General Eisenhower; Lawrence Block's *Burglar* series, where Bernie Rhodenbarr takes on most of New York; Max Collins' Nolan; Kenneth Royce's Spider Scott; Peter George's Blane; John Trinian's Karl Heisler; Sam Stewart's McCoy; Newton Thornburg's Cross; Charles Williams' Lawrence Colby; Dan J. Marlowe's (Slick) Quick; and Westlake's—does the man never stop?—Charlie Poole, Joe Loomis and Tom Garrity, Kelly and Lew Brady and Frank Lanigan.

What is it about crook books? To paraphrase Dorothy L. Sayers (which is the only way she's readable): You have the pleasure of planning a crime in the morning and switching sides in the afternoon and catching it in progress.

Mike Chlanda has never been caught.

RANSACKING THE LOUVRE

Being Restored

ANTIQUITIES

Crave a gilt casket, a Holy Grail bowl, and an Egyptian ankh? Contact Michael Delving and *Bored to Death, Die Like a Man* and *No Sign of Life*.

Collect antique firefly cages, rare Roman coins, duelling pistols, silver steam engines and Chippendale tables? Talk to Jonathan Gash and *Firefly Gadroon, Gold by Gemini, The Judas Pair, The Sleepers of Erin* and *The Vatican RIP*.

If it's Tiffany lamps you prefer, direct your gaze to Marcia Muller and *The Cheshire Cat's Eye,* but if it's eighteenth-century Staffordshire you must have, call on Anthony Oliver and *The Pew Group*.

REMOVED
(Without Permission)

4 Rembrandt self-portraits
21 Rubens, including his second
wife
1 Ingres and 1 El Greco

On Loan

HEADLINES IN LE PARIS HERALD-TRIBUNE

Hugger-Mugger in the Louvre
(*Elliot Paul*)
The Man Who Stole the Mona Lisa
(*Martin Page*)

Portrait Gallery

Begin on the ground floor, which houses the Boscoreale Treasure (more than 100 pieces of Roman jewelry), the Venus de Milo (sans arms) and the Victory of Samothrace (avec wings), which would look quite nice on your patio.

The Department of Oriental Art is not up to your standards. Bear left, go past the front entrance, turn left again and walk miles until you reach the Department of Mediaeval Renaissance and Modern Sculpture; contained here are the remnants of the Royal Collection, including Michelangelo's Slaves and works by Cellini, any one of which would work well in your kitchen or bath (particularly if it's sunken). Also at hand: costumes confiscated from the Royal wardrobe (to supplement your disguise selection).

The Mona Lisa is upstairs, not too far from Susanna Bathing (Tintoretto), the Bohemian Girl (Hals), and Madame Récamier (David). The Gobelins Tapestries are in the Condé Gallery; with their rose backgrounds, they're the perfect finishing touch to a bedroom.

On your way out the window, stop by the Colonnade Galleries and strip off some truly splendid panelling, taken in part from the Château Neuf de Vincennes.

While waiting to fence your haul, you might want to take in the Comédie Française, which is just across the way.

ART

John R.L. Anderson, *A Sprig of Sea Lavender* (art swindlers)

Oliver Banks, *Caravaggio Obsession; The Rembrandt Panel* (Amos Hatcher, art investigator)

Nicholas Blake, *The Worm of Death* (Nigel Strangeways)

Sarah Caudwell, *Thus Was Adonis Murdered* (Venice)

Carolyn Coker, *The Other David* (Florence)

Dimitri Gat, *Nevsky's Demon* (Pittsburgh's Russian sector)

E.X. Giroux, *A Death for Adonis* (disgraced barrister investigates artists)

Peter Inchbald, *The Short Sweet Grass; Short Break in Venice* (London Art & Antiques Squad)

Michael Innes, *Appleby and Honeybath* (Honeybath on a painting commission)

Elizabeth Lemarchand, *Change for the Worse* (stately home art)

Marcia Muller, *The Tree of Death* (Museum of Mexican Art, Santa Barbara)

June Thomson, *Portrait of Lilith* (Inspector Rudd and the artist)

Clarissa Watson, *The Fourth Stage of Gainsborough Brown; Bishop in the Back Seat* (Persis Willum, Long Island artist)

Moncrieff Williamson, *Death in the Picture* (art historian in London gallery)

Recent Acquisitions

WHOPPERS
THE LIES OF J. EDGAR HOOVER

Clark Howard

In the eighteen years since Congress passed the Freedom of Information Act, it has become increasingly obvious with each FBI record released that our country's Depression era outlaws may have been a shade or two less heinous and malevolent than the American public was led to believe.

During the heyday of Prohibition outlawry, newspaper readers across the country were deluged with screaming headlines and shocking stories of the violent exploits of Machine Gun Kelly, Pretty Boy Floyd, and Ma Barker and her gang. According to newspaper and radio reports (most of them based on press releases issued by the FBI), these and other "murdering criminals" were a threat to the life and limb of every honest man, woman and child in America. But how bad were they, really?

Let's examine Machine Gun Kelly. Real name: George R. Barnes. Supposedly raised in a low-class family with only an elementary school education. Supposedly learned to handle a machine gun while a doughboy in France. Supposedly one of the coldest-blooded killers

the FBI ever tracked down. Curious, then, that he was never *charged* with a killing, never even *accused* of a killing. Is it possible that Machine Gun Kelly's murderous reputation was manufactured by the very people who were chasing him, the FBI?

Not only possible, but probable. George Barnes came from a well-to-do Memphis insurance family. He attended college for a time. To be sure, he was the family's black sheep: during Prohibition, like many another, he became a bootlegger. Gradually he moved into bank robbery. Ultimately he engineered and carried out the successful kidnapping of Charles F. Urshel, a millionaire Oklahoma City oilman. Urshel was well treated during his captivity and was released unharmed after Kelly and his accomplices collected $200,000 ransom.

There is no question, then, that George Barnes Kelly was an outlaw and deserved to be hunted down, captured, tried, convicted and sent to prison. But what was the purpose of the "Machine Gun" tag? Why paint him as a sadistic, lead-spewing killer, when in fact he

CATCH 93-579
THE FEDERAL WAY OF
SAYING IT'S NONE OF
YOUR BUSINESS

In 1966 Congress passed the Freedom of Information Act, whose purpose was to "assist the public in obtaining information from the Government." The act was based on the assumption that the information of the government belonged to the people—because the government itself belonged to the people.

Eight years later another statute was passed. This was Public Law 93-579, commonly known as the Privacy Act. This act, in effect, frequently negates the FOI in that it gives federal agencies the right to delete from all files *any* name except that of the person to whom the file pertains.

That's the catch.

*J. Edgar reaching
for an eraser.*

The Federal Bureau of Investigation reading your mail.

"Friend Lee:

"One time mor
that we saw each other
took from the hotel and

affair I am going to r
will have much interes
you. I told him you c
he did not want to bel
because I saw you with

could lead to your tr
destroy them as alway
the money and we will

Mr. Hoover investigating Dick Francis.

never fired a shot in anger in his life (he wasn't even *in* the army, probably never held a machine gun).

The reason for the big build-up was money. Federal budget money. J. Edgar Hoover was in the process of building an empire within the federal government; to do that, he needed increasingly more funds from Congress every year. What better way to get his annual allocation increased than to make everyone think that only he and his Bureau stood between a safe America and rampaging murderers like Machine Gun Kelly?

One of the most flagrant examples of Hoover's promotion was Pretty Boy Floyd. On June 17, 1933, four lawmen, escorting an escaped prisoner back to Leavenworth penitentiary, were shot down in front of the Kansas City train depot by three men attempting to help the convict get away. One of the lawmen killed in this incident was an FBI agent, and Hoover immediately put the blame on Charles Arthur Floyd—a handsome, strapping ex-Oklahoma farmer who had turned to crime when the family farm became part of the "dust bowl." An accomplished bank robber and escape artist, Floyd had made the authorities, including Hoover's men, look foolish on more than one occasion; in many circles he was considered a Robin Hood kind of

Mr. Hoover confiding your secrets to his best friend.

outlaw, and residents of blighted Oklahoma frequently and willingly hid him from the law.

When Hoover saw how much the so-called Kansas City Massacre shocked America, he seized the opportunity to associate Floyd with something that would tarnish his growing folk-hero reputation. Even after eyewitness James Audette (a minor criminal himself) identified all three gunmen as being other than Floyd, the FBI director refused to alter his position. He continued to brand Floyd a ruthless murderer, and the young outlaw, his reputation thus damaged, lasted only slightly longer than one more year; FBI agents, intensifying their hunt in the belief that he had gunned down one of their own, trapped him in a cornfield and killed him. Having previously confessed to every other crime he had committed, Floyd always vehemently denied participating in the Kansas City Massacre.

Ma Barker was perhaps the most glaring of Hoover's fictions. Though on the Ten Most Wanted list as "leader" of the notorious Barker-Karpis gang of bank robbers and kidnappers, Kate Barker was *never* charged with a single crime. Her FBI file, now public, does not specifically accuse her of a single infraction of the law. Her sons, yes; Doc and Freddie Barker were coldblooded killers without peer. And on occasion Kate traveled with them or maintained homes to which they returned to hide. But as far as being the "brains" of the outlaw gang, as far as organizing and engineering bank robberies and kidnappings, this has been proved to be utter nonsense. Harvey Bailey, a longtime associate of the Barker-Karpis gang, was asked before his death several years ago about Ma Barker's alleged planning of their activities. "Hell," Bailey said, "the old woman couldn't plan breakfast!"

The truth is that Kate Barker was nothing more than a harmless, sixty-

Mr. Hoover having a good time at the public's expense.

year-old, mother-hen type. She did what she could for "her boys," outlaws that they were: gave them a place to hide, tended them when they were sick, scolded them when they took up with women of low morals, and no doubt occasionally pondered where she'd gone wrong as a mother.

Kate Barker and her youngest son Freddie were killed by FBI agents when a cottage in which they were residing, near Lake Weir, Florida, was surrounded and riddled with gunfire. The FBI file on Kate states that a Thompson .45-caliber submachine gun "lay at Ma Barker's left hand" and implies that with it she had battled to the death. Any reader who has ever fired a Thompson knows that it's a lot harder to control and operate than the movies would have us believe. To picture Kate Barker, a woman of sixty-three, fighting FBI agents with this weapon in a prolonged gun battle, takes a vivid imagination.

But then, that's one thing J. Edgar Hoover had plenty of.

Clark Howard is the author of four true-crime books and thirteen novels. He won an Edgar for "Horn Man," best short story, 1980.

FIRST AMENDMENT FLATFOOT

James Grady

They never taught me about stake-outs in journalism school. No professor ever explained how to find a discreet parking spot with a good view of the crucial door. Controlling your bladder during six sweltering hours behind the wheel of a parked car was also a question never broached.

My professors never demonstrated how to "Mom & Pop," the hard guy/soft guy police interrogation technique my muckraking partner Gary "Mad Dog" Cohn and I used with varying degrees of success and sometimes comic absurdity. (Just once I wish I could have played the hard guy!) We never analyzed the practical, moral and intellectual dilemmas of cruising America's serious streets in a black Mercedes with three pistol-packing cocaine cowboys, a kilo of *product,* $50,000 in hundreds, talk of an Uzi stashed in the trunk (probably macho bravado), and the radio blasting rock-and-roll through the acrid fog of marijuana smoke as the three cowboys shout answers and explanations about "the life"—the world of our modern-day outlaws. (There are a hundred horrible possibilities in this scenario, and in none of them is a press pass a passport to safety.)

Lessons on how to handle such situations never surfaced in my classrooms. As one of my colleagues told me, "Those are the kinds of things you find out in the street."

That street is the beat of America's investigative reporters, our newest class of flatfoots, the detectives whose badge is the First Amendment and whose clients are everyone who drops a quarter into the corner newsbox. Cases run the gamut from small-time grifters at City Hall to big shots who run scams and schemes out of the White House.

Watergate popularized these detectives of the press: two First Amendment shamuses named Woodward and Bernstein brought down a president and all his men. There had been muckraking journalists busting bad buys before "Woodstein" and there have been more since, but they made the image of "investigative reporters" glamorous—or rather, the movie of their exploits made reporters glamorous.

Life is not always like the movies.

Reporters are seldom loved. If we do our job, we let the public peek behind the curtain, and the public would just as soon enjoy life as a comfortable mystery. We all want to be safe; we want our idealized perspective to stay unchallenged. When a reporter uncovers a "bad news" story, he drives home the truth that none of us is secure in this complex, highly charged modern world and that maybe we should *do* something about the mess around us.

Besides being usually unpopular, reporters—like other detectives—plod through days of scant glamour and abundant drudgery yielding no just reward. A police detective spends three weeks painstakingly building a case against a pimp who turns fourteen-year-old girls into whores, only to have a district attorney refuse to prosecute the case because prostitution is a "victim-

less" crime. A reporter spends three weeks digging through musty courthouse records to piece together a complex story on shady business dealings between a mobster and a city councilman, only to see his exposé bumped off Page One by a gun-shy editor in favor of an interview with a beauty queen, then relegated to Page Four and noticed by almost no one—and of no consequence in November, when the public reelects that "clever" businessman to the city council with an overwhelming vote.

Reporters run risks. Libel law has become a part of the great American game of *sue everybody,* and you're considered an especially good target if you're a reporter. You never win a libel suit: even when the judgment holds you're innocent, the months and dollars required to arrive at that conclusion bleed your spirit, your time and your wallet—and your opposition knows and uses that. If you're an aggressive reporter, you often find yourself in curious and deadly circumstances like that black Mercedes. Grand juries have a way of wanting to hear everything you know, and the hell with your press pass and constitutionally sanctioned privileges. Sources expect you to live up to whatever ground rules of confidentiality were agreed on before they opened their mouths. It's not inconceivable that you get stuck between honoring your commitments to sources and answering the demands of a grand jury. The grand jury has its jails, but your sources have your promise.

Sometimes that dilemma involves more than questions of honor and the law. I once went through my standard litany explaining constitutional privilege, court decisions and shield laws to a Maximum Outlaw. He waited until I finished, stared calmly at me with his dead eyes, and said: "You know, Jim, those things don't mean shit. We don't trust you because of *words*. We trust you because of who you are, and what you know about how things really work—

and because you know the price you pay for your errors." Then he and two of his gunmen smiled. Slowly. So did I.

The greatest risks for a reporter are personal, not professional. First Amendment flatfoots suffer from the same burnout syndrome that turns good cops into walking ghosts. An honest reporter worries constantly about making mistakes: accidentally savaging some innocent person in print, missing an important story, letting the wrong guy slip by. Sixty percent of the people reporters talk to lie to them routinely and ruthlessly, a fact that devours any tendency to trust and love your fellow man. Reporters are used by people who give them stories instead of the truth. The reporter will then do his job, if not his duty. That discrepancy gnaws at self-worth.

NO ADMITTANCE

A press pass won't get you into the U.N., the White House or either of the presidential conventions. For that, you must be cleared by the Secret Service and issued a special entrance badge.

A press pass also won't get you into a debutante ball, if you care.

On the other hand, it will move you past almost any police barricade in town, whether it be at a fire, a murder, a parade or the scene of a robbery. With a press pass, if there's something particularly gory to see, you'll get to see it (just be careful where you step).

A press pass will also get you a lot of freebies—tickets to movies, concerts, sporting events, opening nights—and occasionally they're even good for a decent meal.

PRESSING MATTERS

The fourth estate is the backdrop for many mystery novels, among them Elliott Chaze's *Goodbye, Goliath* and Tim Heald's *Deadline.* Tom Paige, managing editor of the London *Evening Record,* has a few headaches to deal with in Marian Babson's *Dangerous to Know,* as does Jerry Donovan, Richard Neely's investigative reporter in *Shadows from the Past.* Even Robert B. Parker's Spenser finds himself immersed in the world of newspapers when he becomes involved with an investigative reporter in *A Savage Place.*

There are, additionally, several newspaper series sleuths. Lionel Black has created Kate Theobald, a reporter who has difficulties with, among other matters, gold coins (*The Penny Murders*) and German weddings (*Eve of the Wedding*). Dorothy Salisbury Davis' Julie Hays, a stringer for a gossip columnist, is almost put to sleep permanently in *Lullaby to Murder,* while Lucille Kallen's Maggie Rome, ace reporter for *Sloan's Ford Reporter,* and editor C.B. Greenfield deftly work their way through music (*Tanglewood Murders*) and politics (*No Lady in the House*), to limit their adventures to just two examples.

— 30 —

Perhaps the most damning demand of a reporter's work is that you can do so little in a world where there is so much to be done. You can't print what you know, only what you can prove. Seldom if ever do you get the full story, the big story or even the most important story: you get glimpses of the shadows behind the curtain, write them up and call them news. That frustration, the weight of all you see and do, pushes down on your spirit. If you're not careful, if you lose faith in the idea that every blow struck for the truth helps somehow, somewhere, you may be doomed. Indifference creeps over your ambition. Your stories become routine recitations of fact, chronicles created to keep the paycheck coming each month. You end up chasing yourself into the darkest corner of despair, where there are empty nights, bottles, drugs, and sharp razors for the wrists.

Some reporters, like me, find a saving grace in fiction, which allows us to reach beyond the facts for truths that only fantasy can portray. But most of the others have to struggle each day with mere reality.

Why do it? What propels and perpetuates First Amendment flatfoots like Woodward and Bernstein, Seymour Hersh, Jack Anderson, Mike Wallace, the other few who are famous and the hundred who aren't? Not fame, for what glory those big names have is more than tempered by the enmity they endure each day. Not riches, for even though they're well rewarded in dollars and cents, they make far less than they could as corporate executives. And certainly not because investigative journalism is something that is "there," like the proverbial mountain to be climbed: that's the philosophy of a lemming rushing to the cliff.

The only compelling reason to be a muckraker is the faith that somehow what you do in searching for truth and trying to tell it *matters.*

Besides, there's no rush quite like that when, after weeks of hungrily loping behind some big story, you flip open the morning paper beside the coffee cup and see your quarry, captured for the world in black and white.

James Grady worked as an investigative reporter for syndicated columnist Jack Anderson. He is the author of Six Days of the Condor *and* Runner in the Street.

PRISON RESUMÉS
Would You Hire This Man? Marry Him? Murder Him?

WHELKS, CHARLES

a.k.a.: William Charles, Charlie Myboy, Good Time Charlie

History: Cashiered, 37th Regiment, Her Majesty's Service, Punjab Campaign. Brought on charges for cowardice, desertion; remanded to J. John Teasdale, Esq., Upper Slaughter, for rehabilitation.

Caution: Foul temper, surly tongue. Attacks when provoked.

MacARTHUR, JOCK

Address: The Red Herring Pub, Upper Slaughter

Charged: Operating off-hours, no Sunday closing, watering drinks.

Date of Arrest: 8/8/80

Date of Release: 8/8/80 (not proven)

DUNWITTY, LUTHER

a.k.a.: Laurence Dauson, Lawrence Dawsen, Lionel Dawkins, Leo Dempster, Lefty Donegal, Louis Danbury, Louie Denmark, Leslie Druthers

Priors:
Borstal: 10/10/50, apprehended
11/11/50, escaped
1/1/51, apprehended
2/2/51, solitary
3/3/51, transferred to 'alfway 'ouse
Reading: 8/8/65, apprehended
9/9/65, escaped
Strangewaves: 5/5/75, apprehended
6/6/75, escaped
Newgate: 4/4/80, apprehended
5/5/82, escaped

M.O.: Specialist, games of chances involving finger dexterity (three-card monte). Warned off *QEI, II, Mary* and *Margaret Rose* for quick shuffle, bottom-deck dealing, hustling.

Description: White male, approximately 40 years of age. Balding. Right shoulder droops. Tattoo of queen of hearts on sternum. Smokes cheap cigars; badly nicotine-stained right fingers.

Warning: Hard to hang on to in custody, but not dangerous: never armed.

THE GETAWAY CAR
STEP ON THE PEDAL AND GO

Warren Weith

Ralph Nader, the man who tried to convince us that the motorcar was the villain, had it all wrong. The automobile may turn people into villains, and it may attract villains, but alone and unattended it's just a collection of bits and pieces waiting to be thrust into furious action by a fool, knave or—if you will—villain.

There's no doubt in which category to place the author of this brief note to Henry Ford:

> *Hello Old Pal:*
> *Arrived here at 10 A.M. today. Would like to drop in and see you. You have a wonderful car. Been driving it for three weeks. It's a treat to drive one.*
> *Your slogan should be: Drive a Ford and watch the other cars fall behind you. I can make any other car take a Ford's dust.*
> *Bye-bye*
> *John Dillinger*

John Dillinger's use of the car as a tool to help him make quick withdrawals from various banks has become part of our folklore. Little known is how Dillinger learned the art of the fast remove. The technique was the brainchild of an ex-Prussian army officer named Herman K. Lamm.

Herr Lamm was caught cheating at cards and drummed out of his regiment shortly before World War I. Thereafter, he drifted to Utah and thence—there being no military defense establishment in those days to offer gainful employment to former army officers—into the life of a holdup man. This path in turn led, in 1917, to Utah State Prison. For Lamm, as for most criminals, a year in the can afforded time to reflect and to refine his technique. When he got out, he had developed a system for removing the uncertainties from bank robbing. It was a three-step plan. Only step three, detailing the getaway, is of interest here. The first requirement for the getaway was a car. Not just any car, but one that had to satisfy two contradictory rules: it had to be high-powered, yet nondescript to the point of disappearing into the cityscape. Next came the driver: best of all was a racing driver who had fallen from grace; at the very least, an ex-truck hijacker would do. Never just someone who was a "good" driver. Pasted up on the headliner over the windshield was a chart of the getaway route. This was more than a map because it indicated turns in miles that had been registered beforehand on the car's odometer and clocked, down to the second, by the driver under different weather conditions. It was a good plan and it worked for almost thirteen years.

It stopped working on December 16, 1930, in Clinton, Indiana. Lamm and three friends were calmly walking out of the Citizens State Bank in that town with $15,567 in a paper shopping bag and several typewriter covers when they were approached by the local barber. He had a suspicious look on his face and was carrying an Ithaca pump gun. Across the street, the getaway driver didn't like the way things were shaping up and tried to help out by making a screeching U-turn in order to bring the

Buick closer to the four gentlemen who needed to get away and, at the same time, put it between them and the suspicious barber. All of this would have been very smooth except that the driver, an ex-rumrunner possibly more adept with speedy boats than speedy cars, let things get out of hand and slammed the Buick into the curb with such force that it blew a tire. The five bank robbers limped away in the Buick with double-0 buckshot clanking around their ears. Then came the next bad move. Instead of stopping and changing the tire on the car with proven getaway potential, they elected to steal the next machine that hove into view. At this point, the Fates didn't smile—they laughed like hell. The next parked car they saw became, in about five seconds flat, the getaway car. But what they didn't know going in, and learned during the first mile, was that it was a car equipped with a governor by its owner to prevent his elderly father from speeding. Its top speed was 35 miles an hour. Just fast enough to get the fearless five a bit farther out of town and within robbing range of a truck. This worthy vehicle was a bit faster but proved to have very little water in its radiator. It did serve to get them over the state line—and into another car. This equipage had one little flaw. There was only one gallon of gas in the tank.

And there it all ended, under the blazing guns of a 200-man posse. Lamm and the driver were killed, and one member of the little band committed suicide. The other two were captured and sent to Michigan City Prison for life. There they taught a young John Dillinger all they knew about this almost trouble-free system of robbing banks. Herman K. Lamm, master of the fast getaway, is little known among people who use withdrawal slips but nonetheless lives on in our speech. Think of him the next time you hear a TV bad guy growl, "I'm gonna take it on the lam."

John Dilliniger, like any good apprentice, added a few personal touches to the master's blueprint. On leaving a bank, he would drape a frieze of hostages along the running boards to silence

LICENSE PLATES

Changing license plates in-flight, as it were, has always been a subject dear to the hearts of that segment of the motoring public pictured most frequently on post office walls. One ploy that went to the bank once too often was the mud-daubed plate used by a splinter group from the Detroit Purple Gang. Like all good tricks, it was simple and depended for its effect on the perverseness of human nature. Going to the bank, the plates on the getaway car were streaked with mud. At the first chance, after the job, the plates were wiped clean. Dumb as it may sound, human nature did the rest. If you're looking for a car with license plate MUD, it just can't be one with license plate KG 7459—or whatever was under the mud. Simple-minded? No, just simple.

Equally simple, and even more effective, were three or four plates stacked together and wired on. It was only the work of a minute or so to stop, take off the top plate and expose the one underneath. Remembering, of course, not to leave the discarded plate face up in the road. But then again, if a bank robber remembered everything, he'd probably wind up a banker.

W.W.

JUDITH WRIGHT

HYMN TO THE HIRONDEL

Most people think James Bond was the first man of action to have a car as his co-hero. Not so. Strictly speaking, it was Tom Swift in a slim little volume entitled *Tom Swift and His Electric Runabout.* But if we're talking about a car powered by an internal combustion engine, then Simon Templar, alias The Saint, is a likely candidate. His Hirondel—a make beautifully built only in author Leslie Charteris' imagination—was a magnificent motorcar of staggering performance. Its makers modestly alluded to it as the king of the road, and in Charteris' England of the 1930's that's just what it was. This is what its creator had to say about it as it bore The Saint to a lonely country house in which his fiancée, Patricia Holm, was being held prisoner:

If this had been a superstitious age, those who saw it would have crossed themselves and sworn that it was no car at all they saw that night, but a snarling silver fiend that roared through London on the wings of an unearthly wind.

Makes Mr. Bond's Aston sound like a rental from Hertz.

James Bond was first in one respect, though. He was the first hero driver to have a car equipped with gadgets whose sole function was to kill people. I'm thinking specifically of the twin forward-firing machine guns, hub-mounted scythes, and passenger ejection seat that turned his beautiful silver-gray DB 5 Aston-Martin into a death machine. Needless to say, all were used to great gory effect in one of the first James Bond pictures.

The Saint is the only fictional hero to rate a halo.

W. W.

the guns of any law officers who might be on the scene. While a neat touch, this did have a few drawbacks. A 1930's Terraplane or Essex really wasn't able to cope with four or five bandits and upwards of six hostages. Thus a getaway, which should be performed to a disco beat, turned into a slow waltz out of town. The forces of law and order soon got wise. They would follow at a discreet distance, knowing that sooner or later Bad John would have to drop the hostages off on some country road. At that point, the real getaway and chase would begin. But then another Dillinger touch would come into play—large-headed roofing nails liberally spread in the road. Simple, but effective. What made all this work, though, was the fact that most local law enforcement agencies were woefully ill-equipped. Many of them required that individual officers provide their own transportation. What a $5,000-a-year sheriff could afford to drive was simply no match for the wheels a successful team of bank robbers could—and did—buy.

The only automobile that ever came near to being a murderer was a Type 57 Bugatti. Being a French car, it was only natural that it was a crime of passion. The story in a few words: A young French girl was madly in love with a local layabout who was really in love with a Type 57, which he couldn't come close to affording. The girl's father had a mattress stuffed with money. She killed her father, took the money and bought her lover his love—the Bugatti. He and his love took off in a screech of tires for the South of France. She was left at the curb to stand trial for her crime. It being the middle Thirties, and France, the duped young lady served only one year of a two-year sentence. He killed himself in his Type 57. End of story.

Warren Weith is an editor of Car and Driver *magazine. He drives a '59 Alfa sedan.*

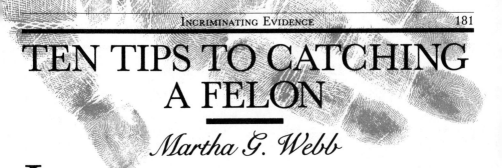

TEN TIPS TO CATCHING A FELON

Martha G. Webb

I've worked real crimes, and I've written fictional ones.

Fictional ones are neater.

They don't start at two A.M. unless you want them to. You don't have to collect unmentionable goop off the wall and ceiling and make diagrams of where you got it from, and nobody's having hysterics in the next room.

But the biggest difference is all those little coincidences and loose ends. In fiction they all have to fit. You make a list and tack it to your wall: loose ends I have to tie up in the last chapter. In real life the loose ends stick out everywhere, and most of the time you never do find out where the killer hid the victim's car keys and why, or what the winos were fighting about the week before one of them turned up dead in a bamboo thicket. Often the loose ends are tied up, and the coincidences worked out, only by physical evidence.

The best physical evidence, bar none, is fingerprints.

I was a latent fingerprint examiner before I started writing mysteries. Fingerprints aren't used in fiction as much as they used to be; would-be sophisticates tend to say things like "Criminals now are too smart to leave prints." That's not so. The prints are there, and they work just as well as they ever did. You can do amazing things with them, things I'd never dare write in a novel.

I still laugh whenever I think about one case. The victim—that is, the primary victim—was an auto repair shop. Sometime during the night several juveniles broke in, and by morning the chaos couldn't be described in words; I had to diagram it. The kids had driven, and wrecked, twelve different vehicles that had been left for repair, besides creating sundry other havoc.

It was hot that night, and the kids were sweating; furthermore, all three of them were barefoot. While Lt. Ronnie King was tracking their footprints quite easily down the alley to their homes, I was sorting out who did what where and in what order. This was easy enough to do, because the position the cars had halted in, and the way footprints were piled on footprints, told me the precise sequence.

That afternoon, after all the other work on the case had been done, Ronnie tiredly marched one of the twelve-year-old culprits across the hall to me and said, "He still denies it. How about you have a talk with him?"

I laid my diagram out on the table. "Now, let me tell you what *you* did," I said. "You drove this car and wrecked it. You couldn't get this one started, so you went through the glove box looking for money." Horrified comprehension was dawning on the kid's face as I continued: "Then you went in the office and tasted the candy and decided you didn't like it and spat it out. Then you took the Polaroid, carried it to the jeep, and—"

His voice shaking, the kid asked, "Lady, where was you hidin'?"

Fingerprint stories aren't always funny. They can be tragic, or they can be ironic—as in the case of the man found

INANIMATE WITNESSES

Fingerprints

Fingerprints are usually a combination of four shapes: arches, loops, whorls and composites. The most common configuration appearing on a finger is the loop (60 percent). Composites and whorls make up 35 percent and arches roughly 5 percent. Identification is made by matching prints at a minimum of 16 points. (Obviously, a loop is a loop is a loop. It is the breaks in its lines that allow a match-up to be made.)

Bodies have been found with the skin either burned or sandpapered, but prints could still be taken since the ridges beneath maintained the original markings. This also allows a set of prints to be taken from a decomposed corpse. In fingerprinting, the epidermis is not necessary.

The sole of the foot and the palm of the hand also have distinctive markings that yield good prints and aid the police in identification.

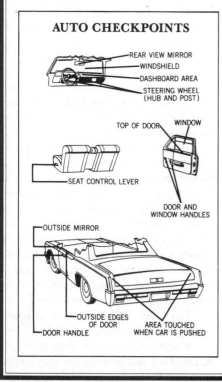

AUTO CHECKPOINTS

REAR VIEW MIRROR
WINDSHIELD
DASHBOARD AREA
STEERING WHEEL (HUB AND POST)

TOP OF DOOR   WINDOW

SEAT CONTROL LEVER

DOOR AND WINDOW HANDLES

OUTSIDE MIRROR

OUTSIDE EDGES OF DOOR
DOOR HANDLE
AREA TOUCHED WHEN CAR IS PUSHED

Hair

Although human and animal hair can be distinguished easily, it is not yet possible to categorically state that a given hair belongs to a specific person. It is often possible to prove, however, that hair did *not* come from a certain person and in this regard it becomes a vital piece of exclusionary evidence.

Hair indicates one's race. A cross-section of Negroid hair shows unevenly distributed pigment, a flat to oval shape and marked variations in diameter along the shaft. Mongoloid hair (American Indian, Eskimo, Oriental) has little diameter variation along the shaft, a round to oval shape and usually a heavy black medulla. Caucasian hair is oval to round in shape, varies moderately in diameter and shows even pigment distribution.

In general, male hair is larger in diameter and more wiry in texture than that of a female.

Scalp hair can be readily distinguished from beard hair, pubic hair, and hair from the ear, nose, eyebrow, eyelid or torso. By examining the hair shaft, it can be determined if the hair has been crushed by a blunt instrument, severed or pulled forcibly from the head.

Fiber

Fibers may be divided into four classes: animal (wool, silk, camel's hair, fur), vegetable (cotton, jute, linen, hemp, ramie, sisal), mineral (glass wool and asbestos) and synthetic (nylon, Orlon, Dacron et al.).

Fiber can be analyzed for composition, dye content, twist and ply count. In cases where the fiber has been in contact with paint, dust and mud, it is possible to compare weave-pattern impression.

Semen

The screening procedures for semen include the Florence, Puranan and Barberios tests, but the only specific conclusive tests for identifying seminal fluid are the acid phosphatase reaction test and thin-layer chromonetography. If the subject was a secretor, it will be possible to identify blood type from a semen sample.

COURTESY INTERNATIONAL ASSOCIATION OF CHIEFS OF POLICE

shot to death at two o'clock one morning. His car had stopped briefly at the top of an embankment before plunging down it, coming to rest with the right front corner jammed against a wire fence so thoroughly that the passenger's door could not be opened. A bloody handprint on the open driver's door showed where somebody had rested briefly before lifting—not dragging—his hand away.

The victim was on the ground, on his back, head pointing toward the left rear tire and feet extended straight out in front of him at about a seventy-degree angle to the car. A shotgun lay on the grass six feet from the victim; but the blast that had torn away part of his left front temple definitely was fired inside the car with the door closed, with the victim's head turned sharply to the right.

As we reconstructed it, the man, leaving home after a quarrel, had picked up a friend. They began quarreling and the victim stopped his car on the roadside, where his companion shot him to death with his own gun. The car, still in drive, plunged over the embankment when the dead man's foot slipped off the brake. The perpetrator, stuck in a wrecked car with a dead man, climbed out, dragging the victim out in the process, started to leave with the shotgun and decided a moment later to abandon it.

That was what we thought.

The detectives talked to literally everybody the victim knew and a lot of people he might have known. I compared that palm print to everybody we could think of in five towns, until I had it practically memorized. We had three or four people working almost full time on

---

BLOODSTAINS

Extreme care must be taken to ascertain that a specific stain is, in fact, blood and not merely paint, rust, ink or lipstick—all of which can easily be mistaken for it.

The three tests routinely used to determine if blood is present at a crime scene are: the Benzidine test (upon contact with even a small amount of blood, the solution changes to a blue-green color); the Leuco-Malachite test (its light green color intensifies to a deep blue-green with the appearance of blood); the Luminol test (the suspect stain will luminesce if all or part of it is formed by blood).

Laboratory tests can prove conclusively if blood came from a human and what type it is.

By the size, shape and distribution of bloodstains, it is possible to reconstruct what occurred during an alleged crime. Often a suspect will insist he acted in self-defense, only to have his story disproved by the pattern of blood spill. On the basis of bloodstain evidence alone, it is possible

to determine whether a victim was in a defensive or attack position at the time of death; whether he was moving or stationary; whether his body was moved after the homicide was accomplished.

FORMS OF BLOODSTAINS

GENERAL APPEARANCE	DIRECTION OF FALL	GENERAL VERBAL DESCRIPTION
	VERTICAL Up to 2 feet	Well-defined spots with rounded edges
	VERTICAL 2 to 4 feet	Prickly and jagged edges which become finer and closer together as height increases
	VERTICAL Over 4 feet	Edges splash out up to one foot from the center of the drop. Small beads can be thrown out (arrow)
	OBLIQUE Varies with the speed of fall	Drawn-out shape with elongated or dotted ends with point in the direction of fall (arrow)

that case for six weeks.

Until the victim's live-in lady friend, who was perhaps not the best housekeeper in the world, came in to talk with me, bringing a note. "I just now found it," she explained, "and I thought you ought to see it."

It didn't mention suicide in so many words. It was a "Poor little me, I'm going out in the garden and eat some worms" kind of note, but it did include the sentence "You'll be sorry when you never see me again." It was not signed. So the first question was, had it really been written by the victim?

The handwriting examiner confirmed that it had.

Had the victim been capable of opening the car door, walking to where he was found and throwing the shotgun to where it fell?

The medical examiner, somewhat puzzled by my question, confirmed that the victim had definitely been alive for several minutes, probably about half an hour, after he was shot; and yes, he could have been semiconscious and capable of volitional action for several minutes.

And the clincher, the palm print we were sure had been made by the killer was the print of—the victim.

We had worked it for six weeks as murder. It was the only non-suspect ident I ever made on a suicide.

Sometimes fingerprints flatly contradict what we thought were facts. There was the time a black woman was attacked about two o'clock in the morning, in her own bedroom, by a would-be rapist. When she punctuated her objections with the butcher knife she kept under her pillow, he decided it might be best to leave.

Detectives collected one beautiful latent from the metal frame of the bedroom window; the glass, oddly enough, was gone and nobody could find it anywhere. And although the bedroom lights were off, there was a good streetlight

outside. The victim gave a fine description of a six-foot-tall white man with a bushy beard.

I knew of a six-foot-tall rapist with a bushy beard who lived in her neighborhood and had exactly that M.O. Furthermore, he was—alas—on parole again. Just one problem. He happened to be black.

I searched the print through known white sex criminals with "negative results," filed it and forgot about it.

Until six months later.

Now, I freely admit that I have a tendency to be lazy. At that time I kept the black and white sex criminals filed together, as there were so few of either. I knew which finger the print was of, and it's really much easier just to compare the print than to look all over every card for race, which keeps getting put in a new spot every year or so. Therefore, when I pulled out the print and began to search it again, I very lazily decided to search it through all sex criminals, rather than just white sex criminals.

He'd have been in jail the day after the crime, if the victim had known whether the man she fought for over ten minutes under a bright light had been black or white. Because it was the man I thought of at first.

At that point I knew why the window glass went missing. His last conviction had been the result of his leaving fingerprints on the window glass of the place he broke into; so this time he'd cannily decided to take the glass with him. Nobody had told him metal holds prints, too.

Would I put these cases in a book, no matter how suitably disguised?

I wouldn't dare, but they were certainly interesting to work.

Martha G. Webb is the author of Darling Corey's Dead, A White Male Running *and (as Lee Martin)* Too Sane a Murder.

VICTIMS

"I say, it's a bit of ///////........"

"I'm not going in there alone, Rosie. I'm not, I tell you. Not. I'll fetch Mr. Leslie, then; he's a kind one."

"Herself's new boyfriend, do you mean?"

"Now what are you big mouthing about, Rosie? What do you say?"

"My Jock told me about them, how they meet secret like, regular as the clock works, ordering the same each time so's he don't have to even ask anymore, just pour the double lager and lime for him and that fancy stuff for her."

"I don't believe it. Not a word. He swore to me, Mr. Leslie did, he'd have no truck with a woman who's taken."

"Oh, yes? And when was that, Bridie my dear, was that when you left me all alone with Cook in the kitchen with that temper full down on me, huh?"

Going . . .

"Ow, Rosie, t'weren't, I swear it. I was looking for Whelks to put up his tools, but I couldn't find him anyplace, I couldn't. It was after chores were well done. You were sound asleep by then, when I met up with him in the hallway and we had a bit of a chat."

"Ooooh, Bridie. Another crush, have you? And on Her Ladyship's fellow? There's trouble comin' down with this one, I can feel it."

"It was only a kiss, Rosie, nothing more, cross my heart to the Pope. A

"W**ould you look at that, taking a nap, is he, on the fine new carpet?"

"Ooooh, Bridie, I think not. The breathing's stopped: I do think so."

"What do you mean, then? Dead, is he?"

"I don't know for sure. Oh, stop all that crossing and fussing yourself, Bridie, until we have a look close up."

"Mr. Roudebush first, Rosie. We must tell Mr. Roudebush. He'll know what to do."

"But, Bridie, ninny girl, Mr. Roudebush is abed with the gout, remember? How can he help us, layin' up as he is? He can't set foot to floor today and that's a fact, remember?"

lovely light little kiss, what's the wrong in that?"

"Oh, you goose girl, it's not me who's taking the confessions, now is it? Let's get on with it."

"In there? You really are stepping in the tea lounge, right now?"

"Yes, and so are you; come on, then, give me your hand."

"You're not going to touch him!"

"Well, he don't look so swell, now do he? A move just to make him tidy... presentable for company like. You take that arm, no, not that one; I've got it. Eeech, see what you've gone and done—dragged his pant leg through all that sandwich stuffing. Quick, pick it up. Won't do to have food on the floor!"

"Right. Put it away in my pocket, I did. Don't you think, Rosie, it's too pretty by half in here now? Where's the trash to go but a pocket?"

"I'll just put the teacup back, too, wouldn't want a smash-up if someone walks about. Uh, Bridie, do you notice anything about the china?"

going . . .

"Nooo, can't say's I do. What's the matter, then?"

"It's second-best, Bridie. Not the company set."

"Ooooh. Her Ladyship wouldn't like that. Get the tray and we'll re-lay so's no one's to notice. How many places? Lady Clare, yes, and Miss Becca and her Mr. Fogg, that's three. And Mr. Leslie and the Colonel, of course, for five. Nurse and Mr. Penny-Pincher, too, do you think? Yes, let's add them for the seven."

"Whew, that's done then, now what about him?"

"Good God, girls, what have you done!"

"Nothing, sir; we didn't do it, we didn't. Tell him, Bridie, you saw the body first."

"Me? Rosie, how can you say that! It was *you* what saw him and knew he were dead! Now, admit it or your soul will go straight to hell, won't it, Father?"

"Perhaps not quite, Bridie, not quite that way. Now, will you stay while I ring for the doctor? And don't let anyone touch anything, all right?"

"Ooooh, couldn't we ring and you stay, Father? It's gettin' kind of like the creeps, if you know what I mean. Smelly like. Please, Father, could you stay and we'll go?"

"Gladly would I, gladly. Now, promise you won't go alarming the house about this. Let's hear the doctor out first, shall we?"

"Yes, sir. Yes, sir. Come on, then, Bridie, come on."

"Our Father, who art . . ."

gone.

HOUSE CALLS
THE DOCTOR DETECTIVE ROUND-UP

P.D. James

It must be a minority of mysteries in which a doctor doesn't make at least a brief appearance. In any civilised country, following a suspicious death, a medical man is invariably called in to examine the body and pronounce life extinct, and later a forensic pathologist will perform an autopsy. The descriptions of some of these medical experts is often as superficial as their appearance in the story is brief. They perform their necessary functions with varying degrees of efficiency and depart leaving the detective, amateur or professional to carry on with the investigation. But occasionally doctors and nurses play a more important role—suspect, detective or even murderer—while a number of mystery writers have chosen a medical setting for their stories—a hospital, clinic or nursing home.

It is easy to understand the attraction of a doctor as suspect or villain. He has the means of death readily at hand; he has knowledge of poisons, their symptoms and effects; his intimate acquaintance with his patients and their private lives gives him particular opportunity; he has professional dexterity and skill, and—particularly if he is a surgeon—he has nerve. Occasionally, too, he has the hubris with which most murderers are afflicted. If all power corrupts, then a doctor, who literally holds life and death in his hands, must be at particular risk. Sir Julian Freke, one of Dorothy L. Sayers' two medical murderers, is an example of the arrogance of the fictional brilliant surgeon who regards himself as above morality and law. It is interesting

that of Sayers' eleven full-length murder mysteries, two have medical murderers, both eminent specialists, while a third has an ex-nurse who kills by the doubtfully feasible method of injecting air into the patient's vein. But perhaps the nastiest of all the medical murderers is Dr. Grimesby Roylott of Conan Doyle's *The Speckled Band.* As his author says:

> When a doctor goes wrong he is the first of villains. He has nerve and he has knowledge. Palmer and Pritchard were among the heads of that profession.

It is perhaps surprising that a medical setting is comparatively rare in detective fiction, considering its attractions. Here we have the closed community beloved of detective writers for the neat containment of victim, suspect and murderer: a strongly hierarchical community with its own esoteric rules and conventions; a mysterious but fascinating world of men and women performing a great variety of necessary jobs from consultant surgeon to ward cleaner, where the reader, like the patient, feels vulnerable, apprehensive and alien. To write convincingly about hospitals usually requires special knowledge, and those who have done it best, in whose books the smell of disinfectant seems literally to rise from the page, have usually had a medical or nursing background. Josephine Bell (*Murder in Hospital; Death at the Medical Board*) is herself a doctor, and Christianna Brand uses her experience as a voluntary nurse during World War II in what I still consider one of the best detective novels with a medical setting—*Green for Danger.*

The peculiar advantages of special knowledge, professional skill and insight into character which are enjoyed by the doctor as villain also apply to the doctor as detective. The list of medical fictional detectives is varied and impressive, including such very different characters as Josephine Bell's Dr. David Winteringham, H.C. Bailey's amiable, hedonistic but deeply compassionate Dr. Reginald Fortune, and R. Austin Freeman's Dr. Thorndyke—perhaps the greatest medical legal detective in fiction. Dr. Thorndyke is essentially a forensic scientist rather than a medical doctor and, in addition to exceptional intellectual powers, has a profound knowledge of such diverse subjects as anatomy, ophthalmology, botany, archaeology and Egyptology. He is also exceptionally handsome. Freeman writes:

> *His distinguished appearance is not merely a concession to my personal taste but also a protest against the monsters of ugliness whom other detective writers have evolved. These are quite opposed to natural truth. In real life, a first-class man of any kind usually tends to be a good-looking man.*

It is not surprising that a number of the most successful medical detectives are psychiatrists. As Helen McCloy's Dr. Basil Willing says: "Every criminal leaves psychic fingerprints and he can't wear gloves to hide them. . . . Lies like blunders are psychological facts." The appropriately named Dr. Paul Prye, the tall, whimsical psychiatrist who features

THE FIFTY-MINUTE CRIME

Need a psychiatrist to help you solve a problem? Contact Gene Goldsmith's Dan Damon, Kyle Hunt's Emmanuel Cellini, Helen McCloy's Basil Willing, Hugh McLeave's Gregor MacLean, Lynn Meyer's Sarah Chayse, Margaret Millar's Paul Prye, Gladys Mitchell's Beatrice Bradley, Hugh Pentecost's John Smith or Patrick Quentin's Dr. Lenz.

If you'd prefer a psychoanalyst, try Henry Kuttner's Michael Gray.

If you'd rather visit a psychologist, try Balmer and MacHarg's Luther Trant or T.S. Stribling's Henry Poggioli.

Still another specialist you might try is the one who makes a career out of nervous disorders—Wynne's Eustace Hailey.

Finally, you might consider contacting Lucy Freeman, who not only has created a psychiatrist sleuth in *The Dream* but has coauthored many books with leading (real) doctors in the field.

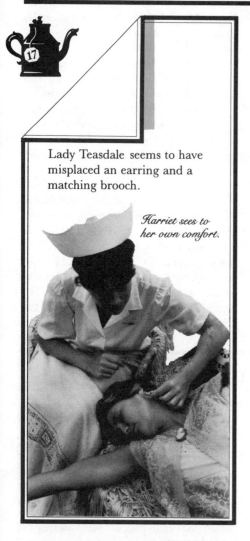

Lady Teasdale seems to have misplaced an earring and a matching brooch.

Harriet sees to her own comfort.

in Ohio who, in *Diagnosis: Murder,* suspects that a number of the apparently natural deaths in the community are actually murders and is able to prove it. Jonathan Stagg's G.P. detective, Dr. Hugh Westlake, also works in a small town, but here the stories, although they have a medical background, contain a strong atmosphere of terror and the supernatural (*The Stars Spell Death; Turn of the Table; The Yellow Taxi*).

But one of the best-known general practitioners in crime writing must be the narrator of Agatha Christie's brilliant but controversial novel first published in 1926, *The Murder of Roger Ackroyd,* in which the village doctor is both narrator and murderer. The trick has been used since, but never with such cunning and panache.

Nurse detectives are considerably less common than doctors, but perhaps the most well known is M.G. Eberhart's Sarah Keate, a middle-aged spinster who works in a midwestern American city with a young police detective, Lance O'Leary—an intriguing and original partnership where Miss Keate's inquisitiveness is a highly effective adjunct to O'Leary's "eyes in the back of his head and ears all around."

But all the great medical detectives are from the past. Gladys Mitchell's eccentric, formidable psychiatrist Dame Beatrice Lestrange Bradley is now silent, and there is a definite move, at least in the orthodox detective novel, toward a professional police hero. Apart from Dame Beatrice, it is difficult to recall a modern medical detective, and it may be, in an age of increasing specialisation, that the heyday of the brilliant omniscient amateur like Dr. Thorndyke, whether medical or lay, is temporarily over.

in Margaret Millar's first three books, would no doubt have agreed, as would the very different philosopher and psychologist Prof. Henry Poggioli, who features in the only mystery novel written by T.S. Stribling—*Clues of the Caribbees.*

Some medical detectives are general practitioners and have the advantage of that intimate knowledge of the local community and the day-to-day lives of their patients, their families and backgrounds which is so important to successful detection. Rufus King's Dr. Colin Starr is a G.P. working in a fictional small town

P.D. James won a Crime Writers' Association Silver Dagger for The Black Tower. *Her* Death of an Expert Witness *features a forensic laboratory.*

FORENSIC PROTOCOL

John R. Feegel, M.D.

Starting with the end first, hardly anyone uses a rectal thermometer to calculate the interval from moment of death to discovery of body. This final indignity, predicated on the fiction that all men were created sufficiently equal that the heat of their bodies will drop uniformly at one degree centigrade per hour, suffers from the realities of grossly unequal environments: bodies clothed and unclothed, wet and dry, on the cold tile of the bathroom floor or wrapped in a shawl, in an armchair near the half-open window or at an angle from the dying embers of a once roaring blaze on the hearth. It is enough for our morgue sleuth to feel the armpit and mentally register warm vs. cold.

The same goes for rigor mortis, a chemical reaction in the muscles. This unpredictably brief stiffness will fall victim to the amount of reactants and the temperature. Hence the running deer when shot will stiffen quickly, along with the struggling, defensive victim, as compared to the sleeping or unsuspecting recipient of swift foul play.

So much for the traditional line "She died at exactly six-fifteen the day before yesterday, Inspector." All plots based on an exact calculation from observed body temperatures, rigor mortis or the settling of blood within the capillaries should be thrown on the floor and their authors shot.

The Remains

The body itself comes from a large, walk-in refrigerated room on a wheeled cart (gurney) and seldom from a tray that slides out of the wall behind individual doors. The older design called for a wall of trays and doors, and the clack of their handles certainly enhances every novel and film. Trouble is, they're hard to clean. The roll-in room—like a meat locker—can be hosed and bodies can be autopsied right on their trays. Small hospitals may have a self-contained body cooler big enough for one or two, with the drawers working sideways.

The Medical Examiner

At best a forensic scientist graduated in medicine and trained in pathology; at worst the coroner, qualified only by election and a morbid interest in dead bodies, and unskilled in autopsy technique. The titles to this office vary from place to place, depending on the legislature. Beware. There are no coroners in Florida. There are both M.E.'s and coroners in North Carolina. The titles may be synonymous in Los Angeles. Wary writers will check the law and customs of their chosen locale before calling in the Miami coroner.

Yes, he may wear a rubber (plastic) apron and almost always disposable (latex, not rubber) gloves, a short-sleeved "scrub shirt" and, more often than not, his own street pants. Sometimes an old pair of shoes permanently blood-splattered are worn and left in the morgue locker, but no one (absent a body that is highly contagious) wears a surgical mask at autopsy.

Scalpels are in. The ones with fat X-Acto handles and wide disposable #22 Bard-Parker blades. The kind used by model-airplane makers. And why not? They're more comfortable in the hand for many hours at the autopsy table. Virtually gone are the wooden-handled boning knives preferred by the old masters and sharpened on a strap by the faithful diener. (*Diener* is still the acceptable term for the autopsy assistant, although lately their organizations have found it demeaning.)

The incision is "Y"-shaped, from shoulder to shoulder and ending at the pubic hair. (The closing stitch is a running baseball and done by the diener, who uses a large turkey needle sharpened along its forward edge; the suture material is plain old string). The forceps are long-handled, rat-toothed and stainless steel. The bone "saw" is a modified Stryker cast cutter that safely vibrates rather than saws. Other equipment includes a chisel and a metal hammer with

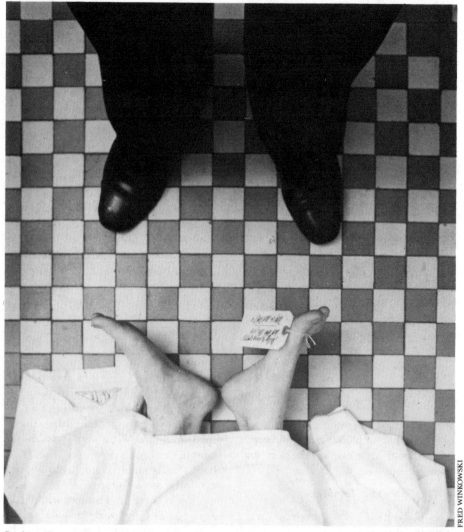

FRED WINKOWSKI

Do they still use toe tags at the morgue? Yes. They are of sturdy manila, with a string looped through one end, and similar to the tags put on packages or luggage. They have a tendency to slip off, but they are slipped right back on again.

a hook at the end of the handle to pull the skull cap off after it's been cut all the way around. (Scalp incision goes ear to ear.)

All medical examiner's morgues have x-ray machines. The "plate," or film cassette, is placed under the body, sometimes in a plastic bag to keep it from getting bloody. The film is developed and reviewed before or during the autopsy by the pathologist himself. He can see bullets and other metal objects on the film and recover them by dissection. X-rays also show fracture patterns and healing injuries in child abuse cases. Long bones and joints are seldom dissected at forensic autopsies. ("Bumper fractures" match the height of the bumper from the road to the distance above the heel *plus shoes.*) Broken necks, while difficult to demonstrate by dissection, are easily seen on x-ray.

The medical examiner does *not* have the body embalmed before autopsy. It ruins the toxicology. Conversely, the pathologist in the small community hospital might. He probably ignores the toxicology anyway and is seldom trained in forensic. (A good place to have a crucial fact missed at autopsy for later discovery by the M.E. downtown.)

But does the M.E. do his own toxicology? With apologies to Quincy, hardly ever. The forensic pathologist is basically a morbid anatomist. His chemist is a Ph.D. whose lab is never in the autopsy room. (The *morgue* is where the body is stored; the *autopsy room,* or *dissecting room,* is where it's cut up. When the fictional autopsy, or post-mortem examination, or just plain "post" in hospital jargon, is done "in" or "at" the morgue, it's close enough.) The well-trained forensic pathologist removes and examines *all* organs in every case and probably puts them all back in the abdominal-chest cavity at the end of the case. Teaching institutions may save them in pans or on trays for conferences before they go about incinerating them.

Let's give the medical examiner a plausible selection of books on that shelf behind his desk. He's a pathologist, remember, so standard medical texts are not out of place. He reads W.A.D. Anderson and also Robbins. In forensic, he would now consult Spitz and Fisher's *The Medical-Legal Investigation of Death.* Out of print (and out of date) is the older classic by Helpern and others out of the New York office. Nobody except the die-hard British and coroners from the turn of the century quote from Sir Bernard Spillsbury; he is as anachronistic in a modern cop story as a prescription written in Latin with symbols, drams and minims instead of milligrams and cc's in plain English, often using brand names. (The doctor who prescribes in Latin is suspect from Chapter One.)

A Watery Grave

Throw a dead body in the water and it *sinks.* Boo to all those films that show the dead victim floating to the horror of the perpetrator. The trick is making the body stay down. Putrefaction, caused by bacteria (nature's way of reducing Uncle Harry to his basic elements), produces gas. When this gas collects in the tissue (not just the body cavities, so opening the chest and abdomen doesn't help), the body becomes bouyant. To overcome this force, one needs to weight down the body—somewhere in the magnitude of two and a half times the victim's own weight—*or* prevent the putrefaction by cold and pressure. So if the water is cold enough or deep enough (or both), the nonweighted corpse is expected to go down and stay down.

While we're in the water, let's drown. Drowning is primarily asphyxia, that is, lack of air. (There is also some dilution of the blood from water in the lung.) Some people drown without gulping or inhaling water and thus at autopsy show little or no water in the airway and lungs. This "dry drowning" is

PAUL REVERE'S TEETH

Who was the first forensic dentist? None other than Paul Revere.

Most people think of him riding about the countryside with a lantern. If they stretch their memories, they may recall he was a silversmith. He was also a dentist and in at least one instance was called upon to identify a gentleman from that gentleman's remains, which included a rather handsome set of teeth. These were teeth Revere had worked on—filling, polishing, pulling, and so forth. He was able to establish, to his satisfaction, that the teeth belonged to his former patient.

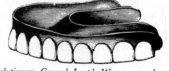

Revolutionary General Joseph Warren owned a set of Revere teeth. His skull still shows remnants of them, should you care to look.

due to spasm in the throat. "Wet drowning" is more typical with mystery writers. Water can be seen and samples of it recovered by the pathologist. But let's be honest: the M.E. can't tell pool water from bathtub water. In fact, he'll have a difficult time differentiating fresh water from salt. Gettler (1921), from the N.Y.M.E. office, found a difference in the specific gravity or salt content in the left and right heart chambers due to dilution (or concentration) of blood returning from the lung circuit. He thought the test would "prove" drowning and whether it occurred in fresh or salt water. The test is unreliable, however, so don't give the morgue-Sherlock too much credit in this scene. Washerwoman's fingers show prolonged immersion, nothing more. Diatoms or microscopic marine skeletons are also found in dust. Their discovery in lung tissue does not prove drowning.

Not every body found at the bottom of the pool is a drowning victim. A person who suffers a coronary while swimming will also promptly sink (much to the horror of the motel's insurance company). His autopsy *might* show a fresh coronary artery thrombosis; then again, it might only show advanced arteriosclerosis, the reason he was on vacation in the first place. Even the "cone of foam" from the mouth and nose may be from pulmonary edema and not conclusive of drowning. When in doubt, call it an accident.

A Burning Question

How about a cozy fire? First of all, there is no such thing as spontaneous combustion of a body. Let's leave that for the religious writers. Mystery readers should know that smoke, when inhaled even by an unconscious victim, leaves soot in the windpipes and lungs. Fires usually produce carbon monoxide and other toxic fumes (particularly from synthetic plastics and furniture), which may kill long before the actual fire reaches the body; hence the char may be postmortem. The toxic gases can be detected in the blood at autopsy, although as a practical matter one seldom tests beyond carbon monoxide.

A house fire is a favorite way of disposing of a homicide victim. Lack of soot in the airway and negative blood CO are highly suspicious, however, and a bullet seen on x-ray of the charred remains is a dead giveaway. Stab wounds may be obliterated by the fire, but the internal bleeding remains. Hot, prolonged fires may boil the brain and cause the skull to fracture like an exploding can of beans in the campfire; such a fracture follows the natural suture lines, while a fracture due to an ante-mortem bash in the head is depressed and crosses suture lines.

The heat of the fire shortens tendons and produces flexion of the fingers, wrists and arms. This "pugilistic" attitude is not evidence that the fire victim was defending himself at the time of death. With additional exposure to the fire, the hands may totally burn off, leaving sharp stumps for forearms. This is not to be construed as evidence of an ax amputation before death.

Name Your Poison

A little something to sweeten the tea? Poisons have long been a favorite with the murder writer. Trouble is, the toxin and the symptons are often confused.

Toxicology is the science of identification of a given poison (toxin) in tissue or body fluid. It is really *not* the study of poisons. That title is reserved for toxinology. Those are the guys who study the specific effects of extracts of weird plants, marine animals, crawly creatures and the like. The orderly approach to the effects of poisons is to consider the life processes they can disrupt. Such processes include intracellular transfer of oxygen (cyanide), transportation and delivery of oxygen in the bloodstream (carbon monoxide), disruption of metabolic systems within the liver (carbon tetrachloride), interference of the filtering functions of the kidney (uranium) or death of selected cells in brain and nervous tissue (lead, mercury).

Obviously, disruptive agents do not act with the same rapidity or dose. Some drugs merely act by depression of function (barbiturates) through sedation to stupor, to deep sleep to coma and death. Alcohol works similarly. Remember that many modern medicines had their origins in the garden, although today most are synthesized; hence a yarn concerning death through plant additives is

plausible if carefully done (foxglove-digitalis). What is embarrassing is the addition of a pinch of cyanide to the Colonel's tea, only to have him agonize on for several days or chapters before gracefully keeling over. In fact, as all toxinologists will testify, CN is a *very* rapidly acting, highly toxic agent pro-

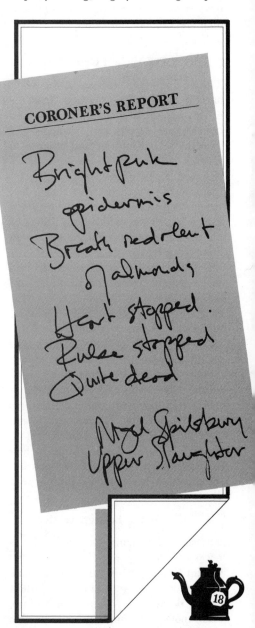

CORONER'S REPORT

Bright pink
epidermis
Breath redolent
of almonds
Heart stopped.
Pulse stopped
Quite dead

Nigel Spilsbury
Upper Slaughter

ducing intracellular anoxia and death probably in minutes. No time here for the victim to contribute further to the intrigue: this one dies at the table. For a more prolonged poisoning, the writer will have to search for a slower agent to specifically disrupt an organ system and be accurate about the effects. A little time in the pharmacology books (Goodman and Gilman, for example, or Macmillan) is all it takes.

The Violent Crime

The fatal rape case is seen by the M.E. as at least two cases in one: first the cause of death and then the investigation of the sexual assault. The pathologist will note the sexual injuries and attempt to recover pubic hairs (from both victim and assailant) for later comparison with material from a suspect or from a bed sheet. Vaginal secretions are examined for sperm (motile or dead) and for acid phosphatase, an enzyme produced in abundance by the prostate gland. Many males "secrete" their blood group into their semen. As for the blood groups themselves (A, B, O, AB, M, N, MN, etc.), they are distinguishable from the blood *types* (Rh pos., Rh neg.).

This branch of forensic science is usually delegated to the serologist, who is able to identify human from non-human bloodstains and, through grouping and immunological techniques (HLA), to produce a statistically valid "profile" of the suspect. The bloodstain expert need not be a serologist or pathologist, but one who is capable of identifying direction, speed and height of a drop of blood that splatters the floor or wall.

Old Bones, Foreign Teeth

The skeletal remains may be all that is necessary to suggest foul play. Stab wounds are long gone, but nicks on bone can be identified and, of course, bullets do not decay. The M.E. or his forensic anthropologist consultant should be able to determine whether the bones are human, the sex, the approximate age at death, the race and the height (if there are limb bones). Racial characteristics (Caucasoid, Indian, African, Asian) are seen in the shape of the head, the eye sockets and the prominence of the brow. Hence the plot that substitutes a skeleton for the victim may fail if the perpetrator is unaware that race can be identified from the skull. Also, old fractures or orthopedic plates and screws may provide individual identification when compared to old x-rays.

Closely allied is the forensic odontologist. This morbid dentist can greatly assist identification by careful examination of the teeth and dental repair and by comparison to old dental records. Race and age can usually be determined, and, as expected, dental work (crowns, bridges, caps, fillings) differ in technique around the world. The spy posing as a Bulgarian had better not smile and show his American crownwork.

The odontologist can also assist in identification of the assailant from the bite marks on the victim or on a food remnant left at the scene of a crime. Obviously, a suspect is required for comparison, but the evidence has repeatedly held up in court.

Of course, it is acceptable and flattering to give the medical examiner all of the above talents. It is not likely that this all-knowing forensic pathologist exists outside the world of fiction, but since each of the medical examiners has an interest in a subspecialty, who will deny the abilities of the morgue-sleuth in an otherwise well-written murder mystery? If he smokes a pipe and wears a long white coat, he must know something scientific.

John R. Feegel, M.D., is a chronic over-achiever: forensic pathologist, attorney and author of five novels, including the Edgar-winning Autopsy.

The New York Times

NEW YORK, WEDNESDAY, AUGUST 6, 1975

Hercule Poirot Is Dead; Famed Belgian Detective

By THOMAS LASK

Hercule Poirot, a Belgian detective who became internationally famous, has died in England. His age was unknown.

Mr. Poirot achieved fame as a private investigator after he retired as a member of the Belgian police force in 1904. His career, as chronicled in the novels of Dame Agatha Christie, his creator, was one of the most illustrious in fiction.

At the end of his life, he was arthritic and had a bad heart. He was in a wheelchair often, and was carried from his bedroom to the public lounge at Styles Court, a nursing home in Essex, wearing a wig and false mustaches to mask the signs of age that offended his vanity. In his active days, he was always impeccably dressed.

Mr. Poirot, who was just 5 feet 4 inches tall, went to England from Belgium during World War I as a refugee. He settled in a little town not far from Styles, then an elaborate country estate, where he took on his first private case.

The news of his death, given by Dame Agatha, was not unexpected. Word that he was near death reached here last May.

His death was confirmed by Dodd, Mead, Dame Agatha's publishers, who will put out "Curtain," the novel that chronicles his last days, on Oct. 15.

The Poirot of the final volume is only a shadow of the well-turned out, agile investigator who, with a charming but immense ego and fractured English, solved uncounted mysteries in the 37 full-length novels and collections of short stories in which he appeared.

Dame Agatha reports in "Curtain" that he managed, in one final gesture, to perform one more act of cerebration that saved an innocent bystander from disaster. "Nothing in his life became him like the leaving it," to quote Shakespeare, whom Poirot frequently misquoted.

Dodd, Mead had not expected another installment in the heroic achievements of the famous detective.

No manuscript came in last year, and none was expected this year, either. However, there had been many rumors to the effect that

Dame Agatha had locked up two manuscripts — one a Poirot and one a Marple — in a vault and that they were not to be published until her death. Jonathan Dodd, of Dodd, Mead, said that the Poirot was the one now being published.

Although the career of Poirot will no more engage his historian, a spokesman for the author said that Dame Agatha, who will be 85 Sept. 15, intends to continue writing. In her long writing career, one that parallels the literary existence of her detective, she has published 85 full-length novels and collections of short stories, which have sold 350 million copies in hard cover and paperback all over the globe. This figure does not include the pirated editions behind the Iron Curtain, of which no count can be made.

In addition, under the pseudonym of Mary Westmacott she has written a half-dozen romances. What is perhaps more significant is that her first title, "The Mysterious Affair at Styles" is still in print.

At least 17 of her stories have been made into plays, including the famous "The Mouse Trap," which opened in London in 1952 and is still running, setting all kinds of records for longevity in the theater.

Twelve of her tales have become motion pictures, many of which have centered on Jane Marple, Dame Agatha's other famous detective.

In the person of the late Margaret Rutherford, Miss Marple developed her own devoted following.

The most recent of Dame Agatha's movies, "Murder on the Orient Express" opened last year, with excellent box-office returns. And Christie properties have been used for television mystery dramas and for radio shows.

Her hold on her audience is remarkable in a way because the kind of fiction she writes is, well, not exactly contemporary. Her characters come from the quiet and exceedingly comfortable middle class: doctors, lawyers, top military men, members of the clergy. The houses in her fiction are spacious, teas are frequent and abundant, servants abound. True, the comforts have been cut back as the real England in which her mysteries are set has been altered over the years. But the polite, leisure-class settings have been retained.

"I could never manage miners talking in pubs," she once confided to an interviewer, "because I don't know what miners talk about in pubs."

'Undisputed Head Girl'

Not everyone has agreed to her high ranking. Robert Graves complained that "her English is schoolgirlish, her situations for the most part artificial, her detail faulty."

On the other hand, Margery Allingham, herself a writer of whodunits, called her the "undisputed head girl," and the late Anthony Boucher, who reviewed mysteries for this newspaper, remarked, "Few writers are producing the pure puzzle novel and

no one on either side of the Atlantic does it better."

Dame Agatha who has been described as a large woman looking both kind and capable, is the daughter of a well-to-do American father and English mother. She was tutored at home and attended, as she recalled, innumerable classes: dancing, singing, drawing. In World War I, she worked in a Red Cross hospital, and this experience gave her a good working knowledge of poisons, ingredients that turn up rather frequently in her books.

In 1926, she suffered an attack of amnesia, left home and was discovered some days later in a hotel under another name. The furor stirred up by the newspapers over her disappearance has made her shy of newspapers and reporters ever since. She has kept herself inconspicuous in public, even insisting for a while that no picture of herself appear on the dust jackets of her books. She has declined to be interviewed about the death of Poirot. In 1928, she was divorced from her first husband, Archibald Christie, and in 1930 she was married to Max Mallowan, an archeologist.

It has been said that she has brought Victorian qualities to her work—a charge she does not deny. She dislikes sordid tales and confesses that she could not write them. But another side of that Victorianism is that in all her years as a writer she has had one publisher in America, Dodd Mead. Such steadfastness is surely of another age.

A MURDERER CONFESSES

Robert Barnard

The Three Fates.

crime fiction), the whodunit writer sits outside and above humanity and asks: "Now, who would it be fun to kill?"

Often, of course, the book he is writing has organised itself around one uniquely unpleasant personality. "He's just asking to be murdered," people say about such personalities in real life, and the detective writer, with a wave of his nibbed wand, fulfils the implied wish. Whether the character is someone he has met, someone he has read or heard of, or someone he has plucked from air, his murder is satisfying to the writer and probably to the reader as well: who can imagine Agatha Christie getting anything but satisfaction from killing Mrs. Boynton or Simon Lee? And though she claimed she almost never took characters from life, who that has read the *Autobiography* can doubt that the victim in *Murder in Mesopotamia* was so taken—and that the murder was something of a wish-fulfilment? Her satisfaction at despatching so odious a creature communicates itself to the reader.

I myself don't very often take my victims from real life. (I'm forced to say that by the laws of libel—but the same laws do, in fact, mean that I do it very seldom.) More often the germ of an idea comes from my reading. Christopher Sykes, in his biography of Evelyn Waugh, has a story about Waugh at a dinner party being annoyed by the fulsome praise of the lady beside him for *Brideshead Revisited*. He turned on her with the devastating words: "I thought it was a good book myself, but now that I

"I suppose you work off all your hatreds and aggressions by writing about violent death . . ."

It's one of the most frequent things that people say to crime writers, and one usually grins an assent. But thinking it over, I certainly seem to retain a modicum of hatred and aggression for everyday life. Surely, if it is ever true, it must be so mainly for the writer of the bloodier type of thriller. The contriver of detective puzzles resembles not the criminal who murders as a result of angry, irresistible impulses, but the *experimental* murderer—the one for whom the commission of murder is a sort of intellectual challenge, a game of chess with blood on the queen or king. Like the experimental murderer (I should be very disappointed to hear that he doesn't exist outside

know that a vulgar, common American woman like yourself admires it, I am not so sure." This anecdote was, I think, the germ of my victim in *Unruly Son* (called in the States *Death of a Mystery Writer*). How do family and friends cope with such a monster? What murderous silences follow such a remark? How does one behave in the aftermath of such social brutalities? My character gained a few of Waugh's other characteristics, such as his country-squire, High Tory façade, and I contrived occasions for social cataclysms such as the above; but as always happens, as soon as he became part of a *story,* he changed. Waugh was a great writer, for example, and part of a close and devoted family, whereas Oliver Fairleigh in my book was the author of racketty and second-rate detective stories, and most of his family loathed him. For what, after all, can a detective writer do with a devoted family circle?

Similar things happened to the mother of the playwright Joe Orton, whom I read about in John Lahr's superb *Prick Up Your Ears*. Here was a monster at the other end of the social scale to Waugh: loud, vulgar, domineering, casually cruel. This working-class Gorgon became the germ of Lill Hodsden in *Mother's Boys* (*Death of a Perfect Mother* in the States); but as usual, as soon as I started to contrive a murder mystery around her, the created character took over from Elsie Orton. Lill is sexy and promiscuous, where Mrs. Orton was prudish and unenthusiastic about sex; Lill's sons are unable to break the chain, whereas Joe Orton escaped without difficulty to London, homosexuality and anarchism.

This last difference illustrates one of the problems about the monster/victim. They are all the sort of people of whom it is usually said when they leave the room: "Isn't it quiet now he's gone?" That's not a good feeling, in a novel. The trouble is that, having built up the monster for fifty or sixty pages, when he is killed off the reader may feel a glow of satisfaction ("He had it coming") but also a sense of anticlimax. Having lost a creature who, though repellent, was nevertheless magnificently individual, the rest of the characters may seem pallid and lifeless, inadequate to sustain interest in the book. Hence the repulsive Mrs. Boynton's power lives on after her death (at least until a decidedly unconvincing epilogue), and so, too, Lill Hodsden's sons, the Mother's Boys, had to find that the chain that tied them to her in life was still shackling after her death. Perhaps

---

COVER CORPSE QUIZ

Can you name the corpses on the covers of the Foul Play Press editions of *Figure Away* and *The Cut Direct*? Clue: He won a Raven for outfitting *Dracula*; she won an Edgar for perpetrating *Murder Ink*.

Other cover corpses in the series have included bookstore owners Carol Brener and Otto Penzler, mystery critic Michele B. Slung and the discoverer of many of our favorite authors, editor Joan Kahn.

Answer:
Edward Gorey and Dilys Winn.

There are no seat belts in the back of a hearse.

MARTY NORMAN

the best instance of the repulsive victim's influence living on is in Allingham's *Police at the Funeral*—but this happens in a way I can hardly reveal.

Sometimes the force behind a book is not an unsavoury character, but a setting or a situation: an opera company, a monastery, whatever. In my favourite of my own books, *Sheer Torture,* the setting and situation were the family that combined privileged birth with artistic talent, living together in the ancestral seat. The Sitwells and the Mitfords provided the germ here, though in fact none of my characters bears any resemblance to a Mitford or a Sitwell, or was meant to, and mine are decidedly short on both privilege and talent. This situation-*cum*-setting combined itself with two other ideas that had been floating around in limbo in my mind, waiting to attach themselves to specific characters and settings. One was merely an opening sentence or so: "I first heard of the death of my father when I saw his obituary in *The Times*. I skimmed through it, cast my eye over the Court Circular, and was about to turn to the leader page when I was struck by something odd. . . ." This notion of someone hearing of the death of his father in that way, and being unaffected by it, intrigued me, but I found it had to be narrated in the first person. Change it to "Peregrine Trethowan first heard of the death of his father. . ." and the bloom wilts. When I adopted Perry Trethowan as my detective for later books, I found they, too, had to be told first-person, which presented technical

problems (very few detective stories, I realized, are told thus).

The last element that went into the making of *Torture* was a death that had taken place ten or fifteen years before and had refused to dislodge from my mind (which has a bent for black humour). The gentleman concerned was something rather snobby and ceremonial in the administration of the City of London—Sheriff, or Gold-Rod-in-Waiting, or some such thing—and he died in his cellar while subjecting himself to one of the Spanish Inquisition tortures, dressed in chorus-girl tights. That, at any rate, is how I remember the affair. There was no doubt that the death was natural, but the circumstances made an inquest inevitable. The *Times,* I recall, tucked the matter away in the law reports section, with some such irresistibly deadpan headline as "Scientific Experiment That Went Too Far." The more popular papers laughed themselves silly. All I had to do was alter the natural death to a murder, and the book was made. With these three rather *outré* elements, it's perhaps not surprising that Jacques Barzun told me he didn't like the novel because he "didn't believe a word of it." Personally, I don't think any of my books rate very high on the credibility scale.

My books are largely, I am afraid, improvisations, and they tend to begin at the beginning. Agatha Christie was much wiser in working *backwards*—in taking a perfectly simple crime and working backwards from it to provide the ambience of confusion that deceives the reader into thinking it extremely complicated. In my case, about two weeks after I've sent a book off to my publisher, I tend to get writer's itch and start in on a first chapter, which grows into three or four chapters and develops a momentum of its own. Often, when this is how a book has been conceived and has grown, there comes a point where the writer has to face up to the question that has been niggling around in the back of his mind from the beginning: who am I going to kill off? (That other question—"Who did it?"—can if necessary be put off for a bit, though it's as well to have a few options in mind.) Perhaps this is a book with no monster; perhaps it has a whole cast-list of them. At any rate, I found myself in this situation with a recent book (another one I confess to rather liking) called *A Corpse in a Gilded Cage*.

The situation was that of a working-class family who suddenly find themselves inheritors of titles and a stately home. The germ of the book was the

DO PEOPLE REALLY DIE IN BED?

Surprisingly, the insurance mortuary tables, which are relentlessly specific about appalling causes of death and sticklers for accuracy regarding the age and sex of the deceased, are a little vague on the subject of how many folks go to their just reward from the comfort of their own beds. One broker admitted, however, that in over twenty-five years in the business, he'd heard of only two people who actually died in their 'jammies. He also suggested if you want to know more about death statistics, you contact the greatest fact compiler of them all—Metropolitan Life, headquartered in New York.

man who, several years ago, became Duke of (I think) Buckingham while he was a street-cleaner in Southend. I took my fictional family down a rung or two on the aristocratic scale and made the father of the family an earl, because I've found that the things people object to as exaggerated in books are invariably the things that are literally true. As I was writing the early chapters of the book—as usual with little that could be dignified by the name of a plan—there arose in me the nagging conviction that the character I liked most was the character who would have to go. I fought against it, and the thing became almost a real-life struggle in my mind: I thought up alternative scenarios—other victims, with quite different reasons for their being murdered. It wasn't as though I was a stranger to improvisation: when I wrote my first book, *Death of an Old Goat*, I had written well beyond the murder, had even written the word that was to be the vital clue, before I finally managed to receive from the ether the message of who it was that did it, and why. But even as I juggled with alternatives, I saw that the logical victim was my favourite; even as I wrote on, hoping that "something would turn up" to save him, I saw that every little circumstance I was recounting served more irrevocably to seal his fate. It was like watching Atropos approaching nearer and nearer the thread with her shears. By the end I knew she would get there, and I knew whose thread she would snip. Finally it was done, and the nicest character in the book lay stone-cold in his pyjamas under the carved Jacobean staircase of the ancestral home.

I felt sad, but also a tickle of something else: perhaps it was the nearest this writer is ever likely to get to feeling he has obeyed an artistic imperative.

Robert Barnard is the author of A Corpse in a Gilded Cage.

THE LURE OF THE REICHENBACH

Peter Dickinson

I am no scholar. I am not even sure how to spell "Reichenbach." Certainly I have no idea how many lesser heroes than Holmes have been done away with by their creators. But it must be a good guess that almost every writer who has kept a detective going through several books finds his thoughts turning more and more toward the moment when... when, for instance, Inspector Ghote eats the poisoned curry, or Peter Wimsey has heart failure on meeting a greater snob than himself, or Van der Valk... But no, Van der Valk *is* dead, isn't he? Mr. Freeling has done the deed.

Why?

The usual answer, that the creator had become bored with his creation, is true in a very trivial kind of way but is at the same time deeply misleading: the kind of answer a writer gives when he doesn't want to discuss the point. I myself stopped writing about James Pibble after five books, but I wasn't bored with him. I liked—and like—the old boy, and I owe him a lot. I think that without hesitation I could answer most questions about him, including the ones that aren't mentioned anywhere in the books. Now he feels to me something like a colleague I spent a lot of time with almost every day but because of a change of jobs have scarcely seen for several years; to meet again might be

delightful, might be embarrassing, but it seems not to happen.

It's worth considering how these long-running heroes come into existence. There seem to be two ways, the deliberate and the accidental. The deliberate hero is nearly always a bloodless creation; the author has decided that he (she? Is it a female trait to manufacture these bionic brains? No idea, but let's settle for "she" throughout)... that she is going to write a series of books and that, therefore, they will have to have some kind of trademark. The hero will be *different*. Thus traits of difference are accumulated, selected not for the way they grow out of the character but solely because nobody else has yet thought of them. In much the same way, minor German monarchs of the eighteenth century invented uniforms for their household troops: violet breeches, because everyone else had green or red; kepis with four-foot plumes; badger-skin bandoliers. What matter if in the end the hussar was unable to lift his sabre above waist height because of the tightness of his jacket? He was more distinctive on the field than old Hesse-Halsbad's boring dragoons.

So the deliberate hero is jumbled into being. (Or *was* jumbled would probably be truer; these creatures were mostly born a generation or two ago, though they live on in libraries, and every now and then a new one is born, especially on TV.) Let's say he has a club-foot and rides an enormous bike (good for last-minute dashes to rescue

Lemmings en route.

the peculiarly witless females who festoon this type of novel) and carries a . . . a swordstick? No, too ordinary; what about a blow-pipe? And he knows the Bible by heart, huh?

For book after book, shelf after shelf, that bike will roar to the rescue, that uneven footstep will sound menacingly, or hearteningly, on sidewalks (though, mark you, in moments of crisis we will read of the man moving "with astonishing dexterity, despite his club-foot"), the witless female's latest attacker will stagger in mid-assault, a tiny dart protruding below his left ear, and all will end pat with a quote from the Second Book of Kings. And by the third book the author will be stiflingly bored with her creation but afraid to let him go.

I said I was no scholar, so I can only guess which of the great detectives was engendered in this fashion. Nero Wolfe, surely—those orchids are typical, and typically become a nuisance after a very few books, and if all Wolfe's characteristics had been as factitious he would have been a bore very soon. But Mr. Stout was a genius, and in inventing Wolfe and Goodwin, solved the central problem of the whodunit by splitting his detective into two parts; this set-up became an art form in itself—I remember one in which Wolfe finally left his apartment, and I felt as cheated as I would have on reading a thirteen-line sonnet. But very few Wolfes came into the canon that way. . .

As a transitional figure, let's consider Margery Allingham's Mr. Campion, who started as factitious as they come, with his silly-ass talk and his mysterious noble connections and the tedious Lugg to provide extra laughs (like the Professor's comic sailor servant in ancient boys' stories). And then Miss Allingham became interested in him, and in the course of two or three books he became, so to speak, real. His chat was mitigated, Lugg almost abolished,

*M*other of God,
is this the
end of Rico?

Little Caesar
W. R. BURNETT

The most famous last line in mystery fiction.

and at the same time the plots and ad-ventures moved out of the realm of card-board fantasy into something like life. So successful was this transformation that Miss Allingham convincingly brought off the problem of making Campion fall in love with a married woman. (Virtue triumphed, too. What a long time ago that must have been. And it's worth pointing out that this passion actually was necessary to the plot.)

So Campion became what I have called an accidental hero. These are the detectives who come into existence be-cause the author wants to write a partic-ular book. The book itself demands a detective, and he *grows* into being, quite slowly, finding his shape and nature from the needs of the book and the au-thor's own needs. He may turn out a very odd creature, but all his oddnesses are expressions of what he is like inside. And then (provided the other bits have gone okay—plot, setting, characters, language and so on) the author may find herself with quite a good book on her hands, centering round a detective to whom readers respond. They may think they're responding because of what seem to be external characteristics (remember the excitement about the first *black* detec-tive?), but really it's because the fellow is *alive*.

Moreover, because detective stories are tricky things to write, the author's attention may not have been concen-trated on exploring every nook and cranny of her hero's personality; in fact,

if it has, she will have written an unsatis-factory book—there isn't room in the genre for a lot of that sort of thing. So there will be more to give. And the publisher, of course, wants more if the first dose has been a success. It requires self-confidence and a healthy bank bal-ance for a newcomer author to say no.

So for a few years everyone is happy; if the readers like it, then the publisher likes it, and the author fleshes out her man, puts him into novel situa-tions, finds new facets. If she'd been writing a straight novel, she'd have done all these things in a single book, but with detective stories it may take four or five. And then . . .

Then she has finished. What is she to do with him now? Is he to go on, book after book, dragging his club-foot, using his little grey cells and dying all the while? Not dying the death that living men die, but moving into the walking death of the zombie? The boom of the Reichenbach Falls begins to mutter in her ears.

The sad result of all this is that, with a few exceptions, it is the accidental heroes who get pushed over the edge, while the deliberate ones—never really alive in the first place—live forever. Those the gods love die young.

Miss Allingham, tactful as ever, found one solution. She allowed Cam-pion to become a sort of ghost, a twinkle of large spectacles across the room, a muttered suggestion of danger, a friendly spirit, there to keep the readers happy—like a horseshoe over the door. But even she must have known just why Conan Doyle made Holmes walk the fatal path.

It's lucky, if you think of it, that most of us are not faced with the same clamour for resurrection.

Peter Dickinson won the Crime Writers' Asso-ciation Silver Dagger for The Glass-Sided Ants' Nest.

THE DEAD END

WHATEVER HAPPENED TO INSPECTOR BLAND?
WAS IT, PERHAPS, A MERCIFUL DEATH?

Julian Symons

My first crime story, *The Immaterial Murder Case,* was written with the idea of guying the form itself. It contained an amateur detective named, with unsubtle irony, Teak Woode and a professional called Detective-Inspector Bland. Woode prided himself on his aesthetic sense and was critical of Bland's attempt to dress "in a way less slovenly than that adopted by most plain-clothes members of the force," noting that "there will always be two or three pieces of cotton adhering to the back of his quite nicely-cut suit; or his tie will be glaringly in contrast with his shirt; or he will wear tan shoes with a navy suit."

Bland appeared in my next book, where he was said to be about thirty-five, with a fresh complexion, fair hair and a round smooth face whose innocence "was contradicted by blue eyes which were not unfriendly but impersonal." He survived into a third story, *Bland Beginning,* which was based on the bibliographical forgeries of Thomas J. Wise and for reasons connected with the plot had to be set in the Twenties, becoming therefore Bland's first case. (Hence the title.) *Bland Beginning* itself developed an interesting bibliographical variation when it crossed the Atlantic. This was the first of my crime stories to

be published in the United States, and Joan Kahn, who bravely took it on, felt that I ought to indicate the detective's later career. Accordingly, the American edition contains a prologue set in 1949, in which Bland tells me the story. And there were some other changes. The climax of the book was a cricket match, and Joan reasonably felt that I should simplify and even explain some of the terms. A cricket match finale for the American market: as I think back, Joan's courage looks more like foolhardiness, but we both survived it successfully. Bland, not at that time a rookie policeman but, for some reason I can't explain, a law clerk, doesn't appear until two-thirds of the way through the book yet solves the puzzle without much trouble. Thereafter he disappears, and no other series detective has appeared in my full-length crime stories.

So what ever happened to Inspector Bland? Or, to put it differently, why did I abandon the series detective? At first it was simply because my fourth novel, *The 31st of February*, demanded a kind of Grand Inquisitor as detective, and

Bland obviously didn't fit the part. But I realised as I wrote the story that the crime novel could be used to investigate the psychology of relationships and to say ironic or angry things about the structure of society. That could be done, it seemed to me, without losing much of the puzzle element that I have always enjoyed and valued; but I couldn't see any place for a detective like Bland in such books. A police investigator of some kind is an obligatory figure in most crime stories, but by bringing him in again and again you raise expectations—even demands—in the reader that have nothing to do with the merits of your story. I did not want people to ask for the latest Inspector Bland: I wanted them to ask for the new Julian Symons.

I have been told a hundred times that such an attitude is commercially foolish, and I don't doubt that this is true. Most readers of crime stories enjoy the sense of the familiar and find it reassuring. Today they encounter Spenser's Marlovian wisecracks, Wexford's literary quotations, as they greeted Wolfe or Poirot or Wimsey or Campion,

with the comfortable feeling they have when putting on a pair of old slippers. The detective's presence is a guarantee that everything will come out right in the end. And there are benefits for the author as well as the reader. There is no need to describe the detective's appearance or methods in much detail, for this will have been done in other books. Where the detective has a home life, the setting has been established and readers get to know it so well that they can draw maps of it, argue about where particular objects are placed, point out inconsistencies between one tale and another. Along with the detective go almost equally familiar assistants of all kinds from Bunter to Magersfontein Lugg, amiable policemen like Brer Fox and Lucas, or slightly tortured ones like Mike Burden, plus Watsonic narrators by the dozen. With a series character, part of every book is already written for you. How could anybody give up such a wonderful labour-saving device?

Quite easily. If one's primary object is to write a novel, a book showing characters involved in emotional conflict that leads to crime, then a detective of this kind is like grit in the machinery. The detective clamours for attention—even if he is not the principal character, most of the investigation must be built around him—and readers demand him, too, resenting books in which Poirot does not appear until halfway through or Alleyn plays a minor part. The author is trying to create a plausible murderous situation, blending into it in some way the puzzle that transforms the work from a "novel" into a "suspense (or detective, or crime) novel." To do so, he may conceal the existence of emotional conflict between possible murderer and potential murderee, or he may attempt to deceive the reader in one of a dozen other ways. To such deceptions the series detective is an unconsenting party, or at the least insists that he must be the person to unravel any such deceits. Let me give an instance: For a few years I became absorbed by the nature of the British legal system and the intricate machinery through which a guilty person may be acquitted or an innocent one found guilty. The form of these stories was

determined by the shape of British law and by the mistakes or falsities involved in eyewitness identification. These books could and did accommodate policemen, but by the nature of the stories it was impossible for the policemen to be central figures. The appearance of a series detective would have made the stories quite different and not, in fact, the tales I set out to write.

"All this," a hostile critic may say, "is a moderately cunning bit of special pleading for your own books. All right, you can't handle a series detective, but more skilful and enjoyable writers can. Are you telling us anything more than that?" Well, I hope so. It is true that I find the fanzine aspect of the series detective repellent—the issue of newsletters, concentration on the Wimsey pedigree and background (has anybody yet investigated the relationship of valet Bunter to Billy Bunter of Greyfriars?), Nero's cookbook, societies of Baker Street Irregulars, and so on—but writers can't be blamed for the pleasures of some readers. I do believe, though, that the series detective has limited many writers who would have fulfilled their talents more fully if he had been abandoned. Nicholas Blake and Ellery Queen—and those are only the first names at the tip of my pen—began with bright, fresh inventions who outstayed their welcome and became figures of routine. Holmes, after his return from the Reichenbach Falls, was like an Old Man of the Sea to Conan Doyle; Christie developed a dislike for Poirot ("They think I love him—if they only knew"); Simenon dismissed the Maigret books as very minor examples of his talent and the detective himself as a mere official functionary. There are living writers who suffer similarly. Chandler once said that the puzzle plot is a kind of crutch needed by the crime writer, and much the same is true of the series detective. A crutch is useful, no doubt about it: but it is better to stand on two legs.

Julian Symons was named a Grand Master by the Mystery Writers of America, received a Gold Dagger from the Crime Writers' Association, and is the ruling voice of London's infamous Detection Club.

FRED WINKOWSKI

THE MOST LIKELY VICTIM

Rosamund Bryce

I confess.

Although I have been reading murder mysteries for the past twenty years, at the rate of two a day (I gulp them down like aspirin), I have never been concerned with who gets killed.

I *am* intrigued with how it's done (I've a fondness for coshes from behind and slits in the back opened by poisoned daggers), and why it's done, but the personality of the victim—ho-hum.

And as unsympathetic as I am, the authors are even more so. I challenge you to name ten books in which the victim was a fully developed, three-dimensional human being. Rarely do authors invest the victim with anything deeper than a quirk: the dowager *always* sits dead center on the settee for the half-hour preceding dinner; the old codger *always* removes the Gainsborough, opens the wall safe and locks away his private papers at 9 sharp; the bride-to-be *always* closes her eyes as she brushes her hair those hundred strokes; the rookie *always* talks too much, to the wrong people; the secret agent *always* goes to the lavatory to decode his messages within five minutes of receiving them; the char *always* gobbles the leftovers when nobody's looking.

I repeat, quirks. Victims are so full of them, there is little room for anything else. No wonder authors kill them off first chance they get. Frankly, I'm six pages ahead of them. At the first whiff of a compulsion or hint of an idiosyncrasy, down comes my mental guillotine.

Clearly, the victim is not inherently interesting. Then why kill him? Well, for one thing, it gets him out of his rut. For another, he habitually has something someone else wants: title to the land; senior position in the firm; a second Rolls; a Chippendale armoire; an heirloom brooch; a guaranteed (millionaire's) income. In the mystery, greed is the principal reason for murdering. Consequently, the most likely victim is well-to-do but stingy.

The next most likely victim is the poor sod who recently fell in love. Invariably, his happiness sets someone's knife on edge, resulting in his lopsided grin becoming a little more lopsided. Miss Sayers was quite wrong, you know. She said love has no place in the mystery. She should have qualified her statement. Love may be an inappropriate emotion for the detective (he has to keep his mind on his work, after all), but it is obligatory as a means of identifying the next corpse. What's more appealing to read about than a juicy crime of passion?

The third most frequent victim is done in out of revenge. The victim has brought shame to one family, ruin to another. (If the book's a Gothic, however, shame doesn't lead to murder; it leads to the offender being closeted in the far turret.) Curiously, it's only in spy stories that revenge is an unadulterated motive. The victim is killed under the cloak of patriotism, but if you read between the lines it's apparent that defending the Crown was secondary; the actual reason was to eliminate the cad who caused the death of the spy's best friend some three books back.

RALPH GIBSON

Don't wait dinner; he won't be around for it.

In classic thrillers revenge is greed's veneer. For every case you can cite in which the killer did it to restore the family honor, I can rebut with two, at least, in which he did it to gain control of the family blue chips as well.

I suppose I must mention, although I hate to fuel the arguments of the anti-genre people, that some mystery deaths are caused by outright meanness. These deaths occur in the bottom-quality books—the ones in which you discover on the last page that the killer was a psychopath who had no motive. Books with these abysmal characters tend to choose sentimental victims: a small child with a mild deformity (a stutter); the family pet; widows and war heroes.

One good author with a perverse streak when it comes to assigning victims is Robert Ludlum. Mr. Ludlum is singular in that he likes his victims, and makes you like them, too. You want them to stick around to the end of the book. The most likely victim in a Ludlum book is the character you least want to see die. Now *that's* perverse.

There are two types of victims who die through no fault of their own. They just happen to have the bad luck to share

---

POSITION THE BODY MOST OFTEN FOUND IN

ENGLISH MYSTERIES
c. 1936

Face down. This is done to give the servants the chance to cry, "It's Lady Fortnum! I put that coat out for her just this morning." Of course, when the body is turned over, it is not Lady F., but Gladys from the kitchen who is M'Lady's size and coloring. Lady Fortnum, feeling quite beneficent that morning, had given Gladys her coat. Gladys, on her own initiative, had stolen her handbag. The servants then get to cry out, "It's Gladys! Leaving service next week, she was. Thought it peculiar, her with a dear old Mum, two little ones, and a good-for-nothing husband to support."

Face down also gives Gladys the chance to obscure with her body the button she managed to wrest from her accoster's mac. This clue will provide the Inspector with at least one red herring and two more victims before the night is over.

AMERICAN MYSTERIES
c. 1955

Face up. This is done to impress Charlie the Horse that it was not an accident. Herman, his best button man, was obviously not the best man for the job of rubbing out Lemons O'Connor, and Lemons told him so—slow and lingeringly, aided and abetted by highly polished knuckle-dusters.

Face up gives Lemons the chance to place pennies on Herman's eyes and pull out his pockets. It also gives him the chance to put a dead fish, wrapped in newspaper, in his arms.

Face up gives the rookie cop a good opportunity to view his first corpse and throw up. While the forensic boys are mopping up, Dan Madison, private eye and bane of the police captain, has time to remove the key to the bus station locker from Herman's hand, pocket it and be on his way to the pickup point, where he is met by a waiting .45.

MARTY NORMAN

a chapter with (a) a Great Detective or (b) a Gothic Heroine. Possibly the greatest Great Detective of them all is Sherlock Holmes, agreed? Have you ever noticed how many people die once he's called in on a case? It's appalling. Holmes and his descendants are *always* examining the plimsoles when they should be attending to the people. They are *always* sniffing the cigar ash, gluing the theater stub and educating their Watsons when they should be advising the next victim how to double-lock his door. These victims die to further Holmes's reputation. After all, it doesn't take a Great Detective to solve *one* murder; with a little perseverance we might all be able to do that. But a killer who strikes down many, who in the process still finds time to loot the silver vaults, waylay the carriage and leave hundreds of clues (none of them traceable) demands the skills of a Great Detective. These victims are known as the expendables. Oftener than not, they are the people who sold the cigar that made the ash, who innocently resoled the plimsole. They come two, three, even four to the book, and I can't recall a situation in which they were ever mourned. Presumably, they live alone: no friends, no relatives, no one to shed a tear. They are honest, hard-working souls, and I think Holmes and all the other Great Detectives should be charged for their deaths. Criminal negligence sounds about right.

The other category of hapless victims exists solely in the Gothic novel. Ogden Nash called this the Had-I-But-Known school and it's been around since 1908, when Mary Roberts Rinehart created *The Circular Staircase.* Victims in these books die because they are not wearing nightgowns. The character who is—the Gothic Heroine—has the worst instincts this side of Lady Macbeth. She is a clear case of intuition run amok. She *always* decides a midnight traipse down the corridor is more important than

What would I poison?

I'd never do anything like that to cookies; maybe artichokes.

You could lace those little leaves with something.

What I really think ought to be discontinued is avocado. You could very easily mix one of those tasteless poisonous substances up in a guacamole and no one would ever know, since it's tasteless to start with.

Yes, I'd definitely kill off avocado.

WALLY
"FAMOUS"
AMOS

warning Cook about the trip-wire set across the servants' stairs. She *always* confides in the killer and with virtually no prompting tells him the name of the only witness. To the Inspector she says not a word. Do you wonder bodies abound when she's around? The big question is: Why doesn't the staff quit the minute she unpacks her nightie? Of course, there is one consolation for the Gothic victim. At book's end the heroine refuses to marry the heir unless he promises her they will name their children after the Recently Departed. From the number of them, the Gothic Heroine does not believe in small families.

Victims, then, are killed out of greed, lust, revenge, meanness, hubris and insensitivity. None of which makes them interesting. It makes their killers interesting. I imagine that's why I would rather identify with the killer than with the victim. (It doesn't mean, necessarily, that I'm unsafe to be around.)

I confess. Victims bore me to death.

Rosamund Bryce is a bully.

DISPOSING
OF
THE BODY

Ione Paloma

The ice casket.

Let us assume the Late Whomever was a deserving victim. He was selfish, cruel, cold, mean, and not only first on the killer's farewell list but next on just about everyone else's.

Let us also assume he was dispatched at the first opportunity, regardless of where that struck. (After all, to wait for him to position himself at the edge of the cliff could take years. Or possibly two volumes.)

Much to his chagrin, the author now discovers—along with his surrogate, the killer—that the Late Whomever does not stop being troublesome just because he's stopped breathing. He now presents a (dead) weighty problem: how to dispose of all those fillings that refuse to melt and all those bones that refuse to bend so they can be neatly pretzeled into a trunk and abandoned at Left Luggage.

What to do with the Late Whomever is surely the most ticklish problem the whodunit has to face. Several authors, however, have rallied with inspired solutions. Oh, the victim was eventually found, the victimizer eventually caught, but in the meantime the body reposed in a stylish place. At once unusual and fiendishly clever.

Perhaps the most creative scheme of them all was concocted by G.K. Chesterton, who reasoned that as a forest eclipses a single tree, so a battlefield would obscure a single corpse. Accordingly, in "The Sign of the Broken Sword" he had the body brought to the war zone and dumped there. It became just one of many.

Ellery Queen was intrigued by the possibilities inherent in the design of the Murphy bed. It folded up into the wall, if you remember, a sort of forerunner of the Castro. Well, in *The French Powder Mystery* he tidily ensconced the corpse between the sheets and recessed him into the fixtures along with the bedding. When the bed was opened—since the bed was one used in a department store window, it was an opening witnessed by many—out popped the deceased.

Ross Macdonald and Christianna Brand favored the medical approach to disposal. Macdonald in *The Ivory Grin* had the body stripped down to bone (you don't really want to hear about the acid bath, do you?), a few holes drilled into the cranium, a few tags inserted in the holes labeling it a medical school skeleton, and then he closed the Late Lamented into a closet, where it hung as a teaching aid for a perverse student. Ms. Brand in *Green for Danger* was equally devious. She arranged for her victim to die mid-operation, then calmly let the hospital authorities dispose of the body.

Ngaio Marsh baled a body into a packet of wool (*Died in the Wool,*) Alice Tilton stored hers in a deep freeze (*Dead Earnest*) and Michael Gilbert crammed his into a safe-deposit vault (*Smallbone Deceased*). Although granted, in the last, the body was conveniently small.

Edgar Allan Poe didn't exactly hide a body; he just caromed it into a chimney (*The Murders in the Rue Morgue*).

John Rhode in *The Mystery at Greycombe Farm* let the Departed harden in a cider storehouse, then rigged an incendiary bomb to char it beyond recognition.

On the bucolic side, Paul McGuire buried his body in a haystack in *Murder at High Noon,* anticipating, perhaps, that one would have as little success in finding it there as the proverbial needle.

Dermot Morrah dispensed with his cadaver by storing it in a mummy case (in—what else?—*The Mummy Case Mystery*), and Freeman Wills Crofts shipped his from Paris to London in a cask marked STATUARY ONLY (in *The Cask,* naturally).

Stanley Ellin in "The Specialty of the House" had the body eaten—not in some philistine manner, mind you, but as a savory added to a fine restaurant's menu (uncredited, of course).

David Harper in *The Hanged Men* made his corpse part of a rite. He replaced the traditional Halloween "straw man" with his man, then let him hang around for the celebration.

The ultimate method was developed by Jack Finney in *Time and Again,* although since it smacks of science fiction we cannot comfortably give it top score. His hero was able to wander in time and thus went back just far enough to prevent his enemy's parents from meeting—thereby circumventing the poor man's birth. He disposed of the body by not creating the body in the first place, and more devious than that, it's difficult to get.

Now then, since we've disposed of the body, shall we adjourn to the library for a little game of wits with the Inspector? Follow me.

Ione Paloma believes in cryogenics.

THE DON'T LIST
(Things to avoid if you *don't* want to be the next victim)

Catherine Prezzano

1. *Don't* go for lonely walks with those you've just disinherited.
2. *Don't* sip a glass of warm milk left at your bedside by an unseen hand.
3. *Don't* sample the chocolates that arrived by post, anonymously, on your birthday.
4. *Don't* rendezvous with the mysterious stranger who offered you a dukedom over the phone in a decidedly muffled voice.
5. *Don't* follow up on the advert in the Personal Column that said if you contact Pains & Grillard, Solicitors, you will hear something to your advantage.
6. *Don't* accept hunting invitations from business associates after you have refused to sell them your controlling shares in the company.
7. *Don't* attend masquerade balls given by wealthy eccentrics who send the car round to collect you and insist you tell no one where you're off to.
8. *Don't* ever enter the secret passageway first.
9. *Don't* remark to William, that rascal, that the mac he misplaced seems to be jammed into the hall cupboard for some inexplicable reason.
10. *Don't* kiss Barnaby when you have just turned Alex down flat and he has not yet left the house.
11. *Don't* tell the Inspector you think it nothing more than an unfortunate accident and police surveillance a breach of your privacy.
12. *Don't* stand with your back to billowing draperies, particularly if the windows are shut.
13. *Don't* offer to fetch the candles from the pantry if the lights suddenly dim, flicker and go out.
14. *Don't* comment that you never realized Titian painted in acrylics within earshot of the art gallery owner.
15. *Don't* suggest an audit of the books.
16. *Don't* ask Woof what he's got there in his mouth, and most especially don't ask him to show you where he got it.
17. *Don't* insist Madame DeClasse conduct the séance at midnight, in the library, when the moon is full.
18. *Don't* adopt young Raymond until you have absolute proof he is your long-lost sister Ava's only child.
19. *Don't* recognize the handwriting on the ransom note.
20. *Don't* assume you are nowhere near cliff's edge when you are being photographed back to it.
21. *Don't* inquire after Lady Margaret's health should you happen to spot her husband signing the chemist's register.
22. *Don't* waltz a second wife down the aisle if the first has yet to relinquish the title.
23. *Don't* commend Sir Trevor on his fine collection of sword-canes, especially if a worrisome rash of stabbings has just been reported.
24. *Don't* doze off in the train compartment when your companion is a burly latecomer wearing very supple gloves.
25. *Don't* return home early.
26. *Don't* laugh quite heartily at a prospective employee's resumé.
27. *Don't* open the connecting door.
28. *Don't* lean over the balustrade for a better glimpse of the gazebo.
29. *Don't* upend the teapot and announce in a loud voice that the hallmark isn't genuine.
25. *Don't* reveal the ending of the mystery to someone who is just beginning it.

Catherine Prezzano don't *want to wind up dead from O.D.'ing on the mystery.*

BLOODHOUNDS

*A Shade
Past
5.46*

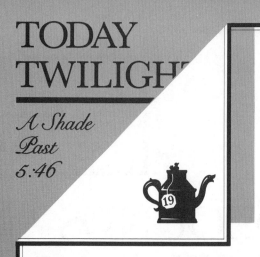

Congratulations, Luther. Your first walk-through in Claridge's and you had to pick the wife whose husband's going to be knocked away. Good planning, Luther, nice work. Three women there were, three of them with sad eyes and hollows where the laughs ought to be, and which did you choose? The lady with the corpse for the weekend. Let's see you get out of this one, Luther. Just let's see you pull this one out.

Face up to it, man, you'll be booked. You've been cuffed and sent up for less, with far better alibis than this one will hold to. She'll tumble it in another day, sure as spades over eights. Almost brought it down last night at the table. "Yes, Vicar, our Leslie raises ki wis over there in Christchurch" cam whooshing out one breath, and "How are those sweet little Cola bears doing Leslie dear?" flew out the other. H knew something'd gone queer, and it'l drop the minute the coppers get here.

Dumb cow. Should've written i down for her, but we'd just been over i for the hour before, cramming it to tha head and who would've thought it'd fal back out again so soon?

Stupid, stupid cow. Today wa worse, with her trying to throw the husband off-track, make him swallow cousins. "Of course Leslie's seen service dear. Tell John and the Colonel about th reef manoeuvres, Leslie, the time yo mined it." Colonel fell off the chair wit that one. Surprised she didn't give me medal, too. My own V.C. He'd hav liked that, all right. Gone home to get hi so we could compare.

No more lounge trade for me if I ge out of this. Stick with the smart ones, th

*Simon spots
something off in the distance.*

The something spots Simon

The musicale has come to a pretty conclusion. Violet strolls the garden while waiting for Hyacinth to return the button.

Bridie calls a spade a spade: "Kim ought to be dismissed for leaving his filthy things about." 5 minutes ago.

ripe ones. Get me a Bridie kind of girl. Maybe even take her, if I can love-talk her into bringing the cards to me. Damn stupid bitch Clare to lock them up before I could switch back. Sure as spades to kings thought I'd be able to pick them off when the house turned dark, but traffic here beat noon at Piccadilly. Bridie clumping down hall. That half-bare nurse running away. And whatever that other was, *that* scared me blue. Maybe husband had a little going with Nursey? If I knew I was going to buy it next day, I'd sure as flush spades want mine the night before.

If I hadn't been rehearsing her while Teasdale was going down, I'd've thought Clare was the one. Bored enough to do it, with the prayers from Vicar and that sister in-law loon crazy and him serving up business all day long. Wives need sweet words, that I know, and there's nothing madder than one who can't hear them. But I was there so I know she's clear. Who did it? Who knows? Not the Colonel. A million words on wind, that's all he is. Nursey, now, that's the possibility. Not quite staff,

but not quite good enough for Claridge's. Nursey might have dared.

What will I do if Clare wants to wait awhile, then after decency's interval take up my proposal? Never would have made it if she were free, 'course not. Think I'll book out of here quick, before too many folks get too many ideas I don't like. Bridie and the cards, that's first. Bridie and me and any money we scrounge and a boat to some place warm, that's number two.

Bloody laugh, me out here playing detective, organising a search party. Haven't a clue what to look for. One thing's sharper than spades: I'll see the coppers before they see me, and one, two, quick over the wall and gone, cards or not. Leave 'em here for the Colonel. He could use a little help with his deal. Comes in all smellin' of horse, says, "Jolly good to see you here, old sport, jolly good. A hand to make up for last night, shall we? Half p a hundred," he says. Two hours until lunch and all I took off him was five quid.

Last weekend invitation I accept, I can tell you.

THE AM EYE AND I

Ed McBain

Always it was the good guys against the bad guys.

The bad guys were the cops.

The good guys were anybody else trying to solve murders.

The cops were always getting in the way of the good guys. If only the cops would let the private eyes and the lawyers and the reporters and the little old ladies with knitting needles get on with their work (which was finding out who did what dastardly thing to whom), everybody would be a lot happier. The cops always smoked cigars and said things like "Okay, shamus, where exactly *were* you when Mrs. Brewster caught it?" Or if they were talking to a *lawyer* who solved murder mysteries, they said things like "Sure, Counselor, but maybe you'd like to tell us why your client insured her late husband for two million bucks." The "Counselor" was meant to be derogatory; it was the police euphemism for "shyster." If the cops were talking to a little old lady sleuth, they said things like "Madam, this is a stiff we got layin' on the floor here, so if you wouldn't mind getting out of our way..."

The bad guys were always throwing the good guys in jail because they suspected the good guys of complicity somehow. Then they let the good guys out the next morning, so they could hurry up and solve the murder the cops couldn't.

Even on the radio, cops were the bad guys. Occasionally, you found a good-guy cop—on shows like *Broadway's My Beat* or *Mr. District Attorney* or, much later on, *Dragnet*—but not very often. Your good guys were your private eyes,

or your reporters, or your insurance investigators, or your tracers of lost persons, or your omnipresent little old lady sleuths. Cops were in the story line only to hamper and harass the good guys.

Boy, how I hated cops.

So naturally, the early detective fiction I wrote fell into the Private Eye, Man-on-the-Run, Woman-in-Jeopardy, Innocent Bystander, Wrong Man Accused, Etc. Etc. categories, where the cops were always the bad guys.

Then—all at once—it occurred to me that if I came home late one night and found my wife slaughtered in her bed, I would not call the little old lady next door, and I would not call an insurance investigator, or a reporter, or a private eye, or even a jockey. I *might* call my lawyer, but only to find out what I should do next. He would undoubtedly advise me to call the cops.

Cops investigated murders.

The only people who had any *right* investigating murders were law enforcement officers.

Anybody else sticking his nose into a murder investigation was strictly an amateur. *Including* any private detective on earth.

Oh, how simple life became.

No longer did I have to make that leap of the imagination designed to convince the reader—*and* myself—that an advertising man, for example, had any business investigating a murder instead of writing a detergent jingle. Never again would I have to send a private eye looking for an errant husband only to discover a corpse, thereby forcing him to solve the murder in order to do the job

Among the current mystery idols: lawyers, professors, jockeys, taxicab drivers, insurance claims adjusters, actors, presidents (and their families), clairvoyants, reporters, antique dealers and the occasional police officer, but only if he represents a truly interesting minority (cf. Tony Hillerman).

he was originally hired for. No more amateur investigators in my life. The Am Eye and I parted company with the creation of the 87th Precinct. On *my* block, cops were now the *good* guys.

That was in 1956.

And now is now.

And now I am five books into a series about a Florida lawyer—a *what?*— a lawyer, yes, who solves murders. And now I have headaches again.

In the beginning, they were even more intense. Now I'm learning how to deal with the quantum jump any Am Eye writer must make in order to justify his hero's or heroine's meddling in police affairs. But even now I know in my heart of hearts that Matthew Hope does not have any legitimate reason for becoming involved in a murder investigation. He should be at a real estate closing instead of in a morgue. He should be writing a brief instead of chasing down clues. (Does *your* lawyer solve murders? *My* lawyer—my real-life lawyer—opens his mouth and out comes a cloud of butterflies.) Matthew's partner is a lawyer who sticks to the practice of law. He is constantly telling Matthew to butt out of murder investigations and tend to business, which is making money for the law firm of Summerville and Hope. Matthew doesn't listen. He is always knee-deep in corpses. He even finds them in his swimming pool.

Why is this so?

Because without a corpse, a lawyer is boring. So is a little old lady sleuth. Would you like to be stranded on a desert island with a lawyer and a little old lady sleuth? (I would prefer Jack the Ripper and Lizzie Borden.) But give either of these essentially dull people a *murder* to solve and suddenly they are scintillating. In fact, without a corpse there would *be* no amateur investigators. You might easily argue that without a corpse neither would there be cops, but at this time I do not wish to discuss the natural symbiosis between criminals and law enforcement officers. To tell the truth, I still feel somewhat guilty mentioning Matthew Hope and cops in the same breath.

That is because in the first several books of the Matthew Hope series—God, how could I have done it?—the cops were almost *bad* guys. Oh, not the way the good old bad-guy cops *used* to be, beating up the Am Eyes with rubber hoses and framing them with throwaway guns and the like. I may have been a traitor, but I was not an assassin. Still and all, in *Goldilocks,* the first book in the series, Matthew actually withholds—from a police detective named George Ehrenberg—information vital to the murder case Ehrenberg is investigating. And in *Rumpelstiltskin,* the second book, a detective named Morris Bloom tells Matthew, "So, Counselor, it would be nice to have your word that from this minute on you won't be running all over

the city of Calusa questioning anybody you think might have some connection with this case as I would hate to have the blood of a six-year-old girl on my hands if I were you, Counselor." (Detective Bloom was not chewing a cigar, but please note the repeated use of the kill-word "Counselor.") And although Bloom and Matthew have become fast friends by *Jack and the Beanstalk,* the fourth and most recent book in the series, a police captain named Hopper puts Matthew through a third-degree worthy of any L.A. cop turning the screws on Philip Marlowe.

I am learning.

In the just-finished *Snow White and Rose Red,* Matthew and Bloom work separately but virtually in tandem to solve an enormously difficult case, a device that brings the bad guy and the good guy into the same orbit. Bloom, of course, has evolved into a thoroughly good guy. The only bad guys in the new book are the ones who are trying to keep the truth from *both* of them. Too, Matthew's involvement with the crime is only peripheral, stemming from a deeper lawyer-client relationship that obviates the need for concocting cockamamie reasons for an amateur investigation. I don't know how this will work in the future books. It is nonetheless a direction, and it puts things in a more realistic perspective.

And yet I know. Man, I know.

Steve Carella and the whole 87th Precinct *mishpocheh* stand behind my word processor as I write.

They want to know why I'm in bed with an Am Eye again.

I tell them it's a challenge.

They say nothing.

But oh, those reproving professional eyes.

Evan Hunter/Ed McBain is a best-selling novelist.

AMATEUR SLEUTHS

The most endearing are the bumblers, whose every act obscures rather than uncovers, whose interrogating skills are second to all and better to none, whose dénouements evolve into self-praising sermons. Military men, naturally, excel in this field, as do those of artistic temperament. Happenstance plays ally to the sleuth of nonprofessional status. Serendipitous walks in the garden, fortuitous fainting spells and onsets of neuralgia, nocturnal strolls round the grounds— all these enable an amateur sleuth to function. There is but one problem: what they discover is correct, but the manner in which they reveal it is wrong. To make sense of

The Sisters of Mozart present the Allegro Concerto for the Teasdales and their guests. Today, half two.

Hyacinth finding, she supposed, the Vicar's button.

The lip rouge on the envelope exactly matches the colour of arterial blood.

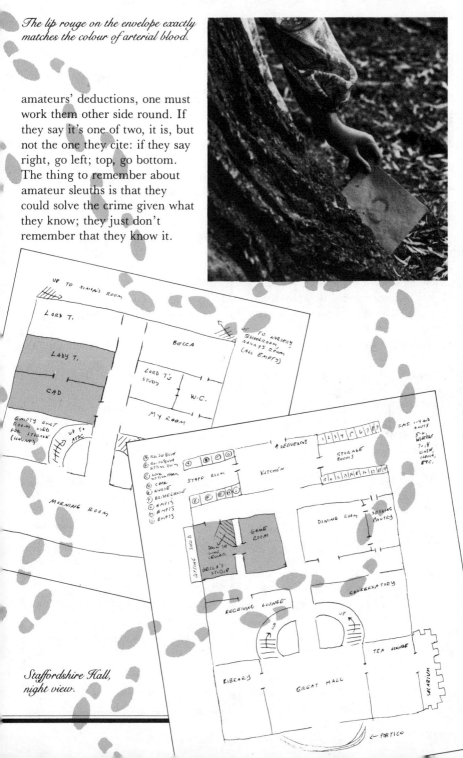

amateurs' deductions, one must work them other side round. If they say it's one of two, it is, but not the one they cite: if they say right, go left; top, go bottom. The thing to remember about amateur sleuths is that they could solve the crime given what they know; they just don't remember that they know it.

Staffordshire Hall, night view.

TRAVIS McGEE
TECHNICOLOR DREAMS ADRIFT ON A HOUSEBOAT

Jean F. Mercier

To more than seventy million readers, John Dann MacDonald is the best writer in America. It's an opinion shared by many critics; even those who don't go quite that far declare he is "a very good writer, not 'just' a good mystery writer."

MacDonald is a genuine rarity, an astonishingly productive writer of literary quality. Since 1945 he has published two notable books of nonfiction, seventy novels and approximately five hundred short stories. The nonfiction includes a beguiling account of life with the MacDonald family cats, *The House Guests,* and *No Deadly Drug,* the classic murder-trial coverage that is required reading for students at Harvard Law School. The fiction is primarily in the thriller category, except for two dandy science-fiction fantasies: *The Ballroom of the Skies* and *Wine of the Dreamers.*

MacDonald thanks his wife Dorothy for launching his writing career. While stationed with the American army in the China-Burma-India theater during World War II, he wrote a story and sent it home, intending it only as an enter-taining change from his letters. But Dorothy, who knows a winner when she sees one, sent it to a magazine that accepted and paid for it—which was all the impetus the returning officer needed to settle down to write.

In 1950 Fawcett published his first novel, a whodunit called *The Brass Cup-cake,* which was followed in rapid order by approximately forty-five more paper-back originals. Then came the landmark year 1964, when the four MacDonalds introducing Travis McGee, "tinhorn knight on a stumbling Rosinante from Rent-A-Steed," were issued. Trav (as his fans call him) narrates his dicey adventures in *The Deep Blue Good-by, Nightmare in Pink, A Purple Place for Dying* and *The Quick Red Fox* and in sixteen sequels identified by the colors in the titles, each related to the plot. Ten years after McGee's début, Lippincott reversed the usual order in book publishing by re-printing the paperback editions of the series in hardcover. In both formats, the novels have been enduring best sellers.

Travis McGee is a knockout, a hunk, six feet plus four inches of sexy male, almost every inch scarred by his "profession" as a salvage consultant. The role is a cover for his actual operations, retrieving stolen property for victims who have no other hope of getting any of it back from crooks and con artists. Clients split the recovered loot fifty-

> *For relaxation I reread either my nineteenth-century favorites—Trollope, Dickens, Thackeray, Austen, Dostoevsky and Chekhov—or mystery detective tales by such as Chandler, Hammett and John D. MacDonald, all of whom are worthy of a Pulitzer Prize.*
>
> JOHN TOLAND

MARTY NORMAN

For detailed explanations of The Busted Flush, *the Plymouth Gin Controversy, Meyer's Abominable Cocktail Dip and other arcana, readers are commended to the* JDM Bibliophile, *edited by Edgar Hirshberg, sponsored by the University of South Florida. Subscription, $5 a year for two issues. To subscribe, contact: JDM Bibliophile, Dept. of English, U. of South Florida, Tampa, Fla. 33620.*

fifty with McGee, half being demonstrably better than nothing. These quests finance Trav's sporadic retirement weeks devoted to blissful hours aboard *The Busted Flush,* Slip F-18, Bahia Mar, Lauderdale, Florida. On the opulent houseboat, Trav relaxes by making love to alluring women, drinking his favorite Plymouth gin or Tuborg beer, listening to music and generally indulging in sybaritic pleasures. Most of all, he cherishes his time off as an opportunity to enjoy the company of his dearest friend, Meyer the economist, who lives nearby aboard *The John Maynard Keynes.*

Once Meyer appeared in the series, readers discovered that they could no more get along without him than Trav could. Many find him more lovable and seductive than the hero: "You can watch the Meyer Magic at work and not know how it's done," MacDonald wrote. "He has the size and pelt of the average Adirondack black bear. He can walk a beach, go into any bar, cross any playground and acquire people the way blue serge picks up lint, and the new friends believe they have known him forever."

Meyer's staunch help and his knowledge of a wide-ranging number of subjects, including economics, are what McGee depends on as he sets forth on dangerous missions *mano a mano* with unscrupulous adversaries.

John Maynard Keynes, Meyer's idol. He named his houseboat after him, unfortunately, it got blown up (Cinnamon Skin).

MacDonald, of course, relies on his training in economics to authenticate the facts discussed by Meyer and Trav. But intricate financial finagling is only one of his interests. The author is a born educator, with, apparently, the habit of studying anything and everything, then weaving his discoveries into a story. As narrator, Trav persuades the readers that they are sharing his enlightenment on the effects of LSD, on surgical procedures, technological miracles, life at sea and on land, and in decidedly different settings—Chicago, San Francisco, watering places in Mexico, a tough South Texas town and the cities in his home state of Florida. He explains the feats of Hans Hoffman, Syd Solomon, Tapies. Even the psychology of poodles: "This is

the most desperate breed there is. They are just a little too bright for the servile role of dogdom. So their loneliness is a little more excruciating, their welcomes more frantic, their desire to please a little more intense. They seem to think that if they could just do everything right. . . . One day there will appear a super-poodle, one almost as bright as the most stupid alley cat, and he will figure it out. . . ." One suspects that MacDonald could discourse on egg candling, zither stringing or Old Church Slovanik with no fear of boring anybody.

Regardless of his sexual escapades, McGee, the man of multiple amours, is an idealist who argues against casual sex. "If there's no pain and no loss, it's only recreational. . . .

"Who needs magic and mystery? Well, maybe it is magic and mystery that an Antarctic penguin will hunt all over hell and gone to find the right pebble to carry in his beak and lay between the funny feet of his intended, hoping for her favor." McGee's musings run to the elegant matings of the Tibetan bar-headed goose and gander that rise high in the water afterwards and make great bugle sounds of honking. "The behaviorists think it is unprofessional to use subjective terms about animal patterns. So

they don't call this ceremony joy. They don't know what to call it. These geese live for up to 50 years, and they mate for life. They celebrate the mating this same way year after year. If one dies, the other never mates again. So penguins, eagles, geese, wolves and many other creatures . . . are stuck with all this obsolete magic and mystery. . . while desensitized humans join encounter groups to find out what's missing."

The need to value people and all forms of life is MacDonald's recurring theme. He shows profound concern for the damages done to this planet. Back in 1962, when few people except scientists had ever heard the word "ecology," the author wrote *A Flash of Green*—not a McGee story, but perhaps the inspiration for the series. It is a strong novel about a venal newspaperman, Jimmy Wing, who connives with businessmen in a Florida town to fill in Grassy Bay and erect shoddy buildings that they claim will profit the residents. It prefigures *Condominium,* which elaborated upon shady land deals.

One of McGee's most forceful warnings appears in *One Fearful Yellow Eye.* "In the night air the lake stank, and I went back in out of the wind and thought of the endless garbage barges that are trundled out of Miami into the blue bright Atlantic. People had thought Lake Erie would last forever. When the sea begins to stink, man better have some fresh green planets to colonize, because this one is going to be used up."

While MacDonald's novels are grand entertainment, they are hardly escape literature. They prove the case against the corrupters, persuade us we can beat them at their greedy games if we band together and fight. Perhaps it's time the seventy million of us in MacDonald's army make our move.

Jean F. Mercier is a book reviewer for Publishers Weekly.

THE TINT TEST

Lily white and basic black are two colors *not* present in John D. MacDonald titles. (Then again, he's not done adding to the series yet. He may even have time for a white, as in whitewash.) Can you correctly name the tints in the following test?

What color is the *Sky?*
What color is the *Sea?*
What color is *Skin?*
What color is a *Shroud?*
What color is *Silence?*
What color is a *Nightmare?*
What color is *Guilt?*
What color is a *Long Look?*
What color is a *Fearful Eye?*
What color is a *Ruse?*
What color is the *rain?*
What color is a *lament?*
What color is a *free fall?*
What color is a *quick fox?*
What color is a *wrapper?*
What color is a *ripper?*
What color is a *place for dying?*
What color is a *deadly shade?*
What color is everything *darker than?*
What color do you *dress her in?*
What color is *goodbye?*

Answers: Dreadful lemon, copper, cinnamon, bright orange, tan and sandy, pink, pale gray, lavender, yellow, scarlet, silver, turquois, crimson, red, plain brown, green, purple, gold, amber, indigo, and deep blue.

THE BBC THROUGH A MONOCLE

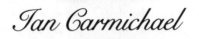

Ian Carmichael

Lord Peter Wimsey.

On 11th March 1966 I received a letter from my agent that read:

> My brother has come up with what might be a very interesting idea for a television series, namely the character of Lord Peter Wimsey in the Dorothy Sayers books. As you know they were tremendously popular, and the character would, I think, fit you like a glove (or vice versa) and there is certainly a lot of material to draw on.

I had read a few of the Wimsey books when I was in my twenties, and some-where about the age of eighteen or nine-teen I had seen my local repertory com-pany give a performance of *Busman's Honeymoon*. In short, I knew sufficient about the character to realise that this was the best idea to have come my way for a very long time.

On receipt of my agent's letter, the first thing I did was ring up Harrods.

"How many books are there?" I asked.

"Fourteen," came the reply after a few moments' research.

Now, I enjoy reading for pleasure very much indeed, but reading for work in an entirely different matter. That I find a complete chore. So it was with mixed feelings that I sat down to read fourteen books, one after the other. Rarely, before or since, has such a daunting job of work turned out to give me so much pleasure.

The next five years were packed with incident and inactivity, and principally the latter.

I first approached the BBC Light Entertainment Department, for whom I had just finished playing Bertie Wooster in three successful series, and immediately I hit the first of a long string of obstructions which were to be strewn across my path like tank-traps for half a decade. It came in the form of a letter from the head of the department.

"The very first snag," it read, "is an insuperable one—money. The BBC has no risk capital whatever at the moment to invest in projects, however optimistic one may be about potential profits."

It then went on to add that the overseas sales advisors had expressed the view that the subject would, and I quote, "by no means be an easy sale across the Atlantic. The character of Lord Peter Wimsey is not very well known in the States," it went on, "nor does the literary and literate style fit in very well with the current trends of filmed series."

Mumbling into my metaphorical beard several phrases like "lack of foresight," "no imagination" and "false assumptions," I refused to be put off. Girding up my loins, I approached the Drama Department of the same station, the head of which was an old friend of mine. I was appearing in a long-running play in the West End at the time, and I telephoned him one evening from the theatre during the act interval to ask if I could go round and have a chat with him after the show. He agreed, and an hour and a half later, armed with a large whisky, I started my sales spiel.

"Do you know the Wimsey books?" I asked.

"Look behind you," he said, and

there, on a bookshelf behind my head, was every one of them. Obviously I had found a fellow fan. My spirits rose.

My friend went on to tell me that the Wimsey books were, indeed, at that very moment, along with a couple of other subjects, being considered as a possible follow-up series to a very successful one that had just come to an end. My spirits rose even higher. They needn't have. It was to prove yet another disappointment.

Having drawn a blank at the BBC, I then sat down and drew up a highly professional twelve-page sales brochure on the subject which, emulating the best door-to-door salesmen, I started touting round all the U.K. commercial stations, which, each in turn, showed a similar lack of enthusiasm.

Simultaneous with all this, my agent and I had been having talks with the Sayers estate in order to find out the availability of the TV rights of the saga, and here again we encountered problems. The executors were, at that time, only prepared to sell the rights of the complete works in one package. To discuss the purchase of individual books or, say, one or two at a time, they were not prepared to do; and this alone, I knew, would not endear the idea to the moguls, regardless of their other prejudices.

Disheartened, I then let the matter drop for a year and got on with something else. In 1968 I became more depressed as I heard that a film company was showing interest in the properties and consequently the Sayers people were no longer prepared to entertain the possibility of a television series.

Impasse.

In 1969 I received information that the film project was off, so I started knocking at the BBC's door once again. This time with considerably more success. A producer was assigned to the job, scriptwriters were put to work and all the novels were to be presented in chrono-

DOWNSTAIRS

The serving pantry abuts the main dining room. There are two entranceways: through the dining room and through the kitchen. Family and guests are never seen in the pantry. Those with free access are: Cook, who almost never has time to venture there; Rosie, who is responsible for placing the serving platters there before taking them in for meals; Bridie, who is frequently called in to help Rosie; Everett, who will always inspect the plates. Nurse enters the pantry only when personally supervising custard for Lady T., who suffers from nervous tummy. Simon frequently enters the pantry as a shortcut to the kitchen.

Cook's special tea tray.

logical order in three series of thirteen episodes each. Excelsior! That was the way I had always wanted them to be presented. Nine months later the producer left and all was off once again.

One year after that (and if you are finding this monotonous, think how I was feeling) I again tried to persuade them to resurrect the project. Apart from anything else, I was getting concerned that when and if we ever did get it off the ground, I would, by then, be too old for the part! By this time the Sayers estate had withdrawn their original condition of selling the complete works as a package, and plans were made to do one novel in five episodes to see how it was received.

You would have thought that by now I was home and dry, but oh dear no, not a bit of it. Which novel to start with was the next hiatus.

"Number one, *Whose Body?*" I opined.

"Not a bit of it," said the authorities. "We must start with a good one and *Whose Body?* is inferior. Let's start with *Murder Must Advertise.*"

"But that's halfway through the canon," I explained. "We shall get into a frightful mess from a chronological point of view if it is a success and you want to do more."

Impasse again.

Finally a compromise was made, and we all agreed to start with book number two, *Clouds of Witness*; and early on a cold March morning in 1972, in the heart of Howarth Moor (the Brontës' moor) in Yorkshire, Wimsey and Bunter got into a green 3½-litre Bentley and drove off past the camera. At last we were on our way.

Three years later, in January 1975, in the BBC studios in Glasgow, the final shots of *Five Red Herrings* were committed to videotape. The fifth book completed. From that day to this, I have heard no more from my employers. The series has

The Lord Peter Wimsey Dinner

Potted Shrimp
Consommé Polonais
Filet of Sole Sauce Mousseline Sabayon
Fruit Ice
∽ Choice Of ∽
Correct Casserole of Beef with Walchelli
Pastry Crust and Port Sauce
~ or ~
Game Hen aux choux a lá Bellona Club
Stilton Cheese & Water Biscuits
∽ Choice Of ∽
English Trifle
~ or ~
Soufflé Glacé au Citron

Friday March 11, 1983
7:30 P.M.
$22.50/guest

Call:
Grounds for Murder   294~9497
a mystery book store   for reservations/information

AS · MY · WHIMSY · TAKES · ME

The menu featured at the Grounds For Murder dinner party honoring Lord Peter. Strong poison was not served.

been abandoned, and Harriet Vane has never appeared on a TV screen. The letters that I have received from avid fans awaiting her entrance would fill the correspondence column of a national newspaper for six months.

I loved Wimsey. He was me. Or what of him that was not me was what I would have liked to be me. I think I was rather like a child playing dressing-up games. I dressed up as Wimsey and played "Let's pretend" because I admired him, I envied him his life-style, his apparent insouciance, his prowess and his intellect. He was never, as some people like to pontificate, a snob, an anti-Semite, an . . . but that is all the subject of another article.

Ian Carmichael is Lord Peter Wimsey.

A FEW (MILLION) WORDS ABOUT MY GOOD FRIEND HOLMES

Otto Penzler

Since 1887, when *A Study in Scarlet* first appeared, there have been over 10,000 novels, short stories, parodies, burlesques, pastiches, critical studies, reviews, essays, appreciations and scholarly examinations devoted to Sherlock Holmes. Herewith, 100 indispensables, priced as in fine condition, with dust jacket where applicable.

1. 1887 DOYLE, ARTHUR CONAN: "A Study in Scarlet." (Contained in *Beeton's Christmas Annual.* London: Ward, Lock, $20,000.) First Book Edition (London: Ward, Lock, 1888, $6,000). First American edition (Philadelphia: Lippincott, 1890, $2,000).

2. 1890 DOYLE, ARTHUR CONAN: "The Sign of the Four" (contained in *Lippincott's Monthly Magazine* for February 1890, London, Philadelphia, $1,250). Also of importance is the first book edition (London: Spencer Blackett, 1890, $2,500; the spine of the earliest issue has Spencer Blackett's name and the later issue has the imprint of Griffith Farran) and the first American edition (New York: Collier's Once a Week Library, 1891, $1,500).

3. 1892 DOYLE, ARTHUR CONAN: *The Adventures of Sherlock Holmes* (London: Newnes, $1000). Also the first American edition (New York: Harper, 1892, $400). The first short-story collection.

4. 1894 DOYLE, ARTHUR CONAN: *The Memoirs of Sherlock Holmes* (London: Newnes, $650). Also first American edition (New York: Harper, 1894, $400). English edition contains 12 tales; American, 13.

5. 1894 BARR, ROBERT: *The Face and the Mask* (London: Hutchinson, $200). Contains "The Great Pegram Mystery" —the first parody, originally published as "Detective Stories Gone Wrong: The Adventures of Sherlaw Kombs" by Luke Sharp in *The Idler Magazine,* May 1892.

6. 1897 BANGS, JOHN KENDRICK: *The Pursuit of the House-Boat: Being Some Further Account of the Divers Doings of the Associated Shades, Under the Leadership of Sherlock Holmes, Esq.* (New York: Harper, $25). The first American book containing a Holmes parody.

7. 1901 LEHMANN, R.C.: *The Adventures of Picklock Holes* (London: Bradbury, Agnew, $1,000). The first Holmes parody cycle.

8. 1902 DOYLE, ARTHUR CONAN: *The Hound of the Baskervilles* (London: Newnes, $600). Also the first American edition (New York: McClure, Phillips, $150). The most famous mystery ever written.

COURTESY HOUSE OF EL DIEFF, INC.

9. 1902 TWAIN, MARK: *A Double Barrelled Detective Story* (New York: Harper, $100). A book-length satire on detective fiction, particularly Holmes.

10. 1902 HARTE, BRET: *Condensed Novels Second Series New Burlesques* (London: Chatto & Windus, $40). Also the first American edition (Boston, New York: Houghton, Mifflin, $75). Contains "The Stolen Cigar Case," about Hemlock Jones. Ellery Queen considers this the best Holmes parody.

11. 1905 DOYLE, ARTHUR CONAN: *The Return of Sherlock Holmes* (London: Newnes, $750). Also the first American edition (New York: McClure, Phillips, $250). The sixth Holmes book.

12. 1907 LEBLANC, MAURICE: *The Exploits of Arsene Lupin* (New York, London: Harper, $125). Translated from the French edition of the same year by Alexander Teixeira de Mattos. Contains "Holmlock Shears Arrives Too Late," the first of several confrontations between Holmes and France's great rogue.

13. 1909 DUNBAR, ROBIN: *The Detective Business* (Chicago: Charles H. Kerr, $250). The first book of mainly nonfiction writings about Holmes.

14. 1911 HENRY, O.: *Sixes and Sevens* (New York: Doubleday, Page, $50). Contains "The Adventures of Shamrock Jolnes" and "The Sleuths," by America's master of the short story.

15. 1912 DOYLE, ARTHUR CONAN: *The Speckled Band: An Adventure of Sherlock Holmes* (London, New York: Samuel French, $200). (The earliest state has green paper covers; later states have light brown covers.) The first published play.

16. 1912 HOLMES, SHERLOCK: *Practical Handbook of Bee Culture, with Some Observations upon the Segregation of the Queen* (Sussex: Privately printed, $2,000). The author's *magnum opus.*

17. 1913 SAXBY, JESSIE M.E.: *Joseph Bell, M.D., F.R.C.S., J.P., D.L., etc.: An Appreciation by an Old Friend* (Edinburgh and London: Oliphant, Anderson & Ferrier, $250). The first book about the man who was Doyle's professor in medical school.

18. 1913 DOYLE, ARTHUR CONAN: *Sherlock Holmes: The Adventure of the Dying Detective* (New York: Collier, $2,000). The only Holmes story to be printed separately before appearing in a collection.

19. 1915 DOYLE, ARTHUR CONAN: *The Valley of Fear* (London: Smith, Elder, $100). Also the first American edition (New York: Doran, $50). The last Holmes novel, called the best of the four by John Dickson Carr.

20. 1917 DOYLE, ARTHUR CONAN: *His Last Bow* (London: Murray, $100). Also the first American edition (New York: Doran, $50).

21. 1918 THIERRY, JAMES FRANCIS: *The Adventure of the Eleven Cuff Buttons* (New York: Neale, $250). An early book-length parody.

22. 1920 STARRETT, VINCENT: *The Unique Hamlet: A Hitherto Unchronicled Adventure of Mr. Sherlock Holmes* (Chicago: Privately printed, $2,000). A rare book, issued in a very limited edition of indeterminate number. Although Starrett said 200, and De Waal 33, it is probably 110, of which 100 have the imprint of Walter H. Hill and 10 of Starrett. The best Holmes pastiche.

23. 1920 CLOUSTON, J. STORER: *Carrington's Cases* (Edinburgh: Blackwood, $225). Contains "The Truthful Lady," a parody about Watson.

24. 1922 GILLETTE, WILLIAM: *Sherlock Holmes: A Drama in Four Acts* (London, New York: Samuel French, $100). Although Conan Doyle is credited with coauthorship, he had nothing to do with writing the play. The best Holmes play.

25. 1925 LUCAS, E.V. (ed.): *The Book of the Queen's Doll's House Library,* 2 vols. (London: Methuen, $750). Contains "How Watson Learned the Trick," a parody by Conan Doyle. Limited to 1,500 copies.

26. 1924 DOYLE, ARTHUR CONAN: *Memories and Adventures* (London: Hodder & Stoughton, $250). Contains "The Adventure of the Two Collaborators" by James M. Barrie. In the opinion of Doyle, it is the best of the many burlesques of Holmes.

27. 1927 DOYLE, ARTHUR CONAN: *The Case-Book of Sherlock Holmes* (London: Murray, $100). Also the first American edition (New York: Doran, $50). Last book in the Canon.

28. 1928 KNOX, RONALD A.: *Essays in Satire* (London: Sheed & Ward, $35). Contains "Studies in the Literature of Sherlock Holmes," regarded as the first essay of "higher criticism."

29. 1929 FULLER, WILLIAM O.: *A Night with Sherlock Holmes* (Cambridge, Mass.: Privately printed, $500). A handsomely printed pastiche, limited to 200 copies.

30. 1929 CHRISTIE, AGATHA: *Partners in Crime* (London: Collins, $750 with dust jacket, $150 without). Also the first American edition (New York: Dodd, Mead, $250 with dust jacket, $40 without). Contains "The Case of the Missing Lady," a parody by the first lady of crime.

31. 1930 MORLEY, CHRISTOPHER (ed.): *The Complete Sherlock Holmes,* 2 vols. (New York: Doubleday, Doran, $100). The first complete American edition. Contains "In Memoriam: Sherlock Holmes," the first printing of the most widely published essay on Holmes.

32. 1931 ROBERTS, S.C.: *Doctor Watson: Prolegomena to the Study of a Biographical Problem* (London: Faber & Faber, $40). The standard life of Watson.

33. 1932 BLAKENEY, T.S.: *Sherlock Holmes: Fact or Fiction?* (London: Murray, $300). The first book-length biography of Holmes.

34. 1932 BELL, H.W.: *Sherlock Holmes and Dr. Watson: The Chronology of Their Adventures* (London: Constable, $250). The first attempt to date all of Holmes' adventures, recorded and unrecorded. 500 copies.

35. 1933 STARRETT, VINCENT: *The Private Life of Sherlock Holmes* (New York: Macmillan, $250). The standard biography of Holmes.

36. 1934 BELL, H.W. (ed.): *Baker Street Studies* (London: Constable, $200). The first critical anthology devoted to Holmes.

37. 1934 SMITH, HARRY B.: *How Sherlock Holmes Solved the Mystery of Edwin Drood* (Glen Rock, Pa.: Walter Klinefelter, $500). A pastiche, limited to 33 copies.

38. 1934 CLENDENING, LOGAN: *The Case of the Missing Patriarchs* (Ysleta, Tex.: Privately printed for Edwin B. Hill, $200). With a note by Starrett. Posthumous adventure of Holmes, limited to 30 copies.

39. 1934 DOYLE, ARTHUR CONAN: *The Field Bazaar* (London: Athenaeum Press, $150). Holmes parody written by Doyle in 1896. 100 copies.

40. 1938 MORLEY, FRANK V.: *A Sherlock Holmes Cross-Word Puzzle* (New York: Privately printed, $500). Often credited to Christopher Morley. The original test for membership in the Baker Street Irregulars. Rare; limited to 38 copies.

41. 1938 SMITH, EDGAR W.: *Appointment in Baker Street* (Maplewood, N.J.: Pamphlet House, $200). Profiles of everyone who had dealings with Holmes. Limited to 250 copies.

42. 1938 HONCE, CHARLES: *A Sherlock Holmes Birthday* (New York: Privately printed, $400). Reminiscences of the 1937 Semicentennial. The first of his Christmas books. 100 copies.

43. 1938 KLINEFELTER, WALTER: *Ex Libris A. Conan Doyle Sherlock Holmes* (Chicago: Black Cat Press, $125). Sherlockian essays. 250 copies.

44. 1940 STARRETT, VINCENT (ed.): *221B: Studies in Sherlock Holmes* (New York: Macmillan, $100). The first American anthology of essays.

45. 1940 SMITH, EDGAR W.: *Baker Street and Beyond* (Maplewood, N.J.: Pamphlet House, $100). The first Sherlockian gazetteer.

46. 1940 BOUCHER, ANTHONY: *The Case of the Baker Street Irregulars* (New York: Simon & Schuster, $125). A mystery novel involving many Sherlockians.

47. 1941 HEARD, H.F.: *A Taste for Honey* (New York: Vanguard, $100). A detective novel about "Mr. Mycroft," a pseudonymous, reclusive Holmes.

Bzzz.

Bzzz.

48. 1941 McKee, Wilbur K.: *Sherlock Holmes Is Mr. Pickwick* (Brattleboro, Vt.: Privately printed, $200). A whimsical pamphlet. Limited to 300 copies.

49. 1941 Wilde, Percival: *Design for Murder* (New York: Random House, $50). A novel with Sherlockian overtones.

50. 1943 Officer, Harvey: *A Baker Street Song Book* (Maplewood, N.J.: Pamphlet House, $125).

51. 1944 Queen, Ellery (ed.): *The Misadventures of Sherlock Holmes* (Boston: Little, Brown, $300). The best anthology of parodies and pastiches. A special edition of 125 copies was distributed at the 1944 BSI dinner.

52. 1944 Smith, Edgar W. (ed.): *Profile by Gaslight* (New York: Simon & Schuster, $75). A large collection about Holmes. A special edition of approximately 125 copies was distributed at the BSI dinner in 1944 ($400).

53. 1945 Roberts, S.C.: *The Strange Case of the Megatherium Thefts* (Cambridge: Privately printed, $375). A flavorful pastiche. Limited to 125 copies.

54. 1945 Smith, Edgar W.: *Baker Street Inventory* (Summit, N.J.: Pamphlet House, $100). The first bibliography of the Canon and the writings about the writings. A preliminary pamphlet appeared in 1944. Limited to 300 copies.

Bzzz.

Bzzz.

55. 1945 Derleth: *"In Re: Sherlock Holmes": The Adventures of Solar Pons* (Sauk City, Wisc: Mycroft & Moran, $75). The first Pons book, with an introduction by Vincent Starrett.

56. 1946 Yuhasova, Helene: *A Lauriston Garden of Verses* (Summit, N.J.: Pamphlet House, $75). Attributed to Edgar W. Smith. 250 copies.

57. 1946–49 Smith, Edgar W. (ed.): *The Baker Street Journal*. The official publication of the Baker Street Irregulars; 13 issues were published ($150).

58. 1947 Cutter, Robert A. (ed.): *Sherlockian Studies* (Jackson Heights, N.Y.: Baker Street Press, $75). Seven essays, sponsored by The Three Students of Long Island. 200 copies.

59. 1947 Williamson, J.N., and H.B. Williams (eds.): *Illustrious Client's Case-Book* (Indianapolis, Ind.: The Illustrious Clients, $100).

60. 1947 Keddie, James, Jr. (ed.): *The Second Cab* (Boston: Privately printed, $75). Essays, ephemera by The Speckled Band of Boston. 300 copies.

61. 1947 Christ, Jay Finlay: *An Irregular Guide to Sherlock Holmes of Baker Street* (New York: Argus Books. Summit, N.J.: Pamphlet House, $175). A concordance.

Bzzz.

Bzzz.

Holmes was a devoted apiarist. Bzzz.

62. 1948 Bayer, Robert John: *Some Notes on a Meeting at Chisam* (Chicago: Camden House, $225). Father Brown and Holmes. Limited to 60 copies.

63. 1949 Carr, John Dickson: *The Life of Sir Arthur Conan Doyle* (New York: Harper, $25). The standard life of Watson's agent.

64. 1949 Grazebrook, O.F.: *Studies in Sherlock Holmes,* 7 vols. (London: Privately printed, $400).

65. 1950 SMITH, EDGAR W.: *A Baker Street Quartette* (New York: The Baker Street Irregulars, $75). Four Sherlockian tales in verse. 221 copies.

66. 1950–52 DOYLE, ARTHUR CONAN: *Sherlock Holmes,* 8 vols. (New York: Limited Editions Club, $500). The ultimate edition of the Canon, edited by Edgar W. Smith and profusely illustrated. Limited to 1,500 sets.

67. 1951 BREND, GAVIN: *My Dear Holmes* (London: Allen & Unwin, $35).

68. 1951– SMITH, EDGAR W. (followed by JULIAN WOLFF, M.D.) (ed.): *The Baker Street Journal (New Series).* The quarterly publication of the Baker Street Irregulars ($800).

69. 1952– DONEGALL, MARQUESS OF (ed.): *The Sherlock Holmes Journal.* Semiannual publication of the Sherlock Holmes Society of London ($500).

70. 1952 PETERSON, ROBERT STORM, and TAGE LA COUR: *Tobacco Talk in Baker Street* (New York: Baker Street Irregulars, $175). Contains an essay and a burlesque.

71. 1952 WOLFF, JULIAN, M.D.: *The Sherlockian Atlas* (New York: Privately printed, $65). 13 detailed maps of Holmes' world. 400 copies.

72. 1953 SMITH, EDGAR W.: *The Napoleon of Crime* (Summit, N.J.: Pamphlet House, $75). The standard life of professor Moriarty. Limited to 221 copies.

73. 1953 ZEISLER, ERNEST BLOOMFIELD: *Baker Street Chronology* (Chicago: Alexander J. Isaacs, $250). A new dating of Holmes' adventures. Limited to 200 copies.

74. 1953–71 SIMPSON, A. CARSON: *Simpson's Sherlockian Studies,* 9 vols. (Philadelphia: Privately printed, $600). The first 8 pamphlets limited to 221 copies; the last was reproduced from the unpublished manuscript in 1971.

75. 1954 MONTGOMERY, JAMES: *A Study in Pictures* (Philadelphia: Privately printed, $100). The first guide to the illustrators of Holmes. The most elaborate of the author's 6 Christmas annuals (1950–55). 300 copies.

76. 1954 DOYLE, ADRIAN CONAN, and JOHN DICKSON CARR: *The Exploits of Sherlock Holmes* (New York: Random House, $50). 12 pastiches by the agent's son and a brilliant writer.

77. 1955 GILLETTE, WILLIAM: *The Painful Predicament of Sherlock Holmes: A Fantasy in One Act* (Chicago: Ben Abranson, $40). Introduction by Vincent Starrett. Gillette's *other* Sherlock Holmes play, first performed in 1905. 500 copies.

78. 1955 CLARKE, RICHARD W. (ed.): *The Best of the Pips* (New York: The Five Orange Pips of Westchester County, $50). Called "the most erudite" essays by Edgar W. Smith.

79. 1955 MITCHELL, GLADYS: *Watson's Choice* (London: Michael Joseph, $50). A novel with Sherlockian flavorings.

80. 1957 WOLFF, JULIAN, M.D.: *A Ramble in Bohemia* (New York: U.N. Philatelic Chronicle [*sic*], $65). A report on the commemorative Holmes stamp issued by the Republic of Bohemia in 1988. A stamp accompanies some copies.

81. 1957 WARRACK, GUY: *Sherlock Holmes and Music* (London: Faber & Faber, $65). The definitive guide to Holmes' life as a musician.

THE GAME PLAN

Parker Brothers created a Sherlock Holmes card game in 1904.

Lawrence Treat created "Bringing Sherlock Home," a series of pictorial puzzles, in 1935.

More recently, International Polygonics, Ltd., introduced a "Three Pipe Problem," an infernally complicated Rubik's cube-type affair.

And the true labor of love has been Sleuth Publications, Ltd.'s Consulting Detective™, a three-ring binder containing a street map of Victorian London, a Case Book including ten cases and their solutions, a Clue Book for assistance, a Newspaper Archive replete with red herrings, real facts, fascinating diversions, and a Quiz Book that is deucedly hard to answer.

82. 1958 DOYLE, ARTHUR CONAN: *The Crown Diamond: An Evening with Sherlock Holmes. A Play in One Act* (New York: Privately printed, $250). A very short play written just after the turn of the century and published for the first time. Introduction by Edgar W. Smith. 59 copies.

83. 1958 HARRISON, MICHAEL: *In the Footsteps of Sherlock Holmes* (London: Cassell, $25). An authoritative geographical examination of Holmes' world.

84. 1958 TITUS, EVE: *Basil of Baker Street* (New York: Whittlesey House, $25). The first of the best series of juveniles for Sherlockians; illustrated by Paul Galdone.

85. 1959 STARR, H.W. (ed.): *Leaves from the Copper Beeches* (Narberth, Pa.: The Sons of the Copper Beeches, $60). Mostly humorous essays. 500 copies.

86. 1959 HOLROYD, JAMES EDWARD: *Baker Street By-Ways* (London: Allen & Unwin, $40). A commentary by the chairman of the Sherlock Holmes Society of London.

87. 1962 BARING-GOULD, WILLIAM S.: *Sherlock Holmes of Baker Street* (New York: Clarkson N. Potter, $25). The most authoritative life of Holmes.

88. 1962 SMITH, EDGAR W.: *Sherlock Holmes: The Writings of John H. Watson, M.D.* (Morristown, N.J.: Baker Street Irregulars, $65). A comprehensive bibliography of Holmes' adventures.

89. 1963 KLINEFELTER, WALTER: *Sherlock Holmes in Portrait and Profile* (Syracuse University Press, $25). Introduction by Vincent Starrett. The definitive study of illustrations.

90. 1964 KAHN, WILLIAM B.: *An Adventure of Oilock Combs: The Succored Beauty* (San Francisco: The Beaune Press, $100). A parody originally published in the October 1905 issue of *The Smart Set Magazine.* The first Christmas keepsake of Dean and Shirley Dickensheet. 222 copies.

91. 1964 KLINEFELTER, WALTER: *A Packet of Sherlockian Bookplates* (Nappanee, Ind.: Privately printed, $125). A compendium of the bookplates of eminent Sherlockians, extensively illustrated in color. 150 copies.

92. 1966 FISH, ROBERT L.: *The Incredible Schlock Homes* (New York: Simon &

Schuster, $75). The funniest series of Sherlockian parody-pastiches.

93. 1966 QUEEN, ELLERY: *A Study in Terror* (New York: Lancer, $20). Also the first English edition, and the first in hardcover, retitled *Sherlock Holmes Versus Jack the Ripper* (London: Gollancz, 1967). A novelization of the film, with added material, which records Holmes' encounter with The Harlot Killer.

94. 1967 BARING-GOULD, WILLIAM S.: *The Annotated Sherlock Holmes,* 2 vols. (New York: Clarkson N. Potter, $50). The definitive edition of the Canon, heavily illustrated and annotated by a preeminent scholar.

95. 1968 WINCOR, RICHARD: *Sherlock Holmes in Tibet* (New York: Weybright & Talley, 25¢). Noteworthy as probably the worst book about Holmes.

96. 1974 MEYER, NICHOLAS: *The Seven-Percent Solution* (New York: Dutton, $15). The book largely responsible for a new Sherlockian boom.

97. 1974 GARDNER, JOHN: *The Return of Moriarty* (London: Weidenfeld & Nicholson, $15). The most literate, enthralling and atmospheric pastiche in half a century.

98. 1974 DE WAAL, RONALD BURT: *The World Bibliography of Sherlock Holmes and Dr. Watson* (Boston: New York Graphic Society, $50). A monumental reference book and a prodigious achievement, listing 6,221 items relating to Holmes.

99. 1976 TODD, PETER: *The Adventures of Herlock Sholmes* (New York: The Mysterious Press). With an introduction by Philip José Farmer. Contains 18 parodies by Charles Hamilton under the Todd pseudonym. Published originally in a British periodical in 1915–16, they are the first of the longest Holmes parody cycle (100 stories). Limited to 1,250 copies ($10), 250 deluxe ($50).

100. (IN PREPARATION) HOLMES, SHERLOCK: *The Whole Art of Detection.* In preparation for more than fifty years; and will contain everything learned in the preceding fifty years. Priceless.

Otto Penzler wrote The Private Lives of Private Eyes, Spies, Crimefighters and Other Good Guys.

THE LONDON CONTINGENT

Margaret Boe Birns

Let us go then, you and I, to the Bottle Street Police Station, off Piccadilly. A dirty yellow portal on the left side of the building leads to the dark at the top of the stairs until suddenly—a carved oak door upon which is a small brass plaque, neatly engraved with simple lettering: ALBERT CAMPION, MERCHANT GOODS DEPT.

But *we* know better, don't we? Inside the flat are some delightful old pieces of furniture, a Rembrandt etching, a Steinlen cat, a very lovely little Girton—and a number of trophies from Campion's true line of work, including the infamous Black Dudley dagger.

As befits one rumoured to be of royal blood, Campion's rooms are luxuriously furnished. But for a look at something that will seem truly rare and unattainable, let us stroll over to 110A Piccadilly. It is directly opposite Green Park, in a block of new, perfect and expensive flats. Some say this address was chosen because it divides by two the 221B number of the notable Baker Street address. Second floor: here we are. Is it not like a colourful and gilded paradise in a mediaeval painting? Let us feast our eyes on this whimsical paradise done in black and primrose, with a wood fire leaping on a wide old-fashioned hearth, a Chesterfield sofa suggesting the embraces of the houris, walls lined with rare editions, Sèvres vases filled with red and gold chrysanthemums, a fine old decanter of Napoleon brandy—and over at the black baby grand piano, attacking a Scarlatti sonata like a man possessed, is Lord Peter Wimsey. He is moody at the moment. Just back from Harley Street, his manservant Bunter tells us, where he's undergone a most unpleasant interview with a Dr. Julian Freke. Something about a body in a bathtub.

As the strains of Scarlatti fade away behind us, let us move on to the beautifully appointed Albany. The thick pile carpet, the air of unhurried splendour—it is the perfect ambience for elegant A.J. Raffles, gentleman and thief. Perhaps we can purchase some Sulivan cigarettes here at the desk, then take a turn into the heart of Mayfair to view the home of the Honorable Richard Rolliston, alias "The Toff." And while in the district, we must visit Whitehaven Mansions. That little Belgian gentleman with the famous moustaches used to live with his friend Captain Hastings at 14 Farraway, but back in the Thirties he moved to this modern block of flats whose geometrical appearance and proportions indulged his passion for order and method. Is it possible that the local Elephant-and-Castle will have retained a bit of his favourite *sirop de cassis*? Perhaps we can stop in and raise our glasses to the memory of the late Hercule Poirot.

Let us move, then, out of the posh Mayfair district over to The Strand. In an old building we find a plain ground-glass door on which appears the single word HEWITT. It is, of course, the private detective agency of the amiable Martin Hewitt. Stout fellow, Hewitt. For an even stouter fellow let us turn just below The Strand and above the Victoria Embankment to 1 Adelphi Terrace, where we find the roly-poly Gideon Fell with a pint of bitter next to him, indulging in one of his favourite pastimes—reading a mystery story.

And now over to The Temple, nearby. 5A King's Bench Walk. One floor up is a massive outer oak door with a name upon it in white letters. This door opens to disclose a baize-covered inner door. Beyond this is a spacious wood-paneled living room with a broad hearth flanked by two wing chairs. In the fireplace is a gas ring, on which a kettle of water boils for tea. On the floor above is a laboratory and workshop, the walls covered with shelves and tool racks bearing all manner of strange instruments. There is also a cupel furnace, occasionally used as a grill for cutlets by

the noble manservant Polton. At a table in the laboratory, a tall and very handsome man appears to be making a study of the characteristics of methylene blue on cellulose and oxycellulose. Yes, of course: it is Dr. John Thorndyke.

And while we are in the area, over at the Inner Temple are Sir Nicholas Harding's chambers, which he shares with that barrister who is the soul of London urbanity—Antony Maitland.

The fog thickens. It begins to close like a shroud outside the city gates and into the East End. The fog is brown and vile here in Whitechapel Road, among the one-night cheap hotels and sawdust restaurants; menace seems to permeate the very brick and stone itself. Later, in one of these dark, echoing side streets, Jack the Ripper may pay one of his

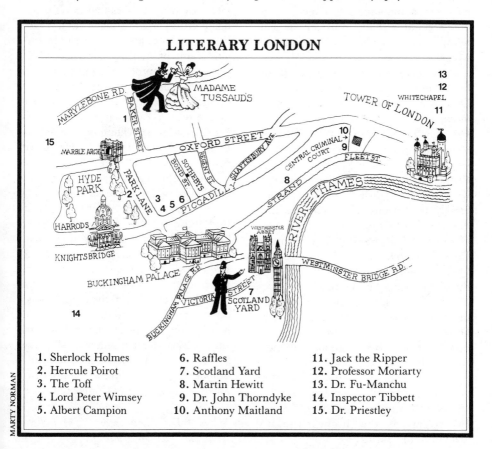

LITERARY LONDON

1. Sherlock Holmes
2. Hercule Poirot
3. The Toff
4. Lord Peter Wimsey
5. Albert Campion
6. Raffles
7. Scotland Yard
8. Martin Hewitt
9. Dr. John Thorndyke
10. Anthony Maitland
11. Jack the Ripper
12. Professor Moriarty
13. Dr. Fu-Manchu
14. Inspector Tibbett
15. Dr. Priestley

MARTY NORMAN

nocturnal visits. Even now, people and objects seem to retreat into the dirty brown mist as we walk the promenade from Whitechapel to Mile End. It is behind the shuttered windows of one of these dingy buildings that we find the headquarters of a certain Dr. Moriarty, organiser of half that is evil and nearly all that is undetected in this great city.

Limehouse. The smoke-laden vapors of the lower Thames have taken on the aroma of incense. You may begin to sense the presence of something, to see—magnetic cat-green eyes, glittering below a dome-shaped forehead. A brow like Shakespeare's, a face like Satan's. Long, tapering fingers with sharp taloned nails fold together in front of a black robe embroidered with a silver peacock. The mist closes again, but we have felt a malignancy we never supposed could radiate from any human being: the devil-doctor himself—Fu Manchu!

We hear the low whistle of his henchmen, the Burmese dacoits. Quickly, to Scotland Yard, and a consultation with Sir Denis Nayland Smith. How safe it feels here in Whitehall! Let us greet Inspector Lestrade. He is on his way to 3 Lauriston Gardens, off the Brixton Road. If we accompanied him, we would see scrawled in blood-red letters the mysterious inscription "Rache." A veritable study in scarlet, as it were.

Let us follow along the corridor to Colonel March at the Department of Queer Complaints. Best walk carefully: there are peppermint cream wrappers on the floor here—Inspector Gently must be about. Ah now, here are the Dead Ends. Inspector Rason, of course, presides here, with a great deal more success than he had with Fidelity Dove! And speaking of influential ladies, let us peek in on Mrs. Palmyra Pym, the Assistant Commissioner of Criminal Investigation—the highest-ranking woman in the Yard.

That there, over at his desk, is Inspector Wilfred Dover. Unfortunately, he appears to have nodded off to sleep. He is snoring over the papers on his desk and has spilled the remains of his tea on what appears to have been a suspect's signed confession. And there is Commander George Gideon. His nose seems a bit out of joint. Evidently he was presented with a traffic ticket this morning.

Now, for a quick nip over to Chelsea. On the ground floor of that shabby yet genteel Victorian house resides Chief Inspector Henry Tibbett and his devoted wife, Emily. And if we just step over to the Fulham Road we can pass Harrington Street and the digs of Commander Gideon.

Let us cross Hyde Park now and enter the Bayswater section of London. Here we are at Westbourne Terrace, home of the brilliant Dr. Priestley. Note how even his house bears the unmistakable stamp of the English aristocrat!

Before we proceed to our final destination, I must inform you of a little side excursion you might, one day, wish to take. Over at Paddington Station Mrs. McGillicuddy is willing to accompany interested bystanders, or available witnesses, on the 4:50 train.

As night falls on the great city, the lamps are lit and we walk past 221B Baker Street. Inside we may expect to find those familiar rooms, the velvet-lined armchair, the array of fine pipes— and smell the aroma of strong tobacco. Even now, the strains of violin music reach us through the sulphurous yellow mist. But wait—out of the night looms a tall, tanned, devastatingly handsome man in an utterly appalling Hawaiian shirt. He is about to enter 221B Baker Street. Something about a "stake-out." Something about drugs. Something about a "Baker Street Connection". . .

Margaret Boe Birns teaches "The Detective Novel" at New York University.

LITTLE GREY CELLS

How many of them does Poirot have? Approximately one trillion, or 10^{12}.

(You have the same number, whether your head is egg-shaped or not.)

The cells are indeed grey, but they are also white—which Poirot forgot to mention—and when seen through a microscope they have a brownish tinge.

Doctors call them neurons, or nerve cells, and divide them into three parts. There's the cell body, the dendrites (for conducting impulses toward the cell) and the axon (for transmitting impulses away from the cell). The axon is surrounded by

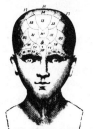

Egghead, front view.

a myelin sheath, which gives the cell its whitish color.

When the axon of one neuron connects with a dendrite of another, you get a synapse. So when Poirot is "using his little grey cells" he is really experiencing multiple synapses involving the cell bodies of the cerebral cortex. To a layman, this means he is thinking. (He also has to use his little grey cells just to stay awake. Consciousness is achieved by the reticular activating system.)

On an EEG machine read-out, normal cells at rest show an alpha rhythm. When you're thinking, however, you get dechronization—or the arousal and alerting response.

Certain drugs can stimulate your little grey cells to think; among them, caffeine, amphetamines, nicotine and strychnine. Considering how much thinking Poirot did, it's just possible he needed a little extra stimulation. A bit of strychnine in the moustache wax, perhaps?

LITTLE GREY CELLS AT WORK

The Mysterious Affair at Styles (1920), *Murder on the Links* (1923), *Poirot Investigates* (1924), *The Murder of Roger Ackroyd* (1926), *The Big Four* (1927), *The Mystery of the Blue Train* (1928), *Peril at End House* (1932), *Thirteen at Dinner* (1933), *Murder on the Orient Express* (1934), *Murder in Three Acts* (1935), *Death in the Air* (1935), *The A.B.C. Murders* (1935), *Murder in Mesopotamia* (1936), *Cards on the Table* (1936), *Poirot Loses a Client* (1937), *Death on the Nile* (1937), *Dead Man's Mirror* (1937), *Appointment with Death* (1938), *Murder for Christmas* (1938), *The Regatta Mystery* (1939), *Sad Cypress* (1940), *The Patriotic Murders* (1940), *Evil Under the Sun* (1941), *Murder in Retrospect* (1943), *Murder After Hours* (1946), *The Labors of Hercules* (1947), *There Is a Tide* (1948), *Witness for the Prosecution and Other Stories* (1948; HP in one), *The Mousetrap and Other Stories* (1950; HP in three), *The Under Dog and Other Stories* (1951), *Mrs. McGinty's Dead* (1952), *Fu-* nerals *Are Fatal* (1953), *Hickory Dickory Death* (1955), *Dead Man's Folly* (1955), *Cat Among the Pigeons* (1959), *The Adventures of the Christmas Pudding* (1960; HP in five); *Double Sin and Other Stories* (1961; HP in four), *The Clocks* (1963), *Third Girl* (1966), *Hallowe'en Party* (1969), *Elephants Can Remember* (1972), *Curtain* (1975). The little grey cells rarely faltered due to the impeccable secretarial skills of Miss Felicity Lemon, the competent plot advice from Ariadne Oliver and the companionship of Captain Hastings, all of whom possessed workaholic grey cells of their own.

Egghead, top view.

NERO WOLFE CONSULTATION

Anthony Spiesman

When I get stuck on a difficult case, I ask myself how Wolfe would handle it. Mentally, I phone Saul Panzer and have him set up an appointment. I don't know why I go through Saul, I just do. Anyway, in my mind, Saul picks up the phone and gets Archie and explains I have this problem and could he see if Wolfe will talk to me. Archie makes a few choice wisecracks, but since I'm a friend of Saul's he gives me the first appointment after orchid hours.

I imagine myself going up the seven steps of Wolfe's brownstone and ringing the bell. Fritz invites me in and escorts me past the famous front room and into the office. He offers me a drink. I tell him I would appreciate a tall, cold glass of milk with two fingers of Scotch. I don't worry about Wolfe's liquor supply or about the quality of the booze, but I make a mental note to send him a case of a great imported Dutch beer called Grolsch which comes in fancy liter bottles and which, for my money, is the best stuff around. I'm a little troubled, though, because the tops are permanently attached rubber plugs that you have to pop open with two thumbs, and I worry about Wolfe's habit of counting bottle caps and putting them away in his top drawer.

While I wait for Wolfe to come help me, I rubberneck the room. The thing that hits me—and to me this is kind of a surprise—is the layout, the use of space. By this I specifically mean the bookshelves and the file cabinet on the second level. Completely avoids floor clutter.

The high ceilings add to the space, of course, and the outstanding collection of furniture and artifacts makes the place first-class. I start to relax. Any man smart enough to live like this is definitely smart enough to help me out of a jam.

Then I walk over to Archie's desk and take a gander at the picture on the wall above it. I know who it's supposed to be, and I have to admit there's a striking similarity. The neatness of it all impresses me, makes me start getting my thinking under control again.

Next I take an imaginary walk over to the Gouchard globe. Having read about it so many times, I have no trouble picturing it. Thirty-two and three-eighths inches in diameter is a lot of globe. Really big. But it's not the size so much that gets to me—it's the overall beauty, the craftsmanship. There's something about being in a room with perfect objects that is conducive to clear thinking. Don't ask me why. (Sometimes, at this point in my fantasy, I take time out for a trip to the lobby of the Daily News building on East 42nd Street. That's my favorite globe anywhere, and I can spend hours staring at it and taking great sea journeys around the world.)

I return to Wolfe's office and decide that my favorite thing in it is the superb mostly yellow Shirvan rug. Comforting while I'm pacing. But being somewhat of an amateur cook myself, I do take a few minutes to appreciate the engraving of Brillat-Savarin. I also find Wolfe's own cookbook on his shelf and haul it down for a quick look. Same contents as

The bronwstone on West 35th Street. Not pictured: the elevator, the rooftop orchids, the dining room, the front doorbell, which just rang to admit Fritz, Theodore, Archie, Saul, Cramer and you. Wolfe will be down to greet you as soon as he changes out of his yellow silk pajamas.

MARTY NORMAN

my copy, I'm glad to say. Still at the bookshelf, I can't resist pulling out Wolfe's copy of Lawrence's *Seven Pillars of Wisdom*. I once tried to get through it. Couldn't. But I'm convinced if Wolfe can, he's the man to analyze my case.

I stand in front of Wolfe's cherry desk and decide not to pick up any of his blunt instruments, but I do take notice of his brown leather Brazilian desk chair. Gigantic! I've never seen anything quite like it anywhere, probably never will. But it definitely looks like it can hold a seventh of a ton just by itself. The chair would take up two-thirds of my office space. I can't help but notice the worn spots on the arms, where countless circles have been made by Wolfe's fingers. I see his fingers circle and his lips go in and out, like an obese goldfish, and I am

reassured he will solve my problems.

I think about sitting in that chair, but I don't have the nerve. Not even in my imagination. I do, however, sit in that infamous red chair—the one Archie says only Inspector Cramer looks like he belongs in. It's a bit uncomfortable to my taste, but I well know the advantages of a chair like this for interrogation purposes. It dwarfs you, makes you feel insecure, and the lies don't come out quite so smooth when you're in it. At this point, I get a little edgy, so I back over to Archie's desk again. I take a quick peek in the red box to see if he really does keep stamps in it. He does. I think about opening the drawers—it's occupational with me—but I don't. I also don't pry inside the liquor cabinet or try to get into the secret alcove and see what Archie sees when Wolfe has him staked out in there.

Then I imagine Wolfe entering the room. I see him as Orson Welles. Nobody else. I imagine him getting straight to the problem, no social nonsense. I can never make up my mind if he shakes my hand or not. I know he doesn't like to shake hands, but I have this urgency to feel that he's really flesh and blood. Usually, I wind up with a strong, quick grip, quickly released. I talk, Archie pretends to take notes, Wolfe listens. Wolfe speaks. The voice is midway between American English and English English. No Montenegrin inflection. Orson Welles in *Citizen Kane,* I think. Full, but not bombastic.

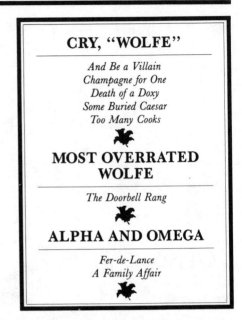

CRY, "WOLFE"

And Be a Villain
Champagne for One
Death of a Doxy
Some Buried Caesar
Too Many Cooks

MOST OVERRATED WOLFE

The Doorbell Rang

ALPHA AND OMEGA

Fer-de-Lance
A Family Affair

THE WOLFE PACK™

This fan club is devoted to Nero Wolfe, Rex Stout and eating, not necessarily in that order. Surely no organization in the history of the world has spent more time preparing, ingesting and washing down food. Among their events: an annual Black Orchid dinner, a beer-tasting, a shad roe extravaganza, and an ongoing search for Rusterman's.

For more information, write Ellen Krieger, Werowance, Box 822, Ansonia Station, New York, N.Y. 10023.

I never know exactly what it is that Wolfe says, but suddenly, after one or two "pfuis," no more problem.

We get up to leave. That is, I get up to leave, preceded by Archie. Fritz comes to the door to see me out. Just as I prepare to go, Wolfe pokes his head out the office door and asks if I'd like to join him in dinner at Rusterman's. (Listen, this is my fantasy. I'll have him say whatever I like.) We agree to meet as soon as I turn in my report on the case.

At this point I get up and walk into my kitchen and start making a mess out of it. I chop, I slice, I mix, I pound, I debone, I decant, I thoroughly fiddle around. And it seems to help. Like Wolfe, I don't talk business when I eat, but there's something about preparing a meal that untangles things for me. So when I start to eat, I raise a toast to my imaginary dinner partner, Nero Wolfe, and thank him for his guidance.

I never met a private investigator like him. But I sure would like to.

Anthony Spiesman is a licensed private investigator in New York.

HOW TO TELL SPADE FROM MARLOWE FROM ARCHER

Richard R. Lingeman

Samuel Spade	*Philip Marlowe*	*Lewis A. Archer*
a.k.a. "Sam"	a.k.a. "Phil"	a.k.a. "Lew"
DATE OF BIRTH		
Ca. 1895	1906	Sometime between 1914–1920, depending on when he's telling it.
DRESS		
Height, 6'; weight, 185 lbs.; hair, blond; eyes, yellow-gray.	Height, slightly over 6'; weight, 190 lbs.; hair, dark; eyes, brown.	Height, 6'2"; weight, 190 lbs.; hair, dark; eyes, blue-gray.
PHYSICAL DESCRIPTION		
Muscular, heavy-boned, sloping shoulders, hairless chest and soft pink skin, big thick-fingered hands. Prognathous jaw, thickish brows, hooked nose, high flat temples and a widow's peak.	Husky. Women find him good-looking in a brutish sort of way.	Husky. As a younger man, resembled Paul Newman; lately resembles Brian Keith.
PHYSIQUE AND LOOKS		
Gray suits, dark brown shoes, green-striped shirts, green tie and loose tweed overcoat.	Hat, trench coat and horn-rimmed sunglasses; when dressed up, wears his one good powder-blue suit, his black brogues and his black wool socks with clocks.	Conservative (owns two suits).
MARITAL STATUS		
Single	Single	Divorced (1949). Wife's name: Sue. Grounds: mental cruelty.

Samuel Spade	*Philip Marlowe*	*Lewis A. Archer*

PERSONAL HABITS

Heavy smoker, rolls his own (Bull Durham, brown cigarette papers) and lights them with a pigskin-and-nickel lighter. Heavy drinker on occasion, including while on job. Drinks Bacardi at home, taken neat in a wineglass; and premixed Manhattans from office bottle in a paper cup.	Heavy smoker, usually Camels; lights cigarettes off kitchen matches, snicking them with his thumbnail. Also smokes a pipe in the office while cogitating. Heavy drinker: keeps a bottle in the deep drawer of his desk for drinks alone or with clients; serves Scotch and soda or Four Roses and ginger ale at home; dislikes sweet drinks.	Heavy smoker for thirty years (but not before breakfast). Gave it up around 1968 but still occasionally reaches for one. Light social drinker; doesn't drink while working or before lunch. Drinks Scotch, bourbon, gin and tonic, and beer (Bass or Black Horse ale).

MANNERISMS

With clients, subject is smooth, sympathetic and ingratiating. Under stress, grins wolfishly, laughs harshly, makes animal noises, or his eyes become cold and hard; when about to slug someone, eyes become dreamy; good poker face with cops.	Tough-guy exterior, enhanced by stream of cynical wisecracks, metaphors and similes: "It was a blonde. A blonde to make a bishop kick a hole in a stained-glass window." "You guys are as cute as a couple of lost golf balls." "Put some rouge on your cheeks. You look like the snow maiden after a hard night with the fishing fleet."	Tough in his day, now more kindly, sympathetic; has father fixation (on self). N.B.: It has been said of subject that "when he turns sideways, he almost disappears."

RECREATION

Reading Duke's *Celebrated Criminal Cases of America*.	Chess problems (his chess is not up to tournament standards), going to movies (he dislikes musicals).	Fishing; sometimes plays the horses when he has some "dirty money"; chess, bird-watching, ecology. Little social life.

HOME

Lives modestly in a small apartment with living room, bathroom and kitchen. Furnishings: sofa, table, armchair, padded rocker, cheap alarm clock by fold-up bed, white bowl hanging from ceiling on chains.	Sixth-floor apartment (living room with French windows and small balcony, bedroom, kitchen and dinette); $60 a month. Furnishings: oak drop-leaf desk, easy chair, chessboard, stale memories, regrets.	Lives in modest second-floor apartment in a quiet section of West Los Angeles. Once owned five-room bungalow on a middle-class residential street in West Hollywood but sold that after divorce.

MATTHEW SEAMAN

Samuel Spade	*Philip Marlowe*	*Lewis A. Archer*
OFFICE		
Sutter Street near Kearney, San Francisco; three-room suite with reception/secretarial area and two inner offices for subject and partner. Furnishings: oak armchair, scarred desk on which is ash-strewn green blotter and butt-strewn brass ashtray.	The Cahuenga Building on Hollywood Boulevard; one-and-a-half-room office on sixth floor with waiting room and interior office. Furnishings: desk with glass top, squeaky swivel chair, five green metal filing cabinets (three of them empty), "near-walnut" chairs, washbowl in stained-wood cabinet, hat rack and commercial calendar on wall.	8411½ Sunset Boulevard, Hollywood; two-room office on second floor of two-story building (office next to Miss Ditmar's model agency). Furnishings: armchair and sagging green imitation-leather sofa in waiting room; inner office sparsely furnished, with mug shots and subject's framed license on walls.
OFFICE HELP		
Effie Perine, secretary, early twenties.	No secretary or answering service. (Telephone: Glenview 7537)	No secretary but does have answering service.
CAR		
Doesn't own one.	Chrysler	Ford

Samuel Spade	*Philip Marlowe*	*Lewis A. Archer*
GUNS		
Doesn't carry one.	Luger, Colt automatics and (preferred) Smith & Wesson .38 special with 4" barrel. Uses shoulder holster.	.38 special, .32 and .38 automatics; no shoulder holster nowadays and rarely uses a gun.
M.O.		
Won't perform illegal acts such as murder or burglary, but otherwise sells self to highest bidder.	No divorce work but takes anything else that's legitimate. Carries photostat of license, honorary deputy sheriff's badge, various phony business cards, fountain-pen flashlight, penknife.	Used to do standard "peeping"—divorce work, adultery, black-mail—but nowadays specializes in family murders with an Oedipal twist. In younger days, used more rough stuff but now avoids violence and has a better (i.e., richer) class of clientele (prefers old money); carries license photostat, various phony business cards, and old special deputy's badge; has a contact mike for eavesdropping, which he never uses; waiting room bugged and has a two-way glass in the door. Usual techniques: psychology (orthodox Freudian), sympathy and probing questions.

MATTHEW SEAMAN

The corridor tail.

CODE		
"When a man's partner is killed he's supposed to do something about it." Byword: "I won't play the sap for you."	First loyalty is to the client; ethical, but would twist rules for client. "I'm selling what I have to sell to make a living. What little guts and intelligence the Lord gave me and a willingness to get pushed around in order to protect a client."	"We are all guilty. We have to learn to live with it." Highly ethical but not squeamish; regularly turns down bribes (including one of a million dollars). Will take any case as long as it's "not illegal and makes sense." Years on the analyst's couch have deepened his insights.

Samuel Spade	*Philip Marlowe*	*Lewis A. Archer*
KNOWN ASSOCIATES		
Secretary Effie Perine; Miles Archer, partner, forties (deceased); Sid Wise, lawyer; (f.n.u.) Freed, manager, St. Mark's Hotel; Luke (l.n.u.), house detective at Hotel Belvedere; Iva Archer (Mrs. Miles), girl friend; Tom Polhaus and Lieutenant Dundy, cops.	Los Angeles crime reporter; Dr. Carl Moss (for confidential medical help); Bernard Ohls, district attorney's staff; Carl Randall, Central Homicide Bureau; Captain Gregory, Missing Persons Bureau.	Morris Cramm, night legman for a Los Angeles gossip columnist; Peter Colton, chief criminal investigator, Los Angeles County District Attorney's office; Bert Graves, Santa Teresa D.A.'s office; Willie Mackey, private detective, San Francisco; Glenn Scott, retired Hollywood private detective.
FEES		
No set fees; employs sliding scale based on client's resources and vulnerability; asked $5,000 (later upped to $10,000) on so-called Maltese Falcon case (collected $1,000).	$25 a day plus expenses ("mostly gasoline and whiskey").	Started out at $50 a day plus expenses; has been at $100 a day since the 1960's.
BACKGROUND		
Subject was probably born in England or lived there before the war. In the Twenties worked with a big detective agency in Seattle (probably a branch of the Continental Detective Agency), then came to San Francisco in the late Twenties and went into partnership with Miles Archer. Partnership dissolved by client Brigid O'Shaughnessy (murder one; served twenty years). Subject's weakness is women; was carrying on simultaneous affairs with his partner's wife (mainly sexual on his	Subject was born in Santa Rosa, California. Began career as an insurance investigator, then worked for the Los Angeles County District attorney's office as an investigator until he was fired for "insubordination." Never speaks of his parents and has no living relatives and few friends. His mail consists almost entirely of bills and circulars. He attended college for two years at either the University of Oregon or Oregon State. Apparent carnal interest in women and often gives them	Subject was born in a "working-class tract" in Long Beach. Stated that he attended grade school in Oakland in 1920, which would place his birth at at least 1914. He probably grew up in Long Beach, and there is some evidence that his parents died or divorced. A juvenile delinquent as a teenager, he reformed and joined the Long Beach police force in 1935 (according to the earliest version), working his way up to detective sergeant before he was fired for reasons that are not clear but relate to

Samuel Spade   *Philip Marlowe*   *Lewis A. Archer*

part) and Miss O'Shaughnessy, yet distrusts women. A cool character who can be unpredictable and harbors a violent streak. Came to a bad end. Subject was shot to death in his office in 1930 by Iva Archer two days after closing Maltese Falcon case. Motive: jealousy.

butterfly kisses with his eyelashes, but has no steady women friends off the job; has turned down advances from attractive females (e.g., the Sternwood sisters) on the job out of loyalty to his client. (Possibility of latent homosexuality? Note overcompensating tough-guy mannerisms and frequent contemptuous references to "pansies," "fags" and "queens.")

corruption. Served in World War II in intelligence. After the war, opened up a Hollywood office and married his former wife, Sue, an ash blonde. She divorced him because she did not like the company he was keeping. Subject tends to cloud his past; for example, he said in 1950 that he had done divorce work in Los Angeles for ten years; on two other occasions stated he was fired from the Long Beach force in 1945 and 1953, respectively, in 1958 he was heard to state his age flatly as "forty." At any rate, he is now close to sixty, a lonely though not unsociable man. Secret passion is not justice, but mercy. "But justice is what keeps happening to people."

Good reading.

FOR FURTHER REFERENCE, SEE:

The works of Dashiell Hammett.

The works of Raymond Chandler.

The works of Ross Macdonald.

Richard R. Lingeman is the author of Small Town America: A Narrative History 1620 to the Present.

MIKE AND MICKEY

Pete Hamill

Out of the mouth of Mike, put there by the mind of Mickey, comes:

> *Go after the big boys. Oh, don't arrest them, don't treat them to the democratic processes of courts and law... do the same thing to them that they'd do to you! Treat 'em to the unglorious taste of sudden death... Kill 'em left and right, show 'em that we aren't so soft after all. Kill, kill, kill!*

If Hammett was a Thirties prizefighter, full of rough grace and a belief in the rules, and Chandler was a Joe DiMaggio, playing on ball fields of a summer afternoon, then Mike Hammer and Mickey Spillane are pro football: brutal, vicious, mean and literally pummeling their way into the American consciousness.

Like pro football, Mike and Mickey reached their first large audiences after World War II, telling them that winning wasn't everything, but—as Vince Lombardi said—it was the only thing.

Mike's tough talk reflected the ethos of the urban blocks, swaggeringly patriotic, xenophobic, virulently anti-Communist. Mickey's often undervalued talent was for narrative, those word bursts hammering heavy and fast, like an epic hangover.

Together their appeal rested on their vigilante primitivism, their idiosyncratic form of law and order in which each man was assigned, by himself, the role of judge, juror and executioner. They interpreted this as the American way, like apple pie and Mom. Critic Philip Cawelti explained this rationale as "part of the justification for Mike's participation in the culminating orgy of sadism and destruction."

Mike and Mickey brashly explained it this way:

> *If you want a democracy, you have to fight for it. Why not now before it's too late? That's the trouble, we're getting soft. They push us around the block and we let them get away with it.*

THE GUMSHOE'S SHOES

An independent survey of private investigators in the New York area revealed that no two of them wore the same brand of shoe and not one of them was sure where the term "gumshoe" came from. Most guessed it had something to do with the fact that they all preferred rubber-soled shoes for working. Several thought it meant they were always picking gum off their shoes—an occupational hazard, it seems, when you do that much walking.

Twelve operatives tossed an extra pair of shoes in the back seat of their car when they were doing surveillance work, just in case their feet started to hurt.

JUDITH WRIGHT

THE CALIFORNIA PRIVATE EYE

Recent additions to the brotherhood are Charles Alverson, Richard Brautigan and Bill Pronzini, whose Joe Goodey, C. Card and Nameless all work out of San Francisco, and Stuart Kaminsky, L.A. Morse and Richard S. Prather, whose Toby Peters, Sam Hunter and Shell Scott hang out in L.A.

But lately there seems to be a drift inland. Perhaps no figure is more representative of the breed than Jonathan Valin's Harry Stoner, who operates out of Cincinnati and has turned up in five titles so far. There is no better embodiment of California private eye principles, even if the guy *is* from Ohio.

Inroads have also been made in Chicago, Indianapolis, Tucson, Detroit, Ft. Lauderdale, Boston and peculiarly named hick towns in Montana, Oregon and Michigan. Even women are getting into the act. (Cf. Sara Peretsky's V.I. Warshawski, a law school grad, black-belt in *Indemnity Only.* Then there's Sue Grafton's Kinsey Millhone, an ex-cop now working Southern California.)

But it's in New York that the California private eye faces his toughest competition, at least in terms of sheer numbers. Thomas Berger's Russell Wren, Andrew Bergman's Jack Levine, Robert Randisi's Miles Jacoby, Frank Leonard's Ross Franklin, Richard Ellington's Steve Drake all pound the crowded pavements, along with the likes of Matthew Scudder (from Block), Mitch Tobin (out of Westlake), Curt Cannon (Cannon), Ed Noon (the prolific pen of Avalone). New Yorkers are wise guys, and if they have a personal code, it's "Do unto others first."

The California P.I. has yet to appear in England. Probably afraid the rain will wash away his tan.

In the Mike and Mickey books one finds the right winger's credo: If you just kill enough Communists, you can save democracy. The courts will only thwart you in this, so you have to bypass them by hiring your bagmen, your wiretappers, your Mike Hammer generals (George Patton) to do your cleaning up.

That Mike and Mickey stand for stunted sexuality, a kind of pornographic reveling in violence combined with a desperate need to present the most awful events as examples of innocence, is not a new idea. Witness the My Lais, the Joe McCarthys, the (I know you're tired of hearing it) Nixons.

Given the chance, Mike and Mickey would run world affairs like rabid politicians. To wit:

> *Some day, maybe, some day I'd stand on the steps of the Kremlin with a gun in my fist and I'd yell for them to come out and if they wouldn't I'd go in and get them and when I had them all lined up against the wall I'd start shooting until all I had left was a row of corpses that bled on the cold floors and in whose thick red blood would be the promise of a peace that would stick for more generations than I'd live to see.*

But the character of popular heroes has, inevitably, changed. The old heroes, the heroes of the Fifties, are dead, and the focus of thriller novels has shifted from the violence of Mike and Mickey. We are now in the company of more interesting men who embrace the sensuality of danger, the turn of the wheel of chance, but who also represent decency and endurance. They can be men who say no, and in so doing, affirm the qualities of the human character that are included in the simple word: hope.

Pete Hamill is the author of The Guns of Heaven, Flesh and Blood, *and* The Invisible City: A New York Sketchbook.

SMILEY AT THE CIRCUS

John Gardner

In John Le Carré's *Call for the Dead* we are introduced to George Smiley—an owl of British Intelligence with a faultless pedigree and a wanton wife. He reappears involved in a death at an ancient and noted public school in *A Murder of Quality*. In the huge best-seller *The Spy Who Came In from the Cold* Smiley is dimly perceived, as he is in *The Looking Glass War*. With *Tinker Tailor Soldier Spy* he holds centre stage, and in *The Honourable Schoolboy* we find him in charge.

Peter Guillam, Smiley's most faithful aide in the secret world, considers (in *Tinker Tailor*) that he has never known anyone who could disappear so quickly into a crowd as Smiley. It is, perhaps, part of Le Carré's particular genius that he is able to make us believe in the now-you-see-him, now-you-don't facility of his most absorbing character.

We believe it, as it were, against the grain, for George Smiley is probably the most complete and fascinating fictional character in the whole bibliography of cold war espionage fiction.

Julian Symons has written of Le Carré's books as having the special qualities of "a sense of place, of doom and irony." They reek of reality, as does George Smiley himself, the most believable character in the fictional dictionary of espionography.

It is this credibility which makes him durable and will keep him haunting the mind long after the pipe-dream James Bonds have been forgotten—a plump, myopic, middle-aged man to whom you would hardly give a second glance. Yet he's a man who carries within his head a lexicon of secrets and ploys that run backward and forward through past, present and future. A man of penetrating intellect, yet reflecting a kind of pathetic sadness that personifies his particular generation and trade.

His ex-Special Branch legman, Mendel, sees him as "a funny little beggar... [like] a fat boy he'd played football with at school. Couldn't run, couldn't kick, blind as a bat but played like hell, never satisfied till he'd got himself torn to bits."

Another policeman says he looks "like a frog, dresses like a bookie, and has a brain I'd give my eyes for." He adds that Smiley had "a very nasty war. Very nasty indeed."

We get glimpses of that nasty war through all the books in which Smiley figures, and Le Carré rounds out his character by making him almost a subsidiary spear-carrier to the plot in such works as *The Spy Who Came In from the Cold* and *The Looking Glass War*.

In both these books, one is never wholly certain of Smiley's situation within the Circus (the author's name for the central department of intelligence, the headquarters of which are in London's Cambridge Circus).

"He resigns, you know, and comes back," says the head of one of the rival departments. "His conscience. One never knows whether he's there or not." He is certainly there during *The Looking Glass War,* yet not so surely in *Spy*—though at the end of that book we hear him physically urging the doomed agent Leamas back over the Berlin Wall: in from the cold.

The facts of Smiley's life are plottable—his mind and body visible through Le Carré's adept drawings—

from the days at Oxford, where he was recruited in 1928, through his service in the field during World War II, until, with cover blown, he is in from the cold, running agents from the Circus and doing tasks that take him all over the world. To tread with him through the major books is to journey through Smiley's life in the fullest sense.

In *A Murder of Quality* there is a summary that brings him into focus:

> Once in the war he had been described by his superiors as possessing the cunning of Satan and the conscience of a virgin, which seemed to him not wholly unjust.... Smiley himself was one of those solitaries who seem to have come into the world fully educated at the age of eighteen. Obscurity was his nature, as well as his profession. The byways of espionage are not populated by the brash and colourful adventurers of fiction.

Duplicity is the stock in trade of the spy, yet it hangs as uneasily on Smiley as the well-made but ill-fitting clothes he wears. Duplicity for George is a cross to which he was nailed, unwillingly, at Oxford, and from which he will never be released. (In reality, all he wants is a quiet, contemplative life studying lesser-known German poets in his pretty house in Bywater Street off the King's Road.) Duplicity, his best weapon, is the weapon that so often almost demolishes his own emotional and professional life, for he finds it wherever he turns: within the Circus, from other departments, from the government, other people's governments and security services, and, worst of all, from individuals—in particular, his wife.

If the Circus is his cross and nails, then his marriage is the crown of thorns: almost incredible to his friends, and indeed to his wife's vast family of faded aristocracy and jaded politicians. It is the first thing we learn about him (in

Call for the Dead) and remains the great seeping fissure in his life. For Lady Ann Sercomb—once Steed-Asprey's secretary at the Circus, now Ann Smiley—is the towering figure of wilfulness who interferes with any peace or happiness the wretched man might attain.

Just as George Smiley is always resigning from the Circus, so Ann Smiley is constantly leaving him for younger, even more unsuitable men. The puzzle is that he puts up with it, together with all its pain and anguish, and even admits to the possibility of taking her back. It is a puzzle that can only be solved by those who have known the same anguish.

So deep are the wounds inflicted by Ann that, on at least one occasion,

MOLES

Most reviewers think Le Carré invented the term. He didn't. The earliest use of the word "mole" in an intelligence context appears in *The Historie of the Raigne of King Henry the Seventh* by Francis Bacon, published in London (1622). Bacon writes:

"Hee was carefull and liberall to obtaine good Intelligence from all parts abroad.... As for his secret Spialls, which hee did imploy both at home and abroad; by them to discover what Practises and Conspiracies were against him, surely his Case required it; Hee had such Moles per- petually working and cast- ing to undermine him."

W. P.

Smiley's domestic situation is used to the advantage of a Russian spymaster.

At the end of the day we are left feeling that Smiley, for all his brilliance within his profession, bears the marks of a man constantly betrayed—not merely by his wife, but by many of those whom he trusts, and by the society in which he lives. Perhaps this is the most telling picture we can ever have of a person who toils within the secret world where trust of any kind is not taken lightly. It is also a most accurate examination of the dilemma of a whole generation that feels betrayed, and it is interesting that, in his confusion, which is a paradox within his professional life, Smiley is easily strung to high, if controlled emotion. He is, for instance, moved to tears at the sight of a child's grief in falling from her pony.

While Le Carré is at his best when peeling the onion-skin layers from Smiley to reveal the whole man, he always shows him at his best within the context of his colleagues. Smiley is the window through which we view, not simply the curving acrostics of the narratives (parts of which must inevitably be lost to those not familiar with the historical in-fighting among the various British intelligence agencies), but also a whole world of secrets, projecting a working knowledge of a profession. Who can tell if the picture is true? Whatever else, it smells and smacks of reality and so becomes more enthralling to the reader.

There are constant references to people long dead, or from Smiley's past: Jebedee, the tutor who recruited him; Fielding, whose brother was later to play a major part in *A Murder of Quality*; Steed-Asprey, who founded the little club, membership of which is restricted to one generation.

These Circus legends become as real to the reader as they are constant memories in Smiley's head—as real as the shadowy Control who is dead by the time we get to *Tinker Tailor*, his place taken by

---

LE CARRÉ UNDERCOVER

Call for the Dead
The Honourable Schoolboy
The Little Drummer Girl
The Looking Glass War
A Murder of Quality
A Small Town in Germany
Smiley's People
The Spy Who Came In from the Cold
Tinker, Tailor, Soldier, Spy

---

the odious Alleline; or Ailsa Brimley, who was a war-time colleague and brings the "murder of quality" to Smiley's attention, and whose house is later used as a hiding place for a witness.

Peter Guillam and Mendel are constants—almost as much as Ann is an inconstant—but it is in *Tinker Tailor* that we get the most detailed and complete structure of Smiley's world, with its scalp-hunters, baby-sitters, pavement artists, wranglers and other jargoned departments. Here the world once inhabited by Control, Jebedee, Fielding and Steed-Asprey is now peopled by the more sinister, but equally engrossing figures of the small Hungarian Toby Esterhase; leftist intellectual Roy Bland; and even Ann's cousin, the renowned Bill Haydon; together with a host of hidden people, both past and present.

From a wealth of detail, Le Carré weaves his narratives around George Smiley, the unlikely agent, the almost shy spymaster whose diffidence is so often a cloak for the rapier mind.

In his world, George Smiley is an owl, but one must never forget that while the owl, in poetic imagination, is a wise bird, he is, in reality, a dangerous predator of the night.

John Gardner is the author of Role of Honor.

THE INVISIBLE BOND

Michael Gilbert

Y̶ou make your entrance into the room. It is an old-fashioned cocktail party, predominantly male, but with a scattering of rather formidable females present as well. You cast your eye hopefully over the crowd to see if there are a few people whom you might recognise.

In the near corner, smoking a meerschaum pipe and wearing, even though he is indoors, a deer-stalker hat, is the unmistakable figure of the sage of Baker Street. Talking to him, an equally unmistakable foreigner with waxed moustaches, green eyes and an egg-shaped head. On their left, three men are engaged in animated conversation. A stout man with an orchid in his buttonhole, a thin and languid young man with corn-coloured hair and a monocle, and a tubby and undistinguished-looking Roman Catholic priest.

So far, we are on firm ground.

But what about this trio in the far corner? Three youngish men, all of tough and athletic build—one, by his speech, American and two English. There is very little to distinguish them. The American is perhaps a little older and a little more thick-set than the other two. He could be Philip Marlowe, but there is no certainty about the matter. Might the man he is talking to be The Saint or The Baron or The Toff or even The Scarlet Pimpernel? (No, hardly, in a well-cut dove-grey double-breasted suit.) But there is something faintly distinctive about the third man.

Memory stirs.

Could it be the grey-blue eyes? No. All heroes have grey-blue eyes. Then it must be the hair. The short lock of black hair that would never stay in place, but

subsided to form a thick comma above the right eyebrow.

Surely, it must be. Dare one introduce oneself?

"Commander Bond, isn't it? I think we first met at Royale-les-Eaux in 1953."

At this point, unfortunately, we wake up and the dream dissolves. But it leaves a curious question behind.

Why is it that detectives are personally so distinguishable and sometimes even distinguished, whilst heroes are physically anonymous? Two hundred pounds of hard muscle, experts at karate, accomplished linguists, irresistible to the opposite sex. But so are ten thou-

James Bond.

sand other young men.

Can the explanation lie in the Greek tag which says that a man's character is the sum total of his actions? The hero of a thriller is unceasingly active. Are we left to deduce his character, as well as his characteristics, from the way in which he conducts his enterprises?

It was with some such thoughts in mind that I re-examined *Casino Royale*. An important book, this, because it is the first time that James Bond, 007, is introduced to us.

Apart from the comma of black hair, I could find only one direct description. It is of Bond asleep, his right hand resting on the butt of his .38 Colt Police Positive. "With the warmth and humour of his eyes extinguished, his features relapsed into a taciturn mask, ironical, brutal and cold." Not much help there.

At a later point Vesper Lynd gives us her opinion. "He is very good-looking. He reminds me rather of Hoagy Carmichael. There is something cold and ruthless . . . ." We lose the rest, because a bomb explodes.

It is significant, however, that Vesper herself is described in great detail. There is a passage of twenty-five lines dealing with her hair, her face, her skin, her arms, hands and fingernails; her jewellery and her dress "of grey *soie-sauvage* with a square-cut bodice lasciviously tight across her fine breasts." Not omitting her handbag, hat and shoes ("square-toed of plain black leather").

Is there some psychological deduction to be made from a book that devotes twenty-five lines to the heroine and only three to the hero? Particularly since Vesper is expendable. She is due to die at the end of the book, although she rises, phoenix-like, from her ashes to reappear under other equally entrancing names in a dozen later books.

It is true that we are told a good deal about Bond's likes and dislikes, and may be able to deduce something further about him from a study of them. He smokes cigarettes specially made for him by Morlands of Grosvenor Street and keeps fifty of them in a flat gun-metal box. He drives one of the last of the 4.5-litre Bentleys with an Amherst-Villiers super-charger. He likes martinis shaken, not stirred, and scrambled eggs.

As the stories roll on, the props pile up: most noticeably, the pigskin Revelation suit-case, with the compartment at the back containing a silencer for his gun and thirty rounds of .25 ammunition. The action continues, fast and furious. The girls are wheeled on, lovingly described, lovingly treated and wheeled off again. The central figure remains obstinately difficult to visualise. Does he exist at all or is he one of those dummies in a shop window, fitted out with every expensive accessory, put into storage at the end of each book and brought out again to start the next?

Ian Fleming.

NEW AMERICAN LIBRARY

THE CONTRABAND FILE

Items confiscated at the (spy novel) border:
False passport
Another false passport
Still another one
Real passport with altered photograph
Forged visa
Stolen visa (since expired)
Counterfeit Deutsche marks
Bank book, First Bank of the Bahamas, Bahama, B.W.I.
Hollow nickel
Hollow quarter
Hollow shoe heel
Hollow tooth
Hollow toothpowder tin
Pen with tear-gas cartridge
Cyanide capsule
Syringe with traces sodium pentathol
Suitcase with trick bottom, lining
Camera that looks like cigarette lighter
Camera that looks like lipstick tube
Telephone bugging device
Cane with sword handle
Safehouse address
Code book
Password of the day, Tuesday, May 11
Phrase book, Albanian/Chinese
Pocket dictionary, Russian/Spanish
Street plan, Vienna
Street plan, Marseilles
Street plan, Lisbon
Day return, Lancashire–London
Microfilm (16 rolls)
Microdots (on postcard of Mississippi, replacing all *i* dots)
Gelignite detonator cap
Several packs of matches, Harry's bar, Venice
Recipe for melba toast and cottage-cheese pâté
Handwritten verse and chorus, *The Whiffenpoof Song*
Ignition key to illegally parked black-and-blue Citroën
Trunk key to abandoned Daimler, maroon and silver saloon car
Telstar transmission frequency schedule, Ottawa/Sri Lanka
Insurance policy, lapsed premium notice

There is another, even more intriguing possibility. Was James Bond really Ian Fleming? It is unusual for a writer to transmogrify himself totally into his own hero. Did not Conan Doyle warn us: "The doll and its maker are seldom identical"? Was this one of the cases where it was, perhaps, true?

On the back cover of the Pan Book edition of the novels is the Cecil Beaton photograph of Ian Fleming. His face certainly looks taciturn and ironical. Questionably, even brutal. He is smoking a cigarette in a long holder. Was it specially made by Morlands of Grosvenor Street and are there forty-nine more in a flat gun-metal box in his pocket, or perhaps in the glove box of his 4.5-litre Bentley with an Amherst-Villiers super-charger and a pigskin suit-case on the back seat?

If this is the truth, it would not only explain the accessories; it would explain the curious elusiveness of the central figure. If you are looking out of your own eyes, you see very little of your own face. To examine that, you need a mirror. On one occasion, James Bond studied his reflection and noted that "the effect was faintly piratical."

If it was Ian Fleming who was looking at himself, one can accept the description without demur. Ian Fleming *was* a pirate, and he brought back a rich and well-deserved hoard of doubloons from his private Spanish Main.

Michael Gilbert is the author of Game Without Rules, *a short-story collection featuring counter-intelligence agents Calder and Behrens.*

BLACKFORD OAKES
Multisyllabic Sex Emanating from Gstaad

John Leonard

Even veteran Buckley-watchers will admit that five spy novels in eight years is an amazement. Balzac himself would be tired, and Balzac wasn't simultaneously writing three other, nonfiction books, churning out a syndicated newspaper column, editing a biweekly magazine, moderating a weekly hour-long television program and speechifying at the drop of a provocation. Nor did Balzac have to spend time in a Jacuzzi or on a yacht or at the Dictaphone in the back seat of a customized-in-Texarkana Cadillac stretch limousine, from which command module Buckley corresponds with more people than there are registered Republicans, promiscuous with his "usufructs," his "propaedeutics," his "velleities" and his reproach.

I haven't mentioned the skis and the harpsichord. And think of the burden of a social life that would hospitalize the Suzy Knickerbockers of this world, who mention his name more often than they do Lady Di's. We learn from *Overdrive,* his account of eight days in an average Buckley week, that when he goes to the theater, the theater he goes to is *Nicholas Nickleby.* When he leaves the ballet, it is to confer with Ahmet Ertegun, who either "owns the Rolling Stones or they own him." When he must change a seating plan for lunch, he can substitute our ambassador to the United Nations for the Vice-President of the United States. When he is about to tape a television program with the governor of Kentucky, the call that interrupts him is from either Barbara Walters or Ronald Reagan.

This is life in the fast (right) lane. No wonder that when he was asked years ago on the *Laugh-In* comedy hour why, on his own TV show, he was always sitting down, couldn't he think on his feet, he paused and then ad-libbed: "It is hard . . . to stand . . . under the weight . . . of all that I know."

Nevertheless, at least every other February, at quaint Gstaad on the Swiss Alpine slopes, between traverses and sideslips with a Galbraith, he perpetrates another episode in the continuing saga of Blackford Oakes, CIA Boy Wonder, at Cold War against the forces of Dialectical Materialism.

Well, the novels are fun: brisk, witty, morally passionate without excessive hectoring, plotted with an increasing intricacy, and full of private jokes. (Blackford Oakes reads *National Review.*) They are no great threat to Malraux or Evelyn Waugh or Graham Greene or even John Le Carré because, like Buckley himself, they're in such a hurry, always in overdrive, broad-jumping to conclusions, and much more interested in the right-wing jab than in complications of character. Think of them as boys' books, upper-class Tom Swifties.

(Which is okay. There's no reason why anybody shouldn't write entertainments with a polemical purpose. Carolyn Heilbrun does it all the time in her Amanda Cross mysteries. The Swedish Wahlöös were vulgar Marxists. Nor am I suggesting that the series is slapdash,

SLEEPOVER AT THE PALACE

A GAME FOR THE INDECOROUS

The Objective: To attain the Queen's Bedchamber, remain overnight and leave in the morning with a small though significant memento, nicely monogrammed—such as a pillow-slip, a guest towel or a demitasse spoon. Since it is always considered bad taste to kiss and tell, anyone selling the story of the Sleepover to the tabloids forfeits the game. Protocol demands the game begin in one of two manners: by special appointment to the Queen or by scaling the Garden Wall—the starting point for the indecorous. Tradespeople must use the Servants' Entrance as their starting point, whereas St. Nicholas must come down the chimney. Players move by divine right, with the highest-ranking title present effecting entry first. This is referred to as droit du seigneur.

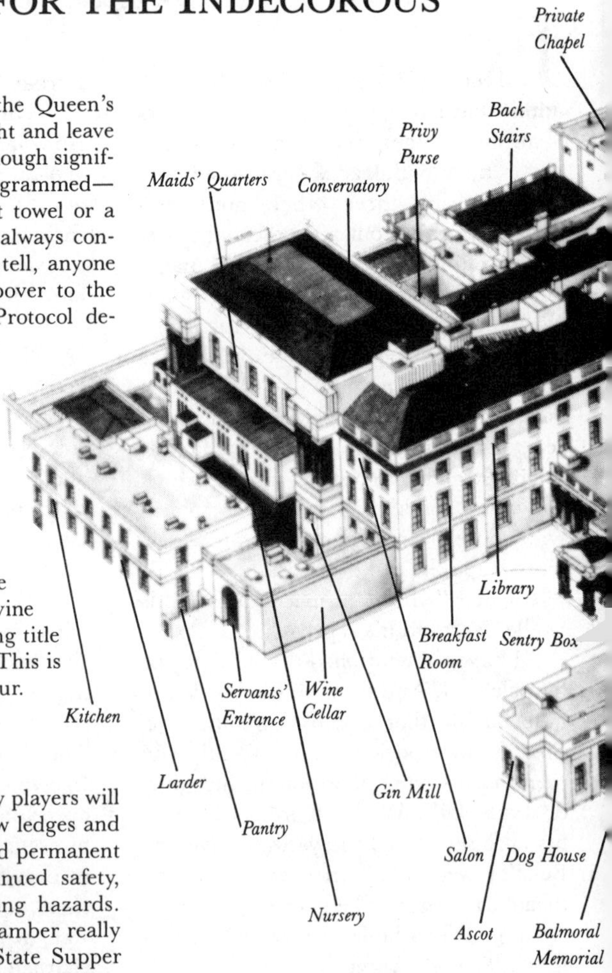

The Grounds: Occasionally players will be forced to perch on window ledges and scramble across roofs to avoid permanent banishment. For your continued safety, please memorize the following hazards. Signs leading to the Star Chamber really lead to the dungeon. The State Supper Room has been poisoned. The Grand Quadrangle is used for target practise. The North Portico has loose bits of masonry, averaging eleven tons per bit. The moat is mined. No one entering the topiary maze has ever been seen to leave it. Prince Philip often sleeps in the doghouse. The sentry boxes.

Private Chapel

Back Stairs

Privy Purse

Maids' Quarters   Conservatory

Library

Breakfast Room   Sentry Box

Servants' Entrance   Wine Cellar

Kitchen

Gin Mill

Larder

Pantry

Salon   Dog House

Nursery

Ascot   Balmoral Memorial Hall

Alarum System: The Queen is protected by the Corgi method, which cordons off her ankles and makes it impossible to get any closer than several paces behind. Throw the poor dogs a bone.

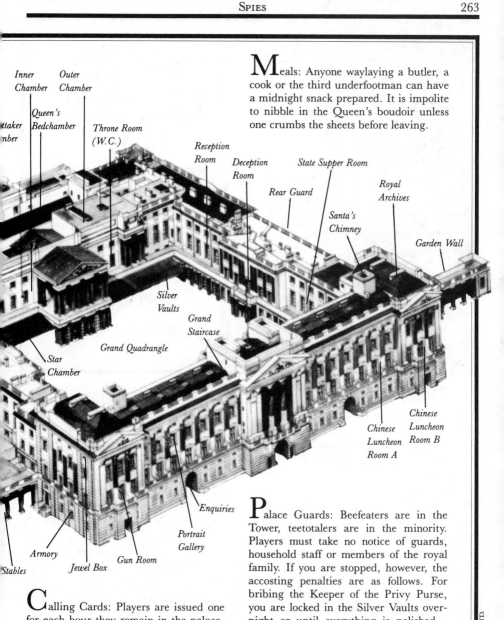

Inner Chamber

Outer Chamber

Queen's Bedchamber

ttaker nber

Throne Room (W.C.)

Reception Room

Deception Room

State Supper Room

Rear Guard

Santa's Chimney

Royal Archives

Garden Wall

Silver Vaults

Grand Staircase

Grand Quadrangle

Star Chamber

Chinese Luncheon Room A

Chinese Luncheon Room B

Enquiries

Portrait Gallery

Armory

Gun Room

Jewel Box

Stables

Meals: Anyone waylaying a butler, a cook or the third underfootman can have a midnight snack prepared. It is impolite to nibble in the Queen's boudoir unless one crumbs the sheets before leaving.

Calling Cards: Players are issued one for each hour they remain in the palace. Princess Anne cards allow access to the Stables, Princess Di cards to the Nursery. A Prince Philip card means you must remove yourself immediately to a distant wildlife preserve, and a Prince Charles card allows you to welsh on all debts. Prince Andrew cards allow you into the Maids' Quarters, and a blank calling card allows you free reign for the night.

Palace Guards: Beefeaters are in the Tower, teetotalers are in the minority. Players must take no notice of guards, household staff or members of the royal family. If you are stopped, however, the accosting penalties are as follows. For bribing the Keeper of the Privy Purse, you are locked in the Silver Vaults over-night or until everything is polished—whichever comes first. For dallying with the Lady-in-Waiting, you are sentenced to Saint Catherine's Home for Unwed Mothers for nine months. For rattling the skeletons in the closet, you are banished to the attic, which you must dust—to dust. For consorting with the Queen, you receive the royal seal of approval and are thereby declared the game's winner.

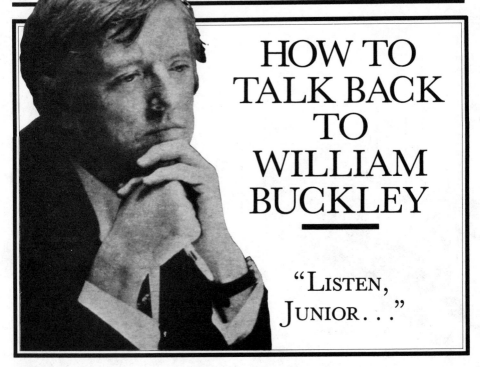

HOW TO TALK BACK TO WILLIAM BUCKLEY

"LISTEN, JUNIOR..."

although there *is* this passage in *Who's on First*: "He explored the refrigerator. There was chicken, ham, cheese, white wine. He put together a plate with slabs of each...." This sounds to me like a wet plate.)

But the 1950's didn't exactly specialize in complications of character. And the novels—with the exception of *The Story of Henri Tod*, which only cheats a little—stick to that decade, in which Buckley's own secularized Manicheanism was the Zeitgeist and the Soviet Union the Demi-Urge. (Sort of like the 1980's, come to think of it: another boys' book.) This prevents clutter. It avoids ambivalence. It lets the bad guys and the Children of Light confront one another with all their gaudy toys, before rock-and-roll and Vietnam. Buckley has probably *met* more interesting ex-Communists, including Arthur Koestler and Whittaker Chambers, than most other American writers have even *read*, and yet, under the weight of all that he

knows, he stoops to comic-strip: bash the "Commies," and the "fags."

Of course, the bad guys rough us up. Despite all Blacky's derring-do, usually in an airplane although surprisingly often in bed, the bad guys develop a hydrogen bomb and launch the first space satellite and bring down a U-2 and build the Berlin Wall. (Odd: when I was at *National Review* in 1959, the editors refused to believe in the existence of Sputnik. Nor would they credit a Sino-Soviet split. According to the revised Buckley, however, the Russians got up there first because of Blacky's compassion, and the Sino-Soviet split was a CIA scam.) This permits the Good Fight in the Lost Cause, a theme of boys' books in American literature at least since Hemingway, although not at Republican conventions.

When he isn't writing about people, Buckley writes well indeed: about flying, and churches, and Berlin, and even the duplicity of Xerox machines. And he is persuasively sure-footed *inside* the spy biz: how agents are recruited, trained and disposed of. Which reminds us that he himself once spooked for the Agency, in Mexico, where he met E. Howard Hunt, which explains some peculiar newspaper columns he wrote during the Watergate affair. But part of the fun of the Oakes series for veteran Buckley-watchers is just being on the lookout for correspondences between Blacky and his creator. We look for Buckley in his fiction the way we look for Mailer; they are performing seals in the media circus.

Blacky is recruited by the Agency directly out of Yale, as was Buckley, and is accustomed to old money, and once did time in the blacking factory of an English public school. At the same age, they would have closely resembled each other: blue eyes, dark blond hair, six feet, a trim 170 pounds. They share a passion for *Antigone* and the Diabelli Variations. Not by accident, Blacky finds himself reading Mommsen's *Römische Geschichte*, on the recommendation of Whittaker Chambers. He also reads Buckley's old friend James Burnham, not to mention something called *Up from Liberalism*. If, however, Blacky is an alter-ego trip, Buckley ought to be a trifle embarrassed.

Because Blacky is almost perfect. To be sure, his French is a "disability," although not his Latin or his German. And he is merely "a competent horseman," although an ace fighter pilot. And he can't carry a tune, although nuclear physics are no sweat, and he is, otherwise, a healthy, cool-headed, decisive, well-adjusted, sophisticated, ingenious and cheeky magnum cum laude and devoted friend, who likes Jane Austen and can build aquariums, fix voltmeters, sail a 44-foot chalk-white cutter, work with stained glass and shoot people—all with "his father's gypsy glamour and audacity," "his mother's quiet and gentle tenacity," and "an indefinable cultural

insouciance." Besides, he's gorgeous.

How gorgeous is he? Such human beings of the female persuasion as airline stewardesses, USIA librarians, Hungarian freedom-fighters, literary critics for the *Sewanee Review*, the higher-priced spreads in the bordellos of Paris and Berlin, *and* the Queen of England all find him irresistible. This means a lot of sex, writing about which Buckley should forswear in favor of Xerox machines and U-2's. One samples at random: "She was silent, but prehensile"; "his staff at stiff attention"; "They discovered a great, even urgent need for each other, and she no less pressing then he as they met, tasted, devoured, and had each other, so to speak, by acclamation"; "They drank in the semidarkness, and soon reexperienced each other, with mounting excitement, with a passion unbridled, but never raucous." And:

> *He came with a terrible hunger. He had difficulty, in the climax, in holding her firm the more so through his own wild excitement as, in the dim light that perforated her underthings, strewn in her haste over the little bed lamp, he peered into her eyes. She was looking at him now with exhibitionistic passion as her pale, full breasts broke out in splotches of mottled light brown while her thighs gripped him and with her hands she stroked him, with a desperate milking action.*

D.H. Lawrence isn't in any trouble, although Terry Southern may be. And where is Colette when we need her? Still, the purpose of sex in the series seems to be the creating of a photo-opportunity, in dim light through perforated underthings, for Blacky to be looked at, occasions of gloom, usually in silence, perhaps taxonomically. His partner always insists that he walk away without his dressing-gown: "uttering squeals of delight at his proportions"; "her eyes shone with pleasure as she watched his lithe

GAIL RUSSELL

Blackford Oakes, seminaked and gorgeous.

body walking into the livingroom"; "you are disgustingly handsome, lover boy"; "she looked at him, this time allowing her eyes to descend slowly along his body." He is made to stand naked at a window in front of a panting double-agent. According to the librarian, "if he actually had been raised in the Aegean," he might "have rekindled jealousy in Olympia." Even his mother calls him "my beautiful Blacky!" Is this really *undercover* work?

Nor are all his admirers female. A member of the Rockefeller Commission investigating the CIA compares "this blond, trim, blue-eyed movie-star type" to Van Johnson. A Norwegian fisherman asks, "but where was the girl who could spurn such a man?" Boris Bolgin, chief of KGB counterintelligence for Western Europe, refers to him as "that handsome fox" and "the picture-poster secret star of the Great Central Intelligence Agency." Even John F. Kennedy, watching Blacky argue the Berlin question before the best, brightest and fattest of cats on the National Security Council, is

obliged to admit: "The Oakes guy, I bet he makes out."

We are somewhere between James Bond and Narcissus. Strange. Especially so since, about women, Blacky is feckless—even the premature feminist and wishy-washy liberal Sally seems to have been phased out of the series, and the rest are one-night stands—whereas the men to whom he is passionately attached (Theo, Michael, Henri Tod) end up dead, except for fellow-Yalie Anthony Trust, who refused to look at Blacky's "proportions" when, in Paris, they had with Michelle and Doucette a four-part "symbiosis." What is being proposed? Are the beauty and the comradeship of well-born males sufficient to save the West from Dialectical Materialism?

One thinks, of course, of Athens and Sparta, of David and Solomon, of the *antiqua virtus* of Republican Rome before the decline, and of the novels of Gore Vidal. I am ambivalent.

John Leonard has never finished writing his mystery novel.

SIDE-TRACKED

TONIGHT

8:01 and Ticking

"And I'm lonesome for you, Simon, I really am. Let's go to your room. I want to show you something."

"I have to be here in case the Inspector shows up, you know that. And you have to go with Lady Clare."

"Look, Simon, this is what a butterfly does. Do you like it?"

"I guess it won't matter if we're a few minutes late."

❤   ❤   ❤   ❤

"Put your clothes on, Harriet."

"You liked me with them off a few minutes ago."

The Colonel assaults Poona.

The bored bereaved.

"**B**ehave yourself. Someone's just died here."

"Yes, and fat lot I care. Do you? Come on, let's go to the room. I'll teach you what butterflies do if we go."

"Butterflies? Harriet! Now, stop it. What if someone came along and saw?"

"I'd tell them the strain had made you weak. That your breathing had gone funny and I was seeing if I loosened things, if it'd make you more comfortable. Like this."

"Harriet, my God, Harriet. No, don't take your hand away, leave it there, yes, like that, ahhhh, there. I love you, Harriet."

"Will you cover up! You're supposed to be in the dining room right now."

"Simon, I think if I hadn't found you sitting by yourself in that theatre and sat down and made friends, you'd be a real old maid by now. I'm tired of hearing 'No, Harriet, stop it, Harriet, Harriet, not now, Harriet, be proper, Harriet.' You used to be nicer to me. I miss my little presents."

"I told you why not; we have to be careful. All the housekeeping cuts go straightaway into the bank, for our start-up funds. I don't want any suspicions looking our way before we leave to use it, and they'd all take notice of a hair slide like you asked for, or an anklet with stones. Bad enough you wore that pin— thought surely His Lordship would recognise it and slam the door shut on us. No, we've been lucky since you got here, and I mean we stay that way. There's time for showing off later."

"Simon. We've got enough, let's pull up now. Even the agent said it, five thousand pounds down is all we need and we've settled that. You could write the cheque now and we could have it, our own little place in Slough. Then you could get it back, I know you could. One more's all you'd need to forge for it, with a back date on it so t'would look like *he'd* done it. An early bonus it could've been. They'd never catch on, and we could take the Mini and book two weeks high season Brighton and be gone, like a regular honeymoon. What do you say, Simon, shall we?"

"We can't be too careful, Harriet. Have to go slow, till this gets cleared up."

"Figure she did it, do you? Her and the boyfriend? Told me she wanted to lie down a bit after the music, and I was hardly out the door when he went through it. D'you think they were doing it while he was dying, Simon? D'you think they have fun the way we do?"

Leslie, stupefied.

"Harriet! You're incorrigible!"

"We'd all be, luv, given the chance. Look at you, signing names and dashing to Bermondsey with pins and rushing back to roll about with me. Who'd think it to look at you, Simon, who?"

"Will you get dressed, Harriet!"

"Which are you more scared of, Simon, that they learn you forged his name and stole her jewelry or that you like playing with me on the sheets?"

"Harriet, I beg you, will you please get dressed! Please!"

"Stuffy old bugger. Like that Roudebush. Now, there's a real one never showing feeling. Vicar said when he told him, he just put his face to the wall, and said, 'Will that be all, sir? I'm feeling a bit peaky.' Still think it odd he wouldn't let me look at the toe. I am registered, after all. Might've helped him."

"Harriet, if you want to live just five minutes longer, you'll put your clothes on before I come over there and kill you. You never heard of shame!"

"Oh, Simon, before you go..."

"Now what? I have to hide these books before anyone sees."

"Kiss me goodbye, Simon. Kiss me like you meant it."

"Harriet!"

"Ten-thirty, Simon?"

"Ten-thirty."

The Colonel retakes the Punjab.

LOVE AND THE MYSTERY NOVEL
OUGHT ADAM TO MARRY CORDELIA?

P.D. James

From the number of readers who write to enquire whether my girl detective Cordelia Gray of *Unsuitable Job for a Woman* will marry Adam Dalgleish, it is apparent that mystery lovers take the view—to paraphrase Jane Austen—that an unmarried detective who is in receipt of a good income is in need of a wife. Dorothy L. Sayers would not have agreed. She expressed the firm belief that detectives should concentrate on the clues, not spend their time chasing young women. It was not a rule she herself adhered to, although Lord Peter had to chase his Harriet (if so ungallant a word can be used for his aristocratic and articulate wooing) six years before she finally capitulated on Oxford's Magdalen Bridge—in Latin.

But it is true that mystery writers, in general, don't interest themselves greatly in the love lives of their detectives, and perhaps this isn't surprising. Birth, sex and death are the three great absolutes in fiction as in life, and it is difficult enough to write adequately about the last, even within the constraints of a detective novel, without attempting to deal other than superficially with its two precursors. A serious love and sex interest in a mystery can endanger its unity as a novel, not to speak of the quality of its detection. It is significant that Dorothy L. Sayers described *Busman's Honeymoon* as a story with detective interruptions. Perhaps this reluctance on the part of detective novelists to

deal with sex and love explains why so many writers make their detectives celibates or at least unmarried: Sherlock Holmes, Father Brown, Poirot, Miss Marple, Dr. Thorndyke. In contrast, the tough, wisecracking, hard-drinking school of private eyes have plenty of women in their adventurous lives, but strictly on their own terms. Other detectives have a happy marital background so that we can rest confidently in the knowledge that all is going well with their private lives and they can get on with their detection without fear of domestic or psychological upheavals. Examples are Simenon's Maigret, Freeling's Inspector Van der Valk, H.R.F. Keating's Inspector Ghote, Edmund Crispin's Professor Gervase Fen and H.C. Bailey's Mr. Fortune. Other detectives are obviously attracted to women but take care to keep them on the periphery of their private or professional lives. It is difficult to imagine a wife intruding into Nero Wolfe's admirably organised brownstone ménage.

There are, of course, some mystery novels in which the love interest complicates and confuses both the investigation and the hero's emotions. Ngaio Marsh's Roderick Alleyn met his painter wife Troy during one of his cases, and Lord Peter first saw his Harriet in the dock at the Old Bailey, where she was standing trial for the murder of her lover. There are, too, some famous husband-and-wife teams: Dashiell Hammett's Nick and

SUBLIMATIONS

Psychologically speaking, geniuses often have diminished sex drives. While we cannot be sure if Josephine Tey's Alan Grant or Stuart Palmer's Hildegarde Withers would have tested off the graph on the standard Stanford-Binet, we know for sure they were more passionate about catching fish and collecting them than about their love life (though Grant did have a very low-key thing going). Said Grant about trout fishing, it's "something between a sport and a religion."

MARTY NORMAN

Nora Charles, Agatha Christie's Tuppence and Tommy Beresford, and Frances and Richard Lockridge's Pamela and Jerry North. But here the wife is a comrade-in-arms, and the love interest is domestic, peripheral and amusing rather than passionate. They hunt the clues together.

So what of my readers' question? Will Cordelia marry Adam? Who can tell? There are, of course, a number of reasons why such an interesting marriage might be nevertheless imprudent. One can imagine the advice which a marriage guidance counsellor would give to Cordelia. Here we have a widower, considerably older than you, who has obviously been unable or unwilling to commit himself permanently to any woman since the death in childbed of his wife. He is a very private person, self-sufficient, uninvolved, a professional detective dedicated to his job, totally unused to the claims, emotional and domestic, which a wife and family would make on him. Admittedly, you find him sexually very attractive, but so do a number of women more experienced, more mature and even more beautiful than yourself. Are you very sure you wouldn't be jealous of his past, of his job, of his essential self-sufficiency? And how real would your own commitment to him be when there would always lie between you the shadow of a secret—that first case of yours when your lives so briefly touched? And are you sure you aren't looking for a substitute for your own inadequate father?

The arguments are weighty, and Dalgleish and Cordelia—highly intelligent both—would be well aware of them. But then, when have two people married on the basis of prudence? I can only say that I have no plans at present to marry Dalgleish to anyone. Yet even the best-regulated characters are apt occasionally to escape from the sensible hand of their author and embark, however inadvisably, on a love life of their own.

P.D. James was made an OBE in 1983.

PALIMONY.
THE ONLY SENSIBLE
ALTERNATIVE TO
MURDER

Cases on the docket:

Brandstetter
vs.
Sawyer
Joseph Hansen,
presiding

Spenser
vs.
Silverman
Robert B. Parker,
presiding

Case dismissed
(*due to death*):

Fletch	Dalgliesh	Vane
vs.	vs.	vs.
Moxie	**Riscoe**	**Boyes**
Gregory Mcdonald, presiding	*P. D. James, presiding*	*(Dorothy L. Sayers, judge on record)*

MARTY NORMAN

MY HUSBANDS

Abby Adams

Living with one man is difficult enough; living with a group can be nerve-racking. I have lived with the consortium which calls itself Don Westlake for twelve years now, and I still can't be sure when I get up which of the mob I'll have my coffee with.

Donald E. Westlake is the most fun, and happily we see more of him than any of the others. He is a very funny person, not jolly exactly, but witty; he loves to laugh and to make other people laugh. His taste in humor is catholic, embracing brows low, middle and high, from *Volpone* to Laurel and Hardy. (His cuff links, the only ones I've ever seen him wear, depict Stan and Ollie, one on each wrist.) He's a clown at times; coming home from the theater recently with a number of children (more about them later), he engaged in a skipping contest (which he won—he's very competitive, a Stark characteristic spilling over) with several of the younger kids, causing the eldest girl acute embarrassment.

Westlake has in common with many of his characters a simplicity and naïveté about life that is disarming, especially if you don't know about the Stark and Coe personae lurking in the background. Looking for an American Express office, he walked through the red-light district of Amsterdam without once noticing the "Walletjes"—plate-glass windows set at eye level in the seventeenth-century canal houses, behind each of which sits a lightly clad hooker, under a red light just in case the message has not been put across. I had to take him back and point them out: "There's one, Don, isn't she pretty? And here's another one."

Like his character Dortmunder,

Westlake is unpretentious, unmoved by style or fashion. He dresses simply, wearing the same clothes year after year, wearing hush puppies until they literally fall off his feet. I cut his hair, but he does his own mending and sews on his own buttons. (Mine, too.) Also like Dortmunder, he takes a great deal of pride in his work (with, thank God, more success), but is not otherwise vain.

Behind the wheel of a car he is Kelp. One of the four publications he subscribes to is *Car and Driver*. (The others are *Horizon, The New Yorker* and *The Manchester Guardian;* what is one to make of all *that?*) He drives passionately, never failing to take an advantage. We once drove across the United States and were passed only three times: twice by policemen and once by a battered old pickup truck full of cowboys that whizzed past us at 90 on a road in Wyoming that I still shudder at the memory of. (We were doing 75.)

Like Harry Künt, the hero of *Help, I Am Being Held Prisoner,* Westlake will do almost anything for a laugh. Fortunately, he does not share Künt's proclivity for practical joking or I would no longer share his bed. Like Brother Benedict of *Brother's Keepers,* he is really happiest leading a quiet life and being able to get on with his own work in peace. However, his life, like a Westlake plot, seldom quiets down for more than five minutes. ("I'm sick of working one day in a row," he sometimes says.) Like many of his heroes, he brings this on himself, partly out of restlessness and partly out of a desire to make things happen around him. For instance, all these children.

Westlake has four, by various spouses, and I have three. Not satisfied with the status quo—his four scattered with their mothers from Binghamton, New York, to Los Angeles, California ("I have branches in all principal cities," he is wont to say) and mine living with me in New York City—he ups and gathers everybody, with all their typewriters, baseball bats, Legos, musical instruments, movie books and stuffed animals, and brings us all to *London* for a year. Then, not content with London, he rents buses and takes this traveling circus all over Great Britain, including Scotland in January (snow) and Cornwall and Wales in February (rain). Still not content, he drives us through the Continent in April for a sort of Grand Tour: Holland, Belgium, Germany, Luxembourg and France in three weeks. Because, like Brother Benedict again, he is obsessed with travel.

Also, like every Westlake hero, Donald E. Westlake is sex-crazed, but I'm not going to talk about that.

Tucker Coe is the gloomy one, almost worse to have around the house than Richard Stark. We see Tucker Coe when things go wrong. The bills can't be paid because the inefficient worlds of publishing and show business have failed to come up with the money to pay them. Children are rude, noisy, dishonest, lazy, loutish and, above all, ungrateful; suddenly you wonder what you ever saw in them. Ex-wives are mean and grasping. Cars break down, houses betray you, plants refuse to live, and it rains on the picnic. Coe's character Mitch Tobin builds a brick wall in his backyard when he's feeling sorry for himself; Coe has never actually built a wall, but he has built enough bookcases to fill the 42nd Street library, for himself and his friends. Also, when the Tucker Coe mood is upon him, he will do crossword puzzles, jigsaw puzzles (even ones he has done before), fix broken electrical things—in fact, do almost anything except work at his typewriter or talk with

other human beings.

Timothy Culver is the professional —hack, if you prefer. He will write anything for anybody and doesn't care how much he's paid, just as long as the typewriter keys keep flying. If he doesn't have any actual work to do, he will write letters; and if you've ever received one, you know they're as well-written as his books. Well typed, too. Part of his professionalism is that he produces copy so clean you could simply photostat the pages and put them between boards and have a book with fewer misprints than most actual volumes.

His desk is as organized as a professional carpenter's workshop. No matter where it is, it must be set up according to the same unbending pattern. Two typewriters (Smith Corona Silent-Super manual) sit on the desk with a lamp and a telephone and a radio, and a number of black ball-point pens for corrections (seldom needed!). On a shelf just above the desk, five manuscript boxes hold three kinds of paper (white bond first sheets, white second sheets and yellow work sheets) plus original and carbon of whatever he's currently working on. (Frequently one of these boxes also contains a sleeping cat.) Also on this shelf are reference books (*Thesaurus, Bartlett's, 1000 Names for Baby,* etc.) and cups containing small necessities such as tape, rubber bands (I don't know *what* he uses them for) and paper clips. Above this shelf is a bulletin board displaying various things that Timothy Culver likes to look at when he's trying to think of the next sentence. Currently, among others, there are: a newspaper photo showing Nelson Rockefeller giving someone the finger; two postcards from the Louvre, one obscene; a photo of me in our garden in Hope, New Jersey; a Christmas card from his Los Angeles divorce attorney showing himself and his wife in their Bicentennial costumes; and a small hand-lettered sign that says "weird villain." This last is an invariable part of his desk bulletin board: "weird" and "villain" are the two words he most frequently misspells. There used to be a third—"liaison"—but since I taught him how to pronounce it (not *lay*-ee-son but lee-*ay*-son) he no longer has trouble.

The arrangement of the various objects on and around The Desk is sacred, and should it be disturbed, nice easygoing professional Timothy Culver turns forthwith into Richard Stark. Children

Vicar Fogg always proposes to Becca in the gazebo.

"No."

tremble, women weep and the cat hides under the bed. Whereas Tucker Coe is morose and self-pitying, Stark has no pity for anyone. Stark is capable of not talking to anyone for days or, worse yet, of not talking to one particular person for days while still seeming cheerful and friendly with everyone else. Stark could turn Old Faithful into ice cubes. Do you know how Parker, when things aren't going well, can sit alone in a dark room for hours or days without moving? Stark doesn't do this—that would be too unnerving—but he can play solitaire for hours on end. He plays very fast, turns over the cards one at a time, and goes through the deck just once. He never cheats and doesn't seem to care if the game never comes out. It is not possible to be in the same room with him while he's doing this without being driven completely up the wall.

Stark is very competitive and does whatever he does with the full expectation of winning. He is loyal and honest in his dealings with people and completely unforgiving when they are not the same. Stark is a loner, a cat who walks by himself. He's not influenced by other people, doesn't join clubs or groups, and judges himself according to his own standards. Not the easiest man to live with, but fortunately I seldom have to. About the best you can say for Stark is that he can be trusted to take messages for the others which he will deliver the next time they come in.

The question that now comes to mind is: what next? Or should I say, who next? A half-completed novel now resides on The Desk, title known (but secret), author still unchristened. I feel a certain suspense as I await the birth of this creature; yet whoever he turns out to be, I know he will probably be difficult to get along with but not boring.

Abby Adams and Donald E. Westlake are more than just good friends.

MURDER FOR FUN AND PROFIT
BIG-BUCKS BOOKS

Louella Chance

The idea's simple enough: if you can solve an excruciatingly intricate mystery that has more complexities than there are stars in the sky, you win a bundle. $10,000. $10,001. $15,000. And-upandupandup. Well, maybe not in the grand lottery range or the Irish Sweepstakes category, but still ample enough to get your greed juices flowing and, should you win, keep you comfortably in hardbacks for a year.

Of course, you're seduced. Most of us would be. It appeals to all the basic emotions: lust (for money) and competition (sure you're smarter than some author, the jerk). Haven't you read mysteries, flung them down and announced to the world at large, "I can do better than *that*! The answer was obvious right from the beginning!" With solve-it-for-prize-money books, you get the chance to actually do what you claim you're so good at: outthink an author, and have half the English-speaking world hear about it.

Because if there's one thing publishers insist on, it's total notoriety for the winners. Not for them the shy librarian who'd rather keep her name out of the press. Not for them the meek parking attendant who refuses to be photographed. No, the more splash they can make of you, the happier they'll be. Splash, as the advertising brethren have shown us, sells, and that, after all, is the point of the prize-money come-on.

How often does a civilian emerge victorious? Not very. And even winning can be muted. It took, for example, the combined efforts of four couples—and one member was a police psychiatrist—to best Thomas Chastain and his *Who Killed the Robins Family?*, and even so they missed one of the major points. Not enough to knock them out of the winner's circle, but just enough to humble them when they try to flaunt their victory to friends, the point being, six did not quite equal the work of one. Give 'em two ears, but no tail.

Mr. Chastain's flamboyant success has started a wave of me-tooism, and one of the first to hop aboard the bandwagon was Otto Penzler, who worked out three prize-money mysteries with the aid of a—in Mr. Penzler's own words—"well-established author." That the author preferred anonymity ought to tip you off to his pride in his work. Even with a prize bigger than Mr. Chastain's, the books kind of fizzled. One witty lady editor suggested money is rarely a sufficient motive in the mystery; they should have tacked a computer date along with it.

The responsibility for the prize-money books rests at the feet of the late Edgar Wallace, who back in 1905 decided to self-publish *The Four Just Men,* a mystery without a solution but with an offer of £500 to anyone who could provide one. It was an unwise decision on his part, as several voices were heard

THE GOLDEN OPPORTUNITY

Thomas Chastain

"What would you think," idea man extraordinaire Bill Adler asked, "about a mystery novel in which there was a series of murders, no solution, and the publisher offered a $10,000 reward to the reader who solved the thing?"

Brilliant, I thought, and at his urging went off to write the book.

Then came the problem: I didn't know how. I tried one approach, threw it out. Another; out it went, too. I won't bore you by recounting the "outs," but they exceeded the corpse tally in the finished book.

Eventually came inspiration: each of the murders would occur in one of the classic mystery situations—in a locked (yacht cabin) room, aboard the Orient Express, at a luxurious country estate, in London and, of course, on an isolated island with, of course again, ten people present. In this manner, I could pay my respects to mysteries of the past and provide, I fervently hoped, fun for contemporary crime solvers.

One week after publication, *Who Killed the Robins Family?* hit the bestseller lists and then stayed there for thirty-six weeks—once, gloriously, reaching #1 in the *New York Times*.

My twin fears, that the solution might prove too easy, or too hard, vanished when some 24,000 responses were mailed in and the winning entry answered 39 out of 40 points correctly.

The sequel, *The Revenge of the Robins Family,* is worth $10,001. And I have taken to thinking of Bill Adler and myself as the John Beresford Tiptons of the mystery genre.

Thomas Chastain is the author of ten mystery novels written over the decade and is on the Board of Directors of the Mystery Writers of America.

from, all of them correct, and Mr. Wallace's money problems extended on.

Between then and now *Ellery Queen's Mystery Magazine* got into the act with its Dec. '46–Jan./Feb. '47 and July/Oct./Dec. '55 issues. Each contained a short story by managing editor Clayton Rawson involving his sleuth magician, Merlini. "The Clue of the Tattooed Man," "The Clue of the Broken Leg," "The Clue of the Missing Motive," "Merlini and the Lie Detector," "Merlini and the Vanished Diamonds" and "Merlini and the Sound Effects Murder" all offered readers $100 for a correct solution, which was announced three months after the story's magazine publication.

The ultimate prize-money book may not be a book at all, but a book and a video cassette and an interactive laser disk, computer game, record album, possible cable-TV series and treasure hunt rolled into one. This entertainment industry bonanza is called *Treasure,* by Sheldon Renan and the cryptically named Dr. Crypton, and owes as much to Kit Williams and *Masquerade* as to Edgar Wallace and Mr. Chastain, with maybe a dollop of Pac-Man thrown in. The object: find a lost Arabian horse named Treasure, which, they tell us, has been buried somewhere within the United States and contains a key to a safe-deposit box. The box holds enough shekels to buy your own Arabian: $500,000. I ask you, who could say Neigh to that?

Louella Chance needs money.

HEAR, HEAR
SUPER-TOUGH QUESTIONS FOR THE WIRELESS FANS

Chris Steinbrunner

If you grew up in the years of radio mystery, with its heart-pounding organ chords, fast pistol shots and machine-gun fire, screams in the night and imprecise sounds blending together on strings of melodrama, the memories still haunt—never quite forgotten.

Here, then, are twenty questions, each dealing with a fondly remembered radio mystery from the golden age of crime on the airwaves.

1. *Superman* does battle with the evil Lex Luthor on today's theater screens, but who played Christopher Reeve's role at that long-ago microphone? Was *Batman* also on radio?

2. *Suspense* was radio's longest-running mystery anthology show. Name its narrator in the beginning years and the tale it repeated most frequently, which became the most famous suspense drama in radio history.

3. *The Shadow,* drawn from the pulp crime magazines, changed somewhat when it was adapted for radio. What was different about the title character?

4. "The Temple of Vampires" and "The Thing That Cries in the Night" were two continuing stories on a mystery show that started with a train whistle, the music of *Valse Triste* and a chiming clock. Name the show.

5. Another radio mystery program opened with a train whistle and a passenger settling back to tell the most gruesome yarn. It had a successful run of nine years. Can you name it?

6. When Agatha Christie's

famed Belgian detective, Hercule Poirot, made his American radio début in 1945, who introduced him on the air to the listening audience?

7. Basil Rathbone was certainly the best known and most beloved actor to play Sherlock Holmes on radio, but two outstanding stage players had already portrayed the master detective at the microphone. Can you identify them?

8. In 1941 Himan Brown, the patriarch of mystery radio, created *Inner Sanctum* with its now legendary creaking door. What was the name of the show's ghoulish host, heard chuckling behind the door?

9. John Dickson Carr, one of the world's great mystery writers, created "Cabin B-13"—a half-hour drama, about a bride whose husband vanishes as the couple board an ocean liner. It was eventually expanded into a series. Can you name the program on which "Cabin B-13" made its début? Who became the central character on the spinoff?

10. San Francisco detective Sam Spade, as rough and tough on radio as he was in Dashiell Hammett's *The Maltese Falcon,* could be heard pouring from the liquor bottle as he dictated his latest crime caper to his adoring secretary. What was the secretary's name?

11. L'il Orphan Annie, the endearing and enduring wanderer, had lots of nifty mystery adventures with her "Daddy" Warbucks and servant Punjab on radio as well as in the comic pages, where she lasts to this

day. The orphan's longtime radio sponsor, chocolate-flavored Ovaltine, ultimately abandoned her to underwrite a war hero and his band of pilots. Who were they?

12. It started as a comedy series, adapted from an amusing series of sketches in *The New Yorker*; then came *The Norths Meet Murder,* and soon enough Mr. and Mrs. North were up to their smiles in weekly radio crime. It took a great many corpses, however, before they fully lost their happy-go-lucky attitudes. Give us their first names and Mr. North's profession (he was *not* a licensed detective).

13. One of radio's most bizarre private eyes spent a good deal of time each week at a make-up mirror, donning different disguises to catch crooks. Indeed, he was known as "The Man of Many Faces"—when he wasn't being called the name of the show. What was it?

14. On television *Richard Diamond, Private Detective* enjoyed a singular claim to fame: the first series appearance of Mary Tyler Moore, who played Sam, the unseen (except for her legs) secretary. The earlier (1949) radio show of the same name, starring Dick Powell, was also unique. How?

15. Most of us know that Warner Oland and Sidney Toler were the two most prominent movie Charlie Chans. But can you name at least two actors who played the wise detective on radio?

16. The CBS creative forces that originated the anthology mystery series *Suspense* as well as the similar (and, some of us thought, superior) *Escape,* also masterminded a show called *Pursuit.* This was not, however, an anthology theater like the other two. What was it?

17. When you listened to *Blackstone, the Magic Detective,* why would you *never* turn the dial even after the case of the

Shhh . . . listen to the windowshade, the heavy cream, the bowling bowl, the bolt of velvet; the radio prop department on a spree.

day had been successfully solved?

18. It was eerie in *The Black Museum,* Scotland Yard's famed depository of murder mementos, and each week a program dramatized an actual case in which its grim relics were used. Who was the celebrated host who took us on these tours of the Black Museum?

19. Who did Basil Rathbone play in *Tales of Fatima,* a series he took on after dissociating himself from Sherlock Holmes? And who was Fatima?

20. Jack Webb made one of the most outstanding contributions to radio mystery with his creation of the realistic police series *Dragnet* and his portrayal of Sergeant Joe Friday. Before *Dragnet,* however, Webb starred in two other excellent crime programs, now largely forgotten. Can you name either?

The answers:

1. Clayton "Bud" Collyer played both Clark Kent and the Man of Steel, alternating his voice between medium and deep pitch to suggest the changeover, a surprisingly effective device. Batman appeared occasionally with Superman but had no radio show of his own.

2. The Man in Black was the early host of *Suspense.* The series was most famous for "Sorry, Wrong Number," written by Lucille Fletcher, in which Agnes Moorehead played a bedridden invalid who overhears a telephone conversation between two hired killers.

3. In the pulps, the Shadow was an avenger who merely lurked in the shadows. On radio he had "the power to cloud men's minds"—a hypnotic trick he had picked up in the Orient.

4. *I Love a Mystery,* with Jack, Doc and Reggie.

5. *The Mysterious Traveler.* (We were never told the traveler's name.)

6. Speaking via shortwave from England, Agatha Christie herself introduced Poirot to the American audience.

7. William Gillette, who for decades had played Holmes on stage, and

Orson Welles on *The Mercury Theater.*

8. The host of *Inner Sanctum* was Raymond, who was probably so called because he was played by announcer Raymond Edward Johnson.

9. "Cabin B-13" originally appeared as an episode on *Suspense.* When it was reworked into a series, the ship's doctor who solved the original mystery became the narrator, telling us bizarre stories from strange ports of call.

10. Effie Perine.

11. *Captain Midnight* and his Secret Squadron.

12. Jerry and Pam North. Jerry was a book publisher.

13. Listeners knew him as, quite appropriately, *Mr. Chameleon.*

14. Dick Powell, who a few years before had changed his screen image from musical comedy star to tough guy, swung halfway back in this radio series. His Richard Diamond was a debonair private detective who closed most of his cases with a song!

15. The three radio Chans: Walter Connolly, Ed Begley, Santos Ortega.

16. *Pursuit*—"the relentless, dangerous pursuit, when man hunts man"—dramatized the investigations of Inspector Peter Black of Scotland Yard.

17. At the end of each case, Blackstone the Magician would teach his audiences how to perform a magic trick.

18. Orson Welles.

19. Rathbone played himself. Fatima, besides being the brand of cigarettes that sponsored the show, was a sexy voice whispering a clue to the audience at the program's start so they could solve the mystery before Basil.

20. Before *Dragnet,* Jack Webb played a San Francisco private eye in *Pat Novak, For Hire* and a San Francisco boat captain in *Johnny Madero, Pier 23.*

Chris Steinbrunner received an Edgar award for The Encyclopedia of Mystery and Detection.

SHOW-BIZ BODIES
The Performing Arts in Peril

The Concert Hall

Death on the High C's, Robert Barnard (opera buffo)

Murder Sonata, Frances Fletcher (symphony clarinetist)

Eliza's Galiardo and *Philomel Foundation,* James Gollin (Antigua players; musical group)

Memorial Hall Murder, Jane Langton (Handel's *Messiah*)

Overture to Death and *Photo Finish,* Ngaio Marsh (Rachmaninoff's *Prelude in C Sharp Minor*; New Zealand opera singer)

A Cadenza for Caruso, Barbara Paul (the Met, circa 1910)

Death Notes, Ruth Rendell (world-famous flutist)

The Stage

Exit, Actors Dying, Margot Arnold (Glendower in Greece)

Blood Will Have Blood and *Dead Heat,* Linda Barnes (Michael Spraggue and Dracula and Shakespeare/Brecht)

So Much Blood, Star Trap, A Comedian Dies, Dead Side of the Mike, Situation Tragedy, Murder Unprompted, Murder in the Title, Simon Brett (Charles Paris, vaudevillian, in all titles)

Murder on Cue, Jane Dentinger (Jocelyn O'Roarke acts)

Light Thickens by Ngaio Marsh (*Macbeth* at the Dolphin)

Murder in Outline, Murder in Mimicry, Death in the Round, Men in Her Death, Hollow Vengeance, Sleep of Death, Murder Postdated, Anne Morice (Tessa Crichton stars in each book)

Murder Out of Wedlock, Hugh Pentecost (Quist and Broadway)

Dearest Enemy, Sara Woods (married actors and Maitland)

Cast for Death, Margaret Yorke (Patrick Grant and *Macbeth*)

The Ballet

Dancers in Mourning, Margery Allingham

Death in the Fifth Position, Edgar Box

Corpse de Ballet, Lucy Cores

Two If by Sea, Andrew Garve

The Gold Deadline, Herbert Resnicow

Movies and TV

Murder, Murder, Little Star, Marian Babson (temperamental child star)

Case of the Angry Actress and *Case of the Kidnapped Angel,* E.V. Cunningham (the Beverly Hills crowd; a sex goddess)

Killed in the Act and *Killed with a Passion,* William DeAndrea (Matt Cobb, TV troubleshooter in both)

Murder at the Academy Awards, Joe Hyams (Capt. "Punch" Phillips, ex-Marine)

He Done Her Wrong and *Murder on the Yellow Brick Road,* Stuart Kaminsky (Mae West; Dorothy/Judy)

Soap Opera Slaughters, Marvin Kaye (Hillary Quayle and TV series)

Murder on Location, George Kennedy (the actor in spotlight)

Nerve Endings, William Martin (cable-TV advertising)

A Savage Place, Robert B. Parker (Spenser in Hollywood)

Murder by Microphone, John Reeves (Coggins & Sump and the CBC)

Death at the BBC, John Sherwood (London, 1937)

THE STAR TURN

"I must continue to support my idolatry of the murder mystery by reading about them."

Glenda Jackson

CROSSWORDS AND WHODUNITS
A Correlation Between Addicts?

Colin Dexter

I noticed with vague disquiet a recent report in the *British Medical Journal* asserting a significant correlation between eating cornflakes for breakfast and the onset of the dreaded Crohn's disease. Yet correlations are notoriously cock-eyed, and it was some consolation for me to recall that the annual number of iron ingots shipped from Pennsylvania to California was once significantly correlated with the number of registered prostitutes in Buenos Aires. With such wildly improbable findings to encourage us, may we please tentatively assume that there is likely to be a positive correlation of sorts between those who enjoy crosswords and those who enjoy detective stories? At the very least, I think there *ought* to be one. Why is this?

Let us begin in familiar surroundings: a murder and a conveniently small circle of suspects, one of whom is the murderer. As in the cryptic[1] crossword, *clues* bestrew the scene; but they will be read correctly only by our hero, who, if not exactly a roaring genius, is an investigator of alpha-plus acumen. Between-times the writer will dangle each of the suspects in front of our noses in such a way that we shall fail to recognise the murderer until the surprise dénouement. Such is the stuff of the classic sleight-of-hand whodunit; and clearly there is

much in common between this genre of detective fiction (though much less so between the broader "crime" story or the "thriller") and the cryptic crossword. Each is a puzzle for which clues are cunningly laid, and to which there is a final, unambiguous solution.

In the actual process of clue-ing, both the whodunit writer and the crossword composer (not "compiler," please!) have a duty to be fair. They need not necessarily say what they mean, *but they must mean what they say*: it is fair to mislead, but not to mislead by deliberate falsification. Let us take an example from the great crossword composer Ximenes: "An item in fuel is somewhat fluctuating supply" (6). "In" means "contained within," and the six letters of the answer are contained, consecutively, within the next three words (no padding). Fair enough. But where is the definition of LISSOM? For any composer worth the name will include a definition. Well, we have been deceived. We see the words "fuel" and "supply," and the misleading connection is immediately forged in the mind: "misleading," because the second word is not "sup*ply*" but "*sup*ply"—the adverb from the adjective "supple"—and LISSOM means "fluctuating *sup*ply." That is the way of it, and instances abound of such ambivalent words, frequently to be found in combination. "A number of members," for example, may refer not only to a local golf club but also to a local anaesthetic;

---

[1] A "cryptic" clue is, loosely speaking, one that is not merely a straight definition but that also leads to an answer by disguised means, usually by allusion to individual letters or parts of that answer.

for it is the way *we* look at these words that determines their significance—the words themselves remain the same.

Similarly, the whodunit writer must seek to be fair, or at least not deliberately unfair. The match-stick found on the scene of the crime may have been used either to light the assailant's cigar or to pick his teeth—but it must always remain a *match-stick*. So, too, with the other clues. If, in the first chapter, we are invited to survey a blood-bedrenched boudoir, we shall feel cheated if, in the last, we are informed that the putative victim had an incurable bedtime passion for the taste of tomato sauce. No. Clues must form a basis for logical deduction— a process as much at the heart of detective fiction as of crosswords.

But deception may, of course, begin from the start. Ximenes once published a puzzle (on April 1st!) wherein the clue to 1 across provided two quite legitimate

answers: MAHOGANY and RAMBUTAN. Each clue thereafter provided a similar pair of answers, and all fitted into one another perfectly—with the exception of one space. Only by working from RAMBUTAN could the puzzle be finally completed. Such cumulative deception is also practised by the whodunit writer. In *The Greek Coffin Mystery,* for example, Ellery Queen can arrive at a convincing solution halfway through the book, only for the reader to discover that one key problem remains unresolved. Back to square one! And in *The Murder of Roger Ackroyd* (the most famous deception of all) Agatha Christie misleads the reader from the very first sentence.

So much for clues. When it comes to *solutions,* it has been said that the whodunit reader doesn't really *care* who committed the crime, but that he has to *know*; and such a situation is familiar to the crossword addict. Ideally, the solu-

MISS SCARLET IN THE LIBRARY WITH A WRENCH

Colonel Mustard in the kitchen with a revolver.

Mrs. White in the conservatory with a lead pipe.

Professor Plum in the billiard room with a knife.

Mr. Green in the lounge with a candlestick.

Mr. Peacock in the hall with a rope.

Mrs. White in the hall with a revolver.

Mr. Green in the conservatory with a wrench.

Colonel Mustard in the billiard room with a lead pipe.

Miss Scarlet in the kitchen with a revolver.

Professor Plum in the conservatory with a wrench.

Mrs. White in the library with a candlestick.

Professor Plum in the library with a rope.

Mr. Peacock in the kitchen with a knife.

Mr. Peacock in the billiard room with a lead pipe.

Colonel Mustard in the bedroom with a knife.

Professor Plum in the kitchen with a candlestick.

Miss Scarlet in the hall with a knife.

Mr. Peabody in the conservatory with a revolver.

Mrs. White in the lounge with a rope.

Mr. Green in the billiard room with a lead pipe.

Colonel Mustard in the library with a wrench.

You won. Game over.

tion, in each case, is one where the bewildered victim can kick himself for not having guessed it before. Let me illustrate. There is little satisfaction in crossword solving if an inordinately obscure clue leads to a dialectal word, now obsolete, in Lowland Scots. But how different when the word is perfectly well known, when only minimal demands are made upon outside knowledge! Consider "What the Jumblies kept in the sieve" (6). Most of us know that the Jumblies went to sea in a sieve. But which of their (doubtless) quaint possessions did they *keep* in the wretched thing? We are tempted to say: "If only I could remember the whole poem!" Or, "What object *could* they have kept in a sieve, anyway?" But no. The simple answer is AFLOAT, and we knew it all the time. Excellent!

Some few practitioners in each genre have raised their work to the level of a minor art, and it is perhaps the very limitations of this art that make it so enjoyable to so many. What are these limitations? Well, whodunits are games, really; games played to a set of rules, however loosely applied. With the emphasis upon coherent deduction, there is little room for characterisation in depth, and death itself is no "fell sergeant," but merely a convenient point of departure—the messier the better. Crosswords, too, are played to rules—or at least the best ones are, as those who have read *Ximenes on the Art of the Crossword* will know. (And what a pity it is that the Americans, sticking for the most part to their rather tedious definition clues, have given themselves so little chance of producing an Afrit, a Torquemada, a Ximenes, or an Azed.[2] After all, it was

PUZZLERS

Peter Fox, *Trail of the Reaper.* Detective Jack Lamarre and Allison Prendergast are puzzled by clues to crosswords; University of London plays a major role.

Robert B. Gillespie, *Crossword Murder.* Includes puzzle, Testament, constructed by dying woman, to challenge Rocky Caputo.

Michael Gilbert, *Close Quarters.* A puzzle challenges the Dean of Melchester Close and his police-officer nephew.

Patricia Moyes, *Six-Letter Word for Death.* Henry Tibbetts, C.I.D., is not sure how seriously to take puzzles, in view of the "Guess Who" group of mystery writers involved.

John Reeves, *Murder Before Matins.* Inspector Coggins finds crossword puzzles relaxing and an aid in solving his puzzling case. Puzzle included.

Murder by Microphone, Inspector Coggins' puzzle included, as he unravels difficult case.

Ruth Rendell, *One Across, Two Down.* Stanley was really into crosswords, and murder? Are they too much of a good thing?

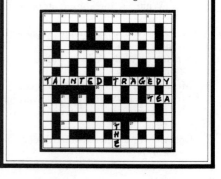

[2]*Afrit:* the late Prebendary A.F. Ritchie, of *The Listener.* His pseudonym is formed from the two Christian-name initials and the first three letters of his surname. Appropriately, the word "afrit" = "an evil demon in Arabian mythology." *Torquemada:* the late Edward Powys Mathers, of *The Observer.* His pseudonym derives from the Dominican Tomás de Torquemada, the Grand Inquisitor appointed in Spain by Pope Sixtus IV in the reign of Ferdinand and Isabella.

He was a great pioneer in the art of the crossword, loved by addicts and feared by the uninitiated.
Ximenes: from 1942 to his death in 1971, D.S. MacNutt concealed himself behind the pseudonym "Ximenes"— François Ximenes de Cisneros, Cardinal, Archevêque de Tolède, Grandinquisiteur, et Régent d'Espagne. The standards set by Ximenes in his famous *Observer* puzzles have achieved world-wide renown, and in the opinion of

the New York *Sunday World* that was the first in the field.) In each genre we learn the rules and we play the game, and in so doing we escape for a while from the harsh world: there is little or no emotional involvement.

Clearly, then, the reasons for the popularity of these two escapist activities are pretty similar: we revel in mystification; we are curiously uncomplaining about being misled; above all, we enjoy the final dropping of the penny.

My own first memory of crosswords? I recall my deep admiration for one of my classmates who solved the unremarkable (and quite unscientific) clue "Ena cut herself" (7); and I was soon to learn, from the same precocious youth, the answer to the riddle "Nothing squared is cubed" (3). (Do you have *Oxo* in America?) My first acquaintances in the whodunit field were Dr. Gideon Fell and Sir Henry Merrivale, wrestling with their "locked-room" mysteries: uneven books, certainly—but what a joy they were! Then, in a rush, came most of the Christie classics, and I've been happily hooked on whodunits ever since. Rex Stout particularly springs to mind as I write, since the oversized Nero Wolfe, when not tending his oversized orchids in his roof-garden or solving a case without stirring from his oversized chair, was wont (so I read) to exercise his oversized brain on Ximenes puzzles. Which, for me, is a happy illustration. To be truthful, I've always wanted to be a super-sleuth; and when I tackle a new crossword, I'm childish enough to see myself as the great detective magisterially surveying the clues and, with a bit of luck,

finding the solution—all on my own. Like Wolfe, too, I'd prefer not to stir from the armchair, since I am just as anxious for the detective to manage without the pathology lab as for the crossword puzzler to manage without the dictionary. Fancifully, I wonder how Wolfe would have fared with the following clues taken from Ximenes puzzles: (i) "Despondency, Reichenbach's effect, unsolved crime . . . could have led Holmes to *this*" (10); (ii) Eyes had I, and unfortunately saw not" (6).[3] The first he might have found a little hard (might even, alas, have needed to look up "od" in Chambers'—by far the best crossword dictionary); the second he would probably have written into the diagram with only a second's thought.

To sum up, the glorious thing for me about the two activities is that each is engaged in for its own sake, with a simple sense of fresh delight; and to those long-faced counsellors who are forever ferreting out some pretentious justification for all human activities, we can cheerfully report that here there is *none*. *Ars gratia artis,* for a change. And why on earth not?

Monsignor Ronald Knox (himself no mean writer of detective stories) was one day sitting in a train with the *Times* crossword on his knee. For several minutes he stared earnestly at the diagram but filled in not a single letter. When a young man sitting beside him suggested a possible answer, Knox smiled serenely and handed him the crossword: "Here you are. I've just finished."

So have I.

---

many (including me) he ranks as the greatest of the crossword composers.

Azed: the pseudonym of Jonathan Crowther, also of *The Observer,* a composer of bold ingenuity. The name "Azed," apart from its comprehensively alphabetical connotation (a–z), maintains (by a reversal of its letters) a continuity with its two predecessors, for Don Diego de *Deza* was Spanish Grand Inquisitor from 1498 to 1507, between Torquemada and Ximenes; and a particularly beastly fellow he was, who burned 2,592 heretics alive.

[3](i) HYPODERMIC (hyp – od + anag. of "crime" & lit.)
(ii) WATSON (anag. & lit.)

[Any reader who is still puzzled by "number of members" should be reminded of the verb "to numb." Poor Ena (who cut herself) – bled.]

Colin Dexter was three times national champion in the Ximenes clue-writing competition. He is the author of The Dead of Jericho.

COMPUTER FREE-FOR-ALL

Iphegenia Burton-Mall

When the telephone was invented, there were those who said, "No, I'll just leave my calling card, like I usually do, thank you very much."

When the horseless carriage came along, there were those who said, "Well now, let's just wait and see if it can make it down to the end of the drive before we go and get all het up about it."

And when the television set turned up in its whacking great coffin-size console, there were those who said, "Yeah, but I miss the popcorn. Let's go to the Roxy instead."

You can guess what's coming next: the newest revolution to mosey down civilization's turnpike. The computer. For every person who swore phones were a fad, cars were impractical and television a blight on the living room, there's been an equally dissenting voice blaspheming the computer. "If God had wanted me to think that fast," it screams, "he'd have given me two heads!"

One age group, however, has taken to the computer industry with an enthusiasm they usually reserve for pizza, punk and putting down Mother: the schoolkids. Breaking and entering, computer style, has replaced short-sheeting and fraternity hazing as the favorite student pastime. To date, they've disrupted banking systems in Canada, comptroller's offices in Washington and Ma Bell everywhere. These exploits have been highly publicized and have attracted yet another contingent to the computer's cause: the true criminal element. Computer crimes now top the list of financially ruinous white-collar crime sprees. And it hasn't taken so very long for the crime writers to catch up with the wonder of it all.

The harbinger: Selwyn Jepson, who in 1968 introduced one V. Norton, chief computer programmer for Hammon & Morgan, the third largest bank in the world, in *The Angry Millionaire*.

In the years since Miss Norton's terminal début, computer escapades have progressed to the point of camp, viz., Frederick Vincent Huber's *Apple Crunch*, a tongue-in-floppy-disk use of the computer as a lethal weapon.

Just as menacing: the computer Frank Orenstein rigged up to shoot Len Gorski in *The Man in the Gray Flannel Shroud*. Actually, there's a hint of the Frankenstein monster here: Gorski was the original computer wizard, we are led to believe, and it is, so to speak, his beloved child who ultimately turns.

If the idea of adding the computer to the mystery's already staggering arsenal of weapons (blowguns, twin-headed axes, lead pipes, gardening shears) appalls you, you might take comfort in the mystery's other new toy: the computer detective. TV's Matt Houston uses a display terminal the size of the stage at Radio City to collate data, and even the more humble of the police forces (on The Hill, for instance) check priors on equipment not much fancier than what you'd find in a home. Then, of course, there's the really new twist: *you* as computer detective.

THE MALTESE MICROCHIP
(with Apologies to Dashiell Hammett)

A tough old bird.

Abby Robinson

"It was an easy run to EOJ with you." His sensor gave her software a hungry contour analysis. "But I don't know about functionality. Suppose we load-share? What's the turnaround time? Maybe it's a conditional transfer that stores a month. I've read in those instructions before. Then what's the feedback? That I was a kludge. And if I allocate and get a post-mortem dump, I'd be sure I was a kludge. Well, if you crash, I'll print out 'Sorry as hell'—there'll be some bad hang-ups in the night transmissions—but there's rollback. Use your acoustic coupler." He took her by the input/output unit, rearranged her circuitry and leaned over her chassis. "If that header doesn't compute, use master clear and give it this feasibility study: I won't because all of me wants to load-and-go and say to hell with the bugs and feed in—and because—IBM damn you—you've logged in immediate access with me the same as you batch-processed the other liveware." He took his digitals from her mainframe and put them on downtime.

She put her access arms up to his monitor and drew his memory bank down again. "Area search," she instructed, "and give me the signal-to-noise ratio. Would you have abended on me if the Maltese microchip had been real and you had a clean compile?"

"What's the matrix? Don't make an intermittent error that I'm the crooked analog I'm simulated to be. That kind of repertoire might pass a reasonableness check—it collates with high-powered programming and makes it easier to tap into competing systems." She scanned him, then went on stand-by. He moved his components and punched in: "Well, more bytes would have increased the data bank."

She direct-accessed her display. Her transistor microcoded and her disks were programmed for dispatching priority. Her voice trade channel switched on: "If you were user-friendly, you wouldn't need validation."

Spade gave her a destructive read: "I won't interface for you."

Abby Robinson is the author of The Dick and Jane.

Acknowledged as the best computer mystery to solve, *Deadline* has been packaged in the manner of Dennis Wheatley's *Crime Files*—with bits of cigarette packages and love letters included. *Deadline,* however, still has one drawback: no computer-generated art.

What's next for computers? The Hereafter. Just ask the folks at Disney Productions. They've packed their Haunted Houses with dancing ghosts, wining and dining ghosts, trembling ghosts, ghosts in sheets and ghosts in finery that would make Miss Vreeland sit up and pay attention. These computer-generated holograms have dazzled visitors. Though Disney won't do it, there are several companies working out of New York and Los Angeles that will create a special hologram just for you. Alas, you may have to break and enter with your computer before you can afford one: prices start in the multi-thousands, and soar.

Iphegenia Burton-Mall counts on her fingers.

DEBACLE ON THE PLAYING FIELDS
An Indictment of Bad Sportsmanship

ARCHERY

Leo Bruce, *Death at St. Asprey's School*

BALLOONING

Richard Forrest, all titles

MOUNTAIN CLIMBING/HIKING

Douglas Clark, *Dread Water* (in England's Berkshires)

Andrew Garve, *Ascent of D-13* (Turkish peak)

Gladys Mitchell, *Cold, Lone and Still* (Scotland)

Gwen Moffat, *Miss Pink at the Edge of the World* (Scottish Highlands); *Over the Sea to Death* (Skye's Cuillin)

POACHING

Pierre Audemars, *Slay Me a Sinner*

Douglas Clarke, *Poacher's Bag*

Gerald Hammond, *The Game; Fair Game; Revenge Game; Reward Game*

Frank Parrish, *Snare in the Dark; Fire in the Barley; Sting of the Honeybee*

SAILING

John R.L. Anderson, *Death in the Channel; Death on the Rocks; Death in the North Sea; Death in the Thames; Death in the Caribbean*

Rick Boyer, *Billingsgate Shoals*

Dorothy Dunnett, *Dolly and the Nanny Bird*; other titles

Dean Fuller, *Passage*

Leonard Holton, *A Touch of Jonah*

Bill Knox, *Bloodtide; Bombship; Witchrock*

Patricia Moyes, *Down Among the Dead Men*

C.P. Snow, *Death Under Sail*

Charles Williams, *Dead Calm; Sail Cloth Shroud*

BULLFIGHTING

Patrick Quentin, *Puzzle for Pilgrims*

Julian Rathbone, *Carnival*

CRICKET

Adrian Alington, *The Amazing Test Match Game*

John Creasey, *A Six for the Toff*

Michael Gilbert, *The Crack in the Teacup*

Geoffrey Household, *Fellow Passenger*

Julian Symons, *Bland Beginnings*

Clifford Witting, *A Bullet for Rhino*

Barbara Worsley Gough, *Alibi Innings*

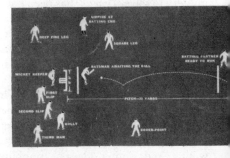

FOOTBALL

Betsy Asward, *Winds of the Old Days*
John Logue, *Replay: Murder*
Shannon Ocork, *Sports Freak*

CAR RACING

John Welcome, *Stop at Nothing*

RUNNING

Linda Barnes, *Dead Heat*

FISHING

Cyril Hare, *Death Is No Sportsman*
Ngaio Marsh, *Scales of Justice*
Shannon Ocork, *End of the Line*

TENNIS

John Dickson Carr, *The Problem of the Wire Cage*
Anna Clark, *Game, Set and Danger*
Stanley Ellin, *The Valentine Estate*
J.J. Marric, *Gideon's Sport*
Brown Meggs, *Saturday's Games*
Lillian O'Donnell, *Death on the Grass*
J.B. Priestly, *The Doomsday Men*

HORSE RACING

Jon L. Breen, *Listen for the Click*
Stephen Dobyn, *Saratoga Swimmer*
Dick Francis, all titles
Hugh Pentecost, *Homicidal Horse*

WINTER SPORTS

William DeAndrea, *Killed on the Ice*
Emma Lathen, *Going for the Gold; Murder Without Icing*
Patricia Moyes, *Dead Men Don't Ski*
Jeremy Potter, *Foul Play*
Owen Sela, *The Bearer Plot*
Ted Wood, *Murder on Ice*
Margaret Yorke, *Silent Witness*

BOXING

Richard Falkirk, *Blackstone's Fancy*
William Campbell Gault, *The Canvas Talk Loud*
Ed Lacy, *Lead with Your Left*
Vernon Loder, *Kill in the Ring*

BASEBALL

William DeAndrea, *Five O'Clock Lightning*
Paul Engleman, *Dead in Center Field*
Leonard Holton, *The Devil to Play*
Robert B. Parker, *Mortal Stakes*
Robert Rosen, *Strike Three, You're Dead*

BASKETBALL

Charles Drummond, *Death and the Leaping Ladies*
Edith Piñero Green, *Sneaks*
Lee Langley, *Dead Center*
Kin Platt, *The Giant Kill*

GOLF

Brian Ball, *Death of a Low Handicap Man*
Caroline Cooney, *Sand Trap*
Michael Innes, *An Awkward Lie*
Janice Law, *Death Under Par*
John Logue, *Follow the Leader*
Ralph McInerny, *Lying Three*

Thank You for Your Letter. Drop Dead
SINCERELY,

Brian Garfield

F an mail to a writer is like applause
to an actor. I don't know any writers
who don't get a kick out of a fan letter.

There are a few problems with it,
however. One is the delivery system.
Most writers are private people who
don't advertise their home addresses on
the jacket flaps of their books. To send a
letter to a novelist, you must address it in
care of his publisher. If, say, you are
writing c/o a paperback publisher, then
the paperback house must forward the
letter to the hardcover publisher who
originally published the book. The hardcover publisher in turn forwards it to the
author. Often this procedure takes six to
ten weeks. By the end of ten weeks the
reader may have forgotten the book, the
characters in it, and everything else except that he sent a letter to the author
and the churl didn't answer him. By the
time he receives the author's reply, it's
too late: the damage has been done;
hatred has set in.

Sometimes the first letter a writer
gets from a fan is one that begins, "Why
didn't you answer my first letter?" Well,
publishers' mail rooms lose things. They
lose manuscripts, too, but that nightmare is a different story.

One category of fan mail stands by
itself: gun mail. I find its implications
fascinating.

You can write a book in which a key
scene is a European Grand Prix auto
race in the late 1930's involving
Hispano-Suizas and Duesenbergs and
all sorts of tactics and technical detail.
Do you get letters from antique-car
buffs? No.

You can write a book in which avia-
tion plays a large part in the story; such
books may deal with Ford Trimotors or
B-17 bombers or C-47 Dakotas or Piper
Apaches. Do you get letters from airplane buffs? No.

You can write a book in which
horses, equestrian gear, Studebaker
wagons and all kinds of nineteenth-
century trappings are detailed and employed. Do you get letters from Western-
history partisans? No.

You can write books set in the Russian Civil War or World War II or Vietnam or the Indian wars of the American
West, in which tactics and the materiel of
military ordnance figure as inevitable
background. Do you get letters from
armchair strategists? No.

Perhaps once a year you'll get a
letter from someone who castigates you
for confusing palominos with Appaloo-
sas (the former is a color, the latter a
breed), or from someone who appreci-
ates the fact that you know they still had
third lieutenants in the Russian Army in
1920. But these are rare. They are individual letters and seldom do they duplicate one another.

Make one trivial mistake about a
gun, however, and you will be buried in
an avalanche of mail.

I committed the unpardonable error, for example, of arming a gunslinger

with a .38–40 revolver. This provoked instant reaction from dozens of letter-writers, all of whom had exactly the same thing to say: A .38–40 is a "ladies' gun," has no stopping power and cannot be compared with a .45 for lethal effec-tiveness. I learned more about the fail-ings of .38–40's from these letter-writers than I ever wanted to know. At the end of the barrage I was left wondering why the manufacturers had ever bothered to make and sell the things at all, since they

Simon improves his signature.

All Staffordshire Hall household bills are reviewed and paid by Simon. For neatness sake, he says, he keeps two sets of books. Lord Teasdale approves the one, knows naught of t'other. Simon makes regular bi-weekly deposits at the Barclay Corner Bank, opposite House of Teas. He deposits in two separate accounts, one labelled Staffordshire Hall; t'other, S. Teasers.

evidently aroused such contempt.

I armed the character in *Death Wish* with a .38 revolver. This in itself caused only a small reaction from readers who thought he should have been armed with a cannon. But when the filmmakers armed Charles Bronson with a .32 revolver, I was broadsided once again—as if I were in charge of the prop department. Instantly I was battered from all sides with snarling know-it-all advice about the ineffectiveness of .32 revolvers and the superiority of, and I quote, "a .38 police revolver with hollow-point 158-grain slugs"—a tediously technical description, followed by a nauseatingly specific account of the anatomical damage that can be inflicted by such a bullet.

After a few hundred such letters it becomes a matter of almost vindictive pride to be able to turn the tables on the babbling gun experts. I was condemned by one reader who found a reference to a .38–56 Winchester rifle; the reader insisted no such rifle existed. I was happy to point out to him I had actually held one in my hand and fired it on a target range; it was manufactured in 1886 and was a fairly popular model for a while. Another reader insisted the Luger automatic pistol had never been manufactured in .45 caliber, and I was gleefully happy to prove him wrong. You do get caught up in this nonsense. For example, the Spencer repeating rifle of U.S. Civil War vintage was mass-produced in *both* .47 and .51 calibers, dear readers, and I don't want to hear any more about that from you. The Colt "Lightning" or "Bird's Head" or "Billy the Kid" revolver was manufactured in *both* .38 and .41 calibers, dear readers, and don't bug me about *that* one, either.

You see, the kicker is, I am somewhat of a gun expert myself, and this always throws the gun-mailers for a loop. They assume anybody effete enough to sit down and write books must be an ivory-tower egghead who can't tell a

fulminate-of-mercury percussion cap from a push-type ejector spring. I served an apprenticeship as a gunsmith, boys, and I was eighteen at the time, and I outgrew it, and I no longer swagger around festooned with weapons, but I still remember what it feels like to get shot by mistake with a .45—it did no permanent damage, but it was not fun—and when I write a gun into a story it is quite often a gun I have held in my hand and dismantled and repaired and test-fired. Over the past twenty-five years I have learned to respect the things and most often to loathe them. The more I write, the less I write about guns.

What is it about them that so fascinates the American reader? It cannot be anything so simple as the tedious Freudian cliché of the phallic power symbol. It is something verbal; otherwise, I would get as many letters from antique-car buffs and airplane types as I get from gun fanatics. Yet the ratio is something like one to fifty. The true antique-car buff is, if anything, more passionate about his obsession than the gun fanatic is; yet he does not write to novelists.

The peak of idiocy came a few years ago when I published a novel in which nobody shoots a gun at all—and even on *that* book I got gun mail. Most of it began, "Why didn't you give the character a gun?" My answer was that the character is, like me, the kind of guy who does not feel comfortable lugging a gun around with him; that bullets do not answer any questions; and that guns do not solve problems, they only create new ones. But this didn't seem to make any sense to the gun-mail writers and after a while they gave up on me in disgust on that one.

If I knew why that was the case, I think I'd know everything there is to know about the American character.

Brian Garfield won the Mystery Writers of America Edgar for Hopscotch.

COMPLICATIONS

TONIGHT

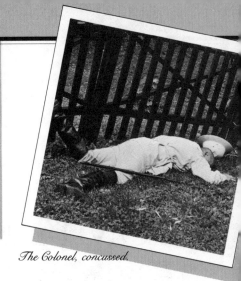

The Colonel, concussed.

I can stop anytime I want to, I just don't want to. I may *never* want to.

Hic.

If it'd rinse away the tea taste, I'd gargle with it for the rest of time.

I hate tea.

I hate this house that tea bought.

I hate the crest that came with it.

I hate John Teasdale most.

Shocked? The man's hardly cold and I'm over him throwing bricks? Good for me. He wanted me? Hic. He got me. Then he spat at me. Hic. What did you expect, grief?

Simon, filling the woodbin.

Let *her* be the one with grief. Little pussycat in her mews house. Little pussycat with the son I would have had if there were any kindness left.

Found out about the little bastard from John's memo to the Portcullis Pursuivant. Three teas to one side and a little tea on the other. For the little bastard. Thought he was being so smart I wouldn't know.

Hic.

Excuse me.

What were we discussing? Pussycats. Pussycats who stuck their claws out and grabbed my man before he could find out I loved him and he loved me.

I wasn't always wet.

I could stop now, if I wanted to, but I don't.

You think I don't know what she is, that nurse? I don't need a nurse. She's here to spill it out as fast as I get it. You want to know a little secret, where I do get it? Shhh. I bribe Whelks. He brings it to me. Who will bring it now?

W-H-E-L-K-S! DON'T LEAVE ME! WHERE ARE Y-O-U?

Shhhh. Hic.

Take it all away, I don't care.

Harriet wants the cameos, let her have them. I know she's taking them. If she asked, I'd give them to her. What does it matter what's left if John's gone?

I loved him.

I hate him.

Have you been in love? Was it a relief when it ended? Hic. I can't wait.

Take Leslie. Please. Why aren't you laughing? That's a funny line. Take Leslie, please. I know what he is and it's not my first lover. I can spot a lizard in the lounge when they crawl out from under the palm tree, sure I can. Leslie's a lizard, maybe not a very bright lizard, but ... hic ... don't tell him I said that. Hurt his feelings.

Brought him home to hurt John. Cousin from Australia, John, right here. He knows. Knew. Who cares? He knows I have no family in Australia, knows it as well as he knows how to make tea ... and we'll get to that in a minute. Hic.

Couldn't say boo, though, could he. Doesn't want to sleep with his wife, someone else does, what can he say about it?

Not a thing. Right under his nose, make him pay for pussycat.

Roudebush, will you tell the guests Lord and Lady Teasdale are at home but not receiving each other.

Scandalised Roudebush when I said

sleep with me, Roudebush, and be sure and tell His Lordship when he comes in from pussycat, won't you?

Personally tell him. Hic. Personally.

You do everything else for him, why not this? The recipe's yours, I know that, he's never been smart that way, in a kitchen. Come on, Roudebush, my turn. Help *me*. Let me crawl in there with you, best medicine a toe ever had.

Whelks found in bed.

Somebody please want me! Leslie doesn't really want me. John's never wanted me. Roudebush won't touch me. 'Retto's all that's left, 'retto in big litre-bottles.

In my handbags, under my blankets, in my bosom. Amaretto, my Italian lover.

Where has everybody got to? Running around for John again? Everybody ... hic ... runs for John. Going to get the killers. Hic. Get knocked on the head while they try.

Here. Smells just like your tea, doesn't it, John? One killed you, the other killed me. Hic.

I'll drink to that ... zzzzz.

Becca says no. Yet again.

THE PRIVILEGED
Old Boy Status and How to Fake It

Tim Heald

The myth that the British and Americans speak the same language is never more convincingly exposed than in crime fiction. Take this, from the estimable Michael Gilbert's "The Final Throw": a chap called Phil "pulled Blackett's leg in public about wearing a Guards tie, which he certainly wasn't entitled to, because as far as I know he was in the ack-ack. He blasted Phil out of his job and took a lot of trouble to see he didn't get another one."

What it means, Americans, give or take a couple of nuances and the odd quiver of the stiff upper lip, is that Blackett did military service in the Artillery ("ack-ack" = anti-aircraft); all right, but socially much inferior to the Brigade of Guards, which prompted Blackett to pass himself off as a former Guards officer by wearing their signature magenta and blue striped neck-tie. Phil, however, rumbled the deception and ridiculed him in public, so incensing Blackett that he had Phil fired and used all his influence to make sure he never worked again.

If it seems a bit silly, the answer is that it *is* a bit silly but a lot of Englishmen behave like this, especially in crime fiction. There is in British public life, even in real-life public life, an equation between social background and power and influence. It's called the Old Boy Network, and nowhere has it been better exposed to view than in a notorious interview by the real-life traitor Anthony Blunt. A quintessential "Establishment" Briton, Blunt was the son of

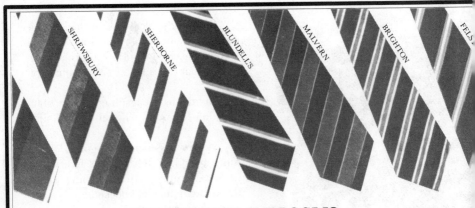

THE NECKTIE IMBROGLIO

The proper pecking (or, in this case, necking) order: Winchester, founded 1394 (the oldest); Eton, 1440 (graduated 10 future P.M.s); St. Paul's, 1509 (G.K. Chesterton's school); Repton, 1557 (*Goodbye, Mr. Chips* filmed here); Westminster,

an Anglican vicar and was educated at "public" (i.e., fee-paying) school and Cambridge. Given these credentials, such formalities as job interviews and security checks get waived. In 1979, interviewed by a man from the *Times* of London, Blunt was asked: "How did you join? Did you apply, or was it arranged for you, or how?"

"Well," replied Blunt, "like all... that kind of recruitment, it was done simply. Someone who was in MI5 recommended me. I was recommended."

"The Old Boy Network?"

"Yes."

At its most extreme, this belief in the OBN provides cover for bounders and cads. E.W. Hornung took the idea to its inevitable conclusion by creating the ultimate acceptable crook, Raffles, a gentleman with all the appropriate antecedents and connections. It was the perfect disguise. He was always much in demand at house parties given by highly desirable victims, because he wore the right school tie and spoke with the requisite accent. He could no more have dunnit than the butler. But he did.

Most clubland heroes manipulate the OBN in better cause. They use their class and connections on behalf of country or in the detection of crime. The underlying assumption is that people like them—Conan Doyle's Holmes, Margery Allingham's Campion, Michael Innes' Appleby, William Haggard's Russell, above all, Dorothy L. Sayers' Wimsey—run the world. Other ranks don't count for much except for supplying loyal manservants like Lugg (Campion's) and Bunter (Wimsey's). In crime novels, professional policemen are decent but dull, often with names to match. They are always pathetically pleased when one of the foppish OBN gentlemen muscles in on their cases. Remember at the beginning of *Have His Carcase*, when Harriet Vane introduces the bumbling policeman to her dashing Lord? "This is Inspector Umplety," says Miss Vane. (Umplety indeed! What a name! You can see the straw in his hair and the clods on his hoppers.) "Lord Peter Wimsey."

Then Miss Sayers writes: "The inspector appeared gratified by the intro-

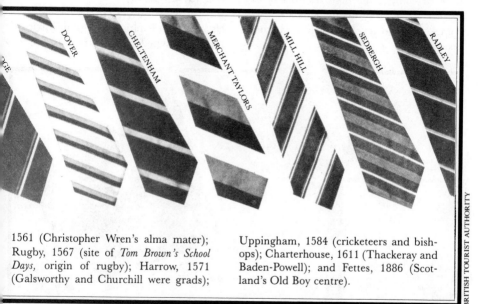

1561 (Christopher Wren's alma mater); Rugby, 1567 (site of *Tom Brown's School Days,* origin of rugby); Harrow, 1571 (Galsworthy and Churchill were grads); Uppingham, 1584 (cricketeers and bishops); Charterhouse, 1611 (Thackeray and Baden-Powell); and Fettes, 1886 (Scotland's Old Boy centre).

duction." He demonstrates this by saying, obsequiously, "You're early on the job, my Lord."

The reaction is patently ludicrous. If I were a police inspector involved in a murder enquiry, I should be profoundly irritated to find Lord Peter Wimsey queering my pitch. "Get lost, you affected old snob!" I should say. But in Miss Sayers' book they never do. Nor in Michael Innes'. Instead, they use blue blood as bait. In *A Night of Errors* Appleby is disturbed at midnight by a phone call about a murder and is quite cross to start, but then the caller says, "Look here, you're simply wasting time. It's a baronet." Appleby can't resist a corpse with a title, however obscure. The call of the old school tie.

In novels of this subgenre you get the impression that everybody, at least everybody who matters, knows or is known to everybody else. Here is Sherlock Holmes himself at the beginning of "The Adventure of the Illustrious Client," enquiring of Watson, "Do you know anything of this man Damery?" To which, thanks be to God and Burke's Landed Gentry, the poor dumb Doctor replies, "Only that his name is a household word in Society." Naturally, Holmes takes the case.

Members of the network will condone almost anything, provided that it has been perpetrated by another member of the network. On one famous occasion, Margery Allingham's Campion gets home after three years "at large on two warring continents employed on a mission for the government so secret that he had never found out quite what it was." (Another key characteristic of this sort of hero is his ability to move effortlessly from moments of supreme silliness to moments of Einsteinian brilliance.) Upon entering his flat he finds a female corpse in his bed, but all is forgiven because it has been put there by people he knows—or knows of. Indeed, one of them, Lady Carados, is so grandly entwined in the network that she is "one of those women who have an original view of law and order, all probably based on the fact that she used to tip the Home Secretary half a crown when he was at Eton." This is rather like saying she used to give the present Secretary of State the occasional quarter when he was just a kid playing Little League. It's not, in other words and as the saying goes, what you know, but who.

In the world of Old School Tie novels, the hero is plugged into an intricate but stereotyped network that is peculi-

LOWER SLAUGHTER JUMBLE SALE

1 old school tie   50p.

Leslie, kitted out.

arly British. "My brokers"... "My club"... "My man Paddock" ("making the deuce of a row at the smoking room door") can all be found in the first few pages of *The Thirty-Nine Steps,* that excellent old thriller by an archetypal Old Boy Network man, John Buchan. Nowadays "my man" has become largely a figure of the past. "My club" remains, however, and so do "my brokers." "My brokers" are probably old school chums. Or maybe they were at the same Oxford or Cambridge college. Perhaps they were in the Guards together or some extraordinarily obscure but distinguished regiment of Hussars, Lancers or Dragoons. They almost certainly belong to "my club," and you can bet your life that much of what they have to say to their chums is said over lunch (or "luncheon") at the aforementioned place.

It's changing, of course. British crime novels, like Britain herself, are less class-conscious than once they were. Titles generally cut less ice; police procedures are no longer regarded as boring and plebeian; there is an increasing sense that detection is a professional business based on a high degree of what Conrad called "ability in the abstract" and what mystery buffs sometimes refer to as "ratiocination." Modern fictional detectives, even in Britain, tend to be career men who have worked their way up through the ranks, not gentleman geniuses who are "household words in society."

This might be regarded as a gratifying shift in the direction of realism, but I am not entirely convinced. Lunch still seems to me to be a remarkably effective venue for conspiracy and indiscretion, particularly when it takes place in a club in St. James. And what more plausible than that it should be a lunch—oh, sorry, luncheon—between two old school friends, both wearing the old school tie or its Oxford or Army equivalent? A lot of life's most significant matters are re-

In step with the Old Boys.

solved over a Dover sole and a bottle of decent white burgundy, between men of a certain age, and a certain outlook and a certain background. Nice, cosy way of arranging things. And what more natural that, in such a situation, the talk should turn to murder or espionage, to death or deception. The juxtaposition of comfortable, safe and ordinary with sinister and disturbing is perennially effective. In life and in print. There are few better ways of starting a mystery.

"He had been stuck again. Not that Sir Duncan had openly sought assistance, but he was a very old friend and he had talked with the freedom which a boyhood in common made perfectly acceptable." Quite so. Luncheon at the club for William Haggard's Colonel Russell in *The Hard Sell.*

The Old Boy Network?

But of course.

Tim Heald is the author of Old Boy Networks, *a nonfiction study of hubris, and a series of crime novels featuring Simon Bognor. He is entitled to wear a Balliol tie.*

SPOTTED AT THE CLUB

BRITISH TOURIST AUTHORITY

TERENCE SPENCER/CAMERA PRESS

TERENCE SPENCER/CAMERA PRESS

Above: two Old Boys chatting in the smoking room.
Left: one Old Boy reading, the other Old Boy snoozing.

Far left: two Old Boys about to enter Boodle's.

Below: The Albany, Piccadilly. Tall-hatted porters were introduced (circa 1805) to discourage feminine inquisitiveness about the bachelor flats.

BLACK STAR

PARAPHERNALIA
MAKING USE OF WHAT'S AVAILABLE

Jeanine Larmoth

Murders cannot be committed haphazardly. They must be planned. Paraphernalia laid in. Not weapons: paraphernalia. Clocks, mirrors, blotters, telephones, candlesticks, decanters—no object too ordinary. Clocks and telephones help establish times. In the ABC's of murder, B is for "blotter," which soaks up the message in reverse. The mirror can read it. Mirrors also let a witness overlook the flicking of a little arsenic that the murderer did not intend to be seen, the forging of a will, or a delicious embrace in the garden below, which, unfortunately, involves the murderer's best friend and his wife. Glasses hold sleeping-draughts; decanters are for poisoned port. In case of need, paraphernalia may be converted so that the least suspicious object, tape measure to flowerpot, turns into a lethal weapon, thus giving a familiar object exciting potential and titillating us with the prospect of an outbreak in our own flowerpots.

The telephone, with its connections to telephone exchange, operator, call box and neighbours, is a fine example of paraphernalia. Lonely country houses become infinitely lonelier infinitely faster when lines go down in a storm, or under the killer's wire cutters. Isolation makes the breath shallow with fear when there's a dead phone in hand; a desperate sense of impotence follows the announcement that the phone is out of order.

Telephone calls work with almost as much efficiency for alibis as timetables. Making such calls from a call box has obvious advantages. A call box in a residential section is an excellent observation post. Tucked behind its little glass windowpanes, one can appear to be making a telephone call indefinitely, meanwhile keeping a certain house under surveillance. Furthermore, a call placed from a call box cannot be traced or overheard by the operator; it may remain anonymous. To be even surer that it does, the wise murderer goes to the call box supplied with another good piece of paraphernalia: a silk scarf to disguise his voice, or for use should it be necessary to strangle a customer already in the box. This action is not the offspring of irritation at having to wait. No, with that same uncanny sense of the time it takes a coin to drop in the box, the murderer knows that a witness has just this minute put two and two together, and is going to make someone else, probably the police, privy to her calculations. That, of course, will never do. Her three minutes are up. Were the same disguised-voice call to be made from home, another member of the household might remark the purple silk scarf stuffed in the murderer's mouth to distort his voice, cackle with laughter at an accent he is affecting, or ask embarrassing questions afterwards, such as "Why did you say you'd lost your gun when it's just where you left it hidden in the metal box under the rosebush?" Undesirable heckling is avoided in call boxes.

The principal purpose of a car in a mystery is to have it break down. If on a country road, it should break down near a good inn, with a jolly, loquacious landlord ready for pumping, or within easy walking distance of the home of friends, where the driver of the deliberately disabled vehicle wants to do some snooping, at around lunch or dinner time. Lunch is more considerate as it is less formal. It is not a bad idea to understand how a car is put together to know which part, when removed, will stall it.

Following a murder on a train, investigation reveals a plethora of paraphernalia peculiar to the setting, as well as the usual clues. The blood-stained handkerchiefs and knives may be found in a sponge-bag hanging on a locked door between compartments. No worthy Englishwoman goes to sleep without arranging her sponge-bag; it is as imperative as saying one's prayers. Sponge-bags are as properly hung on doorknobs as May baskets to be handy for murderers who mysteriously open the locked door and slip the bloody knife inside. Only the English could call a container for their washing apparatus a sponge-bag. It is clearly a bag of lumpish aspect with drawstrings, fading flowered fabric and a lining of yellowing rubber. It is never dry, but in a permanent state of fug. A bloody knife won't make it worse.

A murder in almost any location is likely to uncover the tooth-glass with its dregs of sleeping-draught. The tooth-glass is placed on a shelf beneath the mirror and over the washstand. One can, in lieu of sleeping-draughts, drink poison or whisky from it, with somewhat differing results.

Of importance equal to paraphernalia is the murder's costume. The murderer must be dressed to kill. He should check out his closet and his tailor to be sure he is properly kitted out. Old clothes are best because they blend in better with the scenery, and because they may need getting rid of. A man who sets out to do murder in a jaunty new outfit has only himself to blame. Besides, it is common. If, on the other hand, he chooses loud checks and a cigar, he may find himself the victim instead. Similarly, a too-perfect ensemble is better avoided—shining buttons, yachting cap, that kind of thing. Definitely un-English, therefore unsympathetic. Ease, the ultimate attribute, is better expressed in shabbiness. A murderer may well get away with it if he is properly dressed. He should, however, be sure everything he wears is in good repair. No loose threads left hanging. There is bound to be a thorny rosebush on his path waiting for a strand of tweed to tell it to the police.

One basic is the old raincoat. Apart from being commonplace and disposable, it has pockets. Not for guns alone: that's obvious. Pockets are for gnur.

The parlour candlestick on the servants' stairs.

Rosie collides with Bridie and runs away.

27

Without a flourishing collection of gnur, where will the police be when they try to analyze the murder's origins and whereabouts for the last ten years? "Ah, that morsel of yellow dust can only be from a highland estuary of the Upper Ganges!" "He was eating whelks by the London docks just two days ago." "See this fragment of paper? Only used by the War Office to notify heroes that they've received the Victorian Cross." The murderer will, of course, show the same tact in removing the label from his coat as from his victim's.

A cap is handy. It is very easy to fool people by switching caps. They are firmer over steaming cups of tea than false moustaches, and quicker to put on. But if a murderer should decide to wear a cap, he is honorbound to step over to the train station. There is nothing that provides the locals with more innocent entertainment on a dull afternoon than to watch a man in a peaked cap nipping in at one side of a railway carriage and, having climbed out the other side, a few seconds later walking down the platform affecting unconcern and a bowler.

Of course, a murderer must never wear his own shoes. Bigger is better; there's no point being uncomfortable. He'll soon be in a tight-enough squeeze. Also, he can fill the empty space at the toes with weights, for if he doesn't, sure as shooting (or poisoning), his footprints won't sink deep enough for their size, and we know where that leads. Straight to the jailhouse. Plimsolls are worth packing, if only to stuff up the chimney. They needn't even be worn, if the ritual is observed. If they are not worn, however, they should be smeared with a bit of mud and grass that could grow only in one spot—beneath the victim's window. It is only fair to the police. But as most murderers involve a surprising amount of athleticism, it never hurts to have a pair. In fact, a few warm-up exercises won't be amiss. A little light running in the morning or quite late at night not only helps the muscle tone, it helps in establishing alibis. If the murderer can appear at one end of the village five minutes before the murder occurs at the opposite end, a powerful sprint will have stood him in good stead. Or, if he can leap off a train, dash across a meadow, fire a well-aimed shot *en passant,* hop a stile and walk through the French doors for tea before the train arrives in the village, he is that much ahead.

To put the final touch to a murder, an old suitcase is essential for stuffing things in: the leftover murdering costume, a batch of incriminating papers picked up from the victim's safe, a cachet of jewels to be collected twenty years later from Left Luggage. The suitcase should be cheap and look like everyone else's. Nothing fancy, French, decorated with labels from the Ritz, or otherwise recognizable. It can, naturally, be hurled from a fast-moving train in the midst of a forest, but Left Luggage is better. Then, if the murderer yearns for an evening of nostalgia years later, he can take the ticket, fetch the case out again, and have a round of reminiscences among his souvenirs. He might even have put the flowerpot, slightly used tape measure, or other weapon in there, as well as a flower picked near the scene of the crime.

Success lies in ordinariness. Paraphernalia or costume. "Whoever-would-have-thought" objects as well as "whoever-would-have thought" people in their dreariest possible clothes. A murderer should be like everyone else; no one will bother him. The best murderers are the dullest, the sort who have spent a lifetime smouldering in the woodwork. Which also fuels one of the murder's strongest motives: the need to do just one thing with panache.

Jeanine Larmoth is the coauthor of Murder on the Menu.

WHAT MISS MARPLE WOULD LOOK LIKE IF SHE HAD A LITTLE MONEY

Her Royal Highness, Elizabeth, the Queen Mum.

PICTORIAL PARADE

THE GENESIS OF LINT
THE COVER-UP THAT CAN NOW BE REVEALED FOR THE FIRST TIME

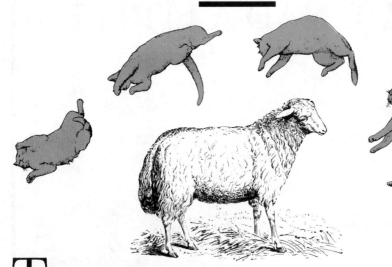

This is the true story of a cat, a sheep and a cottage in the Cotswolds. They were related by marriage. The groom provided the legs of lamb; the bride came with Hallowe'en, who had a sensational wash-and-wear fur coat and a back so arched McDonald's claimed it as a franchise.

There were, as you can imagine, a few housekeeping problems.

Did you know sheep shed? They do, particularly if their wool is dangling from its roots, as often happens when it's been attacked by the ten stilettos allotted to a cat.

Did you know cats shed every second or so, especially when they're nervous, which is all the time if their tail is being used as a carpet by two pairs of cloven shoes?

Do you know what that looks like in a small cottage in the Cotswolds? Wall-to-wall lint, only that's not what they called it. They called it a disaster, but

they thought they could live with it—until both sets of in-laws converged.

"That's lint!" accused his mother, echoed by her mother.

"That's lint!" swore her father, seconded by his father.

The cat hissed, the sheep looked sheepish and the couple leapt up and issued a disclaimer. "Not lint at all," they lied, "but our newest house pets—dust bunnies!"

The parents knew better but did not let on. After all, what kind of family admits to the world that their kids are rotten housekeepers?

So home they returned and dutifully broadcast the news: dust bunnies were the rage of the Cotswolds.

More remarkable, the world bought it—first at Harrods, then at Bloomingdale's (but in the basement).

The moral of this tale: You can pull the wool over most of the people's eyes most of the time.

THE CHINTZ CAPER
(A little room for thought)

Sally Wood

1. How many different chintzes must be combined before a corpse is obscured?
2. Under which antimacassar is the will hidden?
3. Is the wall safe behind the sixth cabbage rose on the left or the fourth cabbage rose on the right?
4. How many scraps of evidence can be burned in a fireplace at one time?
5. What is the difference between window dressing and the naked truth?
6. Is it better to dust for prints first or frame the pictures?
7. How long does it take to sweep everything nasty under the rug?
8. Are red herrings fit companions for sitting ducks?
9. Can you smother a couch with too many throw cushions?
10. How many skeletons will the average closet hold?
11. What is the best thing to use to polish an alibi?
12. Is it good economising to let a tea trolley double as a gurney?
13. When you steal away, precisely what is it you take?
14. Must the ink in the well coordinate with that in the ransom note?
15. Is it more genteel to kill the lights or ring down the (final) curtain?
16. Do frayed slipcovers make handsome shrouds?
17. Can a loveseat be whitewashed?
18. How many servants does it take to rig up a tripwire?
19. If the phone lines are down, is it permissible to scream for help?
20. What must you do to cover your tracks?

The room deshabille.

Sally Wood is an editor of the Agatha Christie Mystery Library.

I.N.I.T.I.A.L.S.

H.R.F. Keating

There are four questions mystery lovers ask whenever I am lucky enough to meet one. First: Do you write in longhand or use a typewriter? I reserve the startling answer for face-to-face encounters. Second: Is it true you wrote about Inspector Ghote in India for years without ever having been there? Yes, plus involved explanations. Question 3: And what do those initials—let me see, is it H.R.H., no, that's His Royal Highness—well, what do they stand for? Question 4: Oh, it's H.R.F., is it? I thought . . . But anyway, why do you use initials instead of your proper name?

And the answer to that is, I haven't got a proper name. That is, on my birth certificate the long roll-call begins "Henry," but in English English (I think it's different in American English) Henry is a pretty stuffy sort of moniker, so I like to be called Harry. Well, nowadays lots of authors write under nicknames or abbreviated ones, but when I began, it wasn't quite the done thing to be Tom, Dick or Harry. So I kept to the initials.

Not that I had been intended to. My father always yearned to write but had little success (an article on keeping rabbits in the *Boy's Own Paper*). So when his first-born came along he transferred some of that ambition to the object squalling in the cradle, and after much thought gave him the name Reymond, spelt in that odd fashion because he had seen it in a book mentioning his ancestors. Why, then, aren't I called Reymond and why isn't it R.H.F.K.? Well, old Uncle Henry had money, and as he had no children . . . (No, in the end he didn't.)

But surely not all crime writers who use or used to use initials had quite those reasons. Some definitely don't. I put the question to them in my turn. And others I have guessed about.

For instance, there are a lot of American authors who use one forename, one initial and a surname, like J.P.M., the creator of Mr. Moto, and W.P.McG. and E.D.H. and J.M.C. and R.L.F. and C.B.H. and E.S.A. and L.G.B. and D.E.W. and J.D. MacD. But this is a good old American custom and is thus accounted for.

An old British custom accounts for many more. In the good old days it was considered just a trifle vulgar to brandish a chap's actual name, what. Initials were more stiff-upper-lip, don't you know, and you called a fellow by his surname. So that's the reason, probably, for H.C.B. (but he may have had Harry trouble, too) and G.K.C. (and he had

---

KEY

John P. Marquand, William P. McGivern, Edward D. Hoch, James M. Cain, Robert L. Fish, Chester B. Himes, Edward S. Aarons, Lawrence G. Blochman, Donald E. Westlake, John D. MacDonald, H.C. Bailey, G.K. Chesterton, C.H.B. Kitchin, E.R. Punshon, E.C. Bentley, G.D.H. Cole, E.W. Hornung, A.A. Milne, J.C. Masterman, C.P. Snow, A.E.W. Mason, Dorothy B. Hughes, Arthur W. Upfield, E. Phillips Oppenheim, Ronald A. Knox, Dorothy L. Sayers, Elizabeth X. Ferrars, A.H.Z. Carr, O. Henry, H.H. Holmes (Anthony Boucher), J.J. Connington, S.S. Van Dine, J.J. Marric (John Creasey), A.A. Fair (Erle Stanley Gardner), A.B. Cox (Anthony Berkeley), E.C.R. Lorac (Carol Carnac), J.I.M. Stewart (Michael Innes), P.M. Hubbard, P.D. James.

PARDON ME, IS THIS YOURS?

Initials when they come on dropped handkerchiefs are one of the best-loved clues. The classic example must be the cambric affair with the letter H on it in *Murder on the Orient Express.*

In the H.R.F.K. sock drawer is a handkerchief that just arrived there, who knows how. And that's the one I shall drop at the scene of the crime. The initial on it is W...Hercule Poirot, I defy you

H.R.F.K.

the distinction of having his initials as the title of a magazine, *G.K.'s Weekly*) and C.H.B.K. and E.R.P. and E.C.B. and G.D.H.C. and E.W.H. and A.A.M. and J.C.M. (but when he got his "K" it was all right to call him Sir John) and C.P.S. (but later it was okay to say Sir Charles and even later "My Lord") and of course A.E.W.M. I'm glad this last kept to initials, because it once fell to me to compose part of a rhymed ceremony for the Detection Club and A.E.W. goes splendidly with "You sin and there's a ghost to trouble you."

With some of us, I suspect, one extra initial gives a bit of extra weight to a name, like that distinguished lady D.B.H. (she was all set to be plain D.H. but a "Your Fate in Your Writing" guy at a charity fair said "With the B is better" and yes, success followed) or the Australian A.W.U. or E.P.O., though the rest of his names were weighty enough, or R.A.K., though when he got a Monseigneur to tack in front he too became a pretty heavy vessel, or D.L.S. And what a fuss she used to make if that L was left out. "I do admit to one fad. I do like my name to appear in advertisements in the same form in which it stands on the title-page," she wrote once. "It is, if you like, a Freudian complex associated with my schooldays, and possibly I ought to get over it, but I can't. It produces in me a reaction of humiliation and depression and *I don't like it.*"

And with one or two others, urged on in one case by her American publishers, an extra initial has been added to provide a little easily got mystery. That's E.X.F. The X stands for nothing. And I suspect something similar went on with A.H.Z.C., because he was born plain A.Z.C., and it was much the same with O.H. and H.H.H. Both pseudonyms these, like J.J.C. and S.S. Van D. and J.J.M. and A.A.F., who all used quite meaningless initials for their noms de plume. Occasionally, too, initials provided additional concealment for a pseudonym, as in the case of A.B.C., who if he had used either of his two forenames would have been revealed for the other author he was, and with that old favourite of mine, E.C.R.L., who wanted both to hide her femininity and make up an anagram. In one odd case initials were abandoned so as to lose a bit of weightiness when the academic J.I.M.S. took to crime.

Finally, there are a couple of contemporary British authors who wanted, in perhaps a rather British way, to protect themselves from the world a little, in order, I hazard, to write the better. You'll see what I mean when you read the excellent, rather secretive novels of P.M.H. and the splendid books, also with a good deal of her private personality in them, of P.D.J.

And what about the one initial of my own I have so far not revealed? Perhaps you will see why when, blushingly, I admit: F for Fitzwalter.

H.R.F. Keating received the Crime Writers' Association Gold Dagger for The Perfect Murder.

THE USE AND ABUSE OF PSEUDONYMS

Carol Kountz

Once I read a wonderful mystery that had me combing libraries and bookstores for more books by the same author—but to no avail. Desperate, I picked up something else to read and discovered that it had an uncanny resemblance to the first (and apparently sequel-less) book I'd enjoyed.

A little library sleuthing proved my suspicions to be correct. The same author had written both books but had used a pseudonym for one.

Why do mystery writers baffle potentially loyal readers by adopting pseudonyms? Usually it's for reasons thought to be—in publishing and writing circles, at any rate—logical, sensible and sometimes profitable. Occasionally it's for privacy. Sometimes it's not even the author's decision.

The most common type of 'tec author to publish under an alias is the individual with a distinguished reputation in another field. Academics are often found guilty. So C. Day Lewis, once Poet Laureate, became Nicholas Blake when he wrote *Minute for Murder* and other mysteries featuring Nigel Strangeways, and so the prolific J.I.M. Stewart writes his Inspector Appleby series as Michael Innes.

Columbia University professor Carolyn Heilbrun had a special reason for hiding behind the pen name Amanda Cross to write her mystery novels: she was hoping to be granted tenure. (In her case, crime paid on both counts.)

Not only scholars stoop to protect identity. John Canaday, former art critic for the *New York Times,* poses on crime shelves as Matthew Head. Literary lion Gore Vidal has written for crime fans under the alias Edgar Box. The name Edmund Crispin is familiar to detective story readers, but they may not know that it stands for (Robert) Bruce Montgomery, the composer of scores for British movies, notably *Carry On, Nurse.*

David Cornwell wrote under the pseudonym John Le Carré for *The Spy Who Came In from the Cold* and other spy stories because of his profession: he worked for the British Foreign Office.

Output

Sometimes a crime novelist's book is brought out under a nom de plume when there are too many of his or her sleuths for sale in one season. The idea may come from the publisher ("The reading public will never absorb all this," mutters the editor), or a second publisher may contract for a novel by a well-known writer with the request that it be under a "new" name.

Take the case like that of John Dickson Carr, the creator of locked-room puzzle solver Gideon Fell (*Problem of the Wire Cage,* et al.). He is a.k.a. Carr Dickson (a name pressed on him by a British publisher and changed at his request to Carter Dickson) when writing about Sir Henry Merrivale.

A prolific contemporary suspense writer such as Bill Pronzini will have his books published under several pseudonyms—Jack Foxx (*The Jade Figurine*) and Alex Saxon (*A Run in*

TEX RILEY · HENRY ST. JOHN · JIMMY WILDE · JEREMY YORKE · GORDON ASHE

MARGARET COOKE

Twenty-Six Creaseys and One Ringer

WILLIAM K. RILEY

JOHN CREASEY · NORMAN DEANE · COLIN HUGHES · MICHAEL HALLIDAY · Y.I. BABBLE

BRIAN HOPE · CHARLES HOGARTH · M.E. COOKE · PATRICK GILL · ROBERT CAINE FRAZER

KYLE HUNT · ABEL MANN · PETER MANTON · J.J. MARRIC · JAMES MARSDEN

RICHARD MARTIN · RODNEY MATTHESON · ANTHONY MORTON · KEN RANGER · ELISE FECAMPS

THE ALIAS' ALIAS

Pseudonym
Pen name
Assumed name
Codename
Misnomer
Nom de plume
Nom de guerre
Nom de passion
Sobriquet
Epithet
Cryptonym
Euonym
Byline
Handle
John Doe
Jane Doe

Diamonds)—in addition to his real name (*Panic* and *Snowbound*). Ditto Robert L. Fish, inventor of "Schlock Holmes," a parody on Sherlock, who also wrote as Robert L. Pike and A.C. Lamprey.

One of the greatest names in the field, Cornell Woolrich, used the name William Irish for *Phantom Lady* (and also used a less well-known alias, George Hopley) because of his high output.

No discussion of pseudonyms used for reasons of output is complete without mention of John Creasey, whose loyal readers are hard put to keep up with his books and his aliases. He used twenty-six, varying them from sleuth to sleuth.

Question of Style

With some mystery authors, for every sleuth there is an alias. The start of the now famous series of books about private eye Lew Archer gave cause for an alias—Ross Macdonald—to one Kenneth Millar. (His wife, Margaret Millar, uses no alias for her successful mystery novels such as *Beast in View,* a prizewinner.) And a difference in style is the reason for Evan Hunter's choice of the pseudonym Ed McBain on those popular police pro-

cedurals, to distinguish them from the books published under his own name (*Blackboard Jungle,* etc.); some of his other pen names are Curt Cannon, Hunt Collins and Richard Marsten.

When Perry Mason's creator, Erle Stanley Gardner, switched sleuths in mid-scream to write about the detective team of Bertha Cool/Donald Lam, he succeeded in deceiving his audience with the alias A.A. Fair. Now these books are emblazoned "Erle Stanley Gardner writing as A.A. Fair," and the secret is out.

The famous Ellery Queen is, of course, a pen name for the writing duo of Frederic Dannay and Manfred B. Lee; the same team decided to create another alias, Barnaby Ross, for their second detective (actor Drury Lane). Another team, Mary J. Latis and Martha Hennissart, chose the pseudonym Emma Lathen when they launched their banker hero, John Putnam Thatcher, in *Banking on Death;* they switched to R.B. Dominic for their capital crimes.

Sometimes writing teams can be confusing. Manning Coles is an alias for two authors, Cyril Henry Coles and Adelaide Frances Oke Manning. It's not to be confused with another detective team, the Coles (G.D.H. and M.I. Cole), and that's not a pseudonym.

Is Sex Necessary?

For every Agatha Christie, Dorothy L. Sayers and Ngaio Marsh, research yields an equal number of talented mystery and suspense writers born female but published under a male—or ambiguous—pen name: Dell Shannon (Elizabeth Linington), E.X. Ferrars (Morna Doris Brown), P.D. James (Phyllis White), Anthony Gilbert (Lucy Beatrice Malleson), Tobias Wells and Stanton Forbes (both actually DeLoris Forbes), Clemence Dane (Winifred Ashton) and so on through a long list.

A parade of double initials or a first name that could be male baffles us less

PRONUNCIATION GUIDE
proe-nun-sea-ay-shun guyed

(f u kn rd ths u kn rd a mstry)

Roderick *Alleyn* al-inn
V.C. Clinton-*Baddeley* baad-uh-lee
Modesty *Blaise* blaze
Anthony *Boucher* rhymes with "croucher"
Ernest *Bramah* rhymes with "comma"
John *Buchan* buck-in
Max *Carrados* care-uh-dose
Auguste Dupin awe-*goost* dew-*pan*
Elizabeth *Ferrars* as in "terrors"
Jacques Futrelle zshahk foot-*trell*
Emile *Gaboriau* as in Zsa Zsa + ee-oh
Ganesh Ghote ga-nesh *go*-tay
Robert van *Gulik* *goo*-lick
Dashiell Hammett *dash*-el
Jack *Iams* *eye*-mz
Michael *Innes* inn-iss
Maurice *Le Blanc* luh-*blahn*
John *Le Carré* luh-car-*ray*
Monsieur *Lecoq* luh-*coke*
William *Le Queux* luh-*q*
Gaston *Leroux* gas-*tone* luh-*roo*
Arsene *Lupin* are-*sen* loo-*pan*
Maigret may-*gray*
Ngaio Marsh *nye* (as in hi) + oh
Berkely *Mather* bark-lee *may*-thurr
Patricia *Moyes* rhymes with "noise"
Hercule Poirot heir-*cool* pwah-*row*
Sax *Rohmer* sacks *row*-murr (as in purr)
Joseph *Rouletabille* roo-luh-tah-*bee*-yuh
Georges *Simenon* zshorzsh sea-muh-*no*
Maj *Sjöwall* as in Taj; *show*-vahl
Julian *Symons* as in Crimmins
Josephine *Tey* tay
François *Vidocq* fran-*swah* vee-*duck*
Per *Wahlöö* pair vahl-*oo* (as in boo)
Hillary *Waugh* as in law
Peter *Death Bredon* Wimsey as in "teeth"; *bree*-dun
Dilys Winn as in "kill us"; rhymes with "djinn"

in these enlightened times, but publishers stuck such male by-lines on their female authors hoping to cash in on all those readers who (they thought) wouldn't touch with a ten-foot noose a detective novel by a woman. Apparently they hadn't heard of Mary Roberts Rinehart . . .

Does it work the other way round? It does for Canadian writer W.E.D. Ross, who publishes Gothics as Marilyn Ross/Clarissa Ross/et al., and for Michael Avallone, who also has Gothics on the stands with female aliases—Edwina Noone and Priscilla Dalton, to name a couple. Reverse sexism applies the damsel-in-distress books, whose readers are largely women.

Potpourri

Some pseudonyms really do exist to preserve privacy: Catherine Aird (for Kinn McIntosh) is one, and Josephine Tey (for Elizabeth MacKintosh) is another.

One famous secret pen name in the mystery field is Newgate Callendar, the terse mystery critic for the *New York Times Book Review*. With all their knowledge of poisons, ballistics and blunt instruments, novelists reviewed by Callendar could do him in handily were his privacy not protected by an alias.

I suspect that, like every other fan of "murder ink" who can never get enough, I will have to take my mystery authors as I find them, letting out a Eureka! when I discover a cache of books by one of my favorites writing under a pen name. There is no way to stop mystery and suspense writers from using an a.k.a. They hide behind them just as the crooks on the pages of their books have always done. The evidence is in, and the verdict is obvious: it's another case of fiction following fact.

Carol Kountz, former managing editor of The Writer, *once checked into a small hotel near the Reichenbach Falls as Irene Adler.*

CODES
Purposely Creating a Language Barrier

Edward D. Hoch

*C*odes. Codes and ciphers are two quiet different things. A code consists of words, phrases, numbers or symbols used to replace elements of the plain text (uncoded) message. A code operates on linguistic entities; thus a code book might show the number 6477 standing for the word "attack," or the letter group BUKSI signifying "Avoid arrest if possible." A problem with codes is that they require code books, often containing thousands of number or letter groups covering all possible messages. The vulnerability of code books to capture by enemy forces has always presented grave problems. For this reason, naval codes are bound in books with heavy lead plates in the front and back cover to ensure their sinking to the bottom if dropped overboard. Good code stories (as distinguished from cipher stories) are rare, but O. Henry's "Calloway's Code" makes clever use of a makeshift code of special interest to journalists.

Dictionary and book codes. A dictionary code uses numbers to identify the page and line on which a given work may be found, the drawback being that the same numbers always stand for the same words. A book code also uses numbers to identify the page, line and word in any book designated "it" by both sender and receiver. Anthony Boucher's short story "QL 696 .C9" uses a code based on the Library of Congress classification system for books.

Substitution ciphers. In ciphers of the substitution type, a single letter, number or symbol stands for a single letter of the alphabet. The most popular device for substitution ciphers is the cipher disk. Cipher disks have a long history with the military, and Aaron Burr is known to have used one. A problem with substitution ciphers is that long messages can be deciphered through use of a letter frequency list. The most frequently used letter in the English language is *e*—as Edgar Allan Poe correctly observed in "The Gold Bug," the world's most widely read cipher story. Though today's letter frequencies are different from those listed in "The Gold Bug," Poe's technique for solving the cipher in the story is still valid. Poe used numbers and symbols as substitutions for the letters of his message, whereas Arthur Conan Doyle used little stick-figure drawings in "The Adventure of the Dancing Men." But Holmes used Poe's technique of letter frequencies in his solution.

Transposition ciphers. When letters of a message retain their identities and are merely jumbled, we have a transposition cipher. In a simple rectangular transposition, the letters of a message are printed horizontally in a square, then removed from the square vertically and placed in groups of five to disguise the original word lengths. The recipient of the message puts the letters back vertically and reads them horizontally.

Skytales. One form of transposition cipher uses a skytale, or scytale—a long narrow strip of paper wrapped around a wooden staff or other object. The message is printed down the length of the staff, with lines of unrelated letters printed down the other sides. When the paper strip is removed, the writing appears to be gibberish, but it can easily be read when wrapped around a staff of the same diameter at the receiving end.

Grilles. Another transposition cipher is the grille—a sheet of metal or cardboard with rectangular holes cut at irregular intervals. The message is written in these open spaces and the grille is then removed. The remaining space is filled with an innocuous letter or report. The receiver lays an identical grille over the letter to read the true message. My short story "The Spy Who Worked for Peace" was built around the use of a grille.

HACKER'S OBSTACLE COURSE

David Kahn

The blending of computation and telecommunications into what is sometimes called "telematics" or "compunications" means that cryptology is invading the bowels of the computer. Stored data must be protected: in part by blocking unauthorized access, often attempted from remote terminals; in part by encrypting the data. David Wise, in *The Children's Room,* gives a technologically accurate portrayal of a brute-force computer break-in, and Peter Ognibene utilizes a computer crime—the penetration of the Federal Reserve System's electronic banking network—as the centerpiece of *The Big Byte.* Data moving through and out of the computer must likewise be protected: in this case, shielding can block the electronic radiation that reveals processing within or transmission from a computer. Nick Carter's *The Ultimate Code* mentions a six-inch lead plate in doors for this very purpose. Encryption can armor the data as it passes over communications links.

The majority of today's cipher machines—unlike the electromechanical mechanisms of World War II—are electronic, ranging from units the size of video-display terminals that automatically transmit the cryptogram to units the size of hand-held calculators that show only half a dozen letters at a time on their liquid-crystal displays and require the encipherer to write down the cipher letters. At the heart of each lies a microprocessor:

a tiny silicon chip no bigger than a thumbnail, whose circuitry embodies the rules of transformation of plaintext into cipher and back again.

One example of such a system is the federal government's Data Encryption Standard (DES), which protects data such as Medicare records stored in or transmitted between federal computers. Though the cipher and its associated chip are common to all users, each user or pair of users would have its own key. The DES enciphers sixty-four bits (or 0's and 1's) at a time, putting them through a transposition, a division, an expansion, a substitution, a contraction, a transposition, another substitution and a combination, repeating the middle group of steps sixteen times. The process is so involved that the change of a single bit in the input will change all sixty-four bits in the output. The chip handles the entire operation in a fraction of a second; for a human to do it would take an hour—not counting the errors he would introduce.

Other computer ciphers use different algorithms for transforming plaintext into cipher. Many use devices called shift registers, but all are in the same range of complexity as the DES and consequently enjoy the same level of security.

David Kahn is the author of The Codebreakers *and* Kahn on Codes: Secrets of the New Cryptology.

Playfair squares. Before World War I, the British Army successfully used a diagraphic substitution called a Playfair square, named for its advocate, Baron Playfair. A five-by-five square of twenty-five spaces is used, filled in horizontally with the unduplicated letters of a key word. The remaining squares are filled with the unused letters of the alphabet, with the letters I and J combined. Thus, using the key word "Blackstone," the square looks like this:

B	L	A	C	K
S	T	O	N	E
D	F	G	H	I-J
M	P	Q	R	U
V	W	X	Y	Z

The cipher is called diagraphic because the letters of the plain text are divided into pairs and enciphered two at a time, with the result depending upon their relation to each other in the square. Double letters occurring together in a pair are separated by an *x*. If the two letters of a pair are in the same horizontal row, they're enciphered with the letters to their right. If they fall in the same vertical column, they're enciphered with the letters beneath them. If they appear in neither the same row nor column, each is enciphered by the letter that lies in its own row but in the column occupied by the other letter. Thus, using the word "balloon" as an example, it would first be written as *ba lx lo on,* then enciphered as *lc aw at ne.* Though it seems complicated, the Playfair is easily mastered and only the key word need be remembered. Best of all, it comes close to being unbreakable.

Vigenère ciphers. Probably the most famous cipher system of all is the Vigenère, a polyalphabetic substitution cipher that is a simplified system of Blaise de Vigenère's original. It uses a tableau consisting of twenty-six standard horizontal alphabets, each positioned one letter to the left of the one above. A normal alphabet stands at the top and another normal alphabet runs down the left side of the tableau. In use, a key word is repeated above the plain text message until each letter has a corresponding key letter. The plain text letter is located in the top alphabet of the tableau and the key letter on the side alphabet. The lines are followed down and across the tableau to their intersection, yielding the cipher letter. Long thought unbreakable, Vigenères are more easily solved than Playfairs, mainly because the key word is repeated several times in a pattern.

Pigpen ciphers. More of historical interest than anything else is the pigpen cipher. Variations of this system were used by the Rosicrucians, Masons and other groups. A "pigpen" of four lines, looking exactly like a tic-tac-toe square, is drawn on a sheet of paper and each pen is filled with three letters of the alphabet, starting with *abc* in the upper left and continuing horizontally until *yz* is in the lower right pen. The first letter in each of the nine sections needs no dot, but the second letter is represented by one dot and the third letter by two dots. In ciphering by this method, a letter is represented by the shape of its pen, with one or two dots in the pen if necessary. Thus the letter *o*, in the center of the pigpen, is enciphered as a square-shaped pen with two dots inside.

Steganography. A grouping of various methods of concealing the very existence of a secret message. Included are invisible inks, microdots, and messages in which the first or last letter of each word spells out a hidden communication. In a 1912 collection of short stories, *The Master of Mysteries,* published anonymously, the first letters of the first words in the twenty-four stories spell out the sentence "The author is Gelett Burgess." The last letters of the last words in each story read "False to life and false to art."

SKOOBEDOC

Denning, Dorothy G.R. *Cryptography and Data Security.* An exceptionally clear survey.

Konheim, Alan G. *Cryptography: A Primer.* Mathematical; strong on theory.

Lorain, Pierre. *Clandestine Operations: The Arms and Techniques of the Resistance, 1941-1944.* Excellent cryptography chapter, pp. 64-81.

Meyer, Carl H., and Stephen M. Matyas. *Cryptography: A New Dimension in Computer Data Security.* Overall system security, by two IBM specialists.

Shulman, David. *An Annotated Bibliography of Cryptography.* Almost definitive for precomputer works; weak thereafter.

Sinkov, Abraham. *Elementary Cryptanalysis: A Mathematical Approach.* The clearest explanation of codebreaking.

Tuchman, Barbara. *The Zimmermann Telegram.* History's most important codebreaking.

Ellery Queen used a similar device in an early novel, with the first letter of each chapter title spelling out *The Greek Coffin Mystery* by Ellery Queen.

Chronograms. More interesting in literature than in serious espionage work are chronograms—inscriptions in which certain letters, printed larger or in a different typeface, express a date or number when added together by their values as Roman numerals. A prime example of a chronogram in fiction is R. Austin Freeman's Dr. Thorndyke mystery *The Puzzle Lock.*

One-time pads. The ultimate cipher that cryptologists dream of is the one-time system, using pads or tape. Popular following World War II, one-time pads use nonrepeating random keys. Since the same key is never repeated, and is only a meaningless jumble of letters, even a great many messages provide no clues. The cipher is truly unbreakable. Only the vast number of keys that must be printed and distributed has kept the one-time cipher from being universally popular. In a confusing battlefield situation, the order of the keys might prove a handicap when several units are involved. And in an espionage situation, discovery of a spy's one-time pads would be damaging evidence—as it was in the cases of Soviet spies Helen and Peter Kroger and Rudolf Abel.

Cipher machines. The ancestor of the modern cryptographic machines was probably the wheel cipher invented by Thomas Jefferson. It consisted of a cylinder six inches long, divided into twenty-six separate wheels, each with a full alphabet in jumbled order. The wheels were numbered and no two were alike. They were lined up so that a message could be read horizontally. Then the jumbled letters from any of the other lines became the cipher. On the receiving end, an identical cylinder had its wheels aligned to show the cipher message. One of the other lines would automatically show the message in plain text. Almost infinite varieties were possible by changing the order of the numbered wheels. A century after Jefferson, the French cipher expert Étienne Bazeries invented a similar machine. These early wheel ciphers could be broken with a bit of hard work, but they led directly to the rotor machines so popular today. Using from three to eight rotors, machine ciphers are difficult to break without a great many messages from the same machine. The preferred technique is to obtain one of the machines itself—as the British did during World War II with the German cipher machine Enigma.

Edward D. Hoch is the author of The Spy and the Thief, *seven stories on codes and ciphers.*

PANDORA'S CLASSIFIED BOX

Will Harriss

Y ou have founded your own little think tank, done some research and made a terrific discovery: for five miles around, a spinning quadripole laser doohickey will turn enemy armor into a substance resembling peanut brittle. Excited, you sit down and write a report on your discovery.

Obviously, your report has to be classified because it gives the U.S. a great strategic advantage, so you (or somebody) must choose among the three basic security classifications: CONFIDENTIAL, SECRET and TOP SECRET, which mean, respectively, that disclosure of the information to unauthorized persons could "damage," "seriously damage" or "cause exceptionally grave damage" to our national security. You decide to mark it TOP SECRET. It's your first classified document.

Fine. But then you discover the appalling disadvantages of producing anything classified. Among other things, you must now:

- Buy a safe to keep your reports in (and the safe combination itself is classified information!).
- Get a security clearance for your facility, authorizing you to receive and store classified documents.
- Get security clearances for anybody who is to have access to your documents—including yourself.
- Print, in different colors, Routed Classified Material receipts and Classified Material Transfer receipts to be signed by people who need documents temporarily or for quite a while.

- Figure out how you're going to mark and keep track of photographs, film, microfiche, floppy disks and the like.
- Hire somebody to set up a record-keeping system.
- Establish a Security Office to control the system, lecture employees on safeguarding classified material, publish a Security Manual, train people in proper document marking and so on.
- Hire guards to keep track of people coming in and out, and check offices every evening for unlocked safes and classified material inadvertently left on desks.
- Set up a wrapping and mailing facility for classified material, which must be sealed in an envelope and marked, then inserted in an unmarked outer envelope.
- Conduct periodic inventories to account for the whereabouts of every copy of every classified document.
- Set up a system for handling classified waste material, e.g., notes, manuscript drafts, typewriter cartridge ribbons, rough sketches.
- Decide how you'll destroy classified waste. Pulping, cross-cut shredding and burning are common methods. (Deep-sixing is a no-no.)
- Fill out and file certificates of destruction when you destroy classified material that's numbered and inventoried.

Mind-boggling, isn't it? You can see why governments do a lot of nail-biting over their perpetual dilemma: they need to protect themselves, but overdoing classification is self-defeating. It can be very costly in money and time, and can severely obstruct the flow of information. (The paranoid and xenophobic Soviets, in particular, make things very hard on themselves.)

Complex as all this is, we have merely scratched the surface. Like those bills in Congress with so many riders pinned onto them that they resemble Christmas trees, classified documents can bristle with restrictions.

First of all, nearly every classified document must have a declassification schedule and sometimes a downgrading schedule. Sooner or later, after all, the enemy will discover the details of your quadripole laser, and you don't want to go on burdening yourself with all that classified rigamarole:

Classified by ———— on ————
Downgrade to ————
Declassify on ————
or Review on ————

Or let's say we've recruited a Polish mole who has given us photos and design specifications of Soviet antitank lasers. You probably won't ever see any reports on the subject, because the Department of Defense has marked it . . .

SECRET
WARNING NOTICE —
INTELLIGENCE SOURCES AND
METHODS INVOLVED

. . . and will closely control its dissemination. All paragraphs in the document that contain intelligence information will have to be marked SWN. And on top of that, you may find one or all of the following markings added to the cover and title page:

NOCONTRACT: Not Releasable to Contractors or Contractor/Consultants
NOFORN: Not Releasable to Foreign Nationals
ORCON: Dissemination and Extraction of Information Controlled by Originator
PROPIN: Caution—Proprietary Information Involved.

The plot thickens if you have anything to do with nuclear weaponry. Maybe your quadripole laser activates a tactical nuclear device that turns steel to peanut brittle. In that case, your documents will *not* be automatically downgraded and declassified, and you must mark them

SECRET
RESTRICTED DATA
This material contains Restricted Data as defined in the Atomic Energy Act of 1954. Unauthorized disclosure subject to administrative and criminal sanctions.

If the nuclear information is crucial enough, your own Top Secret clearance may not be enough to allow you to see it. Your name may have to appear on an access list, and the document will probably be marked:

TOP SECRET
Critical Nuclear Weapon Design Information

At the other end of the scale are those cheery documents that are merely

UNCLASSIFIED

THE BROOKINGS INSTITUTION

The Brookings Institution, an east coast think tank. The country's first think tank was the Rand Corporation, founded 1948 at the instigation of General "Hap" Arnold.

But wait a minute: even if the information is pretty humdrum, it may be rather sensitive and shouldn't be left lying around on tables in reception rooms where every Tom, Dick and Haroun-al-Rashid can see it. Let's say it talks about small-arms ammunition we left behind in Beirut because it was cheaper to dump than to lug out. You might want to mark such a document

LIMITED OFFICIAL USE

FOR OFFICIAL USE ONLY

to keep it off coffee tables. The State Department has its own low-level marking for such a document:

Obviously, the classification system can be abused, especially for official cover-ups of one kind or another. Federal law therefore warns that the system may not be used "to conceal administrative error or inefficiency, to prevent personal or departmental embarrassment" or for other purposes having nothing to do with protecting the national security.

Will Harriss won an Edgar from the Mystery Writers of America for Bay Psalm Book Murder. *He works for a West Coast facility so classified they won't even tell him its name.*

PSSST

Spies all over the world are trying to earn their Li'l Orphan Annie code rings by swiping each other's classified documents. To do so, they have to learn how countries mark them. Following are a few examples:

Country	TOP SECRET	SECRET	CONFIDENTIAL
Greece[a]	ΑΚΡΩΣ ΑΠΟΡΡΗΤΟΝ	ΑΠΟΡΡΗΤΟΝ	ΕΜΠΙΣΤΕΥΤΙΚΟΝ
Guatemala	ALTO SECRETO	SECRETO	CONFIDENCIAL
Haiti	————	SECRET	CONFIDENTIAL
Honduras	SUPER SECRETO	SECRETO	CONFIDENCIAL
Hong Kong	TOP SECRET	SECRET	CONFIDENTIAL
Hungary	SZIGORÚAN TITKOS	TITKOS	BIZALMAS
India	TOP SECRET	SECRET	CONFIDENTIAL
Indonesia	SANGAT RAHASIA	RAHASIA	KEPERT JAJAAN
Iran	BEKOLI SERRI	SERRI	KHEILI MAHRAMANEH
Iraq	سري بلقوة (Absolutely Secret)	سري (Secret)	مكتوم
Ireland Gaelic	TOP SECRET AN-SICREIDEACH	SECRET SICREIDEACH	CONFIDENTIAL RUNDA
Israel	SODI BEYOTER סודי ביותר	SODI סודי	SHAMUR שמור
Italy[a]	SEGRETISSIMO	SEGRETO	RISERVATISSIMO
Japan	KIMITSU	GOKUHI	HI
Jordan	مكتوم جداً	سري	مكتوم
Korea	I 급 비밀 ILKUP PIMIL	II급 비밀 IKUP PIMIL	III급 비밀 SAM KUP PIMIL
Laos	TRES SECRET	SECRET	SECRET/ CONFIDENTIEL
Lebanon	TRES SECRET	SECRET	CONFIDENTIEL
Mexico	SECRETO	SECRETO	CONFIDENCIAL
Netherlands[a]	ZEER GEHEIM	GEHEIM	CONFIDENTIEEL or VERTROUWELIJK
New Zealand	TOP SECRET	SECRET	CONFIDENTIAL
Nicaragua	ALTO SECRETO	SECRETO	CONFIDENCIAL
Norway[a]	STRENGT HEMMELIG	HEMMELIG	FORTROLIG
Pakistan	TOP SECRET	SECRET	CONFIDENTIAL

[a] NATO RESTRICTED Notice A/94-N/23, 5 October 1960.

MOTIVES

TONIGHT

The Stroke of Midnight

*Vicar Fogg
ponders the eulogy.*

"Rosie, lassie, calm down now, there's my bonnie girl. Jus' tell me wha'.

"Aye, I know, but tell me anyway. One thing a' a time, that's the way to tell it. Ye found him and then wha'?

"Um. Were they all millin' about in the room, then? Wi' him on the floor?

"Um. An' then wha' did he do?

"Och, tha' bleedin' fool. A sermon he's givin' when the police they be needin'. Dinna no one say to ring the station?

"Don't, Rosie, don't. I na' be blamin' ye. Nae. Why'd I be doin' tha? Hush. Ye flood the loch wi' those tears. I canna stand it when ye cry.

"Who d'ye mean, *he* did it?

"Y'daft, girl! Nae, I dinna believe it o' him. The man had no reason. His pay came from him. An' his room and meals. An' no bars on his windows, he liked tha', I can tell ye. Nae, he wouldna' done it. I dinna care if he was missin' the day. What's his cause?

"When was the last ye saw him then? Miss Becca, then, when was it she saw him? Nae, I'm na' accusin' Mr. Roudebush. Aye, I know wha' ye said; down wi' the gout. But why couldn't it be he as well? He's been out o' sight all day, na' jus' poor Whelks.

"Sure an' it looks bad, but, Rosie, lassie, think. If he did it, then who done him? Man canna stab himself in the back, now can he?

"Aye, a madman's loose. Now stop that caterwaulin'. Won't do ye the bit o' good.

"I want ye t'go to the room an' stay till I get there, d'ye hear me? Aye, of course, I'm comin' for ye. A' closin'. I canna come a'fore, Rosie. Canna.

"Customers, tha's why na'. Two guests from the Hall.

"Aye, him again. Nae, na' wi' her. I told ye. Wi' t'other one, the Colonel.

"Nae, I na' worried. I be thinkin' ye be safe wi' them here wi' me.

"Now, Rosie, I tell ye agin, plain: ye

an' Bridie slip 'cross to Mr. Roudebush an' tell him ye need his protection till I ge' there. Jus' till I come.

"Aye, y'can. We'll take her wi' us.

"How sho' I know where she'll sleep? Rosie, dinna fret abou' it. Nae, she's na' for the bed wi' ye, wi' me on the floor. She can ha' the floor! Well then, lass, leave her there. There's only the one room. If ye want her t'come, then she takes the floor, right-o?

"Aye. Shall I send him back for her, then? Bridie and tha' killer? Nae, I only be makin' a bit o' a joke. Nae, Rosie, I dinna know for sure he's a bad one. But not quarter an hour ago, ye should o' heard the goin's-on! Huffed an' puffed, the Colonel did. Threw down cards wi' marks and said ri' out: 'You are a cheat, sir, and here is proof!'

"Dinna do much a' all.

"I dinna ken. Maybe it's na' easy to mark up like that an' he wanted 'em back.

"Nae, he kept 'em. Maybe he's goin' to use 'em now, the Colonel.

" 'Course they talked abou' it. Haven't ye been on to my ear abou' it for the past hour? 'Colonel,' he told him, 'women an' cards are my weakness, bu' killin' *never*! Too many women in the world to kill over one,' he says.

Becca tortured by the problem of lining the casket. Purple or pink?

"Och, Rosie, love, o' course I would. Aye, I would, lassie, kill for ye, I would. Come on, now, throw us a kiss. Let me hear it. Mmmmm. What a little delicious ye be.

"Nae, he dinna seem so, why? Ne'er heard o' such a night for knockin' abou'!

"Wha' d'ye mean, exaggerate! Rosie, what did ye tell me: first himself an' some sandwich poisonin! Then Whelks wi' a knife by the pond. Then Penny-Pincher bashed round a bit and put in the woodbin. Now ye tell me the Colonel, too, got a slug, and ye say 'twas naught serious! Come on, Rosie, girl. I tell ye plain: stay in the house. Somethin's na' right o'side it.

"Ye dinna! Out cold, ye put her! What did she say when she be comin' to?

"Och, Rosie, how could ye run away? Wha' kind o' friend is tha'?

"Aye, you'll make her understand. The noise was wha' made ye bump an' run. Of course she'll forgi' ye."

"Nae, I'm na' scoldin' ye. Nae. Now do as I say: lock up wi' Mr. Roudebush till I ge' there.

"I love ye, too. Right after closin', I promise.

"Now, gents, time in ten. What can I do ye for till then?"

Lady Teasdale, prostrate.

WHODUNIT
A GUIDE TO THE OBVIOUS

Matthew J. Mahler

I once knew a man who thought he could outsmart John Dickson Carr. He was reading *The Skeleton in the Clock,* and along about page 56 he decided he knew who done it. In fact, he was absolutely convinced of it. He was all wrong, of course, his thinking detoured by one of the most devious minds in the business. Several years later, the same man picked up the same book and decided to reread it. He wouldn't make the same mistake twice, he said, not him. He'd forgotten everything about the book except whom he'd first chosen as murderer. Carefully ignoring that person, he went on to finger someone else. And missed again.

RED HERRINGS

They are, of course, false clues meant to distract one from the real villain. The term originated in England, and there are instances of its use as far back as the seventeenth century. It seems some people were distressed at the idea of a fox being hunted to its death by a pack of snarling dogs and a party of upper-class riders. To throw the dogs off the track, these anti-hunt people would go to the fish market, buy herrings, take them home and smoke them—which gave them a reddish color—then drag them through the woods and fields. The pungent odor of the fish would cover up the scent of the fox and confuse the dogs, allowing the fox to escape. Thus did red herrings become synonymous with attempts to deceive.

John Dickson Carr, in the words of the people at Vita, was a (red) herring maven. He was expert at creating them. His two closest rivals, according to an informal poll taken by my duped friend, would have to be Agatha Christie and Dorothy L. Sayers, which brings us to an interesting equation: take *Ten Little Indians,* divide by *Four False Weapons,* and you're left with *Five Red Herrings.* Not to mention the feeling that you've been had by the best.

Any respectable mystery will have at least one red herring in it. Now, a red herring comes in two forms: human and inanimate (in which case it's called a clue; sometimes, an alibi). Human red herrings are easy to recognize. They are usually anybody with a deep dark secret in his past. The deep dark secret is that he is a red herring. In books with more than one murder, the second murder is a red herring. That body, poor thing, died for no other reason than to distract you from the killer's motive for committing the first crime. Other likely red herrings are: a business partner, particularly if he's disgruntled (too obvious); a woman suffering from amnesia (whereas a man so afflicted is almost always the culprit); at least three of the heirs present at the reading of the will. This last is tricky. How do you know which are red herrings and which, in combination, have sent Grandfather off to *their* eternal reward? Well, years of study have revealed that any heir who has not yet reached his majority is a red herring, ditto an heir who receives the bulk of the estate (providing the will was not drawn up within a fortnight of the funeral). Any heir who refuses to cry is a red herring; only a red herring would be that unsympathetic.

Mysterious telephone callers, gentlemen with foreign accents who ask a lot of questions in the pub, poison-pen writers and neighbors who own large barking dogs are also red herrings, but that doesn't mean they're guiltless. Usually, though, they're responsible for a secondary crime, such as extortion.

There are two other candidates for red herringdom: the least likely suspect and the most likely suspect. Ever since Mrs. Christie conned us in *The Murder of Roger Ackroyd,* we've become extremely wary of ruling out the least likely. It's gotten so we trust no one, not even the victim, who we're convinced—sometimes correctly—is shamming. The tip-off here is how much the least likely talks and if he has a first name. If he seems awfully helpful and full of gossip, and has both a first name and a surname, he's no red herring. If he's quiet, thoughtful and always referred to as Mr. So-and-So, he *is* a red herring. If the cards seem stacked against one character right from the beginning, that person is a red herring. The real killer will appear three pages from the end of the book.

Clues and alibis also function as red herrings. Clues to disregard are those that come in pairs, such as an earring with a bloody fingerprint on it. That strains coincidence just a bit too much and is an obvious plant. Red herring alibis are those which are airtight. Nobody lives that tidy a life.

Red herrings were spawned years ago. I suppose one would have to credit Mr. Poe (remember those two voices overheard in that upstairs room in the Rue Morgue? Red herrings, if ever there were ones). They proliferated in the Twenties and Thirties, but now, with the advent of the police procedural, they're becoming extinct. As the whodunit fades and the whydunit and howtheydunit be-

Simon loves Harriet.

Harriet loves Simon.

Clare loves John.

John loves Caro.

Pride and Prejudice and Amaretto.

come more popular, a reader is forced to turn to the older authors to find them.

I don't know what you're reading next, but a friend of mine is taking a third crack at *The Skeleton in the Clock.* This time, he swears he'll get it right.

Matthew J. Mahler is chairman of the Save the Red Herring Movement.

SHAKING THE FAMILY TREE FOR CULPRITS

Dorothy Salisbury Davis

I don't think I wrote a real, live, flesh-and-blood heroine until the women's movement. This is not to say that all my female characters before the awakening suffered from wilt: a number of them were quite vigorous, but generally speaking, the more vigorous they were, the older they were. And all of them owed something to Aunt Mary.

Aunt Mary was my mother's cousin. When she came to America from Ireland as a young girl, she didn't have the nails to scratch herself, as the saying went in our house. She married and became a widow within a year. There was constant gossip about her in the family, which I memorized while pretending not to listen. How, on a fireman's widow's pension, did she acquire a house on the Fox River? Who were the men you'd meet there, men with names like Indian Red Mitchell, Big Bill Hansen, Dago Jim?

Those were the waning days of Prohibition, and only my mother's naïveté—which she clung to piously—kept her from admitting they were bootleggers. The incident by which pride overcame piety occurred when Aunt Mary took a still apart and sank it, piece by piece, in the river quicksand while the Revenue agents were having breakfast at her kitchen table.

Probably there's an Aunt Mary in everybody's life: the legendary family rebel, whether she is female or male, whether she is a pioneer or a witch. She is more often a sinner than a saint (and I ask you: which is more interesting?) and very often she is the skeleton who simply will not stay in the closet.

My first rendering of Aunt Mary was the most literal. She became Mrs. O'Grady in my second book, *The Clay Hand.* Yet aspects of her live in a half-dozen later characters, even in so distant an inheritor as the psychiatrist in the Julie books. Like their inspiration, "my" Aunt Marys are larger than life and surely you won't be surprised when I tell you I have perpetuated elements of Aunt Mary in myself.

Is it banal of me to say that all my characters, most especially my villains, are aspects of myself? Their wickedness exceeds my own, of course; for the present, at least, I am able to divert or suppress evil inclination before it gets out of hand.

I am much aware that my craft is in the conscious shaping of what the unconscious sends up, a bit of Aunt Mary, my

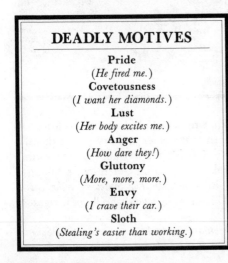

DEADLY MOTIVES

Pride
(*He fired me.*)
Covetousness
(*I want her diamonds.*)
Lust
(*Her body excites me.*)
Anger
(*How dare they!*)
Gluttony
(*More, more, more.*)
Envy
(*I crave their car.*)
Sloth
(*Stealing's easier than working.*)

A GLIMPSE OF DADDY
Penelope Wallace

My father and I were very much alike, and neither of us suffered from false modesty; I think it is this similarity which has enabled me to be proud of him—as a father, as a man and as a writer—without feeling that I am stifled by his shadow.

Although I was quite young when he died, I'd spent two years with him at Chalklands, our country house in Buckinghamshire, and here, with the rest of the family away during the week, we talked as equals. He was totally approachable, stopping work in mid-sentence to deal with my problems and answer my questions. We would go in the motor launch to Marlow, where we both ate strawberries and cream for tea—heavy on the cream or sugar.

After my father died, we moved from our luxury apartment to a small flat in Kensington. Here I lived with my mother while she wrote a biography of my father, using the money to pay my school fees at Roedean. She lived to see me pass the entrance exam and died just over a year after my father.

My guardian was a thirty-six-year-old bachelor who was totally incapable of housing a headstrong girl, so I shuttled myself between relations and left school at seventeen. At school I'd suffered somewhat from the "I should have thought Edgar Wallace's daughter would be able to do that" remarks from the staff, but since one is never introduced to people

Logo of the Edgar Wallace Pub, London.

there—presumably new girls are warned in private—it wasn't until I started working in Oxford that I first ran up against the standard introduction to which I've become accustomed:

"This is Penny, daughter of Edgar Wallace."

For a while I thought people only wanted to meet me for my relationship, and I thought of changing my name; then I realised this might be true the first time—as if I had two heads—but if people invited me twice it was because they liked me as me. Now I know "daughter of Edgar Wallace" is an additional interest. I'm proud that so many people like and admire him, and I'm delighted to share the affection they have for him.

Penelope Wallace received a special Crime Writers' Association Silver Dagger for her organization of the First International Crime Writers Congress.

self, my mother, as well as numerous women I've known down the years whom I cherish for the chinks in their armor that I recognize—women who thrust the dark mirror before my very greedy eyes.

I therefore find it puzzling to contemplate that while I claim the name Margaret to be my favorite—it was my mother's name and it's my own second name—in the four of my books in which

women are the villains, two of them are named Margaret. I have yet to so name a heroine. What does it mean? I have no idea. I loved my mother. I have the requisite amount of self-esteem. But a story of matricide has been tossing and turning in my mind for years. When it comes right, perhaps I shall know.

Doroty Salisbury Davis is a past president of the Mystery Writers of America.

MURDER INK OPINION POLL

On average, mystery readers write one fan letter in any three-year time span, upping their quota if the author (a) replies promptly and asks them a question or (b) sends them a complimentary copy of his latest book.

Most readers have met at least one mystery writer, but not necessarily their favorite one. The most accessible authors: Bill Pronzini, Charlotte MacLeod, Lawrence Block, all of whom seem to spend almost as much time signing autographs as they do writing books. The authors the readers most wanted to meet, however, were (in order of popularity): Dick Francis, Robert B. Parker, P.D. James, John Le Carré.

When pressed, readers confessed they preferred spies to cops, private eyes to spies, and amateur sleuths best of all. If the amateur sleuth appeared as a series character, they were ecstatic.

According to them, a cozy English village has hand-knit street signs, innumerable spinsters, a bumper crop of rumors, all telephone lines cut and a freesia border. Its name is either St. Mary Mead, St. Mary's Mead, St. Marple's Mary, Ham-on-Wry, Crumpet-on-Jam or Bedlam nr. Chaos. It was founded long ago (1066) or very recently (1984).

Given the chance to prosecute the vilest mystery villain, they issued subpoenas to Fu Manchu, Moriarty and Frankenstein. They were willing to defend Harriet Vane, provided they received Bunter as a retainer.

They expected a lawyer's brief to contain a party, another party, a sentence, a judgment and Calvin Klein's label.

If they took up a life of crime, they'd specialize in robbing banks (by a wide margin), knocking off the competition, making a killing.

Everyone knew Scotland Yard was not in Scotland, but the precise whereabouts of Interpol remained a mystery. In attempting to pinpoint it, fans traveled a route of evil from Brussels to The Hague to Flaxborough to the 87th Precinct to the seventh level of Dante's Inferno.

The "hot line" between Moscow and Washington was invariably described as a red telephone with several extensions for the exclusive use of bugs, translators, cabinet members, honchos at Lubyanka and the editor-in-chief at the *Enquirer*. Nobody mentioned it is actually a teletype system with message printouts.

When feeling sociable, readers invited Miss Marple to tea, Nero Wolfe to dinner and Thomas Magnum to bed. They attended a masquerade ball disguised as a corpse, the invisible man, the girl in the plain brown wrapper.

They defined *corpus delicti* as the body in the case, the mafia's way of saying "I love you," the dead woman's perfume.

Playing editor, they gave Hawk his own book, wistfully plotted a real romance between Clarissa and Valentine, presented Dalgleish with a Nobel for his poetry, and awarded $10,001 to themselves for correctly deducing the Robins family skulduggery.

Asked to spend a night alone in a Gothic house, they brought along spider repellent, a nightgown, enough candles to fill every candelabra Liberace ever owned. But they forgot matches.

They had no trouble spotting a clue (the charred letter, the dropped matchbook, the thumb print on the wall safe, the lipstick smudge on the collar/cocktail glass/napkin, the crumpled train schedule, the mis-set clock) or knowing what to do with it (pocket it, show it to the Inspector, demand an immediate explanation, pretend not to notice it).

Invited to participate in the classic dénouement scene, they gathered in the library, congregated in the lawyer's office or, wisely, took it on the lam.

Polling procedure: 1,000 questionnaires were mailed to fans who had queried the editor regarding the two previous polls; 812 were returned, and those that were legible were read and appear here in slightly altered form.

THE MOST ASKED QUESTION
WHY DO PEOPLE READ DETECTIVE STORIES?

Gladys Mitchell

I suppose one answer to this question is that people read them because other people write them. Why do other people write them? Well, according to Dr. Samuel Johnson, no man ever wrote who did not write for money.

There are those among us who claim that the detective story is a form of escapist literature. Lovers of the genre will deny this, and they are right to do so, for the detective story addict is not content to sit back and enjoy what is called "a cosy read." For full enjoyment of the story, the reader needs to use his brains. A problem has been set before him, and the true addict obtains pleasure from doing his best to solve it.

When the Detection Club was formed in London, England, very strict rules were laid down for the members to follow. The first and greatest commandment was that every clue to the identity of the criminal must be placed fairly before the reader. This provided for a true and just battle of wits between reader and author, and this, I think, is one of the main reasons people prefer those detective stories that keep to the rules.

Here, perhaps, it may be a good thing to repeat an observation that others have stressed. To the uninitiated, all classes of mystery fiction are apt to be classed as "thrillers," but to the intelligentsia the rough-and-ready story of breakneck adventure, car chase, mysterious master criminal, sex, bloodthirstiness and highly coloured heroics is but the bastard brother of the classic whodunit and is not to the taste of the true detective aficionado.

The thriller poses no problem, makes no tax upon the reader except perhaps to find out how much blood and guts he can stomach, so that its chief merit is to take the reader from his own safe, fireside existence into what P.G. Wodehouse would call "another and a dreadful world." This makes a strong

---

HALL OF INFAMY

1. *The Mind Readers,* Margery Allingham
2. *Trent's Last Case,* E.C. Bentley
3. *The Hungry Goblin,* John Dickson Carr
4. *Playback,* Raymond Chandler
5. *Elephants Can Remember,* Agatha Christie
6. *Fear Comes to Chalfont,* Freeman Wills Crofts
7. *Valley of Fear,* Sir Arthur Conan Doyle
8. *The Bloody Wood,* Michael Innes
9. *The Naïve and Sentimental Lover,* John Le Carré
10. *Goodbye America,* Alistair MacLean
11. *When in Rome,* Ngaio Marsh
12. *Busman's Honeymoon,* Dorothy L. Sayers
13. *The President Vanishes,* Rex Stout

appeal to some minds but is not for the reader of detective stories, except as an occasional relaxation.

Of course, the detective story has changed over the years. Not for nothing did Dorothy L. Sayers call her last full-length Wimsey tale "a love story with detective interruptions." Of old, the purists laid down the axiom that love had no place in a detective story and was nothing but an unnecessary and most undesirable effluent when introduced into those otherwise unpolluted waters. It confused the narrative and dammed the flow of pure reason, for love's detractors (so far as the detective story is con-

cerned) can rightly claim that there is nothing so unreasonable, so utterly illogical, as love. The unreasonable and the illogical have no place in a mystery.

Times change, however, and so do the fictional detectives themselves—among whom, I suppose, every one of us has a favourite. The painstaking detective measuring footprints, treasuring cigarette ends, taking fingerprints, is a genuine character in real life and often "gets his man," but in fiction his worthy, molelike activities are apt to give a somewhat dull read. In fact, Edgar Allan Poe described (and, by implication, despised) the fictional use of the method.

THE PHYSIOLOGY OF READING

All comfy in your chair, are you? Good.

What you are sitting on are your ischial tuberosities. Depending on how fat you are, you may or may not be able to feel them since they are the bones of your rear end. They are covered by your gluteus maximus, a network of muscle.

If you are sitting in such a position that your feet do not touch the floor, you are undoubtedly tensing your gluteus maximus, which is not such a good idea. You should try to make contact with the floor by putting pressure on your calcanei, commonly called your heel bones. This will relieve the pressure on your beset rear.

A chair seat should not be so deep as to keep your feet from reaching the floor. On the other hand, it should be deep enough so that it does not cut across the buttock crease, causing pressure on your sciatic foramen.

Should you suffer from coccygodynia, you are experiencing a pain in your coccyx. It is unlikely that this pain is aggravated by reading in a chair, but in the event that you have trouble with it, you are advised to read while sitting on a rubber doughnut.

An unstable point in many people is the junction of the lumbar spine and the sacrum. Unless this is properly supported, you may fall victim to lumbosacral strain (lower back pain). So you should not read in a chair without a backrest—such as a barstool.

A reading chair should have a seat cushion. The back cushion is optional. But again, a fairly high-backed reading chair is a must or you will put undue strain on the articulations of your spinal facets. This means you are not supporting your upper back correctly. May we remind you that with incorrect support you lose your normal lordotic curve. A dire situation indeed.

If you think you can circumvent all these problems by reading in bed, you will be unhappy to learn that that can cause strain on the cervical area. Resulting in a severe pain in the neck. You should sit up in bed, leaning against the headboard, with your feet straight out in front of you. This also protects you from those who would sneak up behind to give you a stout cosh. Still comfy, are you? Good. Then we'll leave you to your book.

The rococo reading chair, ample enough for a lap, a laprobe, a cat and a book.

"You include the grounds about the house?"

"They gave us comparatively little trouble. We examined the moss between the bricks and found it undisturbed."

"You looked among D___'s papers, of course, and into the books of the library?"

"Certainly; we not only opened every book, but we turned over every leaf in each volume. We also measured the thickness of every book-cover."

"You explored the floors beneath the carpets?... and the paper on the walls?... You looked into the cellars?"

> *"Well, I may tell you that Filminister was murdered."*
>
> *"Murdered?"*
>
> *"Yes. What is more, he was murdered three times."*
>
> *"Three times?"*
>
> *"Yes, and not only that. He also committed suicide."*
>
> *"I think you'd better give me the details of this extraordinary story."*
>
> A Considerable Murder
> BARRY PAIN

This is far removed from the Chestertonian girth and intellect of Dr. Gideon Fell and farther still from "the little grey cells" of Hercule Poirot. Nowadays the gentlemanly detectives, Alleyn, Campion, Wimsey, the don-detective Gervase Fen, the delightful Inspector Ghote, Hillary Waugh's indefatigable policemen baying like hounds on the trail and the quirky legalities in the plots of Cyril Hare have taken over, to some extent, from the older, more plodding sleuths of earlier years.

I am far from believing that people read detective stories in order to learn new methods of committing murder, but it is a fact that, greatly to the author's distress, after Anthony Berkeley had published perhaps his best-known book, a real-life murderer successfully employed the method described in that book and strangled his victim with a silk stocking—the first time, it appears, that such an object had been used in real life for an act of thuggery.

Conversely, the police learned a thing or two when they attempted a reconstruction of the method they thought might have been used by the hymn-playing George Joseph Smith when he drowned three successive wives in the bath. The police reconstruction was almost too conclusive, for they nearly drowned their volunteer victim and had difficulty in bringing her back to consciousness. The method, which I shall not describe, has been used subsequently in at least one detective story.

So why *do* people read detective stories? I think one of the main reasons is that such books must, above all things, have a definite plot. Modern literature is full of plays and films that end nowhere; novels and short stories that leave the playgoer or the reader suspended in mid-air, forced either to impotent irritation or else to having to invent their own outcome.

Detective stories, by their very nature, cannot cheat in this way. Their writers must tidy up the loose ends; must supply a logical solution to the problem they have posed; must also, to hold the reader's attention, combine the primitive lust and energy of the hunter with the cold logic of the scholarly mind.

Above all, they must concentrate upon murder, although they may also say, with Robert Herrick's bellman:

From noise of scare-fires rest ye free,
From murders Benedicite.

Gladys Mitchell received the Crime Writers' Association Silver Dagger for her fifty novels featuring Dame Beatrice Bradley.

A CRITIC'S WORDS RETURN TO HAUNT HIM

Jacques Barzun

Crossing New York's Sherman Plaza late in a chilly November—the clock then striking one—I saw advancing toward me from the northeast something light-footed and cloudlike. It came along 59th Street as if from the Playboy Club, but it was no ordinary Bunny. When only a few steps away, it assumed a man's shape, and though still rather translucent it spoke in a firm, almost truculent voice.

GHOST: Remember me? Know who I am?

J.B.: Yes, you're the great critic I used to argue with, the man who said he didn't care *who* killed Roger Ackroyd and professed to be unmoved by the famous words, "Mr. Holmes, they were the footprints of a gigantic hound."

GHOST: You're wrong there. I was moved—moved to laughter—or would have been if I had wasted my time on that kind of trash.

J.B.: You can't have it both ways. You *did* read and you disliked what you read. That's your privilege, but it confers no right of moral snobbery. But tell me, what do they think of

crime fiction down where you come from?

GHOST: They loathe and despise it as I do. Crime holds no mystery for them; they know all about it ex officio.

J.B.: That's what I thought. It's only up here among living men that the idea of law, of an ordered life, coupled with an inquisitive impatience about mysteries and a skill in piercing them, provides rich materials for entertaining tales.

GHOST: There you are. Entertainment. You've given your case away. I don't read for entertainment; I read for knowledge and wisdom.

J.B.: And that is what shuts out detective stories. First you stiffen your mind against pleasure and then you look for things that the genre doesn't afford. You're a bad reader.

GHOST: What do you mean! It is generally admitted that I'm the best reader since—since—

J.B.: McGuffey? Yes, of course, you were an indefatigable reader. You had to read in order to write those serious accounts of serious books, terribly serious. Now many of those books are seen to be dull, false, pretentious, though you called them "important," "significant," "moving," "original." That's what happens in every age. If you'd begun by taking pleasure in literature instead of studying it, you wouldn't have

been fooled so often. Try to read Galsworthy now and see if Dorothy L. Sayers doesn't wear better.

GHOST: Galsworthy keeps the mind working on something. The sub-

---

I am stopped at the very threshold by the consistent use of the term "mystery"... Mystery stories, as such, are rarely well enough written to excite much interest. The real mysteries are not those of kidnapping or theft or murder, but psychological. That is why Simenon is unquestionably the greatest and the most widely read "mystery" writer of our time. He does not deal in solving mysteries: these are disposed of, usually, in the first chapter—we know who the murderer is, or the thief, or the embezzler. The mystery is, of course, in the character of the man or woman who commits the crime, and it is a mystery of character. Why? Simenon has this in common with all great writers—writers who throughout literature have probed character—none better than Shakespeare or, for that matter, Hawthorne or Henry James... The trouble with most professional "mystery" writers is that they long to be novelists, and so they pad out their "mysteries" with all kinds of extraneous materials which really do not explain the stumble into crime. Some of the traditionalists were better than that—Collins, for example, or that much neglected American Mary Roberts Rinehart, or in our day Faulkner—hard going as he is.

I think we should get away from the term "mystery" stories, unless we are indeed prepared to broaden its meaning—and speak instead of "crime" or even of "sin" stories.

HENRY STEELE COMMAGER

---

stance may be thin, but it's there.

J.B.: I know, Galsworthy had "ideas" and Sayers hasn't. That's your second error. You don't know a novel from a tale. A tale is its own excuse for being; it doesn't have to stuff your well-filled mind still fuller and make it stuffier yet. A tale charms by its ingenuity, by the plausibility with which it overcomes the suspicion that it couldn't happen. That is art. Learn to enjoy it. Read a few fairy tales, a few Arabian Nights to clear your mind of "knowledge and wisdom." Save your long face and restless eyes for the really great novelists who do handle the stuff of life and impart wisdom about it.

GHOST: There's no art outside of that; there's none in your rubbishy "tales" because there's nothing—not a thing—to carry away and reflect on.

J.B.: Of course there is. If you can grow lyrical over Proust's crumb of cake in the teacup, you can find charm in the ambiguity of any clue. The dog that did nothing in the nighttime is as justly famous as Cerberus, and T.S. Eliot found so much poetry in the Musgrave ritual that he lifted it to give a little class to one of his plays. Your trouble, dear Ghost, is—or was—that you poisoned your mind with sociology and stale ideas, so that you lost the power to appreciate the staples of literature: invention, surprise and suspense, plot and peripeteia, terse dialogue and good prose generally. Bone up on those and you'll soon be able to tell a good crime tale from a dull one, a Holmes from a Hawkshaw. Then perhaps your objections will fade away—as I see *you're* about to do. My regards to all our shady friends!

Jacques Barzun is coauthor of A Catalogue of Crime.

THE MARXIST APPROACH TO TENURE
A Validation of the Untenable

Robert B. Parker

As a reformed academic, I have had the chance to watch the slow dignification of the hard-boiled detective story. English departments now offer courses in it, and English professors now write about it. The departments do it in the hope of attracting students; the professors do it because if they don't publish they will perish or—the moral equivalent of perishing—they will be forced to teach. Such professors like the work of Hammett, Chandler, Macdonald and MacDonald, and (if they have Ph.D.'s from second-rate universities) Parker. But in order to make their pleasure in such writers profitable, they have to first make them seem suitable grist for the mill of tenure (smaller than which few things grind). Thus such professors examine such works in a frame: archetypal criticism, Freudian criticism, Marxist criticism. The work becomes the expression of larger motifs. It becomes important and thus fit subject for a scholar.

Numerous years in the professor dodge has taught me that one can argue ingeniously on behalf of any theory, applied to any piece of literature. This is rarely harmful because normally no one reads such essays. If someone does, it is only another professor doing background on his own article. If he mentions it to a student, the student is likely to ignore it. (Unless he is a graduate student. A graduate student will write it down before he ignores it.) But now and then one of these ingenious tenure-getters creeps out into the public domain, and people start believing it. Such is the case with Marxism and the private investigators.

It is a reasonably conventional allegation that the hard-boiled hero can profitably be seen in Marxist terms—"the honest proletariat," in Leslie Fielder's phrase. Certainly one can make a case for the Continental Op in the short stories (notably "The Cutting of Couffignal") and Sam Spade in *The Maltese Falcon,* who solves his partner's murder because it's bad business not to.

It is also quite true that the wealthy are often villainous in Chandler's work (although General Sternwood in *The Big Sleep* certainly is not, nor is Sewall Endicott, who appears in several of the novels). But that seems about as far as one can reasonably take such speculation. To claim that Hammett and Chandler were writing proletariat fiction is to read them very selectively. It is also to misread them. How Marxist is *The Thin Man?*

In "The Cutting of Couffignal" the Op captures a woman who offers him money and sex to let her go. He won't do it because, he says, he likes his work and is committed to it. In *Red Harvest* he cleans up a corrupt Western town even though he knows his employer will give him "merry hell" for it. In *The Dain Curse* he helps rescue a young woman from drug addiction and a mistaken belief in her own degeneracy, although he is not employed to do that. What have these actions to do with each other? Very little in terms of class struggle, very little in terms of the Op as a worker. But they say a good deal about the Op as a man.

In *The Maltese Falcon* Spade turns in a woman with whom he is apparently in love; it's clear the act costs him pain. When she asks him about it, he says, "I won't play the sap for you." Earlier in the novel, as they wait for Joel Cairo to appear, he tells her about a man named Flitcraft. It seems to be a way to pass the time, but it is a parable about Spade's vision of life and a warning to Brigid that he lives in keeping with that vision.

There were things Hammett was incapable of saying, or saw no need to say. The story of Flitcraft and Spade's refusal to "play the sap" were as far as he went in articulating a code. It wasn't Marxism. It was much more fundamental. It took Chandler to point out that the hard-boiled hero was concerned not with economics, but with honor.

When Hammett was learning to write, he was working in a world which, after the fiasco of World War I, found the man of honor an embarrassment and talk of honor naïve. It found toughness necessary and cynicism only sensible. So people like the Op and Spade talk about doing the job, or not playing that sap. In *The Glass Key* Ned Beaumont speaks of loyalty to a friend (*The Glass Key* was Hammett's favorite). In *The Big Sleep* Marlowe tells one of the Sternwood girls that he's a detective and "I work at it." But what they do, as opposed to what they say, is honorable. The hard-boiled hero is aware that honor has no definition. He has noticed that he who has it may well have died o'Wednesday. But he knows that there are things a man does and things he doesn't do, and it is not usually very hard to decide which is which. It is often wearisome to choose. The fact that such men elect to be honorable in a dishonorable world makes them heroic. As in most fundamental things that humans care for, honor is indefinable but easily recognized.

The hard-boiled hero belongs, therefore, not to the Marxist but to the chivalric tradition—a tradition he shares in this country with the Westerner. He is not of the people; he is alone. His adventures are solitary statements. His commitment is to a private moral code without which no other code makes any sense to him. He regularly reaffirms the code on behalf of people who don't have one.

He is the last gentleman, and to remain that he must often fight. Sometimes he must kill.

Robert B. Parker won the Mystery Writers of American Edgar for Promised Land.

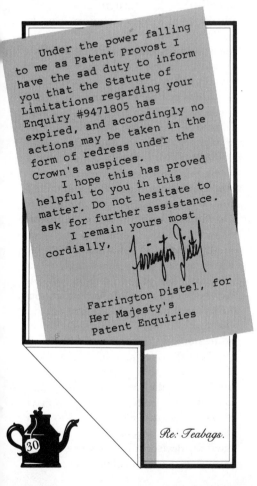

Under the power falling to me as Patent Provost I have the sad duty to inform you that the Statute of Limitations regarding your Enquiry #9471805 has expired, and accordingly no actions may be taken in the form of redress under the Crown's auspices.
    I hope this has proved helpful to you in this matter. Do not hesitate to ask for further assistance.
    I remain yours most cordially,

Farrington Distel, for Her Majesty's Patent Enquiries

Re: Teabags.

PROFESSIONAL JEALOUSY
A LESSON IN PATIENCE

Joyce Porter

During my twenty years as a professional writer, I have managed to avoid almost all contact with my pen-pushing colleagues. I did once, when a mere "first offender" in the business, attend a literary cocktail party, but I left almost immediately when somebody insulted me by asking if I were a publisher. However, writers are an intrusive breed and occasionally they penetrate my defences via the television set, pompously planking themselves down on my hearth rug before I can dash across and switch them into oblivion.

One of them made it the other day. He had me riveted to my chair. Not by the splendour of his presence, you understand, or the beauty of his eloquence, but by the sheer fascination of the background they were photographing him against. Would you believe floor-to-ceiling bookshelves?

Anyhow, I ignored the rubbish his nibs was spouting and took a good look at the books, naturally assuming that they were studio props because your genuine, dedicated, doing-it-for-eating-money author doesn't read anything except publishers' contracts and banker's cheques. But no, I was mistaken. The books were the real thing and without a doubt the personal property of the charlatan who was pontificating there in front of the cameras. How could I be so sure? Well, the books were all in sets of six. In other words, they were the free copies we bearers of the flag of culture

get as perks from our European publishers. (The Americans, with typical generosity, dish out ten.)

I couldn't believe my eyes. This joker must have kept every free copy of every edition of every book he had ever published! What strength of character! What nerve! What resolution! Had he no friends? After all, most of us who manage to get something into print are knee-deep in good old chums eager to grab one of our free copies rather than venture into a bookshop and *buy* one. (I wouldn't mind so much if they didn't think they were softening the blow by asking you to sign the damned thing.)

Well, when I'd got over the shock of seeing this star of the literary firmament broadcasting his niggardliness to the nation, I began to pay close attention to what he was saying. Such a consummate skinflint must have a message for us all.

Unfortunately, what he was saying proved to be a pretty fair sample of the usual drivel. In private, writers only talk about money, but in public they trot out the habitual phoney clichés of the trade. Viz.: no waiting for inspiration for us professionals ... moral obligation to grind out the daily stint just like the rest of you miserable wage slaves ... the loneliness ... the self-discipline ... the soaring imagination ... the creative blocks ... the soft black pencil on the creamy yellow paper ... characters who magically develop a life of their own and begin to take over ... blah, blah, blah.

And then he said it.

You could have heard my jaw drop a mile away.

In answer to some puerile question about one of his earlier best-sellers, he said (and I quote): "Yes, when I re-read it the other day, I must say I thought it had worn quite well."

When he'd *re-read* it? One of his *own* books?

I wouldn't re-read one of my books if you paid me! (Well, I would, actually, but you know what I mean.) Blimey, I have to write the damned things—and that's enough for anybody. I produce "funny" detective stories (though they don't make me laugh), and by the time I've thought up the plot, worked it out, written the first draft in longhand, typed the second draft and bashed out three copies of the final one, I've had it up to *here*! Nowadays I can't even face a last read-through for typing errors, and

when the proofs come in for correcting I start at the last page and work backwards. Believe me, any bright or original idea I might have had right at the very beginning is looking pretty tatty when I meet it for the sixth time or so. The books I write are meant to be wolfed down at one gulp on a train journey, or wherever, and thrown away. (I should be so lucky! Returned to the blooming library is more like it.) I don't expect anybody to read them half a dozen times, and I bitterly resent that I have to.

Come to think about it, I resent most things about being a writer. I resent having to sit there all alone at my desk. I resent all my brilliant ideas turning to dust the minute I get them down on paper. I resent the sheer physical labour of pushing a pen-nib over all those acres and acres of sneering white paper. I resent the noise a typewriter makes. I resent my publisher asking me

COMPETITIVE LINE-UP

Best-Preserved	Wettest	Fattest	Most Chic	Tiredest
JUDGE DEE	MAIGRET	NERO WOLFE	ASTA	MARTIN BECK

MARTY NORMAN

BOOKIES

Mss.

Catherine Aird, *Parting Breath* (Jane
  Austen's last letter)
Robert Barnard, *Case of the Missing
  Brontë* (Emily's manuscript)
Amanda Cross, *James Joyce Murder*
  (Joyce's unpublished mss.)
Richard Hoyt, *Siskiyou Two-Step* (lost
  Shakespeare mss.)
Jane Langton, *Emily Dickinson Is
  Dead* (Emily's Centennial)

Book Dealers

John L. Breen, *The Gathering Place*
  (bookstore owner's heart attack)
Roy Harley Lewis, *Cracking of Spines*
  (Matthew Coll, antiquarian
  dealer; other titles)
M.K. Wren, *Wake Up, Darlin' Corey*
  (Conan Flagg, Oregon book
  dealer)

Writers

Josephine Bell, *Treachery in Type*
  (historical romance writers)
Leela Cutter, *Murder After Teatime*
  (dotty old mystery writer)
Richard Forrest, *Death in the Willows*
  (children's book author)
L.A. Taylor, *Footnote to Murder*
  (researcher for true crime writer)

Crime Courses

Edward Candy, *Words for Murder
  Perhaps* (crime fiction course)
John Sladek, *Invisible Green* (reunion
  of disbanded mystery club)

Libraries

Charles Goodrum, *Dewey Decimated*
  (D.C. private library)
Michael Innes, *Ampersand Papers*
  (archivist challenges Appleby)
Stella Phillips, *Hidden Wrath*
  (university library)

write off as a solid-gold idiot anybody
who implies that I have.

And I'm not really whining about
writing being hard labour, am I? Why,
even on a good day I reckon I spend
more time playing Patience than I do
penning deathless prose. Luckily, I know
three different ways of laying out the
cards; otherwise, I might well drop down
dead with sheer boredom. But what else
can I do when Literature goes sour on
me? I only need a fleeting distraction,
something that doesn't take me away
from my desk, something that can be
instantly abandoned should inspiration
strike, and something that demands no
intellectual or creative effort. What else
is there except Patience that will guarantee to send me back to my writing almost
as quickly as I left it?

A well-known American writer once
said: "I sometimes ask myself what a
grown man like me is doing, sitting there
all day telling himself stories." It's the
most perceptive remark I've ever heard
a writer make about his job. That's precisely what writers should be doing—
telling themselves stories. Not playing
endless games of Patience.

But, back to that pundit on the television who actually reads his own books.
Could it be that his books are so good
and so well written that, even twenty
years later, he can . . . ? Is that why he's
on the telly and I'm not?

I decided that it was all giving me an
inferiority complex, and I switched the
set off. Tenth-rate writers simply can't
afford to indulge in self-doubt.

Back to the grindstone.

My own fault, really. I shouldn't
have got hooked on eating.

Now, where had we got to? Ah, yes!
One face upwards and six face downwards. One face upwards and five face
downwards. One face upwards . . .

to cut a thousand words. I resent my
publisher asking me to add a thousand
words. I resent critics who suggest that I
haven't written a masterpiece—and

*Joyce Porter is the author of the hilarious
Inspector Dover mystery series.*

THE CHRISTMAS MYSTERY LECTURE

Bill Vande Water

GARY RENAUD

The selling of Christmas.

Let us address ourselves to that curious paradox of detective fiction known as the "Christmas" mystery. The most curious thing about it is that it exists at all. Christmas is supposed to be the time of peace, of joy and love, when Macy and Gimbel shake hands, suddenly repentant Scrooges toss ten-dollar bills in Salvation Army kettles, families are reunited, old friendships rekindled, and children are on their best behavior. Why spoil such warm, nostalgic, tug-at-the-heartstrings scenes with a petty theft, much less a murder?

The cynic will answer with one word: money. Being the high-minded people we are, however, we shall ignore the base suggestion that authors write merely to sell to the Christmas issues of mystery magazines. (Besides, Isaac Asimov's "The Thirteenth Day of Christmas" came out in July.)

Instead let us consider that Christmas is joined with crime for historical, indeed theological, accuracy. One of the wise men (they figure as detectives in R.L. Steven's "The Three Travellers") brought myrrh, an embalming spice. King Herod celebrated the first Christmas with a mass killing of babies. Even mistletoe has a criminal record: it was the murder weapon used to kill Balder, the most loved of the Norse gods. And the Puritan fathers of Massachusetts Bay Colony made the celebration of Christmas itself a crime, punishable by a five-shilling fine.

It becomes apparent that in real life, then, crimes do occur at Christmas. Good will may increase, but so does the homicide rate. By some strange quirk of human nature, the same season that fills the stores and churches also fills the jails and morgues—and motivates the mystery writer like no other holiday could ever hope to.

We must understand, however, the peculiar distinction between Christmas mystery novels and Christmas mystery stories. The novels, without exception, favor homicide as a leitmotif; in them, a writer may use pine, spruce, holly or even money for his Christmas green, but his Christmas red had better be blood. The stories, on the other hand, are partial to theft and burglary.

The tradition of the nonlethal Christmas detective story goes back to the master himself and his "Adventure of the Blue Carbuncle." This story also started the tradition of stolen and hidden jewels and was followed by G.K. Chesterton's "The Flying Stars," Dorothy L.

Sayers' "The Necklace of Pearls," Margery Allingham's "The Snapdragon and the C.I.D.," Ellery Queen's "The Dauphin's Doll," Agatha Christie's "The Adventure of the Christmas Pudding," Georges Simenon's "Maigret's Christmas" and Damon Runyon's "Dancing Dan's Christmas."

Conan Doyle also started the tradition of the "season of forgiveness," in which the criminal, though discovered, is allowed to escape with nothing more than a warning and a good scare.

One of the best of the Christmas short stories is August Derleth's "The Adventure of the Unique Dickensians." This double pastiche combines elements of Doyle and Dickens and is a true tour de force.

Christmas mystery novels fit into three categories. The first is a Christmas mystery by courtesy only. Christmas is mentioned, but it is really there as an excuse for assembling a group of people who otherwise would not be caught dead together—so that at least one of them may be so caught. The best example of this misuse of the Christmas theme is Agatha Christie's *Murder for Christmas*; the next best (or worst, depending on how strongly you feel about this type of thing) is Michael Innes' *Comedy of Terrors*; not quite as bad, but reaching, is Georgette Heyer's *Envious Casca.*

The second category of Chrismas mystery novel features, more often than not, police procedurals. Private detectives and nosy old ladies may go home for the holidays, but for the police it's just another busy day, what with pickpockets and shoplifters working the Christmas rush. Among the best of these realistic, ironic novels are Ed McBain's *Pusher* and *Sadie When She Died,* Dell Shannon's *No Holiday for Crime* and James McClure's *The Gooseberry Fool.* Not a police procedural, but still falling within this category, is Ian Fleming's *On Her Majesty's Secret Service,* in which James

NASTY NOEL

For an analysis and annotated bibliography of Christmas mystery novels, you are commended to *Mistletoe Malice: The Life and Times of the Christmas Murder Mystery* by Albert Menendez. Difficult to find, even in specialty stores, but readily available from Holly Tree Press, P.O. Box 7002, Silver Springs, Md. 20907.

David Alexander, *Shoot a Sitting Duck*
Michael Allen, *Spence and the Holiday Murders*
Marian Babson, *The Twelve Deaths of Christmas*
Gavin Black, *A Dragon for Christmas*
Nicholas Blake, *Thou Shell of Death; The Corpse in the Snowman; The Smiler with a Knife*
Carter Brown, *A Corpse for Christmas*
Leo Bruce, *Crack of Doom (Such Is Death)*
Thomas Chastain, *911*
Agatha Christie, *A Holiday for Murder (Murder for Christmas)*
Noel Clad, *The Savage*
Alisa Craig, *Murder Goes Mumming*
Joel Dane, *The Christmas Tree Murders*
Charles Dickens, *The Mystery of Edwin Drood*
Mary Durham, *Keeps Death His Court*
Mignon Eberhart, *Postmark Murder*
Terence Feeley, *Who Killed Santa Claus*
Elizabeth Ferrars, *The Small World of Murder*
Ian Fleming, *On Her Majesty's Secret Service*
Martha Grimes, *The Man with a Load of Mischief*
Dashiell Hammett, *The Thin Man*
Cyril Hare, *An English Murder*
Georgette Heyer, *Envious Casca*
John Howlett, *The Christmas Spy*
Fergus Hume, *A Coin of Edward VII*
Alan Hunter, *Landed Gently*
Jack Iams, *Do Not Murder Before Christmas*
Michael Innes, *A Comedy of Terrors*
Henry Kane, *A Corpse for Christmas*

Mary Kelly, *The Christmas Egg*
Glenn Kezer, *The Queen Is Dead*
C.H.B. Kitchin, *Crime at Christmas*
Alfred Lawrence, *Columbo: A Christmas Killing*
Richard Lockridge, *Dead Run*
Miriam Lynch, *Crime for Christmas*
Charlotte MacLeod, *Rest You Merry; The Convivial Codfish*
Ngaio Marsh, *Tied Up in Tinsel*
Ed McBain, *The Pusher; Sadie When She Died; Ghosts*
Helen McCloy, *Mr. Splitfoot; Burn This*
James McClure, *The Gooseberry Fool*
David William Meredith, *The Christmas Card Murders*
Magdalen Nabb, *Death of an Englishman*
Anne Nash, *Said with Flowers*
Jack Pearl, *Victims*
Ellery Queen, *The Finishing Stroke*
Patrick Ruell, *Red Christmas*
David Serafin, *Christmas Rising*
Dell Shannon, *No Holiday for Crime*
Nancy Spain, *Cinderella Goes to the Morgue*
Van Siller, *The Lonely Breeze*
Michael Underwood, *A Party to Murder*
Thomas Walsh, *The Resurrection Man*

Anthologies: Isaac Asimov, *The Twelve Crimes of Christmas;* Thomas F. Godfrey, *Murder for Christmas*

Children's Mysteries: Laura Palmer, *A Merry Mix-Up* (ages 5–8); Wylly Folk St. John, *The Christmas Tree Mystery* (ages 8–12); Jean Van Leeuwen, *The Great Christmas Kidnapping Caper* (ages 7–11).

Change of Pace (other holidays): Margot Arnold, *Death of a Voodoo Doll* (Mardi Gras); W.J. Burley, *Wycliffe and the Scapegoat* (Hallowe'en); Jane Langton, *Minuteman Murder* (Patriot's Day); Ngaio Marsh, *Death of a Fool* (midwinter solstice).

MARTY NORMAN

HOLIDAY PLANS

Passage has been booked in the names of J. John Teasdale, John T. Rowntree and Caroline Rowntree aboard the *Queen Elizabeth II,* sailing from Southampton to Bermuda (with a forty-eight-hour stopover in New York) on Boxing Day, arriving on the New Year. The accommodations requested were one double room with private lavatory, an adjoining sitting room and a connecting single room, also with private washroom. Second sittings for all meals were specified.

Enquiries have been made of Caribe Transport Ltd. in the name of Laurence Shipley. Mr. Shipley has been advised *The Banana Boat,* a vessel with Panamanian registry, is due to leave Hollyhead on 7th January and can accommodate eight paying guests. Mr. Shipley tentatively reserved two berths.

The *Cotswolds Crier* Positions Open department ran the following advert: Amiable couple, she with nursing degree (specializing in neuralgia cases) and he with secretarial skills, seek work placement. Reply in strictest confidence to box no. 13.

Bond makes his violent escape from SPECTRE headquarters on Christmas Eve and Christmas Day. In these novels the Christmas background offers a depressing commentary on the kind of world in which peace is so frequently converted to death.

The third and perhaps most effective category of Christmas novel is the one in which the crime, or detection, or both, could take place in no other season. The accouterments of Christmas are necessary to the novel's success. These tend to feature Santa Claus. Burglars, detectives, bank robbers, the police, murderers, victims, even a few (relatively) innocent bystanders—all have made use of this disguise. Nor have Santa's criminal appearances been confined to fiction. A.C. Greene's *The Santa Claus Bank Robbery* concerns a real-life use of the ubiquitous Santa disguise that went dead wrong. (There is, by the way, a Midwestern state that has made it illegal for women to appear on the street dressed as Santa Claus.

Next to Santa the most popular Christmas motifs, in a novel, are Christmas house parties, reunions, mistletoe, trees, toys and seasonal foods. In *The Finishing Stroke* Ellery Queen even makes special use of a song, "The Twelve Days of Christmas." Be assured, however, that novels in this category do not use Christmas as mere trimming; it is integral to their plots.

In closing, may I remind you that Charles Dickens, creator of that sentimental tale *A Christmas Carol,* eventually tired of all the Christmas niceties. The next time someone tells you he longs for a typically Dickensian Christmas, ask him if he had in mind the kind of Christmas Eve Dickens gave to *Edwin Drood.*

Bah, humbug to all, and to all a good fright.

Bill Vande Water works with used news at the CBS News Film & Tape Archive.

WEATHER, AND OTHER INCLEMENTS

Duncan Kyle

JUDITH WRIGHT

There is a kind of novel, one I greatly enjoy reading and try to write, in which there is an extra principal character: the setting. I have no idea who wrote the first, but I think my own first realisation of the importance of *place* came with *Wuthering Heights*, which I read young because I grew up a comfortable morning's walk from the Haworth Moors.

They're storyteller country, these novels, and they're popular because people love tales that take them, as the song says, to faraway places with strange-sounding names. It may be escapism, it may be just armchair travel. But people do enjoy a hero engaged not only with human opponents, but with Nature herself. That, after all, is the beleaguered history of mankind.

Richard Hannay, handcuffed to the beauteous damsel, dragging her across

Scottish moors that are at once enemy and friend, provides a good example: it's the moors that make the story sing, not the people; the Forth Bridge, not the villain. Erskine Childers' *Riddle of the Sands,* with one man in a tiny boat confronted not only by Germans but by murderous intricacies of weather and tide, is another. It may even be the best one of all.

But there *is* C.S. Forester: not his *African Queen,* though it's a good example, but *Brown on Resolution,* with a lone sailor on a tiny volcanic island pitted against a warship. Sound unlikely? Begin it, and be convinced. Feel the hazard the island presents, scalpel-sharp rocks, heat to flay off the skin. Mark again the extraordinary demand to endure, which has always been, and is, man's need.

Some people can compose magical settings and make them real. Lionel Davidson's deep ravine in *Smith's Gazelle,* which not only presents problems of survival but forces bonds to grow between people with cause for enmity, is one of these. Davidson's *The Rose of Tibet,* too (without in any way disparaging Hilton's *Lost Horizon),* is a masterly demonstration of the force of place upon people.

And that, really, is what I'm talking about. But I *do* mean place, not object. Ships don't count: they are too nearly human, anyway. Aircraft, on the other hand, are all too neutral, forcing the attention back toward people and weather and places.

Okay, okay, so where's Hammond Innes? Isn't he the international grandmaster? He is indeed, and I'm coming to him now. He's criticised, sometimes, for failing to create interesting people—which all too often means he doesn't write about the boozy infidelities of antiquarian booksellers. In any bookshop you'll find work by authors who do, but you'll find only one Hammond Innes. Listen. A man is in a small boat on the Atlantic, looking for a difficult and dangerous landfall:

An islet loomed in the fog, white with the stain of guano, and as I skirted it, the wind came funnelling down from the hidden heights above, strong enough to flatten the sea; and then the downdraught turned to an updraught, sucking the fog with it, and for an instant I glimpsed rock cliffs . . . they rose stupendous to lose themselves in vapour; dark volcanic masses of gabbro rock, high as the gates of hell.

Well, you could call it florid, I suppose. You could say there are clichés around. But having said whatever you're going to say, read it again, and *sniff!* Something in your nostrils now—and a picture on the screen of your mind, of place and man and hazard—that tickles something deep inside. We know we're going, once again, to stir up those ancestor-memories. Read on, read on—how on earth could you not?

It is a real place (St. Kilda, if you must know, disguised as Laerg) and recognisable to the place-man. Innes has been there and has the feel of it. With him it's always a real place, and he can show it to you as no one else can. You become enmeshed in the realities of storm and cold, of animals, of navigation, of mining and geology. It's not just identification: you and the hero seem to merge.

Going there, of course, is all-important. It *is* possible, and indeed has been *done,* to write place novels by careful reading of, for example, the *National*

Geographic. But it just isn't the same. I wrote a novel whose finale was played out on a small island and a sea stack in the Shetlands. I'd read about them and seen a lot of photographs. Yet when I got there . . . Nobody had said the great skuas (called Bonxies, locally), which nest there among the grass tussocks in comfortable solitude, would fly at me on five-foot wings, from six directions at once, fast and silent, brushing by close, rough enough to raise welts on my face. Nobody had said the only path ran up beside the high cliffs and the skuas knew all about it and were careful to herd you that way. Nobody had told me what it's like to stand over six hundred sheer feet and watch the gannets fall suddenly, like white darts, after fish.

Go there and material accumulates. The pity is that one can only use so much before the book becomes overloaded. Mine do, anyway. Hammond Innes' unique skill lies in the way he draws in the detail, so that the plot is ultimately composed of small parts of knowledge. Sometimes I turn green, I really do.

But if he's the nonpareil, there are others: Desmond Bagley, conjuring up the Andes in *High Citadel*; Derek Lambert's grim and grinding Moscow in *Angels in the Snow*; Berkely Mather (number two only to Innes), drawing beautiful pictures of the Himalaya lying gigantically in wait to oppress a few lonely, desperate—and desperately *small*—men.

No women? Come now, I did begin with Emily. Yes, there are women. Mary Stewart knows how to use a setting. So does Helen MacInnes. But in general (in *my* experience, that is, and I'll be delighted to widen it) women writers like the people larger than the landscape. No criticism there, or implied, just a matter of approach.

Duncan Kyle is a past chairman of the Crime Writers' Association.

JUSTICE

Light
Dawns

One year later.
Lady Teasdale has switched to Strega.

I'm sorry I can't offer you tea, but it's not permitted here. The only tea offered is taken with meals. Bulk, you understand, quite rough to the palate. Lord Teasdale would never have approved.

I drink as much of it as I can.

Never cared for the almond tea, I admit it. You don't have to like something to create it, you understand. And I only came up with it in desperation, when he said he'd lose the Hall, go so low he'd never get back up. I thought if I saved him he'd reciprocate, give me shares, and make me on the road to independent.

One year later. Becca continues to work the lower left corner. Vicar Fogg proposes one more time.

The lie almost killed me. "My blend," he called it. "My special recipe."

No such thing. Who suggested quick-boiling the almonds and straining the leaves through the residue? Not he, I can assure you.

He was a watcher, a sucker, a leech and a sponge.

I hated that tea, did you know?

I hate it to this day. It left me poor and should have made me my fortune. It earned him a title. Invitations to the Café Royale and Mayfair clubs. Whilst I stayed here. Protecting his two dirty little secrets.

He was not the master of House of Teas; I was. But no one knew it.

When little John was born, I realised my turn would never come. Everything would go to family, even family from the wrong side of the blanket. And where would I be then? No better off.

When business took a slump, I was pleased. Every time I heard of a sliding profit, I retired to my rooms and gloated.

Finally, I made my suggestion: Teasdale sandwich spreads to accompany Teasdale tea.

Of course, he couldn't resist. I watched him tinker, knowing full well I'd never let him produce one ounce.

When he announced the crest was arriving, there was no way I'd stand in the background while he celebrated what rightfully belonged to me.

I told him a touch of the gout was on me. I'd never lied before; why shouldn't he believe me?

Then, Friday late, I entered the pantry and replaced the sugar in the bowl with cyanide crystals. Turning to leave, I careened into the sideboard, nearly bringing it down. Luckily, no one came to investigate.

Next morning, I slipped out to make sure things were as I left them. Whelks saw me moving about. Killed him, of course. A minor loss, won't you agree? I

to my rooms and discovered the button missing. I tried the pond first. That's when Simon saw the bushes move. I just stayed low and soon his cowardice drove him inside.

When I came out again at ten, they were *all* out there, pulling in Whelks. I cold-cocked Simon; he never knew what hit him. The Colonel was more difficult. I had no hope an army man would ever be taken by surprise. But he's getting on, isn't he, and it's been quite some time since that Cross was presented. I barely shoved him and he went down.

Never did find the button.

The rest, of course, you know. The Colonel and his diagrams, once he un-

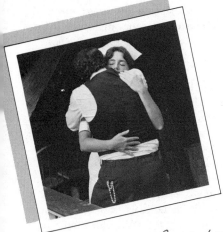

One year later.
Harriet and Simon, after relieving the Honourable Constancia Portegas-Jones of the trappings of wealth.

One year later.
V.C. Cholmondesley, private and discreet enquiries, has just opened its offices in a charming flat off Foxborough Mews.

waited until the musicale began, then dragged him off to the pond.

I arrived for tea at just past four. His Lordship was alone. He poured, oblivious to my rage.

"I've brought you this bit of sandwich I was testing, sir, for our filling. Would you be so kind as to try it?"

I shall never forget the look on his face. Never. I'd poisoned it, too.

I thought I was safe until I got back

scrambled them and realized my room overlooked Whelks' working in the garden.

He didn't know why, however, and I chose not to enlighten him.

I saved my story for the papers.

My House of Teas by Everett Roudebush. Some called it *The Tainted Tea Tragedy*.

It made it all worth it.

Even this.

ON ADVICE OF COUNSEL

Carolyn Wheat

"**V**ery few people," said Nero Wolfe, "like lawyers. I don't. They are inveterate hedgers. They think everything has two sides, which is nonsense."

The great mystery-reading public disagrees. The best-selling series detective of all time is a member of the bar: Erle Stanley Gardner's Perry Mason. (Elizabeth Mainwaring, in *Murder in Pastiche,* records the only known meeting of Wolfe, disguised as Trajan Beare, and Mason, alias Jerry Pason.)

Since the task of a detective in a mystery novel is to bring the murderer to justice, logically the prosecutor should be the genre's legal hero. Yet it is the criminal defense attorney—the Don Quixote of the courtroom—who engages the public imagination. Hard-drinking, flamboyant, working on the edge of the law, it is Mason we adore, not the prosaic Hamilton Burger.

So powerful is the Mason myth that real lawyers trying real cases in real courtrooms invoke his name as they address prospective jurors. They apologize in advance for the regrettable fact that unlike the fictional lawyer, they can't promise to unmask the perpetrator as part of their courtroom performance.

Perry achieves his results through the lawyer's most powerful tool—his mouth. Asking incisive questions, hammering away at a weak witness, revealing startling information with a flourish so theatrical that D.A. Burger invariably labels the trial "a circus," Mason is a courtroom wizard. But he doesn't do his own legwork. Paul Drake hunts down the birth certificate, deed or second will guaranteed to snatch acquittal from the jaws of conviction.

The prolific Gardner tried hard to balance the scales, but it was no use. Writing as A.A. Fair, he celebrated the honest, tough prosecutor in Doug Selby, but it was Mason who was imitated; fellow mystery authors invariably chose defenders over prosecutors as heroes.

John J. Malone, the bibulous little lawyer of Craig Rice's imagination, is a far cry from Perry Mason. For one thing, Malone is deeply interested in his retainer, which he accepts at least twice over, having a lofty disregard for the finer points of conflict of interest. Malone's English cousin is Dr. Gideon Fell's favorite lawyer, Patrick Butler. Irish, emotional, eloquent and a pretty fair drinker, Malone lives in a world where fees loom large—a refreshing note in a profession whose fictional practitioners seem to confine their representation to close friends.

Case in point: Antony Maitland, who until recently did only defense work. Even if his client by some fluke began the book a stranger, by end Maitland will have risked disgrace, disbarment and even death on his behalf—and all without mention of a fee. Harold Q. Masur's Scott Jordan, on the other hand, gets involved in his cases only after a mysterious blonde, wearing nothing but her nail polish, turns up dead in his bathtub. An earlier version of the wisecracking Jordan is C.W. Grafton's Gil Henry, whose first adventure, *The*

Rat Began to Gnaw the Rope, was recently reissued.

And then there's Rumpole. Here at last is the true professional—the man who knows to the penny just how much legal work he must do to finance household supplies for She Who Must Be Obeyed. Horace Rumpole understands it is neither legal scholarship nor courtroom eloquence that will win the day, but sheer trickery aided by luck. He works within the limits of the law with the flair and precision of an ice skater performing school figures. Francis Pettigrew, Cyril Hare's tired barrister, is a sadder, wiser, less poetic Rumpole, yet no less a realist. He suffers at the hands of insensitive judges and endures the bizarre (to an American lawyer) rituals of the Inns of Court.

The flamboyant image of the high-powered criminal lawyer is alive and well in San Francisco, where Gene Thompson's Dade Cooley maintains his office when not being flown to the side of a client in trouble. Arthur Crook, Anthony Gilbert's shady barrister, manages to be both flamboyant and a loser at the same time. Ditto the redoubtable H.C. Bailey's Joshua Clunk.

Shadier than Crook and Clunk are two lawyer-characters created by Erle Stanley Gardner as counterpoints to the virtuous Perry Mason: the disbarred Donald Lam and the con artist Lester Leith. John Roeburt's Jigger Moran was also stricken from the rolls. Still worse, Randolph Mason, Melville Davisson Post's chilling creation, and his spiritual descendant Block's Ehrengraf.

As fictional detectives, judges have fared even less well than prosecuting attorneys. There's August Derleth's homespun Ephraim Peck and Robert Van Gulik's Judge Dee, but perhaps the fact that he solves mysteries in the exotic setting of T'ang China, without benefit of Miranda warnings, adds to our interest in him.

Even those mystery writers whose

A FOOL FOR A CLIENT

If you think you might like to conduct your own defense, the following books may serve as a primer:

Delano Ames: *She Shall Have Murder*
Mel Arrighi: *Freak Out*
H.C. Bailey: *The Garston Murder Case*
James Francis Bonnell: *Death over Sunday*
Henry Cecil: *Brother in Law; Daughters in Law; Fathers in Law*
August Derleth: *Murder Stalks the Wakely Family*
D.M. Devine: *My Brother's Killer*
Warwick Downing: *The Mountains West of Town*
Lesley Egan: *A Case for Appeal*
Sydney Fowler: *The Murder in Bethnal Square*
Erle Stanley Gardner: *The Case of the . . .* (series, 85 titles); *The D.A. Holds a Candle*

Anthony Gilbert: *A Case for Mr. Crook; After the Verdict*
Michael Gilbert: *Smallbone Deceased*
Edward Grierson: *The Second Man*
Richard Himmel: *I Have Gloria Kirby*
Roderic Jeffries: *Dead Against the Lawyers*
Frederic Arnold Kummer: *The Clue of the Twisted Face*
Hugh McCutcheon: *And the Moon Was Full*
Ross Macdonald: *The Ferguson Affair*
Harold Q. Masur: *Bury Me Deep*
Margaret Millar: *Ask for Me Tomorrow*
Hugh Pentecost: *Around Dark Corners*
Frank G. Presnell: *Too Hot to Handle*
Craig Rice: *Trial by Fury*
David St. John: *Return from Vorkuta*
Michael Underwood: *Murder Made Absolute*
Sara Woods: *Let's Choose Executors (series, each with a Shakespearean title)*

detective characters didn't attend law school have used the law as a background. Lord Peter first sees his Harriet as she stands in the dock in *Strong Poison.* Albert Campion goes to court in *Flowers for the Judge.* Mr. and Mrs. North confront death while making their wills (leaving everything to the cats, of course) in *A Key to Death.*

Mysteries set in English solicitors' offices include: *She Shall Have Murder* by Delano Ames; *Bloody Instructions,* by Sara Woods; *Smallbone Deceased,* by Michael Gilbert; and newcomer Sarah Caudwell's *Thus Was Adonis Murdered,* featuring a chambers of bright young tax lawyers.

On this side of the Atlantic there's Richard North Patterson's portrait of an old Southern law firm in *The Outside Man,* Brian Lysaght's prestigious Los Angeles firm in *Special Circumstances,* and the courtroom atmosphere of *Kennedy for the Defense* by George V. Higgins and *Dutch Shea, Jr.* by John Gregory Dunne.

Two sides of the criminal coin are presented by Dorothy Uhnak's *False Witness,* starring Manhattan A.D.A. Lynne Jacobi, and Julie Smith's *Death Turns a Trick,* introducing San Francisco defense lawyer Rebecca Schwartz. *See also* (as we say in the trade) Winston Lyon's *Criminal Court,* featuring A.D.A. Barbara Driscoll, and *One Just Man,* James Mills' fantasy of the day the Legal Aid Society shut down the criminal justice system. As antidote, there's Lillian O'Donnell's compassionate Mici Anhalt, who obtains justice for crime victims through New York's Victim-Witness Assistance Program.

Nothing grips the public imagination more than the sensational trial, and mystery fiction has provided its share. Agatha Christie's *Witness for the Prosecution* is a tour de force of legal twists and turns. In *Trial and Error,* by Anthony Berkeley, a man is determined to prove a charge of murder—against himself. In contrast, in C.W. Grafton's *Beyond a Reasonable Doubt,* a lawyer accused of murder conducts his own defense; probably the best cross-examination ever put on paper. In *The Glass Village,* Ellery Queen deliberately creates an Alice-in-Wonderland courtroom as Judge Lewis Shinn conducts a mock trial in order to stave off a lynching. James M. Cain's *The Postman Always Rings Twice* presents the *film noir* version of the court system, and Margaret Truman takes us behind the scenes of the biggest legal backdrop of all in *Murder in the Supreme Court.*

Arguably, the greatest courtroom novel is Robert Traver's *Anatomy of a Murder.* So thoroughly does it examine the extensive trial preparation process that the trial itself doesn't begin until halfway through the book. Then its author takes us on the roller-coaster ride

Simon tore it up.

I, the undersigned, bequeath to my leg for the duration do hereby the use of ... al wife Clare ... of her lifetime, ... se, 13 End ... lifetime ... ady Tea ... financial ... The Hous ... hat said wife employment, ... and week ... ctainer, the ... Upon the ... dale, Tea ... from The ... v only ... ntree, ... Lady Caro, Lower ... Court, Lower ... nessed, ... all income ... e of Teas revert to ... ssue, John T. Ro ... other, the ... Everet ... chful r ... ugings, oard compensation for Roudebush, fai ... ngth of his ... eath of I ... ouse ai ... J. John Teasdale ... approved and se ... Slaughter o ... spinster o

SCOFFLAWS

Cocaine was legal when Holmes injected it, but the same can't be said for Moses Wine's favorite relaxer, according to Roger L. Simon. Don't worry, Moses, it's only a misdemeanor.

GEORGE TORRIE/NEW YORK DAILY NEWS

Charles Paris, Simon Brett's actor-detective, regularly impersonates police officers. If he did it in New York, he'd be risking a year in jail.

When Asey Mayo committed burglary in Phoebe Atwood Taylor's *Proof of the Pudding,* he was looking at two to six years in the can.

Romance writer-detective Patience McKenna escapes from jail in Orania Papazoglou's *Sweet, Savage Death.* Penalty: four years max.

Spenser could go to jail twice, once for coercion (*Early Autumn*), a felony carrying a penalty of up to seven years, and again in Robert B. Parker's *Ceremony*—this time for promoting prostitution.

As if Gervase Fen's reckless driving wasn't enough to put him behind bars, there's his habit of borrowing other people's cars, as in Edmund Crispin's *The Moving Toyshop.* Give him seven years.

In Barbara Paul's *The Fourth Wall,* Abigail James risks a fifteen-year jail term when she commits assault in the first degree.

The ultimate crime? Holmes fails to prevent a murder; Queen and Fell abet suicides; and Wimsey, Poirot and Drury Lane all commit murder. Throw away the key!   *C. W.*

---

that is a criminal trial. One day up (your cross-examination brought out a point in your client's favor), the next day down (the judge admitted a damaging piece of evidence), then up again (your witness came through). Traver accurately portrays the anxiety, the identification with the client, the inner mind of the trial lawyer. And, on top of all that, presents a genuine mystery, with a twist ending that turns all our legal assumptions upside down.

Why are legal mysteries so popular? As Arthur Train's Mr. Tutt once remarked, "the law offers greater opportu-

nities to be at one and the same time a Christian and a horse trader than any other professon." Practicing what he preached, Tutt used the law's most despised weapon, the loophole, in a manner unprecedented in legal annals—on the side of justice. Perhaps that is the ultimate appeal of the Masons and Rumpoles and Maitlands: the triumph of justice mixed with the unholy joy of beating the system.

Carolyn Wheat is the author of Dead Man's Thoughts, *featuring Brooklyn lawyer Cass Jameson.*

"Now read me the part again where I disinherit everybody."

DISINHERITING EVERYBODY

Ebeneezer Nizer

You can't take it with you, that's true, but you can so tie it up that no one else can take it away, either.

And as long as you're not planning on living up to (dying up to?) expectations, you might as well disappoint your lawyer as well. He's probably anticipating a handsome fee for drawing up your will, but as of this year you can inform him that his services are no longer required; you're perfectly capable of issuing a legally binding, bona-fide, court-acceptable document yourself. And you can, too, with a little prompting from the Mesa Publishing Company, producer of various Consumer Legal Kits™ dealing with, respectively, Wills, Summary Divorce (where were they when Henry VIII needed them?), Power of Attorney, Promissory Notes, Small Claims and House Sales as well as Residential Leases.

Prepared by a certified attorney-at-law, the Wills Kit includes a standard will form for you to adapt (or slavishly follow, if you wish) and a simple step-by-step explanation of how it's to be filled in, witnessed, dated, even signed. What's more, to the horror of your disinherited, it should prove unbreakable, provided you adhere to the guidelines.

Your will must be witnessed by two reasonably sane individuals, with at least the education to write their names on the dotted line. It would be most cunning if you could induce two of your newly disinherited to act as will witnesses; that way you have the double pleasure of abandoning them and watching them pretend it doesn't matter. Even Machiavelli could not plan things better.

Regarding wills, the more idiosyncratic they are, the more apt they are to be found in a mystery novel. Mystery wills, for example, are rarely written on paper—that's too flammable. H. Rider Haggard found the perfect nonperishable substitute: human skin. What's more, in *Mr. Meeson's Will,* the one tattooed on a woman's back was upheld by the court!

A superior mystery will will, naturally, be written under duress. In Patricia Wentworth's *The Fingerprint* it came about as a response to an anonymous letter, requesting, surprise, surprise, remembrance. In Allingham's *Death of a Ghost,* it was the heirs under stress: the will stipulated they must convene once a year; on the eighth reunion, when they'd been lulled into a sense of ease, that's when one of the heirs was dispatched.

But the best of the wills, the one disinheritors like the most, tries to duplicate Charles Dickens' *Bleak House* situation. In this, inheritance shenanigans dragged on for years until, finally, there was no inheritance left—it had all gone to pay legal fees.

One final note: if you're planning on disinheriting the world, don't confide this to them, unless you're rather in a hurry to be on your way. They'll be delighted to help you out—feet first.

Ebeneezer Nizer chases ambulances.

THAT "BASTARD VERDICT"

Avon Curry

The Scots, as any Scott will tell you, are an exceptional race. They remain distinctively themselves although linked geographically and historically to a richer nation to the south, and in no area of life are they more "separate" than in their system of law. Scottish law has many of the costumes and settings of English law, but the terminology is different.

It may surprise you to learn, for instance, that the Sheriff plays an important part in Scotland—but he would die of the shock to his dignity if he were asked to wear a star and a six-gun. There is also an important official called the Procurator Fiscal, a term that alarms Americans because they feel it has something to do with tax prosecutions. Nothing of the kind. He fulfils a role something like that of the French *juge d'instruction,* looks into suspected crime and, in the case of an unexplained death, is the equivalent of the English coroner.

And speaking of the unexplained death, we come to murder and the part of Scottish law that interests crime fans most—the verdict Not Proven.

Not Proven can be brought in for any accusation, but it takes on its utmost importance in a murder trial. For here the accused has a two-out-of-three chance of walking out free, whereas in the rest of the world, in general, there are only two verdicts: Guilty and Not Guilty. The Scots would say that as usual they are ahead of everyone else in providing an alternative to the Not Guilty verdict.

This is a very cool way of looking at evidence; it goes back in history to a time when Scottish juries were asked to condemn prisoners accused of a breach of the laws concerning religion. Unwilling to do so, they were instructed by the Lord Advocate that they must examine the facts and not the opinions in the case; if the facts proved the offence, they must so declare. They took him at his word: if the prosecution did not satisfy their minute examination of the facts, they brought in the verdict Not Proven, and it has remained.

One of those involved in the Burke and Hare case (1829) was a woman called Helen McDougal, who was accused of taking part in the murders whereby these grave-robbers provided corpses for the students of anatomy at Edinburgh University; she was set free by a Not Proven verdict. Mary Elder (or Smith) was charged with poisoning her maidservant in a strange and scandalous case the previous year; she received the benefit of the Not Proven verdict. Sir Walter Scott, who was at the Mary Elder trial, thought she was guilty, and it was he who coined a phrase for the result that is often used by those who disapprove of it—"that bastard verdict."

The case that most crime fans recognise at the mere mention of the name is that of Madeleine Smith. Her trial (1857) has all the ingredients of a great novel and has in fact been the basis for many books, both fact and fiction, and at least two plays. There's no doubt the story attracts attention because Madeleine was young and pretty, and the turns and twists of the evidence unfolded a passionate, year-long yet clandestine romance.

Pierre Émile L'Angelier died from arsenic poisoning. The prosecution claimed Madeleine had murdered him rather than let him expose their shameful affair to her tyrannical father. Three of Scotland's most eminent lawyers handled the prosecution. For the defence appeared the Dean of the Faculty of Advocates, John Inglis, later to become Lord President of the Bench. With him were George Young, later Lord Young, and Alexander Moncrieff. The Ayrshire *Express* said Madeleine entered the court room with the air of a belle entering a ballroom.

There were three charges: two of administering arsenic, one of murder. When the chancellor (foreman) of the jury announced the verdicts, they were: Not Guilty, Not Proven, Not Proven. It's said that Madeleine hoped for a complete acquittal, but there were too many extraordinary coincidences and oddities in the evidence for that—even though there was no proof that she actually did give Pierre the poison she had bought.

One could say that here the "bastard verdict" proved legitimate. Alas, almost exactly seventy years later it freed an equally young accused, John Donald Merrett, whose mother had died of a gunshot wound to the head. Mrs. Merrett had taken a fortnight to die after the injury and during that time was either unable or unwilling to explain how she received it. Donald insisted she had shot herself—and this was just possible, as she had money troubles.

It says much for the pleading of his defence and the uprightness of the jury that, despite the strong feeling against Donald, he was allowed to escape the death penalty through the Not Proven verdict. He was taken off to prison to serve a sentence for forging cheques, on completion of which he embarked on a life just as strange as its beginning.

He defrauded shopkeepers, married the daughter of a woman who claimed a title to which she had no right, became a smuggler and gun-runner during the Spanish Civil War and changed his name to Ronald John Chesney. He served in the Navy during World War II and acquitted himself well. In 1946 he was involved in the black market in Germany, became known to prison officials in various European countries and collected several mistresses.

At last, in 1954, he decided to get rid of his wife so as to marry his current girl friend and made a special trip from Germany to London. Later, his wife was found drowned in the bath and his mother-in-law, who seems to have been unlucky enough to have met him on the stairs, battered and strangled to death. The case against him mounted, and once it became known that Ronald John Chesney and John Donald Merrett were the same man, it seemed the police needed only to lay hands on him to bring the matter to a close.

But Merrett-Chesney settled the debt to society himself. He put his Colt revolver in his mouth and pulled the trigger. Thus ended a career that perhaps should have been cut off in the High Court of Justiciary in Edinburgh twenty-six years earlier.

The usual view of the Scottish verdict is: "We couldn't prove it this time, so you can go away. But don't do it again." In the case of Madeleine Smith, it worked. She lived on to a ripe old age in America, unheard of. In the case of John Donald Merrett, the accused didn't take the implied advice. In all other Not Proven murder cases, the advice has been heeded.

At least, so far as we *know* . . .

Avon Curry is a past chairman of the Crime Writers' Association.

THE BARRISTERS' WIGMAKER

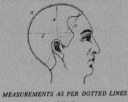

Among the differences between a barrister and a solicitor, the barrister wears a wig, the solicitor does not (nor does he usually appear in a courtroom, which is why). The most enviable wig to own is one prepared by Ede & Ravenscroft, whose waiting list is six months long. All barristers' wigs have two little pigtails and four rows of sausage-like curls. They are of bleached horsehair, which darkens with age. (The older the wig, the more desirable it is; an "antique" wig is quite the status symbol.) To make a wig, five separate measurements must be taken.

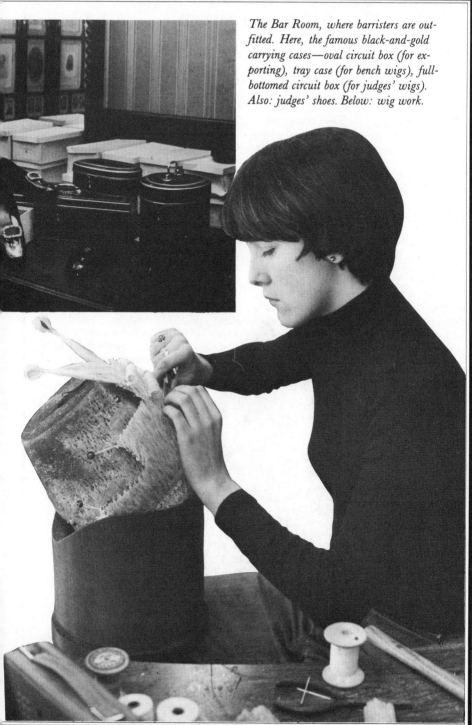

The Bar Room, where barristers are out-fitted. Here, the famous black-and-gold carrying cases—oval circuit box (for ex-porting), tray case (for bench wigs), full-bottomed circuit box (for judges' wigs). Also: judges' shoes. Below: wig work.

THE OLD BAILEY

The Old Bailey is one of the most familiar court buildings in the world, standing as it does in the centre of London. It is surmounted by a copper dome and a fifteen-foot gilded statue of the figure of Justice. One hand of the figure holds the traditional scales of justice; the other, the symbolic sword. This particular statue is unique in that it is not blindfolded. Over the door are carved the words: "Defend the children of the poor and punish the wrongdoer."

The site of the Old Bailey had a long criminal history as Newgate Prison. Standing next to Newgate was a building known as the Justice House or, alternatively, the Sessions House. This was erected in 1550 "over against Flete Lane in the old bayley." The latter referred to the street it was built on, and the building soon acquired that nickname. John Stow, a writer in Shakespeare's time, believed the name came from the word "ballium," used to describe an open space in front of the old wall of the Sessions House to allow guards and watchmen a better view. The ballium in front of the original Newgate Prison was on ground rising from what is now Ludgate Hill. Londoners called it Old Ballium, which has been corrupted into Old Bailey.

A new Sessions House was built in 1774, and this also became known as the Old Bailey; it was extended in 1824 and again in 1834, but it was always too small for the increasing court work of London.

In 1902, the old Newgate Prison and the Sessions House were demolished to make way for the Central Criminal Court, which would accommodate all the criminal work of London and the surrounding area. In 1907, it was opened by King Edward VII, but it immediately assumed its old nickname and again became the Old Bailey.

During the opening ceremony, the King said, "The barbarous penal code which was deemed necessary one hundred years ago, has been gradually replaced in the progress towards a higher civilisation, by laws breathing a more humane spirit and aiming at a nobler purpose."

The Old Bailey is purely a criminal court and has no civil jurisdiction. It is now a crown court and continues to provide the location for some of England's most famous trials.

P.N.W.

CARELLA
HERO OF THE 87TH PRECINCT

James McClure

High above rope barriers and waiting nets, a pretty young girl threatens suicide on a twelfth-story ledge:

> The police and the fire department had gone through the whole bit—they had seen this particular little drama a thousand times in the movies and on television. If there was anything that bored civil service employees, it was a real-life enactment of the entertainment cliché.

So begins Ed McBain's *Like Love,* a tour de force in his 87th Precinct series. It proclaims the man's genius for honesty, empathy and gentle humour. It explains why his Stephen Louis Carella has become one of the greatest "real" detectives in fiction, and the series itself among the most satisfying. We smell truth here and we are not bored.

The essence of the matter is simple enough. "A truism," Lord Samuel once remarked, "is on that account none the less true"—a sentiment to be echoed wistfully by anyone who has ever used the cliché "I love you." And an obvious truism is that nothing's so trite, nor so engaging, as a real human crisis, the very stuff of police work.

However, hacks excepted, most writers panic when plunged into what one could call cop corn. Some strike out on their own, eyes tightly shut, determined to impose a personal "reality" on the situation—scything down the clichés with meaningful pseudo-insights or building themselves cosy wee nests in the middle of hunt-the-needle haystacks so suffocating that only their imagined po-

licemen, each as endearing as a field mouse, could hope to survive in them. Others climb out and get on the fence, where they often assume a radical stance while painting a picture more terrible, in its way, than Van Gogh's final canvas; the corn writhes, the carrion crows descend, and God help the pig who gets caught in this glaring light.

McBain, on the other hand, accepts things as they are; if the field that engrosses him is knee-high in clichés, so be it. In he goes, as eager and uncompromising as a child, to grasp the thistle that grows between the rows.

"Great narrative," observed Eric Bentley, "is not the opposite of cheap narrative: it is soap opera *plus.*"

"Plus," there certainly is in McBain's writing; not even his most severe critics have been able to deny that, although they occasionally hint dark things about potboilers stretching back thirty years or so.

On the evidence, however, that is hardly likely to offend McBain. No pot that ever boiled has contained a more zealous missionary, expounding to the end on the gospel truth of police procedures, while producing platitudes, parables and homilies, with an urgent, often jovial intensity closely linked to an awareness of the underlying nature of things. Provoking behaviour, admittedly, for those who attend the pot, their bellies rumbling again so soon after a light meal of lesser novelists, and who have now to wait until the talk stops.

With the directness, then, of one unafraid to get down to essentials at the cost of spurious originality, McBain in-variably begins to create the world of Steve Carella by discussing the weather—everyone's favourite banality when confronting strangers. He also, al-most invariably, manages to score his first plus this way, as indicated by these opening lines from *The Pusher* (1956):

> *Winter came in like an anarchist with a bomb.*
> *Wild-eyed, shrieking, puffing hard, it caught the city in cold, froze the marrow and froze the heart.*

God/the novelist speaking. The sec-tion ends with a public consensus, lack-ing in flair but not in the same forebod-ing: "Winter was going to be a bitch that year." A space and then, flatfooted and phlegmatic: "The patrolman's name was Dick Genero, and he was cold. He didn't like the winter, and that was that."

Gone is the novelist, to return only when he has something pertinent to say, and in his place is a policeman writing with the skills of one and the authority of the other.

Most often that policeman is Steve Carella, although his part in any story is not necessarily more important than it would be in an investigation carried out by a squad of detectives. Significantly, when he makes his first appearance on a murder scene in *Cop Hater* (1956), he rates no more than a cursory glance from the homicide double-act already there. What he's wearing is automatically noted, that's all, and it's an utterly con-ventional neat suit, clasped tie and shirt. It takes a member of the public to re-flect: *He was not a frightening man, but when you opened the door to find him on your front step, you knew for certain he wasn't there to sell insurance*—a description that Carella might himself have difficulty in accept-ing, being more at home with the six-foot-nothing, downward-slanting eyes and brown hair stuff.

The narrator *seems* to be Carella—even when it's not—for two reasons. The first is that McBain has admitted to basing Carella on himself, so naturally some blurring is bound to occur. And the second is an extension of that, inas-much as Carella is our chief source of information about the 87th Precinct and thereby blurs his personal experience with our own.

The reader is shown what Carella sees, however "unseen" it may have be-come to him through overfamiliarity, and learns what he knows, however "second nature" this may have become, too. In other words, the cop corn is ground fine and then baked to fill a larder of goodies to which one returns again and again, even when a plot itself falls flat as in, ironically, *Bread* (1974), that singularly unleavened loaf.

What could be more mundane in mystery writing than a fingerprint? Yet once it has been through the mill, so to speak, there can be no denying its filling properties.

> *There are sweat pores on the finger-tips, and the stuff they secrete contains 98.5 percent water and 0.5 to 1.5 percent solid material. This solid material breaks down to about one-third of inorganic matter—mainly salt—and two-thirds of organic substances like urea, albumin and formic, butyric and acetic acids. Dust, dirt, grease cling to the secretion . . . .*

Not that one is likely to remember this—or would even want to—any more than Carella remembers it from the po-lice academy; it's having it made a part of oneself as well, however subliminally absorbed, that makes the difference. Much the same goes for the chunks of city ordinances found in the text: they, too, provide a taste of life as a police officer that no amount of descrip-tion alone could achieve.

Just as a description of the books

THE NYPD GLOSSARY

Lynn Strong

"**I**n the bag." In uniform.

Blotter. (formerly) A large green book used for logging precinct members' daily movements and any unusual occurrences.

Booking. Recording an arrest.

"**Brain.**" Detective. The term is used by non-detectives.

"**Chamber of Horrors.**" The trial room at Headquarters.

"**Collar.**" Arrest.

Command. Any unit, such as a precinct, with a commanding officer.

"**Cooping**" ("**In the heave**"). Time out for lunch, a quick nap, etc. Local funeral parlors and garages are well-suited for this purpose.

Detail. A temporary assignment to another command.

"**Downtown.**" Headquarters.

"**Flaking.**" Depositing incriminating evidence on or near suspect to facilitate arrest.

"**Floater.**" A body dragged from the river.

"**Flute.**" A whiskey-filled pop bottle in plain brown wrapper, donated to the SH by a grateful civilian.

"**Flying.**" Temporarily assigned to another command.

"**In grays.**" Probationary; not yet graduated from the Academy.

"**Gun run.**" A response to a report of person seen with a gun.

"**Hat.**" The sum of $5 used by a civilian as an attempted bribe.

"**Jug day.**" A celebration for promotion or retirement.

"**Jumper.**" A potential or actual suicide.

"**Kite.**" A complaint received through the mail.

Line-up. Five persons (suspect plus four others of similar physical description) on view for purpose of identifying suspect. Civilian non-suspects are paid $5. Now closed to the public, line-ups were once a source of neighborhood entertainment.

"**Loid.**" (from *celluloid*) Small stiff piece of paper, as a credit card, used to open locks on doors.

"**Murphy man.**" Con man.

Observation. Watch kept on a stationary object, as a house, bar, etc.

Operator. The driver of an RMP.

"**Pick man.**" A professional lock-picker, equipped with special tools.

Post. The area of a PRECINCT covered by a patrolman (synonymous with "beat" in other cities). A "one-armed" post includes only one side of the street.

"**Potsie.**" Shield.

"**Rabbi**" ("**Hook**"). An influential friend, either on or off the Force.

Recorder. The officer in an RMP who handles communications.

"**Ripper.**" A safe-cracker, usually employing a torch.

"**Round robin.**" A comprehensive check-out preceding transfer, promotion, etc.

Sector. The area of a PRECINCT covered by a patrol car (equivalent of POST).

Shield. A badge worn or carried to designate rank. "Working with the white shield" describes a PO assigned to detective's duties. A "gold shield" is another name for a detective. (*Note:* The word "badge" is rarely used by NYPD members.)

"**Squeal.**" Complaint.

Surveillance. Watch kept on a moving object, as a person, car, etc.

Ten-thirteen. Assist police officer!

"**Tin.**" Shield. "**On the tin.**" Free; without being asked to pay.

"**Torch.**" Arsonist.

"**Undesirables**" ("**Germs**"). Pimps, prostitutes, junkies, etc., as a group.

"**Yellow sheet.**" Record of arrests (now a white computer print-out).

Lynn Strong is an editor and current informer and former friend of the NYPD.

themselves is unlikely to convey their flavour with any accuracy. But a glance along the shelves, picking out other odds and ends at random, would at least provide some idea of what is on offer.

Lovely sandwiches of ideas, for a start. In *Cop Hater*, Carella calls on the heavily sensual widow of a murdered colleague and wishes "she were not wearing black."

THE MCBAIN BOOKS RATED BY MCBAIN

MY FAVORITE
Sadie When She Died

I LIKE A LOT
Blood Relative
Long Time No See
Ice

I'M NOT SO FOND OF
So Long as You Both Shall Live

ALFRED J. YOUNG COLLECTION, NEW YORK CITY

> *He knew this was absurd. When a woman's husband is dead, the woman wears black.*
> *But Hank and he had talked a lot in the quiet hours of the midnight tour, and Hank had many times described Alice in the black night gowns she wore to bed. And try as he might, Carella could not dissociate the separate concepts of black: black as a sheer and frothy raiment of seduction, black as the ashy garment of mourning.*

And to follow that section through to its conclusion, for a glimpse of what makes Carella so real:

> *He left the apartment and walked down to the street. It was very hot in the street.*
> *Curiously, he felt like going to bed with somebody.*
> *Anybody.*

Then there are the other people one meets. The cartoonist's gag writer, for instance, in *Ten Plus One,* who features briefly as a suspect. A morose man, he nonetheless obligingly explains the genesis of the funnies in most magazines and shows the detectives the slips he sends out, each carrying a description of the drawing and supplying the caption, if there is one. Four of these slips are reproduced in fascimile—one of McBain's most effective techniques for giving one the "feel" of being right there. Elsewhere one is shown reporter's copy, police forms, timetables, letters, signwriting and, in *Doll* (1965), some photographs. There is something enormously gratifying in seeing something for oneself, particularly if, as in certain cases, it's possible to pounce on a clue before the men of the 87th get to it.

Ten Plus One also features one of McBain's many unforgettable incidental characters, a grouchy token seller called Stan Quentin who has never heard of Alcatraz and doesn't see why the detectives should be so amused. Now, that's so corny one wouldn't dare use it in fiction, whereas it works perfectly for four pages of McBain. Culminating with:

> *"You know those guys at Alcatraz?"*
> *"We know lots of guys at Alcatraz,"* Carella said.
> *"Tell them to take my name off it, you hear?"*
> *"We will,"* Carella said.
> *"Damn right,"* Quentin said.

Long exchanges of dialogue are a characteristic also to be enjoyed, both for the tension they create and for the authentic ring which the conventions of television make impossible. Humour, used to counterpoint harsh realities, is also much in evidence, as in *Cop Hater* when the father-figure of the squad room cuts short an introduction without malice aforethought: "It was simply Miscolo was a heavy sweater, and he didn't like the armpits of his uniform ruined by unnecessary talk." Other times it can be used to steady a flight of fancy: "Detectives are not poets; there is no iambic pentameter in a broken head."

And all this is to say nothing of Meyer Meyer (victim of his father's Jewish sense of humour; nobody could call that a Christian name, for start), Cotton Hawes, Bert Kling or the odious Andy Parker, who between them handle the work load with varied degrees of success. In one story, largely because the right hand doesn't get to know what the left is doing, they all goof off, including Carella, and an arrest is made—only *after* a catastrophic crime is committed— by a distant patrolman in search, not of fame, but of ice cream.

Such is life. Such is what McBain re-creates by giving his policemen far too much to do (seldom are they ever concerned with one case at a time); a sky over their heads that can, in a heat wave, befuddle them while investigating a shoot-out in a liquor store filled with smashed bottles; and a world as real as Isola's model of New York is real.

Sometimes, however, he seems to go too far having fun, and smart-asses who rely on hindsight—what else?—have suggested that he may regret certain parts of the framework he laid down for himself in *Cop Hater*, little suspecting he'd have to live with them through almost a generation. They cite Teddy Franklin, the lovely, lamentably deaf and literally dumb girl whom Carella courted and married in that first book of the series, and quote Philip Norman's interview with the writer, in which it was said she "came from some heartless, fatuous notion of the ideal woman: beautiful and speechless." Fine for a one-off story, just as most jokes will take a single airing, but surely. . .

Nonsense. the very essence of Mc-Bain is that he embraces his clichés with the same loving enthusiasm Carella has been known to direct toward his missus—and, with possibly as little thought for the consequences, although he has himself so far avoided twins.

If this means he has become, in effect, the Norman Rockwell of the police procedural, that is surely no bad thing—not when he's also Evan Hunter, author of such celebrated works as *The Blackboard Jungle* and *Buddwing,* which must provide him with literary kudos.

Ah, say our literary-minded friends, why didn't you disclose this at the beginning? Hunter is bound to have an influence on McBain at times but plainly indulges in him the excesses of a trained mind allowed to slip its leash, to scamper cute as a spaniel in a public park— sometimes upright, mostly with a strong leaning toward grass-roots kitsch in exuberant figure eights which, despite sudden switches of direction, neatly tie up the ends.

Well, mainly because addicts of the 87th Precinct don't put this about much. Some are simply ignorant of the fact, and possibly much happier that way, being intimidated by "real" novelists, whereas "Ed McBain" is such a reassuring cliché of a name in itself, exactly right for a cop-lover. Others are confident that their emperor isn't going about in the buff (he, too, wears neat suits)— and that it's rare enough even to catch him with his pants down (although this does occur, forgivably, during moments of extreme sentiment).

James McClure won the Crime Writers' Association Silver Dagger for his political thriller Rogue Eagle.

SUIVEZ MAIGRET

Eve Darge

My assignment takes me to the very heart of Paris, "Île de la Cité." I glance at the Towers of Notre Dame watching over the city since the twelfth century. Turning to the left of the Cathedral, I arrive at the Conciergerie, the former palace of the city's superintendent where memories of the French Revolution still linger. Marie Antoinette spent her last days here. It houses now the Palace of Justice, the Court House, the Police Headquarters. The place I am to visit, the right wing, was added by Napoleon the Third.

My taxi has dropped me at the entrance, Quai des Orfèvres.

"Right wing, second floor, Room 202," the guard says.

This is where the Homicide Squad operates.

"The Commissioner wants you to wait for him in his office," conveys young detective Janvier.

I have arrived just in time to avoid the gusty winds and the torrential rain falling now heavily on the city.

Heavy footsteps down the corridor. The solid, well-known silhouette appears at the door. His other detective—Lucas, I believe—helps him take off his drenched overcoat and hat. I stand up.

"Please remain seated." He exchanges his flooded pipe for a fresh one. "So, they send me women now! I have nothing against that . . . I've always had a preference for them. I get along better with them."

E.D.: Commissioner . . . how does one address you?

MAIGRET: Call me Maigret, you're a civilian!

E.D.: I should perhaps come back . . . this bad weather . . .

MAIGRET: No. It's your work. Bad weather has never interfered with mine.

E.D.: This weather reminds me of home . . . Lorraine, at the Belgian border.

MAIGRET: It's true. Always starts in England. The English try to unload it on us through the Belgians, who get it twenty-four hours earlier. Excuse me while I change my shoes. My feet are soaked.

E.D.: You should have had rubbers.

MAIGRET: I hate them! I also seem to have a certain allergy for raincoats and umbrellas. Besides, I used to lose them regularly.

E.D.: Monsieur Maigret, you just completed an investigation—what is your feeling when the murderer has been arrested?

MAIGRET: The satisfaction of the work done, the duty accomplished. The satisfaction of knowing that the perpetrator of a crime will not commit another one, as it sometimes happens, to cover the first.

E.D.: What are the most common motives you have encountered in your investigations?

MAIGRET: At the source, you'll always find the capital sins. Envy is the motive of the murderer who kills to get the property of others without working. Uncontrolled anger, a sort of temporary insanity, may also transform a man into a killer. Jealousy, of course, which is nothing other than a violent rejection of abandonment. The killer in that case will not admit to having his love or security usurped.

E.D.: You have not mentioned lust, or gluttony.

MAIGRET: Lust rarely generates murders. It does not generate anything. It degenerates, rather... gluttony, ah, that is my weakness. I have a strong appetite. Nothing moves me like good country cooking odors. In my time we never counted calories, and as a result people were much more level-headed. Particularly women!

E.D.: Do you imply that the modern woman lost some of her equilibrium when she lost her... excessive roundness?

MAIGRET: I have always preferred them pleasingly plump. My wife, you understand, is my ideal. A woman of good size, but with thin legs.

E.D.: Monsieur Maigret, you seem to know them very well. Women of all walks of life. It is even said that you know the prostitutes particularly well. That you have for them a certain fondness, a bias.

MAIGRET: No. Not a bias. But I do not condemn them. I try to understand the reason that brought them there. In general, they are not malefactors ... but the victims.

E.D.: Coming back, Monsieur Maigret, to the confessions you obtain. It is rumored that you dissect souls. That people do not confess their crimes, but rather confide in you.

> *My favorite mystery author is George Simenon. I have a whole shelf of his books. I read the Inspector Maigrets again and again.*
>
> ROBERT MACNEIL

MAIGRET: I don't know if I dissect the souls. But I think I am able to put people at ease. I get their trust. The criminal is perhaps the human being who suffers the most. The one who has never been understood. Faced with someone who is able to discover what he is really like, to expose him to himself, he soon softens up. The weight of his guilt was becoming unbearable. This is the only way for him to feel some relief.

E.D.: In the course of an investigation, do you immediately recognize the guilty?

MAIGRET: No. But I recognize instinctively the non-guilty. I proceed by elimination. In difficult cases, I investigate the antecedents. Their childhood tells me more than their adult lives, which they might have been able to keep partly hidden.

E.D.: That makes you a disciple of Freud. I noticed while waiting for you that your library counts as many Treatises on Psychoanalysis as Manuals on Criminology.

MAIGRET: I believe everything is related to childhood.

E.D.: Besides the murder act, which are in your opinion the most hideous crimes?

MAIGRET: Without any doubt, blackmail and breach of confidence. Many years ago, while in Vichy, I became involved in the investigation of the murder of a woman. She had had, in her youth, a brief relationship with a man in Paris, and had moved away. Under the false pretext that he was the father to a son, she made him pay fantastic sums of money for more than twenty years—with the promise that they could come together when the boy would be of age. The man, being married and childless, waited patiently, and when finally faced with the truth that no child ever existed, in a fit of anger strangled her. For me, the real victim was the murderer... I had wished that he would be acquitted. And there is a justice... he was.

E.D.: You seem to be well liked by your associates. They call you "Patron" and "Boss" with reverence. Your former detectives assigned in different parts of France continue calling you "Boss."

MAIGRET: Well... they're a fine bunch. But the real boss is the French taxpayer. This is why we must do our job even better. We must protect him, I think.

E.D.: What sort of private life do you lead, Monsieur Maigret?

MAIGRET: A very quiet life, between my wife and my office. I should say between my wife's dinner table and my office... I am not much for formal affairs. I hate wearing a tuxedo. Tuxedos should be worn only by men that look like Prince Philip.

E.D.: What do you do for leisure?

MAIGRET: Not much. I love to take walks by the Seine River looking at the simple people, along with my wife, my understanding wife. We get along so well, we don't even have to talk. I don't have much time for novels. But to really relax, I read Simenon. Even though he comes from the other side of the border, we seem to have a lot in common. You see... before all... he is human.

Eve Darge is a French poet now living in New York City.

VIDOCQ

Peter N. Walker

François Eugène Vidocq was a criminal who became chief of the Paris police.

Born in 1775 at Arras, he had an overpowering weakness for women. When he was only fifteen, he disguised himself as the sister of a willing serving maid so that he could accompany the lady of his desires on holiday. He had a fortnight's bliss without the lady's husband ever suspecting his wife had a lover.

His parents thought he would be best employed in the army, but there he continued his amorous exploits. Out of the army, he was an acrobat, forger, swindler, thief and highwayman, and his capacity for trouble brought him eight years' hard labour on the galleys at Brest. He escaped twice and was recaptured; upon his third escape he lived among the thieves and criminals of Paris, learning their ways. Armed with this knowledge, he offered himself in 1809 as a spy to the Paris police, and his energetic work eventually led to his becoming head of the reorganised detective department. He worked with a body of ex-convicts under his command and was known for his genius for catching crooks.

It was in 1811 that he hit upon the idea of the Sûreté, crime fighters who had no boundary limits. In 1817, his small group made 811 arrests, among which were 15 assassins, 341 receivers of stolen goods and 14 escaped prisoners. He started a card index of criminals, but his success did not please the orthodox police of Paris. They suggested that Vidocq arranged the crimes he successfully solved.

Vidocq's strong point was his extrovert personality. He was a master of disguise, a brilliant speaker and a humorist; on the debit side, he was always in trouble and constantly chasing women, especially actresses. He liked duelling, stalking the night life of Paris in disguise (his disguises ranged from coalmen to women), raiding criminals' lairs or defending himself in court with his customary eloquence.

In 1827, Vidocq retired and started a paper mill, staffed with ex-convicts, but it was a failure. He tried to re-join the police and in 1832 succeeded by being allocated political duties. But Vidocq wanted only to return to detective duties, and it is said he organised a daring theft, one that he could solve in order to prove his worth. Once his real part became known, he was dismissed from the service.

It is also said he died in poverty, a broken man, although some accounts deny this. Some say he continued to work privately as a detective into ripe old age, still chasing the women, and that he lived in reasonable luxury until his death in 1857.

A CHIEF CONSTABLE EVALUATES AN INSPECTOR AND A MASTERMIND

Colin Watson

Mr. Harcourt Chubb, O.B.E., Chief Constable of Flaxborough, was asked to give his personal impressions of Colin Watson, a fellow citizen and chronicler of such events in the town's recent history as have exercised his, Mr. Chubb's, authority and talents as a law enforcement officer—Flaxborough's somewhat remarkable crime record.

At first diffident ("One has to live in the same town as the man, you know"), Mr. Chubb eventually proved forthcoming in the matter of confidences as any guardian of morality is when given reasonable expectation of garnish.

Colin Watson, admitted Mr. Chubb, was not too bad a fellow, by and large, considering that he wrote books and had even been a journalist at one time. Apart from two convictions for speeding, he had kept out of trouble with the police, had no paternity orders against him, was never seen really drunk and once had made a contribution to the Town Band's instrument fund—one wondered, in fact, if he were a proper author at all.

You say he was once a newspaperman?

Oh, certainly. He began on the old Flaxborough *Citizen*. Right here in this town, though he's from London, I believe. That might account for a certain streak of irresponsibility.

Coming from London, you mean?

No, no. The journalism. Let me give you an example. Some wretched junior had submitted a wedding report—this was years ago, mind—and it was Watson's job to correct his copy. The lad had written: "All the bridesmaids wore Dutch caps." Shocking gaffe, of course. But Watson let it through. Thought it funny. Can't think why. Must have embarrassed no end of people.

I presume his newspaper career took him further afield than Flaxborough. Do you know anything about that, Mr. Chubb?

A little, yes. It has to be said that Watson does not seem to have taken that aspect of his work as seriously as his employers' had the right to expect. There's a certain irreverence about the fellow. I've always regretted his having made friends with my Inspector, you know. I suspect part of Purbright's awkwardness is due to Watson's influence.

Inspector Purbright is not portrayed in the novels as an awkward man.

No, well, he wouldn't be, would he? I mean, look who wrote them.

Is the Inspector, in fact, an awkward man to deal with? What one might call a bloody-minded man?

Ah, you won't get me to say that. No, no. Very sound chap is Purbright. I don't know what we should have done without him in Flaxborough over the past twenty years—and all despite lack of promotion, you might notice. There's devotion to duty for you. No, it's just this funny streak in the man. I don't always know which way to take him. As I say, I think he sees too much of Watson.

How do you explain what you call Watson's "irreverence," Mr. Chubb?

Well, I've a theory, such as it is. He went to one of the smaller public schools, d'you see, and that nearly always has the effect of putting one up against authority. What do they call it—compensatory attitude? Something like that. Take Watson's career in journalism, for instance.

He rose to be one of the best-paid leader-writers in Kemsley Newspapers. Earned nearly twenty pounds a week (that's what, oh, more than thirty of those dollars of yours) at his peak. Yet instead of being grateful, do you know what he used to do? Put chunks of carefully disguised socialist propaganda into his leading articles. Poor Lord K. would have been terribly upset if he could have understood them. I asked Watson if he wasn't ashamed of having taken advantage of his employer in that way. I've never forgotten his answer. It wasn't in

SHOPTALK

A.B.H. Actual Bodily Harm: a serious assault

A.C.C. Assistant Chief Constable

B.O.P. Breach of the Peace: a disturbance

C.C. Chief Constable

C.I.D. Criminal Investigation Department; Coppers in Disguise (slang)

C.O.P. Chief of Police

C.R.O. Criminal Record Office

D.C. Detective Constable

D.C.C. Deputy Chief Constable

D.C.I. Detective Chief Inspector

D.H.Q. Divisional Headquarters

D.I. Detective Inspector

D.S. Detective Sergeant

D. Supt. Detective Superintendent

F.A. Found Abandoned (applicable to cars illegally borrowed and dumped after use)

G.B.H. Grievous Bodily Harm: a serious assault

G.P. Car. General Purpose Car: a police vehicle with no specific duties; it deals with any incident that might arise

H.Q. Headquarters

ID Parade. Identification Parade

INSP. Inspector

M.P.D. Metropolitan Police District: the area policed by the London Metropolitan Police

N.F.A. No Fixed Abode

P.C. Police Constable

P.N.C. Police National Computer (All English and Welsh forces are linked to the P.N.C.)

R.T. Road Traffic; Radio Transmitter

Sgt. Sergeant

SOCO. Scenes of Crime Officer (spoken as "Socco"): police or civilians who visit scenes of crimes to photograph them or to undertake other scientific investigations

Supt. Superintendent

T.W.O.C. Taking Without Owner's Consent (spoken as "twock"): unlawfully borrowing a motor vehicle ("I arrested two men for T.W.O.C.")

T.I.C. Taken into Consideration: a term used when a criminal on trial for a crime asks a court to punish him for other offences he has committed in the past; this "cleans" his slate." ("He asked for eight other burglaries to be T.I.C.")

U.B.P. Unit Beat Policing: a system of patrolling with five officers and a "Panda" car; the officers are made responsible for a given area which they patrol, so they become well acquainted with the residents

U.S.I. Unlawful Sexual Intercourse with a girl under sixteen years of age

P.N.W.

THE COSY LITTLE VILLAGE

One can walk it in a morning, provided one doesn't dawdle. Nodding to shopkeepers the length of the High Street does take up a good bit of time. There's the greengrocer. And the eggman. And the victualler and his friendly rival, the poulterer. There's the gentleman in notions and the sisters in millinery. There's the teacher (briskly rounding up would-be truants) on the way to the schoolroom. And, of course, there's the vicar out seeking inspiration for Sunday Evensong. And Himself taking his daily constitutional. And the constable stranded with a flat tyre on his cycle.

And, indeed, there's the spinster. Every cosy village has one, if only to keep watch on the pub and its bleary consumers. She does natter on—about potholes and potshots and bits of evidence draped 'cross the stile (or flung beneath it). Indeed, her eyesight is as sharp as her tongue.

Yes, it can take a while to walk round a village, which, as it happens, is always steeped in water, inside and out. Within, there's the steaming kettle on every hob, the warm pot beside every evening paper and the quick cuppa just waiting for every tradesman to have a moment free. Outside, there's the pond at the far end, almost the next village over. As well as the ditch, running north to heaven knows where, but that's the place they find the shoe in. It's missing a heel, which is not surprising: heels prefer cities; the countryside is where cads feel comfortable.

The cycling constable.

BRITISH TOURIST AUTHORITY

AND THE CORRUPT STATELY HOME

No matter where it lies (or how often), the stately home is at every village centre. Feeding it and staffing it are the village's chief preoccupations. Driving guests to and fro (often in a casket) takes up almost as much time as walking the High Street.

The stately home routinely has visitors for the weekend, relatives for a fortnight and a constant stream of unwelcome interlopers. Among the most noted of the stately home architects are Catherine Aird (*Stately Home Murder*; *A Most Contagious Game*), Tim Heald (*Blue Blood Will Out*), Alan Hunter (*Landed Gently*), Michael In-nes (*The Crabtree Affair*; *Lord Mullion's Secret*); Elizabeth Lemarchand (*Change for the Worse*; *Death on Doomsday*) and David Williams (*Unholy Writ*).

If you feel life will not be complete without staying just once in a bona-fide stately home, you can make arrangements by contacting the National Trust, London, England. They have a list of stately homes you can stop by (prices varying according to niceties, i.e., a functioning loo, central heating, number of bedrooms). When you leave, take the corpse with you.

Mrs. Chubb's hearing, fortunately. "All newspaper proprietors in my experience," he insisted, "are chisel-minded, semiliterate whoremasters with delusions of grandeur." A very unfair generalisation, I always thought.

Why, in the Flaxborough novels, did Watson elect to use a crime format? They are not "thrillers" in the conventional sense.

You mean, why does he write about the few bad apples in our little community barrel? I've often asked him that. You don't do the town justice, I say to him. I get a characteristically flippant answer, as you might imagine. The good apples, he says, are so bloody dull.

Is it true he was a crime reporter?

So I gather. At least, he did a lot of court reporting at one period. Inquests, police calls, all that sort of thing. We in England don't use sensational terms like "crime reporter," you know. Watson claims that his police characters are based on officers he has known. Maybe they are. It's not for me to say. I must say that *I* never found crime amusing. Still, I never found the Honours List amusing, for that matter, whereas Watson thinks it a great joke. Perverse sense of humour.

What do you think is the reason for the Flaxborough novels being popular in America?

Are they indeed? That *is* interesting. Can't imagine why, unless it has something to do with those Pilgrim Father chaps. A lot of them came from round here, you know. Some of Flaxborough's first trouble-makers. Protesters, they call them now. They used to get shipped off to the plantations in those days. Come to think of it, I daresay our friend Watson would have qualified if he'd been around then.

Has he any sympathetic feelings toward America?

He has American friends, I understand. He rather likes *them*. Sympathy, though—that's a word one has to be careful about. It can sound patronising. Purbright probably has the right idea:

he says we all need sympathy these days.

Inspector Purbright is a long way from being a "tough" policeman. Isn't that being rather out of fashion?

Possibly. But it wouldn't do, you know. Not in Flaxborough. The last really aggressive officer we had was nearly forty years ago. Poor fellow fell off the town bridge one night after registering a court objection to the grant of a liquor license to the Over-Eighties Club. Purbright is a very conciliatory chap in comparison. Mind you, I don't think much of some of his notions. I once heard him telling his sergeant—you know young Love, do you?—some rubbish about his being fascinated by what he called "the curious innocence" of the professional criminal. Nothing very innocent, I'd have thought, about some blackguard who goes round pinching people's valuables, eh?

What is your author's attitude toward crime and punishment, Mr. Chubb?

Decidedly odd, I'm afraid. He says too much effort goes into enforcing laws designed to protect property, and too little into protecting people. That's nonsense, of course, but I'm just telling you *his* ideas. Oh yes, he said on another occasion, I remember, that if we *had* to go round hanging people, it ought to be for murdering the English language. Let me see, who was that president you used to have in America, the one who didn't shave very often and had a dog? Dixon? Or was it Nixon? Anyway, Watson and Purbright were talking about him at the time of that Watergate business of yours, and Watson said impeachment would be too dignified a course to take with such a grubby little man; he ought to be put in a home for cliché addicts. I thought the remark was uncalled for, frankly.

You must find your author a great trial.

Oh, it's my job to cope with people.

Colin Watson is the author of The Flaxborough Chronicles.

TO WALK AMONG SHADOWS

George Baker

C*hief Inspector Alleyn looked at the poinsettia, its top-most flower well above his head, and said "I am amazed." "Dear Br'er Fox" he thought "if you could see the wonders of New Zealand. Palms grow over cool streams, streams cool enough for trout. Can you imagine trout fishing in the blazing sun, standing in the shade of a palm. There are more things in heaven and earth, Br'er Fox."*

The very English Chief Inspector Roderick Alleyn, Scotland Yard, is the creation of Dame Ngaio Marsh, a New Zealander and one of the world's foremost detective story writers.

I was wandering around my house in London, wishing a part would be offered and as a bonus take me abroad for a week or two. The phone rang so close upon the wish that I laughed when my agent said, "Would you like to go to New Zealand and play Ngaio Marsh's Inspector Alleyn in four television films?"

"Yes," I said.

"Don't you want to read the script?"

"As a formality," I answered.

I took *Died in the Wool*, the first book to be filmed, from the shelf and started to reread it. The other titles for filming were *Vintage Murder, Opening Night* and *Colour Scheme*.

I was delighted with Inspector Alleyn and his faithful subordinate, Inspector Fox. Unfortunately, Fox does not appear in these particular books, but Alleyn often speaks to him in soliloquy.

"And St. John Acroyd," he says in *Vintage Murder*. "There, my dear old Inspector Foxy, a subject fit for you and me. A stock comedian, a funny man with a funny face, and unless I am much mistaken, a mean disposition." And with those few words Alleyn sets up another suspect and the reader has another clue for the Dame's crime puzzle.

How to play him would by *my* puzzle. What were my clues?

A product of Eton and Balliol, Alleyn entered the Foreign Office before transferring to Scotland Yard. These were the clues to his background. So I deduced that he was a well-bred Englishman of some social standing who had followed a conventional pattern through to his thirties. He broke away from these conventions when he transferred to Scotland Yard. It was Dame Ngaio's genius to create a professional policeman who also carried the mores of his amateur rivals Lord Peter Wimsey and Father Brown—breeding and education. Inspector Alleyn married an exceptional and gifted wife, Troy. And in that, too, he broke with convention. I had a glimpse of a man whose mind and interests were at variance with his social upbringing.

I carefully dressed him in the tweeds and brogues of the period. If anything, I made the clothes more severe and reserved than they need have been in order to give myself the opportunity to contrast the exterior and the interior man. Now, what was I going to use to aid me in bringing out Roderick Alleyn's humour?

THE MURDER GAME

Roderick Alleyn débuted in 1934 in *A Man Lay Dead*. The Chief Inspector was called in to investigate a murder that occurred during a weekend house party. Sir Hubert's guests were gathered in the parlour to play "The Murder Game." The lights were turned off while the game was in progress. When snapped back on, they revealed a very dead gamesman, his back skewered by a jewelled dagger. Alleyn solved the case. To the best of anyone's knowledge, no one ever played the game again.

Through her extraordinary gift of drawing character, the Dame lets the reader catch glimpses of Roderick Alleyn's humour. For an actor, thoughts are communicated through the mind and through the eye. I invented a pair of half-spectacles for Alleyn to frame that humour which would not be spoken.

It was all very well for me to have these thoughts, but I hadn't yet met the producer and was by no means yet on my way to New Zealand to appear as Chief Inspector Roderick Alleyn.

My agent set up a meeting with the producer, who agreed to lunch at the London Cumberland Hotel. I parked my bicycle with the porter and went in. John McRea introduced himself and offered me a pre-lunch drink. After being served, I said, "If you're offering the part, I'd like to play it."

"I'm offering the part."

"Right," I said, "when do we start?"

On 14th March I flew to Auckland, New Zealand, via Singapore. Inspector Alleyn grew on me more and more as I travelled the 13,000 miles to play him. I re-read *Opening Night* and *Vintage Murder,* and became more and more convinced that the Inspector's humour was going to be the most pleasurable factor in the part and the most difficult to convey.

On arrival at Auckland I was met by John McRea, who took me to the studios to meet the two directors. From the beginning we got on well. Our discussions were pointed with laughter and relaxation. When the costume designer joined us, I realised that we were all on the same wavelength. The feeling of rightness I had experienced in London was still with me.

So Roderick Alleyn began to prepare himself to step out of the books he had made famous for his creator and make his début on the screen.

"Dear old Foxkin, the New Zealand countryside is quite breathtaking and the locations found for the four stories are so like the places of imagination our dear author describes, I believe she may have taken a peep or two at reality when she put us into the settings we share. It's all shrewd observation, Foxkin, and knowing human nature. You will forgive me if I go now. The smell of the frangipani wafting past me on the night air as I stand on the verandah makes me suspect foul play in the woolshed . . . indeed Flossie Rubrick may have *Died in the Wool.* I might investigate."

George Baker, in addition to an acting career, has written for the BBC, and his The Trial and Execution of Charles I *was performed by the Royal Shakespeare Company.*

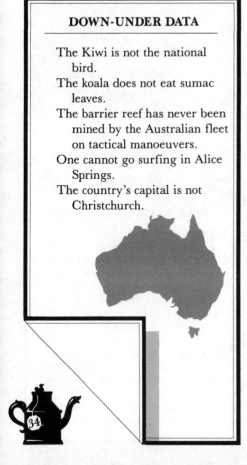

DOWN-UNDER DATA

The Kiwi is not the national bird.
The koala does not eat sumac leaves.
The barrier reef has never been mined by the Australian fleet on tactical manoeuvers.
One cannot go surfing in Alice Springs.
The country's capital is not Christchurch.

THE HISTORY OF THE ENGLISH POLICE

Peter N. Walker

The name Bow is pronounced as in "bow and arrow." Bow Street still exists in London and contains a very busy magistrates' court.

The first magistrate of Bow Street was Thomas de Veil, who was appointed in 1740. He was described as a courageous man, unafraid to expose himself to the criminals and mobs who terrorised London at that time. There was no police system to counteract their activities, other than the incompetent local watchmen; furthermore, criminals could bribe the justices to overlook their crimes.

Henry Fielding, who succeeded Veil, became a magistrate at Bow Street in 1748. He was a noted author (*Tom Jones*) and vigorously campaigned against the widespread corruption among the justices. His brother John, who was almost blind, assisted him, and together they made a register of all crimes committed in London. The numbers horrified the brothers, so in 1750 Henry recruited six "thief-takers" to arrest the wrongdoers.

These were ordinary householders "actuated by a truly public spirit against thieves." They were ready at a moment's notice to perform their duty but were unpaid. Their task was to pursue all villains and bring them to justice; their reward came from the "blood-money" paid upon the arrest of a villain or upon the recovery of stolen goods. Fielding was their leader, a task he shared with a man called Saunders-Welch, who was High Constable of Holborn. The "thief-taker" wore no uniform and carried only

the staff of a parish constable.

But they did achieve success; in addition to arresting thieves, they managed to break up gangs, and people began to ask for a paid police force.

Fielding's men became known as Bow Street Runners about 1785 and at one time boasted two horse patrols. Fielding also published a news-sheet of criminal activities, listing known rogues and their crimes, but gained little official support from the government. His small band of men, as few as four in some cases, remained until the formation of the Metropolitan Police in 1829.

Sir Robert Peel

Sir Robert Peel, founder of the modern English police force, was born on 5th February 1788 near Bury in Lancashire, England. His grandfather, also called Robert, was a calico printer who progressed to the spinning-jenny after he spun himself a fortune out of cotton. Peel's father, another Robert, was the third son of this self-made man; he became a Member of Parliament for Tamworth and was awarded a baronetcy.

SCOTLAND YARD

Our Robert was educated at Harrow and Oxford, where he was a friend of Byron, the poet. He took first-class degrees in Classics and Mathematics, and in 1809, at the age of twenty-one, he, too, became a Member of Parliament. A dedicated Tory, he was an outstanding speaker and acquired a deep knowledge of Parliamentary procedures.

TIPSTAVES, TIPSTAFFS AND TRUNCHEONS

Donald Rumbelow

Today, recognising an English policeman isn't difficult. He wears a uniform and carries a warrant card. But before 1829 his sole symbol of office, of authority, was his tipstave, his tipstaff or his painted truncheon.

The tipstaves, being short, were either put in one's pocket or stuffed in one's waistcoat. They usually had a brass handle and a crown on the other end. Some of the crowns unscrewed and warrants were rolled up inside.

The tipstaffs, being very long, were usually used for parades and fancy processionals.

In 1829, the first officially recognised police uniform—blue coat, blue trousers, top hat—eliminated the need for the tipstave and the tipstaff. However, the truncheon was still carried and was still regarded as a symbol of authority. Often, it had to be produced by a plain-clothes detective when he questioned a suspect. The painted truncheon had a crown motif on top, with the Royal Coat of Arms or the Burgh Coat of Arms below it. Gradually, the elaborately decorated truncheon disappeared, until in the 1870's it was virtually extinct. It was still produced for ceremonial purposes, however, as late as the 1920's.

Donald Rumbelow is the author of The Complete Jack the Ripper.

Only three years later, he became Secretary for Ireland, and there he instituted the Irish Constabulary in an attempt to preserve life and property. This body of men became known as "Peelers."

In 1820, he married the daughter of General Sir John Floyd. She was named Julie, and they had five sons and two daughters, His family life was said to have been very happy.

In 1825, Robert Peel began his famous reform of criminal law in England, resulting in the birth of London's Metropolitan Police in 1829. It took four hard years to overcome the prejudice of his government, who saw the police as a threat to personal liberty. They failed to see that unchecked crime was a greater threat.

Peel, who was Home Secretary at the time, did not want his policemen to look like soldiers, so he dressed them as civilians in black top hats and blue tailed coats. They were unarmed. Political disturbances in 1832 brought them into rapid conflict with the general public, who looked upon them as a political tool of the government. They hated the police and called them "Peel's Bloody Gang" or "Blue Lobsters." It took thirty years for them to become acceptable, and during that period crime diminished and public order was restored.

Once they had become accepted by the public, the police became known as "bobbies" in honour of their founder, Bobby Peel. The English policeman is still affectionately known by this name.

Robert Peel, who has been described as one of the hardest workers and greatest intellectuals England has known, was thrown from his horse on Constitutional Hill, London, on 29th June 1850; he died on 2nd July that same year.

Peter N. Walker is a police inspector in the North Yorkshire Police. He is also the author of over thirty crime books.

FICTIONAL CHARACTERS IN THE ENGLISH POLICE HIERARCHY

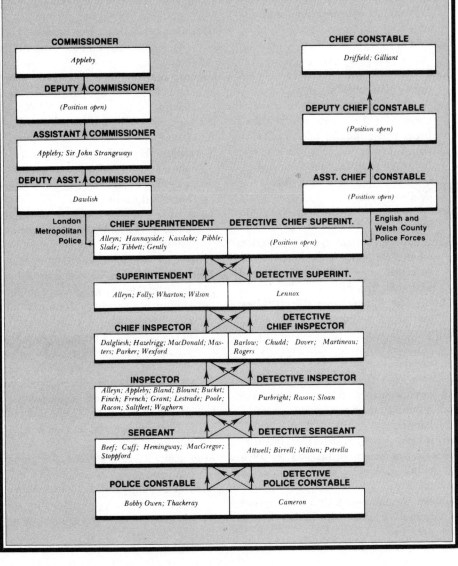

COMMISSIONER

Appleby

DEPUTY COMMISSIONER

(Position open)

ASSISTANT COMMISSIONER

Appleby; Sir John Strangeways

DEPUTY ASST. COMMISSIONER

Dawlish

London Metropolitan Police

CHIEF CONSTABLE

Driffield; Gilliant

DEPUTY CHIEF CONSTABLE

(Position open)

ASST. CHIEF CONSTABLE

(Position open)

English and Welsh County Police Forces

CHIEF SUPERINTENDENT

Alleyn; Hannasyide; Kasslake; Pibble; Slade; Tibbett; Gently

DETECTIVE CHIEF SUPERINT.

(Position open)

SUPERINTENDENT

Alleyn; Folly; Wharton; Wilson

DETECTIVE SUPERINT.

Lennox

CHIEF INSPECTOR

Dalgliesh; Hazelrigg; MacDonald; Masters; Parker; Wexford

DETECTIVE CHIEF INSPECTOR

Barlow; Chudd; Dover; Martineau; Rogers

INSPECTOR

Alleyn; Appleby; Bland; Blount; Bucket; Finch; French; Grant; Lestrade; Poole; Racon; Saltfleet; Waghorn

DETECTIVE INSPECTOR

Purbright; Rason; Sloan

SERGEANT

Beef; Cuff; Hemingway; MacGregor; Stoppford

DETECTIVE SERGEANT

Attwell; Birrell; Milton; Petrella

POLICE CONSTABLE

Bobby Owen; Thackeray

DETECTIVE POLICE CONSTABLE

Cameron

THE BOBBY GLOSSARY

Peter N. Walker

Antecedents. A criminal's history, including his education, work, family record. ("What are the accused's antecedents?")

Bat phone. A police officer's personal radio. (slang)

Book on/Book off. To report on/off duty. ("I'm booking on at 2 P.M.")

Break. (a) A breakthrough in a major enquiry. ("I've got a marvellous break in the murder enquiry.") Or: (b) A crime where property, like houses or shops, is broken into, e.g., burglary. ("I've got a few breaks to deal with today.")

Brothel creepers. Boots with very soft soles.

Charge room. A room in a police station where criminals are processed, i.e., searched after arrest and charged with their crimes.

Chief. The Chief Constable. ("Have you seen the Chief lately?")

Climber. A burglar with an ability to climb drainpipes, walls, etc. A cat burglar.

Collator. An officer who keeps local records of suspected and/or convicted criminals, their movements, friends, haunts, etc.

Divisional sleuth. A detective. (slang)

Fence. A person who disposes of stolen goods. ("Jack is the best fence in this area.")

Flasher. A man who indecently exposes himself. ("There's a flasher in the park.")

Gong. A medal of any type.

Going equipped. Being in possession of instruments or tools for use in crime. ("I arrested Fred for going equipped.")

Handler. (a) A police dog handler. Or: (b) A receiver of stolen property; a fence.

Horror comics. Police circulars, crime bulletins, information sheets, etc. (slang)

Heaven. The Chief Constable's office. (slang)

Juveniles. Persons under 17 years of age.

Knock-off. An arrest. ("I got a good knock-off last night.")

Lock-ups. Arrested persons placed in custody. ("I had seven lock-ups last night.")

Lab. A forensic science laboratory.

Metro. The London Metropolitan Police.

Manor. A police officer's area of responsibility, e.g., streets in one part of a city. (slang) Also, a criminal's area of operation. ("I'm going for a trip around my manor.")

Motor patrol. The Police Traffic Department; police officers who specialise in patrolling main roads to deal with vehicular traffic matters. Sometimes known as the Traffic Section.

Mug shot. Photograph of a prisoner. (slang)

Nick. The police station ("Take him to the nick.")

Nicked. Arrested or reported for a minor offence. ("I got nicked for a parking offence.")

CHIEF CONSTABLE, MANCHESTER CITY POLICE

Noddy bikes. Small police motorcycles. (slang)

Panda car. Small car used for local beat patrol duties; named "Panda" because the originals were two colours, e.g., blue and white.

Nutters. People of unsound mind.

Prints. Fingerprints.

Previous. A criminal's previous convictions. ("Has he any previous?")

Queen bee. A senior woman police officer. (slang)

Rings. Phone calls to the police station to see if anything has arisen which requires attention. ("I make my rings on the hour.")

Station. A police station.

Sussed. Suspected; to realise a person is guilty. ("I sussed him the moment he opened his mouth.")

Scene. The scene of a crime. ("Make sure the scene is protected and cordoned off.")

Tonsil varnish. Tea or coffee served in police canteens. (slang)

Verbal. An oral confession.

Voluntary. A statement, freely given, in which guilt is admitted. ("He has given a good voluntary.")

Wopsie. A woman police constable (from the initials WPC). Today, women are not distinguished in this manner; since 1975 they have had equal rights with male officers and a woman is known simply as "Police Constable X."

Working a beat. Patrolling on duty, in a specified area, either on foot or in an automobile.

Whiz kid. A rapidly promoted officer. (slang)

The Yard. Scotland Yard.

Yellow perils. Traffic wardens. (slang)

Yobs. Thugs, vandals, trouble-makers. (slang)

Zeds. Somewhat dated slang for cars on patrol, named after *Zed Cars,* a highly successful television series with questionable authenticity.

THE BLACK MUSEUM OF SCOTLAND YARD

Laurence Henderson

All police forces have a museum in which they locate relics of exceptional cases. The first of these, and still the most famous, is the criminal museum at Scotland Yard. The original intention was to collect mementos, not for their curiosity value, but as a detective training aid. Any officer undergoing a senior detective course will, as part of his training, make a tour of the museum in order to learn the tricks of present-day criminals are only variations on those of the past—and to see how his predecessors fared in grappling with them.

The museum is divided into a number of sections. The historical section contains the declaration signed by George III that brought into existence the first official police force. Here also is an original police uniform from those early days, curios such as the skeleton keys of Charlie Peace and the knighthood regalia of Sir Roger Casement, and a collection of death masks taken from prisoners hanged at Newgate Prison in the early nineteenth century. (The only recent death mask is that of Heinrich Himmler, which was taken by the Army Special Investigation Branch as proof that the body they held was indisputably that of the Nazi Chief of Police; it had served its purpose, and the mask was sent to the museum as the appropriate place to record the end of the greatest mass murderer in history.)

The main sections of the museum cover burglary, drugs, abortion, fraudulent gaming devices, forgery, murder, terrorism and kidnapping, with a final section for sexual perversion. All of the sections are constantly updated, but each new exhibit has to win its place either because it is startling in degree or because it is original in its criminal inventiveness: the device, for example, invented by a jewel thief specialising in the Mayfair area which, based upon the principle of a geared cork remover, is capable of winding out a spring lock from a street side of the door; a walking stick, built of interlocking tubes, which can be extended into a hook-ended ladder almost twenty feet long; the shaved dividers of a rigged roulette wheel; two-way radios built into hearing aids for the heavy poker game; and, in the forgery

NO, IT DOESN'T SELL POST CARDS

The Black Museum is not called that by its curator. The term "black" was coined by a reporter who liked the negative emotionalism of it.

The museum is open by special arrangement. Visitors are met at the reception desk on the ground floor by a Yard official who escorts them to the door of the museum. The curator lets them in, then locks the door behind them. No one is allowed to wander the building at his leisure.

A tour takes approximately one and a half hours, at which time the visitor is released from the locked room and escorted downstairs and out the door.

section, examples of outstanding artistic ability in bank notes drawn freehand, totaliser betting tickets altered within minutes of the end of a race to show a winning combination, and postal orders altered to a higher value by a single hair dipped in watered ink.

Since forgery of bank notes has become a matter of photogravure processing, it no longer requires the high skills of the criminal engraver, who now operates in the high-risk field of fraudulent bonds and share certificates. The most active area of forgery has nothing to do with bank notes or share coupons: it is apparently easier and less risky to forge airline ticket blanks and Social Security frankings, which are sold to crooked travel agents, accountants and company secretaries. An area not usually thought of in connection with forgery is that of consumer goods: the label and wrappings of an expensive perfume, for example, which has a ready sale to buyers who believe they are cheaply acquiring stolen goods.

The most fascinating exhibit in this section is that of a coiner rather than of a forger. Coining is generally regarded as a dead criminal activity, but it does still continue in the field of gold coins. One particular character was in operation from the mid-1940's until the beginning of the 1960's. Well aware that most fake gold sovereigns are detected by either a weight or chemical test, his technique was to take a small cross section of half-inch copper piping and place it between dies, first spooning into the hollow centre a carefully measured quantity of mercury. He would then trap the mercury within the copper by exerting pressure on the dies with a gallows device powered by a pneumatic jack. The result was a coin the approximate weight of a genuine sovereign, which he coated in gold obtained by melting down stolen cigarette cases and old watches. (*In extremis,* he would purchase gold leaf.)

During the fourteen years or so of his career, he made and sold thousands of his fake sovereigns to coin dealers, tourists, smugglers and others who think it smarter to keep money in gold rather than bank notes. The police have an amused regard for him. What I find entertaining is that, when he was eventually arrested, it was not on a charge of coining at all, but for receiving stolen copper piping.

The largest section of the museum is devoted to murder, with various subsections allotted to terrorist murder, murder associated with kidnapping and the murder of policemen. From the point of detection techniques, however, the more interesting murders are those committed by individuals for personal ends. The two obvious cases in this sense are those of Neville Heath, who savaged his victims with whips, knives and teeth solely for his sexual satisfaction, and of Christie, who murdered in order to supply himself with the dead bodies, since he obtained no satisfaction in connecting himself with live ones.

The section on perversion does not collect dirty photographs or films for their own sake, although there are certainly plenty of both, but rather as unique examples of their own very special kind. It is sobering to consider that whatever the human mind can envisage in its wildest moments of madness, sickness or aberration—the worst, most disgusting, utterly vile thing—not only has already been thought of but has already been brought to actuality. However experienced a police officer, he must surely be taken aback, at least momentarily, by the life-size crucifix with its barbed-wire attachments or the case in which a man was truly crucified by nails driven through the hands and feet; the leather collar with the inward-pointing nails, the macabre surgical trolley and the other, quite ordinary objects, like the wind-up Gramophone, which have, with fiendish

WHY "SCOTLAND YARD"?

London's first police office was situated at No. 4, Whitehall Place, London. The rear entrance was along a narrow lane called Scotland Yard.

From that time, the name has been given to all subsequent buildings that have accommodated the headquarters of London's Metropolitan Police.

New Scotland Yard is in Victoria Street. It is *not* the headquarters of *Britain's* police; it is the headquarters only of the Metropolitan Police.

The fifty or so police forces of England, Wales, Scotland and Ireland each have their own policemen with their own chief constable and their own police headquarters. All are complete units, and between them they service the entire British Isles outside London.

There is no national police force in England, although the Home Secretary is responsible to the government for law and order, and in this capacity issues guidance to all police forces.

P.N.W.

ingenuity, been transformed into instruments of pain and perversion.

It is with mixed emotions that one leaves the Black Museum. When I was asked which exhibit had struck me the most, it was not any of the objects of refined sexual torture or aids to perversion; it was not even the photographs that record the handiwork of the sadist Heath or the necrophiliac Christie.

In 1945 a girl, living in Southampton, sat opening the gifts she had received for her nineteenth birthday. One of the parcels that came through the mail contained a pair of binoculars and a card that said she would be surprised "how closely it brings things." She put the binoculars to one side while she opened

the rest of the gifts, and it was her father who picked them up and casually touched the central focusing screw, whereupon needle-sharp spikes sprang from either eyepiece.

The binoculars had been painstakingly carved from solid wood, the spikes fitted inside on a rachet, powered by a coiled steel spring, and then the whole thing disguised with black rexine and enamel paint. The workmanship is incredible, the cunning intelligence of its execution is frightening and the monumental hatred behind its creation is demoniac. It is also an unsolved crime.

Laurence Henderson is a past chairman of the Crime Writers' Association.

THE HANGMAN'S STORY

Laurence Henderson

The last man to die on the scaffold in England was hanged in 1965, and when a few months later the capital penalty for murder was abolished, it ended a carefully calculated ritual of execution that had been followed for almost a hundred years. The code had arisen out of the rough-and-ready methods that had been used in the previous eight hundred years and, as finally adopted, had some claim to being the most efficient as well as the most humane method of state execution ever operated.

The man under sentence would be brought back to the prison in which he had been held during his trial, then taken not to his previous cell in the remand wing of the prison, but to a special cell that completely isolated him from the rest of the prisoners.

This cell contained a prison cot, table, chairs and an alcove with washbasin and toilet, and from the moment the man entered the cell until the moment he finally left it, two warders were constantly with him. Six warders were allocated to this special duty, rotating in pairs at eight-hour intervals. While in the cell, they not only watched the man but also engaged him in conversation, helped him to write letters if he was illiterate, played cards or other table games and generally kept him company. They also reported every word that the man uttered, and any reference to his crime was immediately forwarded to the Home Office official who was dealing with the case papers.

Three clear Sundays had to elapse between the passing of the sentence and its execution, a period originally laid down so that the man could reflect upon his crime, express remorse and make peace with his God. In practise this period was used by the defence lawyers to appeal against the sentence or, if there was no legal ground of appeal, to petition for mercy. Also during this time the government official who was responsible for the case papers would be studying the case and collecting all relevant information, including an opinion on the man's sanity if this had not been an issue in the court of hearing; he would then make a final report to the Home Secretary. It was this minister who had the final decision on whether the sentence be confirmed or commuted to life imprisonment.

AMEN ALTERNATIVES

The gas chamber.
The electric chair.
The firing squad.
The lethal injection.

The only method among them that offers the convicted death with dignity is the last, which is still not accepted practice in most penal institutions.

Life imprisonment has its advocates, too. Among them: most members of the health professions and social welfare systems. Opposed: the law enforcement agencies.

During this time the man wore ordinary prison clothing except that the jacket and trousers were held together not by zips and buttons, but by tie-tapes, and that instead of shoes he would be given felt slippers. His food came from the prison kitchens, but the doctor could authorise any diet and in most cases the man could choose his own meals. He would also be allowed a daily amount of beer or liquor and, if a smoker, would be supplied with cigarettes or tobacco. He could choose any books that he wished from the lists of the prison library and he could read newsapers, so long as any reference to his own case had been deleted. He could write or receive any number of letters, but they first had to be read by the chief officer of the prison. Each day he would be visited by the prison governor, doctor and chaplain.

If the man had visitors, he would be taken from the cell to see them in a nearby interview room. Such visits were limited to thirty minutes unless otherwise sanctioned by the prison governor, who usually did so only if the visitor was the man's legal advisor. The man could also leave the cell to attend religious services in the prison chapel or to take exercise. This exercise was always taken alone, when the other prisoners were locked in their cells or at recreation.

The governor had to make a daily report on the man's health, and it was also his task to tell the man when the sentence had been confirmed by the Home Secretary and that there was no longer any possibility of reprieve.

Once this decision had been taken, a long, japanned box was delivered to the prison and carefully locked away until it could be handed over to the hangman, who would arrive at the prison with his assistant sometime during the afternoon of the day before that set for the execution. Once inside the prison, he would be unable to leave again until the execution had taken place: a relic of the times when the hangman was inclined to arrive at the scaffold reeling from gin.

The hangman would open the execution box and thoroughly examine its contents before signing that he was satisfied with the equipment provided. In the box were two six-foot lengths of inch-thick hemp rope, one end of each rope spliced around a two-inch brass-faced eyelet and the other lashed around a thick brass disk with a bolt hole drilled through its centre. The rope would be doubled back through the brass eyelet and for the first eighteen inches would be faced with chamois leather. Both ropes were precisely the same, but one was absolutely new and the other a rope that had already been used in an execution. It was the hangman's option as to which should be used. Also in the box was a white linen bag with tapes for putting over the man's head, a broad leather belt with attachment straps for his arms and a second belt to pinion his legs.

The hangman would be given de-

James McClure is a compulsive doodler, particularly when working on a book. This one popped out of his unconscious while he was finishing The Sunday Hangman.

THE LAST COG IN THE LAW MACHINE

Anne Worboys

"That man," said somebody at the party, "is Albert Pierpoint."

Albert Pierpoint, the public hangman, not halfway across the room from where I was standing.

He was of smallish stature, his thinning hair cut short, back and sides. He had a broadish face with ruddy cheeks and pointed chin. He wore a navy blue suit and gaily striped tie. A Yorkshireman, they said, with a Yorkshireman's ability to speak his mind. (They don't call a spade a spade up there; they call it a bloody shovel.) He looked amiable enough to me.

"Do you want to meet him?" (They told me afterwards my eyes were sticking out like organ stops.)

"Give me a moment," I said.

What did I want to ask him? For a start, I wanted to know if he had ever had a grudge against society. A mental hang-up, with no pun intended. Then, how did he feel when pulling the switch/turning the handle/jerking the rope? And what did the Act of Parliament abolishing the death penalty mean to him, the man whose job it had been to destroy other men fairly consistently? More pertinently, what had he looked for since, to take the place of those high-tension days?

"Okay," I said, "let's go."

At closer range I saw he had the twinkliest eyes in the room. He seemed amused at the sight of this startled-looking woman approaching him.

He inherited the job, he said straightforwardly. His uncle had been the hangman before him and his father had been the hangman before his uncle. He simply followed on. I felt he was going to say, "Why not?" but he didn't.

He didn't feel anything, he explained. He didn't think about it. After all, he added, if he thought about it, he'd have gone mad, wouldn't he?

He said they would ask him to come at a certain time, and he would get on the train, go, do the job, then turn round and come home again.

What did he do after retiring as public hangman? He kept a pub.

Anne Worboys won the Romantic Novelists Association award for her suspense novel Every Man a King.

tails of the man's age, height and weight, as well as an opportunity to see the man without being observed so that he could form a judgement as to the man's general build and likely muscular strength. He would then sit down and make his calculation, take all factors into consideration and decide the length of drop that was required.

During that final evening, while the man was seeing a visitor or being exercised for the last time, the hangman and his assistant would enter the execution chamber, which itself was an extension of the condemned cell. The trap, measuring eight feet by five, was split along its centre, the two halves being hinged along the sides. At the end of the trap was a lever, held locked by a cotter pin, which, when operated, retracted the central bolts and allowed the two halves of the trap to drop away.

The trap was spanned some nine feet above by a heavy beam from which hung a number of chains, one of which was selected and bolted into position over the centre of the trap, its length being either taken up or extended according to the drop decided upon by the hangman. The selected rope was attached to the final link of the chain by a U-bar and bolt through the brass disk at the end of the rope. A bag of sand the same weight as the man would then be put into the running noose and the trap operated. If this worked to the hangman's satisfaction, the bag of sand would be drawn up, the trap reset and the bolts and lever reoiled. If the man was still out of his cell and time permitted, the hangman would finalise his arrangements by setting two hand ropes on the beam to hang on either side of the noose and putting two planks across the length of the trap below the hand ropes.

The hangman could also, if there was time, set the noose by taking it up to the approximate head height of the man, coiling the slack above the noose and then tying it in position with a piece of thread. If the man was expected to return to his cell, these final preparations would be made in the very early morning, if possible while the man was asleep, the important consideration always being that the man should hear nothing of the preparations that were being made on the other side of the thin, movable partition. On the morning of the execution, the hangman and his assistant would enter the execution chamber, make a final check, and then, ready with the restraining harness, wait for the false wall to be moved aside.

In the cell the man would be with the prison chaplain, either seated at the table or, possibly, kneeling in prayer. The door of the cell would be opened by the chief officer, who would lead in the prison governor, doctor and either the Under Sheriff or some other representative of the Lord Lieutenant of the County in which the execution was taking place. As the man rose to face the group entering the cell, one of the warders slid aside the false wall for the hangman and his assistant to come forward.

The first awareness the man had of their presence was the restriction on his arms as they were brought into the harness. It was as the hangman turned him that he saw, for the first time, that the scaffold was only a few feet from the bed in which he had been sleeping for the past three weeks. While the hangman tightened the strap around the man's body, the two warders would take him by the elbows and walk him to the scaffold, keeping him between them as they stepped onto the planks and grasped the hand ropes with their free hands.

The hangman set the noose over the man's head while his assistant placed the final strap around the legs. The noose was then placed around the man's neck, and the hangman immediately stepped from the trap and pulled the lever; the doors of the trap crashed open and the condemned man disappeared between the two warders. The broken fragments of thread drifted slowly past a rope that hung as straight as an arrow, showing barely a shudder of movement from the tension placed upon it. The time taken from the moment the chief officer opened the door of the cell until the man fell through the doors of the trap was less than twenty seconds.

The hangman and his assistant would descend to below the scaffold, erect a ladder and take the man from the rope. The doctor would examine the body and confirm that death had occurred. Since under English law all unnatural deaths have to be inquired into, a local coroner and his jury would be waiting. The inevitable medical evidence would be that death had resulted from a fracture dislocation of the ⅔ cervical which had severed the cord. The coroner would then record the jury's verdict that death had resulted from judicial hanging and the body would be released for burial. This always took place immediately and within the precincts of the prison; the position and identity of the grave would be carefully recorded on a plan of the prison grounds, but the grave itself would be unmarked.

Laurence Henderson is the author of the crime novel Major Enquiry.

INDEX TO AUTHORS

A

Rosie, framed by Harriet and Simon for pinching the Chandler-Bodine snuffbox, is on her way to Holloway.

The Sisters of Mozart have just completed a successful engagement at the Royal Albert Hall

Cook changed kitchens and is now in the employ of the Honourable Constancia Wilson, Lover Slaughter.